GREETINGS FROM AAL

To mark the 450th anniversary of the Lutheran Reformation, Dr. Conrad Bergendoff, pastor, educator, theologian, was commissioned by Concordia Publishing House to write this historical survey of Lutheranism. It is probably the most comprehensive work in the English language on the four and a half centuries of Lutheran history.

The author has drawn together many historic threads to show how Lutheranism spread from the countries of central and northern Europe to almost every part of the world, with some personal observations on the present state of Lutheranism across the globe.

Carrying out one of the objectives of its fraternal benevolence program — supporting efforts to accumulate and disseminate information that will contribute to the understanding of Lutheran history and heritage — Aid Association for Lutherans is pleased to present this book to pastors of Lutheran congregations throughout the United States and Canada.

AID ASSOCIATION FOR LUTHERANS

APPLETON, WISCONSIN

THE YEAR OF OUR LORD 1967

The Church

of the

Lutheran Reformation

A Historical Survey of Lutheranism

Conrad Bergendoff

CONCORDIA PUBLISHING HOUSE

SAINT LOUIS

1967

Concordia Publishing House, St. Louis, Missouri

Concordia Publishing House Ltd., London, E. C. 1

© 1967 by Concordia Publishing House

Library of Congress Catalog Card No. 67-16893

MANUFACTURED IN THE UNITED STATES OF AMERICA

To my colleagues and fellow students

at Augustana College

this volume

is gratefully dedicated

CONTENTS

PREFACE

Two misconceptions have distorted the story of the Church of the Lutheran Reformation for those within as well as those outside that church. One of these has regarded the Lutheran Church as a new communion dating from Luther's days. The reformers, however, were not innovators. Rather they sought to restore the church to its original foundations. This volume begins with the early church since the true purpose of the Reformation church can be understood only in the light of the preceding 1,500 years.

The other misconception has considered the Church of the Lutheran Reformation as essentially a German church. This has been due in part to a lack of literature in the German or the English language on the career of the churches in Denmark, Sweden, Norway, Finland, and Iceland. And the story of the Lutherans in all countries, including those on the missionary fields, has rarely been told in comprehensive manner. Despite obvious difficulties in describing scores of bodies throughout the world over a period of four centuries, an attempt is made in these pages to indicate something of the individuality and variety as well as the richness and unity within the worldwide Church of the Lutheran Reformation.

As little as the Lutheran Church can be viewed apart from the past history of the Christian church can it be isolated from other Christian communions. The year 1967 marks the 450th anniversary of the clarion call of Martin Luther to consider what is the true treasure of the church of Christ and the unchanging nature of its ministry to mankind. The purpose of this book is to trace the enduring and universal qualities of the church amid the ceaseless changes in the life of humanity and to relate the Church of the Lutheran Reformation to the church catholic of all ages.

CONRAD BERGENDOFF

Augustana College
Rock Island, Illinois

I

THE CHURCH BEFORE THE REFORMATION

We have introduced nothing, either in doctrine or ceremonies, that is contrary to Holy Scripture or the universal Christian church." So the Lutheran reformers declared in the confession they presented to Emperor Charles V at the Diet of Augsburg in 1530. They considered themselves members of the church of Christ, which had a history of 1,500 years, and their concern was to correct the errors and remove the abuses which through the centuries had weakened and corrupted that church.

THE COUNCIL OF NICAEA

At the very opening of their statement they asserted that "we unanimously hold and teach, in accordance with the decree of the Council of Nicaea." It was at this council in 325 that the Christian church first adopted an elaborate official declaration of its faith, or "creed" (from the opening word *credo* — I believe). This creed was the result of many years of discussion on the question of the relationship of Jesus Christ to the Divine Being. The Nicene Creed clearly stated that Jesus Christ is the Revelation of God to man and together with the Holy Spirit one with the Father in a threefold unity. This Trinitarian doctrine became the teaching of the Christian church everywhere, so that the church was identified by its faith, believing that Christ reveals to man the nature of God, is Himself God, and is the Head of the church. The Gospel that the church set out to make known to all the world proclaimed that Christ was born into the world of the Virgin Mary, was crucified for the sins of the world, raised from the dead, and in heavenly power directs His church until His return to judge all the world and then to reign in His kingdom of glory. His present kingdom includes all who have faith in Christ's atoning ministry and sacrifice and whose sins are forgiven by His grace. They enter into an eternal fellowship with Him.

The Council of Nicaea was called by Emperor Constantine and attended by some 300 bishops. Much early Christian history is revealed by these two facts. They indicate that the churches had been organized under leaders, or supervisors, called bishops, and that they stood in a relationship to the government that enabled the emperor to exercise influence over them. All the Mediterranean world had for centuries been under the Roman Empire. Christ was born when Caesar Augustus was emperor in Rome, and the apostle Paul appealed to a Caesar since he was a citizen of the empire. For over two centuries the emperors persecuted the Christians for their worship of another Lord than Caesar. But Constantine became a Christian and protected the church — his name became forever associated with the Council of Nicaea. During the next half century Christianity became the official religion of the Roman Empire. While its favor enabled the church to grow and prosper, the price paid was the independence of the Christian religion, which became subject to the will of emperors. The relationship of church and state has ever since been a dominant factor in church history — and in the history of states.

The name of Constantine was enshrined also in the capital of the empire — Constantinople. For the center of the Roman Empire was moved to the East, and for 500 years the West was subordinated to the rulers in Constantinople. After A. D. 800 the West again had its own emperor — Charlemagne — and the bishop of Rome, who crowned him, asserted his supremacy over the whole Christian world. The Eastern Empire wasted away under the attacks first of the Moslem Arabs and then the barbarian Turks. The patriarch of Constantinople, who was recognized as the spiritual head of the Eastern churches, lost many of his provinces. In the West the emperors and the popes contended for the mastery of Europe in a struggle that was indecisive and marked by bloodshed and compromise. The pope's pretensions to supremacy over the Eastern Church were violently opposed and repudiated. After 1054 the breach between the two parts of Christendom was complete. The Eastern Empire slowly fell to pieces and after 1455 was only a memory and a hope. While Moscow dreamed of becoming a new Rome, the Turkish hordes pushed on to the very borders of the Western Empire and church and threatened the domains of the Hapsburg dynasty, the imperial power in 1500. The Preface to the Augsburg Confession states that the emperor had summoned a diet "to deliberate concerning matters pertaining to the Turk, that traditional foe of ours and of the Christian religion, and how with continuing help he might effectively be resisted."

Missionary Expansion

While pope and emperor were trying to determine who was the arbiter, the real work of the church went on rather obscurely. The borders of the church were extended by missionaries, both in the East and in the West, whose patient, often heroic labors laid the foundations of civilization and Christianity from the heaths of Scotland to the steppes of Siberia. France and Spain had been Christianized by the sixth century. In Britain a Celtic community around Iona was already flourishing when Augustine crossed the Channel — in time the whole island was brought under Rome. The great missionary to Germany was Boniface, who by the end of his career († 755) had won central Europe for the papal church. In the ninth century Ansgar had ventured into Sweden, but another century was to pass before paganism would bend before the cross. On the borders of the Eastern Church Bohemia and Moravia were won by missionaries from the Bavarian Church, which succeeded in converting also the Magyars. The latter people finally settled in Hungary and became a Christian kingdom under Stephen in the year 1000. The archbishops of Hungary and Poland, which had accepted Christianity from Bohemian missionaries, were related directly to Rome, not to Bavaria and Bohemia. Bulgaria and Serbia owed their conversion to the Eastern Church missionaries Methodius and Cyril, who worked among the Slavs in the ninth century. These border countries wavered between Constantinople and Rome, but finally along with Rumania gave allegiance to the patriarch rather than the pope. Russia, through contacts with Constantinople, became Christian by an edict of Vladimir of Kiev in 988, though any real influence on the life of the people required centuries of effort by consecrated monks. The Teutonic Knights, established in 1198, used both book and sword in bringing the faith to the Prussians and other peoples along the Baltic, who later became known as Lithuanians, Latvians, and Estonians.

3

Bishop and monk represent the victory of the medieval church. When a new area was won for the church, it came under the supervision of a bishop who arranged for the parish life of the members. A building was erected and worship instituted. The clergy conducted the services — the Mass — and brought the people into the sacramental life of the church. This revolved around the seven sacraments that theology and practice elaborated during the centuries. Baptism was the initial rite, followed later by confirmation. Marriage and extreme unction solemnized other experiences of the parishioner. At certain seasons he was supposed to receive the Sacrament of the Lord's Supper, for which confession and absolution — the sacrament of penance — was required. The ordination to priesthood was also a sacrament. Through this series of sacred acts the life of the individual and of the Christian community was ordered and moulded, all under obedience to a nearby bishop and a faraway pope. The priest could exercise influence over the parishioner, especially in confession and absolution, for he could fix the conditions under which sins could be forgiven. In some cases he could ban the person from the sacraments, actually excluding him from the life of the congregation. Only the bishop could confirm and ordain, making all the acts of the church, through the priest, dependent on obedience to superiors.

THE LITURGY

The Mass was essentially a Communion service. In the early centuries Gaul and Spain had used a form of Mass that bore marks of Eastern rites. This order, called the Gallican, fused with an old Roman form from the time of Gregory I (590—604). The result was the Mass that from the time of Charlemagne the missionaries of Rome carried to all parts of Europe. The Eastern Church adopted as its most general form a liturgy that had originated in Syria but after its acceptance in Constantinople was called the Byzantine rite. In the early church all communicants received both bread and wine, but the practice had become normal in the Western Church for the priest to give only the bread. Around the Sacrament had grown an elaborate priestly ceremony considered meritorious before God by mere repetition, even without the presence of communicants. When they were in attendance,

4

they could hardly understand what happened, for the Mass was said only in Latin. Originally the liturgy had made provision for lay responses in word and song, but in time the Mass was looked on as a priestly celebration, and the laity were but spectators. The simplicity of the original Eucharist gave way to an elaborate series of prayers, and the remembrance of those who paid for the Masses overshadowed the remembrance of Him who bade His disciples to eat and drink. Church edifices with ornamental altars were built to enshrine the elements and to provide places for the sacrifice of the Mass — for the act came to be regarded as a sacrifice offered by the church to Christ.

Monasticism

Almost as early as Nicaea we find beginnings of a movement among the devout to withdraw from the common life and to seek Christian peace in solitary places. In the Eastern Church Basil the Great of Cappadocia (†ca. 379) set up regulations for those who wanted to live together in a monastic community. In the Western Church Benedict of Nursia (†ca. 550) laid the foundations of monasticism. Solitude and contemplation were not the only purposes, for the monastery was to give opportunity also for organized work, both intellectual and manual, since it afforded the time ordinary laymen lacked for spiritual meditation and worship. The monk took three vows — poverty, celibacy, and obedience — that placed all his time and energy under the direction of the abbot. The monasteries often became missionary centers for the surrounding region in material as well as spiritual affairs, especially in agricultural regions. They served also as important conservers of an older culture that was being buried under new barbarian manners. In time monasteries banded together in larger fellowships, and the Benedictine Order of Cluny, France, became a great force in the ecclesiastical and international life of medieval Europe. Often the monasteries were the schools of the nation and furnished leaders of thought and action. The ascetic ideal was looked on as a higher type of Christian life and attracted large numbers of earnest and thoughtful individuals.

Central in the monastic life was worship. Here time was available and a theoretical system of seven hourly services was developed (the *horae,* or hours). The Rule of Benedict, which was widely followed,

5

started the day with Vigils at 2 a. m. Matins came at dawn. Then at 3-hour intervals followed Prime at 6, Terce at 9, Sext at 12, and None at 3. Vespers at 6 and Compline at 9 closed the day. In some places a Nocturn was added to divide day and night into eight services — one every 3 hours. The regular recital of the Psalter was the main stem of the hours — around the Psalms grew up the reading of Scripture lessons and passages from the lives of saints, and the music of the church owes much to the monastic services. The adoration of saints and of the Virgin entered into the meditation of the monks and was advanced by them as they later contributed to the education of the laity in their capacity of itinerant members of the Franciscan or Dominican Orders.

THEOLOGY AND PHILOSOPHY

The monastic schools and the schools in the cathedral towns, where the bishops resided, became the intellectual centers of European Christianity. Later, at Bologna, Oxford, and Paris, great universities developed that determined the thought of the times. As the early church spread out into the Greek and Roman world, it had to defend its faith against the skepticism or attacks of ancient philosophy and ethics.

The great work of Augustine was to determine the thought of Christians in explaining their faith and attitude toward the world they lived in. He himself had been influenced by the philosophy of Plato. Later, as the Northern people were educated to the traditions of the church, new questionings arose, especially in the relationship of the human intellect toward the doctrines drawn from Scripture. Aristotle, the other great teacher of antiquity, differed from Plato in his ideas of reality. He stressed less the ideas of the mind and more what the senses taught. His influence led some to question the miracle of the Lord's Supper and the doctrine of the Trinity, since the mind could not reason them out from evidence available to the senses. Anselm of Canterbury († 1109), however, thought he could logically prove both the existence of God and why Christ became man. But Abelard († 1142) doubted this method and claimed that the teachings of the church were in the realm of faith. So the fundamental question was, How do we know? Do we believe in order to know, or do we try to know in order to believe?

What Aristotle was to the ancient world, Thomas Aquinas

(1225—1274) was to medieval European Christianity. He tried to summarize all knowledge within a Christian framework, and his influence still lives on. For him the mind is a gift of God, but it knows naturally only what it learns through the senses. But the works of creation are also the works of God so that what the mind discerns is similar to what faith may know. Yet the mind only deduces truth from the experience of the senses and cannot prove what belongs to a higher sphere, the sphere of revelation. In Scripture God reveals the saving truth — only faith can grasp this, and faith is a gift of God made possible through Christ and the church. For in the sacraments the grace of God is infused into man, and he then becomes aware of a supernatural world. The highest stage is a mystical union of the soul with God wherein a beatific vision of God unveils itself.

Scholasticism

Thomas attempted a synthesis of the natural and the supernatural, of knowledge and faith, of philosophy and theology. It was a combination difficult to maintain, for with various scholars the emphasis would fall on one or the other. Duns Scotus († 1308) gave less place to reason in matters of revelation and based faith more on the authority of the church. God's will was the foundation of truth, and man's will had to be turned to God if man was to fulfill his purpose. In his experience of the natural world man formed abstract ideas in his mind — universals they were called. The ideas were not in the things perceived but in the perceiver, who gave them names. This gave rise to a school called nominalism, which denied the Platonic reality of ideas. Its foremost representative was William of Occam († ca. 1350). But the notion of the independent existence of ideas persisted and found expression in a mysticism that runs like an underground river through medieval thought from Dionysius the Areopagite (6th century) through Bernard of Clairvaux († 1153) to Master Eckhart (1260—1327) and Johannes Tauler (1300—1361). Intuition and contemplation are here the ways to the vision of God, and the mystical union between man and God tends not only to depreciate the intellectual investigation of the world but also to erase the distinction between God and man. Yet a distinctly Christian mysticism originated in the thought of Gregory of Nyssa in the fourth

7

century in the East and is evident in the theology of Bonaventura
(† 1274) and even in Thomas Aquinas in the West.

The 12th and 13th centuries were the high point of theology.
It is called the period of scholasticism because the movement had its
home in the schools of the church, but the name also refers to the
aim and method of theology, which was to exercise the powers of the
intellect in the field of faith so as to penetrate to the depths of religious meaning and to give systematic presentation to the doctrines
of the church. Scholasticism was nourished by great teachers in the
monastic orders, especially the Dominican and the Franciscan, and
its results were embodied in textbooks that became the material of
theological training, such as the *Sentences* of Peter Lombard († 1160).

After the 13th century the University of Paris became a great
center of theological thought and teaching. Influential new universities
grew up in Germany — Heidelberg, Tübingen, Erfurt, and Wittenberg. Oxford was noted for its early interest in investigation and experiment of natural phenomena (Roger Bacon, † 1294). The University of Bologna grew out of interest in law and medicine. Everywhere a new interest in the world around man and in his nature and
history was awakening, and the domination of the traditions of the
church in the realm of thought was being challenged.

EMPIRE AND PAPACY — GERMANY AND FRANCE

The history of the church is inextricably interwoven with that
of the governments under which it functioned. After Constantine the
church in the East devised a theory of "symphony" in which church
and state were conceived of as playing free, independent parts in
harmony. But the conductor of the symphony in the Greek and Russian Orthodox Churches was undoubtedly the emperor. The perfor-
mance was stormy when a strong patriarch such as Photius († 891)
clashed with the ruler.

In the West the church grew up among the ruins of the Roman
Empire. The removal of the capital to the Byzantine territory left
Italy a prey to competing forces. The Germanic tribes that invaded
the capital and were baptized and civilized by their captives could
fashion and centralize new governments in Europe rather slowly. In
the absence of an emperor the Roman pontiff assumed many secular

8

powers and at times was the protector of the capital. He claimed some of Italy as his own and entered into alliances with other powers. By A. D. 800 the pope considered himself strong enough to crown a new emperor in the West — Charlemagne — who had brought a large part of western Europe under a central administration. From the time of Charles I to Charles V, a period of 700 years, the political story of Europe is, from the point of view of the church, a duel between the successors of St. Peter and Caesar Augustus, both of whom claimed supremacy in the Eternal City.

Charlemagne's empire was soon divided into many parts among his successors, but the dream of a united Europe had been born, and for centuries one power or another strove to gain the ascendancy. France was the first to unite many small principalities under a strong central monarchy. By the end of the 13th century, largely through kings such as Philip II (reigned 1180—1223) and Louis IX (reigned 1226—1270), France had warded off the threats of England — which had important lands in Normandy — and had established a respected system of law and taxation, emerging from feudalism to a monarchical state. The growth of the French power was accompanied by a parallel growth of the church, which held vast properties under the king who shared in their income. The monarch needed the church in his contacts with the nobles and richly rewarded the help he received. France had 76 bishoprics, and the king could nominate 22 of the bishops. There were over 500 abbeys, many controlled by the royal house. Archbishops were among the leaders of the nation in secular as well as ecclesiastical matters.

Germany could not match the centralizing movement in France. Its great "stem" lands — Saxony, Franconia, Swabia, and Bavaria — were ruled by dukes who jealously guarded their powers. But the fatal error of the Germans was their illusion that they could inherit the prestige and power of the Roman Empire. This involved them in constant turmoil with the papacy, whose favor they needed but whose power they contested. The imperial name was borne by one after another of the ducal powers, but while the emperor was embroiled in Italian affairs the other dukes increased their power and prevented a German union. Saxony and Bavaria slowly extended their lands eastward among the Teutons and Slavs but had to meet the recurring threats of invaders — Mongols, Magyars, Turks. Saxony and Swabia faced west and south and were involved in the expansion of France in the Netherlands and in the growth of Italian cities in Lombardy. For a century Saxon princes wore the imperial crown, though without much success, and their favoritism to bishops over against the monasteries won them enemies among the Cluniac reformers, especially because of German interference in Italy. The Franconian emperors followed the Saxon.

In 1076 the controversy between pope and emperor came to a head when Pope Gregory VII, who headed the party seeking independence from a secular yoke, forced Emperor Henry IV to seek release from excommunication at Canossa. But the papacy could not enforce its demands nor could the emperor control the pope. In 1122 at Worms a compromise was reached that confined to Germany the emperor's influence in the election of abbots and bishops.

The papacy was everywhere gaining strength. The Fourth Lateran Council (1215) was attended by more than 400 bishops, 800 abbots and priors, and representatives of every kingdom in Europe. And the church boasted of more than spiritual resources. The revenue of the papacy exceeded that of any state. Because of the fear of ban and interdict the rulers of Europe had to come to terms with popes, archbishops, bishops, and abbots. The claims of the papacy reached their high point in the person of Boniface VIII (1294—1303) who declared in the bull *Unam Sanctam* "that submission on the part of everyone to the bishop of Rome is altogether necessary for salvation."

Beyond the pinnacle was an abyss. So tangled were the affairs of the pope that 7 years after the *Unam Sanctam* the reigning pope was forced to flee to France, where for 69 years at Avignon the papacy was really an appendage to the French monarchy. When it returned to Rome, it faced trouble; and for a while there were two popes, with Christendom divided. The cardinals at the Council of Pisa (1409) vainly tried to displace the two popes by a third. Not until the Council of Constance (1414—1418) was the breach healed and a pope elected who commanded the allegiance of all Europe. The result was attained by the influence of the universities and the power of Sigismund, who was the emperor. After another council — at Basel from 1431 to 1449 — both France and Germany won important concessions from the papacy, the French crown virtually gaining financial independence in its realm for the church.

Toward the end of the 13th century the Hapsburgs of southeastern Germany (Austria, Switzerland) succeeded to the imperial name and began to rival the Bavarian and Luxemburg dukes. A notable event in the reign of Charles IV of Luxemburg was the definition of the imperial status in the Golden Bull he issued in 1356. It established the practice of seven electors choosing the emperor — the archbishops of Mainz, Cologne, and Treves; the king of Bohemia; the count of the Palatinate on the Rhine; the duke of Saxony; and the margrave of Brandenburg. The territories were to pass to heirs by law of primogeniture (thus avoiding division), and each elector was to have one vote. On the death of Sigismund in 1437 a son of Charles IV, Albert of Hapsburg, became emperor, and thereafter Hapsburgs occupied the imperial throne for almost four centuries until the end of the empire under Napoleon. When the Reformation broke out, Maximilian I was emperor, to be followed by Charles V. The imperial power, however, was restricted. Germany had more than 300 separate principalities, and the princes were as jealous of their privileges as were the bishops and abbots. The encroachments of all were disputed by the growing number of cities whose councils *(Rat)* obtained various degrees of freedom and independent power.

NATIONAL CHURCHES — ENGLAND

After the Norman Conquest (1066) England was closely bound to France, but it moved toward independence and a strong monarchy. Under Thomas à Becket, the archbishop of Canterbury, the church put up a strong Cluniac resistance. Becket's reward was martyrdom. Popular reaction forced Henry II to recant temporarily. In 1215 the Magna Carta promised canonical elections. By the middle of the 14th century Parliament had grown sufficiently strong to exclude papal appointments and to forbid the taking of lawsuits out of the country. Monasteries and cathedrals were in favor — by the end of the 13th century one third of England's lands were owned by the church. Oxford and Cambridge were centers of learning, both in theology and in science. Its geographical situation saved England from many of the quarrels between papacy and empire on the mainland and allowed the church a steady growth.

SPAIN

In the Spanish peninsula the presence of the Moors had long been an obstacle to a Christian nation. But by the end of the 15th century the enemy was finally driven out by a union of the royal houses of Aragon and Castile. The crown asserted its supremacy over both nobility and church. Although it controlled the appointments in the church, the royal power was loyal to the papacy. How far it was willing to go to enforce uniformity is shown by the organization of the Inquisition. Heretics, Jews, Moslems — all were victims of the inquisitor general Torquemada.

ITALY

Italy remained the most chaotic and dismembered part of Europe. Some areas were claimed by the Eastern Empire. The pope tried to keep his patrimony. The Saracens disputed with the Byzantine rule in southern Italy until they were displaced by the Normans from France. They in turn were driven out by the armies of Spain. In the north the cities of Lombardy, grown strong and wealthy, asserted their independence of the empire and virtually gained it by their defeat of Frederick Barbarossa. Rome itself, the scene of frequent papal elections, was often in turmoil. It was repeatedly invaded by the German forces of the empire. Its attempt to set up an independent republic under Arnold of Brescia (1144) failed. During the Crusades Rome was a center of intrigue and had to counter the alliances and ambitions of Byzantium. In the 14th and 15th centuries it became the home of the Renaissance, which left enduring monuments not only in the plastic and literary arts but also in the arts of free thinking — and loose living. It was a strange context for the purported spiritual center of the Western world.

THE SCANDINAVIAN COUNTRIES

The last corner of the European continent to be drawn into the orbit of the Roman hierarchy were the Scandinavian peninsula and the Baltic lands. The work of Ansgar had been continued from Bremen and Hamburg, but the effective missionary impulses came from

England. The Vikings had conquered parts of the British Isles, but had been conquered by their subjects in religious matters. After the conversion of Canute in the 11th century, Denmark rapidly adopted the new faith. In 1103 an archbishopric was established in Lund (which then belonged to Denmark), with nine bishops. Kings of both Sweden and Norway were baptized in the beginning of the 11th century. In 1153 the Norwegians received an archbishop in Nidaros, and in 1164 the first Swedish archbishop was enthroned at Uppsala. The Norwegian province included ten bishops: five in Norway, one each in the Orkneys, the Faroes, the Hebrides, Iceland, and Greenland. The seven Swedish bishops were in ancient centers of worship and trade.

Olav Tryggveson, with whose name the Christianization of Norway is associated, also had a part in the decision of Icelandic leaders in 1050 to adopt the new faith. A century later there were two bishoprics — one in Skálholt, the other in Hólar. For a long time the clan headsmen were themselves the priests, but after 1275 the church attained independence. Thereafter its wealth grew in monasteries and episcopal lands.

The Danish Church was the first to push through the Gregorian reforms. The freedom it won in 1170 had to be defended in frequent involvements in political struggles. Nicholas Brakespear, a papal legate to Norway, in 1152 secured canonical elections for the Norwegian dioceses, but was resisted in his demand for celibacy of the clergy. A century later another papal legate was present at a church meeting in Skänninge and incorporated the Swedish Church into the papal system, insuring canonical elections, clerical celibacy, the tithe, and freedom from taxation. But in all these countries popes and kings bargained over elections, and the bishops ranked with the nobles in affairs of state. The relative independence of the Scandinavian churches from Rome may be due partly to their distance from the center but partly to the traditions inherited from England, whence the church came to Scandinavia. Notable archbishops were Eskil and Absalon in Denmark, Eystein Erlendsson in Norway, and Jacob Ulvsson in Sweden.

Norway was turned toward the Atlantic, Sweden toward the East. In Finland missionaries from Sweden met missionaries from Germany and England. The first two bishops of Abo (Turku) were of English origin. From the middle of the 13th century Finland was under the Swedish crown, and for a century the bishops were of Swedish origin. After 1366 Finnish bishops were the rule. They had to contend not only with native paganism but also with efforts of the Russians to extend their power and the Orthodox domain, and with representatives of the Teutonic Order in Riga and Dorpat. The Gregorian reforms were partly realized by the able Hemming, bishop of Abo from 1338 to 1366.

Of great importance in the growth of the northern churches was the coming of the Franciscans and the Dominicans. Monasteries of the older orders had been established early in Denmark, Sweden, and Norway, but the gray and the black friars came closer to the people as they built their houses in the commercial centers and spread out on their begging tours. Denmark was the provincial headquarters. Especially the Dominicans stressed the education of their preachers. From the Dominicans arose the early literature of the lands. Peter of Dacia, a Swedish Dominican, was a noteworthy writer. Scandinavian students made their mark at the great universities — a Finnish student became a rector at Paris and later Bishop John II of Abo. The orders brought the architecture of southern lands to the North. The Dominicans brought the first liturgy to Abo. Sweden contributed a new order in that of St. Birgitta (1303—1373), who was also one of the principal religious figures of medieval Sweden. What the Hanseatic League meant for international commercial relationships the monastic orders meant for contacts of the North with the rest of Europe. In the academic world beginnings were made at Copenhagen and Uppsala before the end of the 15th century. Although attempts after 1377 to unite the countries under one crown proved futile, the church and the orders did give Scandinavia after its Christianization a uniting principle.

II

VOICES OF PROTEST BEFORE THE REFORMATION

Any reading of the history of the church for the thousand and more years after Nicaea that gives the impression of peaceful progress in a straight line is false. Even the notion of a united church before the Reformation is unfounded. The removal of the capital from Rome left the pope a freedom he used for gaining power over the Eastern exarchate in Italy. When Nicholas I (858—867) asserted papal supremacy, partly on the basis of forged documents, the Eastern Church resisted immediately, and we have the spectacle of the patriarch of Constantinople — Photius — and the Roman pope excommunicating each other. Two centuries later the legates of Leo IX, after fruitless negotiations, placed a bull of anathema against Patriarch Cerularius on the very altar of St. Sophia on July 16, 1054. From that date the churches of the East and the West were separated despite a series of councils in later centuries that sought reunion both for political reasons and by political means. Not until Vatican Council II was the mutual excommunication of the two churches rescinded in 1965.

THE SECULARIZATION OF THE CHURCH

The alliance between papacy and empire after Charlemagne led to a division between church and states of the prerogatives, powers, and lands of the old empire. The pope became a temporal ruler in Italy. Through the expansion of the church the bishops became powerful lords over temporal possessions, and the monastic leaders — abbots and priors — received lands as fiefs from overlords. Itself free from taxation by papal agreements with rulers, the church received a huge income through tithes and various fees associated with appointment to and holding of church offices. Bishops and archbishops sat in councils of state. As temporal lords they enlisted soldiers and engaged in wars. The pope had the disposition of great

15

wealth, and his treasury was engaged in far-reaching banking ventures. He even held a monopoly on a source of mineral wealth — alum. The monasteries of England were principals in the wool industry. Taxes and bequests made possible great churches, and incomes from pilgrimages built splendid shrines. The dress of the clergy became increasingly elaborate and costly. The retinue of legates rivaled or exceeded that of the ambassadors of states.

It was natural from the very nature of the Christian faith that voices would be raised against the secularization of the church. That criticism of its faults could arise from many and varied motives the course of events amply demonstrated.

THE CLUNY REFORMS

Isolated instances are recorded of protests against the power and lives of the clergy in the 10th and 11th centuries, but it is significant that protests decreased as the church undertook a reformation of its own. In 910 a monastery that was to have wide influence was established at Cluny in eastern France. It was to be free of control by either bishops or princes and to answer directly to the pope, for the monastic establishments of the time were often pawns in the struggle of secular and episcopal rulers for lands and power. And as a part of the feudal system they rendered homage and paid fees to the secular prince who claimed overlordship. Under a series of strong abbots Cluny maintained its independence and undertook a reform of other aspects of monasticism and of the church. The Rule of St. Benedict was strictly enforced. The monks were engaged in teaching in the monastic schools, in improving agriculture in the neighborhood, and in caring for the poor, the sick, the stranger.

About the year 1000 various monasteries associated themselves into "congregations" to further their goals. The abbot of Cluny appointed priors in the single institutions and supervised them. The chief monastic virtue was that of obedience, which enabled a single mind to rule over the order and to enforce the other vows of poverty and celibacy. But the Cluny reformers looked beyond the monastic walls and wanted to improve the life of the church. They insisted on the celibacy of all the clergy, for among other advantages an unmarried clergy would help relieve the church of the problems of inheritance

16

under the feudal system. They attempted above all to shake off the interference of the secular princes in the affairs of the church and denied the right of the rulers to appoint bishops or abbots or to invest them in their office or to veto their appointment. They called this practice of the temporal powers simony (Acts 8:18), or traffic in church business.

The Cluny reforms influenced all church offices, even the papacy. In 1057 Cardinal Humbert of Rome extended the meaning of simony to all secular interference with church elections. Two years later he persuaded a synod to regulate the election of a pope by placing it in the hands of a college of cardinals. Only after election by the cardinals and approval by the clergy (and, theoretically, by the people) would the emperor's confirmation be sought. This was to remove the influence of secular rulers from church elections. While from the church's point of view this was a highly desirable reform, it would not be easy to execute because the church was so deeply involved in worldly business and so many high officials of the church were relatives of princes or members of noble families of great influence.

Hildebrand, a disciple of Cardinal Humbert, in 1073 became Pope Gregory VII and tested Humbert's principles in his contest with Henry IV at Canossa. His ambition was fourfold: (1) to emancipate the papacy from German domination, (2) to reform church life and discipline, (3) to make the church independent of all temporal power, and (4) to be recognized as the supreme ruler over princes and people. In its effort to be freed from interference by the temporal power the papacy was tempted to declare itself above all earthly authority. As successor to Peter, the pope considered himself the lord of the universal church and overlord of all secular rulers, who were to kiss his feet. He alone could appoint and depose clergy of all ranks and have power to convene general councils. He could unseat kings and emperors and free their subjects from obedience to them. He was judge of all, but to be judged by none. Such was the temper of the times that the assertion of these claims overawed both people and rulers. Not until the Reformation of the 16th century was the spell broken.

Aside from its secular aims we should credit the Cluny reform movement with great spiritual gains for the Christian cause. In Italy Pietro Damiani of Ravenna (1007—1072) promoted the ideals of

17

Hildebrand. Branches of the Cluny movement spread to other parts of Europe. Most renowned of the related institutions was the monastery of Citeaux (Cistercium), from which the Cistercian Order took its name. Founded in 1098, it developed the "congregation" of Cluny into a more integrated order in which the life of all the member cloisters was regulated by a superior general and a chapter. Its character was determined to a great extent by its foremost exponent, Bernard of Clairvaux, the founder of a daughter monastery of Citeaux at Clairvaux in 1115. So successful was the order that at the death of Bernard in 1153 it counted 343 institutions. Bernard was a great preacher, hymnist, and literary leader. Of a pious and devotional nature, he was recognized as a saintly figure even by his own generation. He represents the best of the life of the church in the 12th century. The "grey friars," as his monks were called from the color of their garb, were missionaries of the church in Scandinavia, England, Spain, Portugal, and the eastern lands of Europe. Their establishments were simpler than those of other orders but models of agriculture and industry. Their devotional life led to renewal of interest in and new forms of liturgy and church music. The Benedictine motto *Ora et labora* was their program. Their influence led to the forming of a related order of nuns, but its members remained under the jurisdiction of bishops. The stream of religious devotion and fervor that flowed from Cluny in the 10th century was like a refreshing and creative stream through the dry lands of ecclesiastical and political strife of the Middle Ages. We wonder at the pretensions of Innocent III and Boniface VIII, but we still sing the hymns of Bernard and are guided by the aims of an imitation of Christ that inspired the monastic ideal.

The Waldensians and the Lombard Poor

The first organized protest against the way the church of Christ was developing in the Roman hierarchy was led by Peter Waldo, a successful silk merchant of Lyons. Around 1173 he decided to follow the example of Christ and divest himself of all his possessions, including his family, and go about preaching the Gospel. He soon found followers, and the mendicant preachers were known as the "Poor Men of Lyons." At first they wanted to remain within the church, but the pope and the Third Lateran Council (1179) denied their request to preach.

When they persisted, they were branded as heretics in 1184. Undaunted, they went on and formed a separate church, Waldo as bishop ordaining presbyters and deacons. Members were not required to leave the hierarchical church but made confession to their own clergy and joined regularly in a common meal, reserving the Eucharist for Thursday of Holy Week. Waldo had parts of the Bible translated, but his society engaged in a legalistic biblicism that treated the Bible as a book of law for morals and the life in Christ. The externals of the church were minimized — church buildings, cemeteries, altars, the crucifix. Purgatory and intercessions for the dead were rejected.

In some respects the Waldensians resembled the heretical Cathari, or Albigensians, as in their poverty and in their refusal to take an oath or to wage war, with the consequence that they were caught in the Inquisition, which so cruelly extirpated the Cathari. But they rejected the dualistic teachings of the Cathari, whom they considered non-Christian. The main tenet of the Waldensians was the simple life of the follower of Christ who, in poverty and obedience, tried to imitate the Master on the basis of Biblical teachings. In this they followed a tradition deriving from the very beginning of Christianity, appealing in every age to individuals and groups.

When the Waldensians reached northern Italy, they found similar associations of laymen in the Lombard cities. They were within the Roman Church but, mainly craftsmen, had banded together for mutual edification, and this in an ascetic spirit somewhat akin to a monastic organization. They too had been declared heretical at the Third Lateran Council but carried on, though not, like the Waldensians, moving about from place to place. Innocent III succeeded in winning some of them back by adopting a conciliatory policy that conceded them the right of meeting together on Sundays, if taught by sympathetic clerics, and by giving them a sort of rule for their common endeavors. Also some of the Waldensians were regained. We can see in this policy a preparation for the later papal recognition of the mendicant orders. But more forthwith was the consent of the pope in 1256 to the formation of the Order of the Augustinian Hermits, which gave opportunity to those of the laity who wished to travel about in poverty to preach and to aid the needy. It was in this order that Martin Luther was later to become a monk.

After the death of Waldo his followers had to endure persecution in France and Spain. This sharpened their opposition to the clergy, from whom they would not receive the sacraments because of the unworthiness of the administrants. They opposed the ceremonies of the church and rejected its indulgences. In the valleys of the Alps they were able to maintain their congregations, from which missionaries went out to Germany, Bohemia, Moravia, and the Netherlands. In Bohemia they later found kindred spirits among the followers of John Huss and the "Bohemian Brethren." The Reformation drew them into the Herrnhut movement in eastern Europe and to Calvinism in Italy and southern France.

THE FRANCISCANS

A generation after Waldo a more famous itinerant imitator of Christ appeared in the hill country of Italy and started a worldwide movement whose vitality is still felt in the church. Francis of Assisi in 1210 left his well-to-do father, a cloth merchant, to go about to preach the Gospel and help the poor in the cities of Italy. His sympathy for the conditions of the underprivileged in the developing Italian cities, his love of nature, and his mystic abandon were not out of harmony with the rulers of the church. He therefore gained papal recognition of his "Lesser Brethren," or *Fratres Minores,* in 1210. An order of sisters soon followed, and then a third order in 1221 for lay members who stayed at home and continued their work but followed specific rules of discipline and devotion. The poverty of the brothers made begging necessary — this was the beginning of the mendicant orders.

Francis represented a new sense of life, of joy in the creation of God, and an appreciation of the worth of life that soon won adherents, and so the order spread rapidly. Because a missionary impulse was inherent in the order, the Franciscans carried their message and method to every part of Europe, then to Palestine, Japan, and China. Theological study was a part of their interest — also the study of nature — and they could in time boast of such scholars as Bonaventura and Duns Scotus, Alexander of Hales and William of Occam. Differences arose early as to the holding of property. Although the church allowed the orders to own lands and buildings, a more ascetic party, the Spirituals, found themselves rather in sympathy with the Lombard Poor and in opposition to the papacy, thereby incurring involvement in the Inquisition's persecution of heretics. The larger party, however, proved itself an arm of the church in holding the allegiance of cities and in extending the borders of the hierarchy.

THE ALBIGENSIANS AND THE INQUISITION

The church had need of the help of Franciscans and similar orders in meeting the inroads of strange sects in France and elsewhere. The Cathari, or "Puritans," seem to have entered the West from Bulgaria and the other Balkan areas, bringing a mixture of Christian and old Persian teachings wherein all material things were the creation of another power, Satan, and Christ dwelt only in the spirit. A rival church organization was set up, challenging the hierarchy, the sacraments, and even the truth of Christianity. Since the movement gained publicity first around Albi in southern France, the name Albigensian was applied to it. Unable to overcome the sect—which included clergy, officials, nobility, and many women—by argument or ban, the church called in the secular power. The count of Toulouse, Raymond VI, was defiant of the pope, refusing to persecute his subjects. The pope, Innocent III, in 1208 proclaimed a crusade, entrusting to Simon of Montfort the duty of ending the heresy. Political ambitions combined with religious fervor to create a war that saw 30,000 inhabitants of Beziers massacred, Carcassonne captured, the lands of Raymond given to Montfort, and the remnant of the Cathari burned alive. Out of the war grew the Inquisition, a papal commission that examined and tried heretics and then turned them over to the secular authorities for execution, usually at the pyre. Ironically the lands of southern France soon passed to the Capetian royal house, enabling it to eventually unite much of the nation and in time to frustrate the vaulting ambitions of the papacy. Another result was the extension of the Inquisition not only to eliminate heresy but also to prevent reformation.

THE DOMINICANS

Out of the Albigensian crusade came another important order. Dominic of Castile had aided his bishop in fighting the heretics. He had seen the futility of force in attempts to change men's faith. Therefore he conceived of an order to convert men by teaching and preaching. He was acquainted with Francis, but Dominic was of a different

21

nature — an intellectual interested in dogma and reasoning. Like Francis, he was willing to roam the countryside — in poverty — to teach the doctrines of the church. In 1216 he was authorized to institute a "Preaching Order," and the Dominican Order was born. It became primarily an association of mendicant preachers following, like the Fransciscans, the Augustinian rule but giving itself to teaching the clergy rather than the laity. It was renowned for its scholars, among them Albertus Magnus and Thomas Aquinas.

It was to the Dominicans that the papacy turned over the Inquisition, and it was the Dominican Order that proved itself one of the stoutest defenders both of the papal throne and of the theology of the papal church. While the Fransiscans dominated Oxford, the Dominicans were masters in Paris. In the provinces of the order the Dominicans set up schools that developed into universities.

WILLIAM OF OCCAM

Implicit in the emphasis on poverty and preaching, which were practiced by the many orders, was a protest against the worldliness of the church. But the reaction also found expression in theoretical attacks on the place of the papacy in the structure of Christendom. While advocates of the pope could declare, as Cardinal Peter Amelli did, that the pope and the cardinals occupy such a place in the Roman Church that they are the church, voices were raised to give other definitions. Conrad of Gelnhausen claimed in 1380 that the church is the community of the faithful united by the sacraments, and when the pope errs the church must act. John Gerson (1363—1429), rector of the University of Paris, placed the authority of the church in the hierarchy, that is, the bishops, who were to rule the whole body of believers. Such expressions showed clearly the influence of William of Occam, a Franciscan from Oxford, a pupil of Duns Scotus, and a friend of Marcellus of Padua at the University in Paris. In 1322 Occam defended the doctrine of "evangelical poverty" (according to it Christ and His disciples possessed no property), which a Franciscan chapter in Italy had adopted. Pope John XXII opposed the doctrine, and Occam declared him a heretic. Occam was imprisoned but escaped to the court of Emperor Louis of Bavaria.

Louis was engaged in a quarrel with the pope regarding the rela-

22

tionship of secular power to the papacy and succeeded in getting a diet of the empire to assert in 1338 that the elective office of the empire needed no papal confirmation. The pope was termed an "ancient enemy of mankind" and "totally ignorant of Scriptures." We may guess that Occam had something to do with the reasoning of the declaration, for not only did he hold the pope heretical for denouncing poverty but as a pupil of Duns Scotus he distinguished between the articles of faith, which are known through the Scriptures, and the world of sensual experience, where truth is reached through logic. Louis was finally deposed, and Occam was reconciled to the church before his death, but the chasm between the ecclesiastical and political realms was widening as the medieval mind was awaking to a world of nature and history outside Scripture. Occam had appealed from the authority of the pope to the authority of a council, thereby opening a new path for dissidents.

WYCLIF

Only a few decades later another Oxford scholar was opposing the papacy and defending an English crown against Rome. John Wyclif (1320?—1384) too was impressed by the poverty of the Master and of the first disciples as contrasted with the church of his day. He maintained that "it belongeth not to Christ's vicar nor to priests of holy church to have rents on earth." For him the supreme authority was Holy Scripture — and in its translation he was interested. "No custom in the Church, confirmed by popes or observed by saints, is to be praised save in so far as Jesus Christ confirms it." The meaning of Scripture is given us by the Holy Spirit "as Christ declared its sense to the Apostles." The true church is neither the communion of the faithful nor the hierarchy, but in reality is invisible, including all whom God wills to be saved. The power of the church is purely spiritual. In his own realm the king is head of the church and responsible for its reform. Such was Wyclif's teaching.

Before Wyclif died he witnessed a fatal event in the history of the medieval church. For much of his century the papacy had been transferred to France, where it was a virtual captive of the French monarchy. When it sought to return to Rome, a schism developed, and for the next 40 years (1378—1418) the church watched two popes fighting each other and dividing Christendom. The results are apparent in an observer such as Wyclif. He now denounced even the spiritual claims of the pope and declared him the Antichrist and the whole hierarchial system unjustified. Indulgences and pilgrimages were without merit. Wyclif was not interested in a place for art and music in the church but stressed preaching and knowledge of Scripture. The mendicant orders he criticized sharply and opposed them by the character of the preachers he trained to preach and teach and hear confession. "All is of grace," he asserted, "and the ruler who grants us all our all is God." His followers, known as Lollards, carried his message far and wide, but their involvement in social and political struggles earned for them enemies in both church and state. The corpse of Wyclif was dug up and burned after the Council of Constance had judged him heretical, and some of the Lollard leaders were likewise burned as heretics or hanged as rebellious spirits.

HUSS

Even more tragic was the course of events in Bohemia, a land to which the teachings of Wyclif brought enduring fruits. Czech preachers had already stressed Biblical teachings that reflected on a worldly clergy when Jerome of Prague brought back Wyclif writings from his student years at Oxford. In Prague John Huss (1370—1415) came into contact with the teachings of Wyclif. He found himself in accord with them though not willing to go so far as to reject the papacy and the sacraments. His criticism of the clergy was popular since many of these were German and an anti-German spirit was stirring in Bohemia. When the Czech nation gained ascendancy at the university in Prague, a German exodus led to the foundation of Leipzig University. Huss was leader in the Bethlehem chapel in Prague where his preaching won him a wide following. His enemies succeeded in having him excommunicated and his writings burned, but he maintained his influence in southern Bohemia when driven from Prague. From the papal ban he appealed to the true Head of the church, Christ Himself. Emperor Sigismund granted him a safe conduct to the Council of Constance, where he was willing to defend his faith. But Huss was condemned by the council and burned at the stake in 1415, as was Jerome the following year.

The followers of Huss denied they were heretics, for they did not believe subjection to Rome necessary. Patriotism blended with their

24

faith, and social and economic factors influenced their attitude toward the emperor and the Germans. But divisions arose among them, the Taborites assembling for preaching and Communion in the south, the Horebites meeting in the north. They united only when threatened from without. An agreement known as the Prague Compactata was finally reached on four main demands: freedom to preach the Word of God, Communion with both bread and wine (hence the name given them — Utraquists = both kinds), abstinence of clergy from worldly wealth, and secular punishment for mortal sins. Despite bans and crusades the papacy could not win back the Bohemians, who maintained a separate church characterized mainly by the use of the vernacular and the administration of the cup. After the death of the regular Roman archbishop the church was governed by a consistory of clergy and lay members until its absorption in the Counter-Reformation. In 1467 one group separated to become the Bohemian Brethren, with their own bishops and having as their goal an imitation of the simplicity of the primitive church. This group survived the 16th-century Reformation.

THE REFORM COUNCILS

The rival claims of pope and emperor, of secular rulers and ecclesiastical lords, had prompted theories of the relationships of church and state. When the papacy itself produced pope and antipope, interest grew in the doctrine of the church. Men began to question the papal claims, the hierarchical structure, and the nature of the Christian community. At first recourse was taken to the theory of a council of the church. If it was questioned whether the pope possessed fullness of power — the curial theory — or whether the power was distributed among the bishops of the church and their chapters — the episcopal theory — might not the power dwell in the whole community for which pope and bishops existed? And in times of crises, such as those of the 14th century, should not the whole church come together, through representatives, and deal with its problems? But who should call it, and how should it be organized?

The cardinals of the opposing popes met in 1408 and called the Council of Pisa for the following year. It was an assembly of cardinals, bishops, heads of orders, abbots, doctors of theology and of canon law, and representatives of rulers. The council deposed both current popes and elected the archbishop of Milan, with the result that there were now three popes. A cardinal council had failed. The next attempt was made under the auspices of Emperor Sigismund at Constance. It proved to be the largest gathering of the Middle Ages. John Gerson of the University of Paris proposed that the group be organized on the pattern of the "nations" at the medieval universities. This equalized the votes of the many bishops — English, German, French, Italian, Spanish. Each cardinal had one vote. The council, following the theory of Gerson, declared its power was direct from God and extended over the whole church. No moral reforms were effected — these were left to the pope, who was to call another council in 5 years. But the schism was healed and the church again had one pope. The papacy, meanwhile, had been transformed from an absolute to a constitutional monarchy. The idea persisted for a long time that a council could be called to remedy ills, or that a national group could effect reforms.

The difficulty of reform by council became evident very soon. A third council was called for Basel in 1431. When the pope objected and wanted Bologna as the site, he was overruled by a council that declared its own supremacy. But the decrees of the council revealed the real desire of the various "nations," namely, to enhance national churches at the expense of the Curia. The decisions included the following reforms: annual synods were to be held in each diocese; biennial synods in the archbishoprics; a general council was to meet every 10 years. While elections should be canonical, appointments should not be made by the pope. Annates and heavy taxes should not be levied by Rome, and only certain legal appeals could go out of a country. The number of cardinals was fixed at 24. The actions drastically reduced the income of the papacy. In line with such an attitude was the concordat between France and the Curia that almost gave the French Church its independence. The English Church had won equal freedom. Only Germany, by the Concordat of Vienna (1448), was still subject to Rome, and this less because of the papal power than the internal jealousies and divisions among the German princes.

Following Basel a council met first at Ferrara and then at Florence in an attempt to reach a reconciliation with the Eastern Church. A reunion was even proclaimed in 1439, but the proposals were unacceptable to the Greeks, and before further negotiations could be carried

26

on their capital had fallen to the Turks. Thus about all the conciliar movement could produce was a united papacy, which, however, was no longer sovereign but subject to the desires of national churches.

A New Age — Humanism

Behind the scenes of rivalry between the rulers of the church and the monarchs of emerging nations other forces were at work that were destined to change the character of European life. In northern Italy, Germany, France, and England cities were growing that demanded freedom. Trade and industry were their lifeblood, and they resented the exactions of both imperial and ecclesiastical masters. Travels eastward, the Crusades, and contacts with Eastern Christendom widened the horizon and afforded profitable exchange. Venice, Genoa, and Florence became centers of trade, and Italy's geographic position gave her a strategic place in commerce with western and northern Europe. In the north the route of the Hanseatic League was an avenue of exchange of goods and ideas. Men became aware of a created world full of wonders that tempted their curiosity. By observation and experimentation facts were discovered that man had not known before. The overarching arguments about authority made some skeptical of all traditional ideas.

A new humanism arose which found its richest expression in Italy in what was called a rebirth, or renaissance. The discovery of ancient classics after the fall of Constantinople contributed to a new concept of the individual, which had been gradually developing. It found room for free — even licentious — expression in the paganism that flourished during the struggle of the church for power. The use of the vernacular, the achievements in literature, art, and architecture, the study of nature, and a new interpretation of history were some of the expressions of an individualism whose view of life was dictated by one's attainments in life. The framework of the church still stood, its ceremonies were observed, the final sacrament was still desired, but few took seriously the spiritual claims of the papacy. The monks were ridiculed. Historical research revealed the forged documents to which the popes had appealed. The Renaissance popes, who were themselves of great Italian families, employed famous artists and builders to adorn the churches of Rome and Italy. The voice of the preacher was heard, but when

Savonarola attempted a moral reform in Florence, he was as readily burned as he had been made a dictator by political factions.

SPANISH HUMANISM

Almost alone in Europe in seeking reform of the church from within was the higher clergy in Spain. In 1473 a council had effected some improvements, and a translation of the Bible into Spanish was made in 1478. Cardinal Ximenes, who became archbishop of Toledo in 1495, secured permission from the pope to reform his diocese. In 1508 he established the University of Alcala, a center for philological study. A Greek Testament was printed in 1514, and in 1520 a Polyglot Bible in six volumes made available ancient texts of the Scriptures — the cardinal expended $125,000 on its publication. A group of humanists brought honor to Spain — Elio Antonio de Nebrija, Juan de Valdes, Juan de Vergara, Juan Luis Vives — but the light of learning turned into flames of persecution when the torch of the Inquisition was brought in.

HUMANISM IN NORTHERN EUROPE

The Netherlands produced a reform program antedating both the advent of humanism and the influence of Luther. For toward the end of the 14th century Gerhard Groote had preached a life of repentance in accord with the divine image of man and established at Deventer a school of enduring significance. Love to fellowman and imitation of Christ were the motives he sought to inculcate. His disciple Florentius Radewin carried out his ideas in the care of the sick and the poor and in the education of boys and girls. Gerhard Zerbolt gave literary expression to the ideals of the group that came to be known as "Brethren of the Common Life" because of a common fund and a form of life as a company though without monastic vows. Zerboldt was the foremost scholar of the group. His *Spiritual Exercises,* modeled after Radewin's treatise on the same subject, became the basis of a still more famous system — Ignatius Loyola's *Spiritual Exercises.* In the 15th century the influence of the Brethren extended far and wide through the Windesheim monastery, which numbered Thomas a Kempis among its members, and through the schools of John Cele at Zwolle, Alexander Hegius at Deventer, and John Murmellius at Münster. Wessel Gansfort and John Standonck continued the tradition through writings that prepared the way for Erasmus, Luther, and Calvin.

Erasmus was a student in the schools of the Brethren. He imbibed their scorn of the depraved life of the monks and the clergy, their concept of Christianity as a practical obedience of the ethical life, and their love of learning, which included both the classics and Christian literature.

In England More and Colet, in France Faber and Bude, and in Germany Reuchlin accepted the humanist legacy of the Renaissance, hoping that deeper knowledge would result in a purer church.

The time had come for a reconsideration of the relationship of faith and knowledge. From many sources a questioning of the ultimate source of authority among men was arising, and nothing less was involved than the nature and place of the Christian church in this new age.

III

REDISCOVERY OF THE GOSPEL

The story of the Christian church is one of repeated attempts at reformation. For every living organism grows. But growth can be in different directions, and the church is ever tempted to develop away from its true goal. Then it must be recalled from its false tendency and set on its rightful path. The life and work of Martin Luther achieved such a turn in the church of the 16th century.

Whole libraries have been written on Luther. He has been examined from all angles and by all types of scholars — friendly, hostile, neutral. He has been hailed as a hero of Christendom and condemned as a disrupter of the church. Some have made him a saint, some have despised his occasionally vulgar language and boisterous manner. He has been exalted as a German patriot and denounced as a provincial demagog. Each age has judged him according to its standards and used or abused him according as he could be fitted into contemporary programs. He has suffered the fate of many historical figures who find their purposes distorted by their own times and their achievements turned toward selfish gains of their followers.

But our aim is not an evaluation of all the results of Luther's words and deeds. The history of the church is something else than the story of great individuals, however powerful. It is the greatness of Luther's contribution that he pointed to sources of spiritual life beyond himself and in his own experience witnessed to the truth by which the church lives. He is not the creator of a new church but the guide to an understanding of the nature of the true church. At first he had no intention of challenging the existing order of the church in which he grew up. It was only as his own inner experiences in that church opened his eyes to the central fact of the church of Christ that he found himself in opposition to much in his contemporary situation. The

31

church existed in reality not by virtue of what many took for granted as its supports, but by the Gospel, and Luther's reformation was the result of his rediscovery of that Gospel.

LUTHER'S EARLY LIFE AND EDUCATION

The home into which Martin Luther was born Nov. 10, 1483, was probably a typical German household of the lower middle class. When Luther was less than a year old, the family moved from Eisleben to Mansfeld, where the father leased a smelting furnace. There is no doubt but that the parents were dutiful members of the town church. The father, however, wanted Martin to become a lawyer, for law was the way to preferment in the rising economic level of the German communities, and Hans and his wife Margarete had ambitions for this son. He was sent to a Latin school in Magdeburg at the age of 14, then to Eisenach, and to the University of Erfurt in 1501. Erfurt had a law school where a student could learn both the law of the church — canon law — and the law of the state. Luther finished his bachelor and master of arts studies and in 1505 was ready to begin the course in law.

IN THE ERFURT MONASTERY

Then in July 1505 a radical change in plans took place. Luther forsook his law studies and entered a monastery in Erfurt. We can only guess at what lay back of this decision. We do know that two weeks earlier he had become terrified in a storm when lightning struck close to him. He said that he then vowed to enter a monastery. Knowing that this would be against his father's wish, Luther must have had earlier secret thoughts of such a step, which now prompted him to act. The fact that he chose the strictest of the six monasteries in Erfurt suggests that he was in earnest in seeking to become a monk. The Augustinian Hermits were not — despite the name — hermits, but they did carefully regulate the hours of common prayer, work, begging, and meditation. They belonged to the Observant branch of the order, tolerating no laxness in the life of the members. After a year's novitiate Luther became a member of the order and prepared for the priesthood. He was ordained in the Erfurt Cathedral in April 1507.

Much has been written on Luther's motives in this change. Why did he lose interest in law? Why did he thwart his father's plans?

Was he sick in body or mind? Various interpretations have been given. But the simplest seems the most adequate. At the age of 22 he was trying to find himself, and in the Middle Ages the monastery was the natural place for a religious-minded youth who was uncertain of himself, his faith, his career. The earnestness with which he applied himself in the monastery testifies to the genuineness of his religious fervor. He worried his superior by his meticulousness in confession. The rules of the monastic life — celibacy, poverty, and obedience — he sought to fulfill completely. Since the religious, as monks were called in opposition to the laity, strove for a higher state of Christian perfection, Luther followed the prescribed course in the hope of reaching the promised goal. But the more carefully he sought out his sins the more despondent he became. His studies included the writings of Occam and Augustine — the one suggesting that he had a freedom of will to do the best he could, the other confronting him with the idea of predestination with its corollary that some were not ordained to blessedness. Was he among the elect? Had he done all he could? In John Staupitz, the sympathetic and understanding superior, Luther found comfort and help. Staupitz assured him that the grace in Christ was to be set over against the wrath of God caused by his sin. But Luther could not rid himself of his fear and sense of guilt. Even in celebrating the Mass he felt this fear.

In 1510 the order sent Luther and another monk to Rome on business having to do with the order's provincial administration. Luther has been criticized for not showing more interest in the new movements in literature and art and in the monuments of the Renaissance. But many of the edifices were not yet finished or even begun, and it is true that Luther evinced no curiosity about them. Rather he was still seeking the peace promised by the church, and so he attended Mass after Mass at the Roman altars, even climbing the *Scala santa* on his knees. Later he was to express his astonishment over the carelessness of the clergy in their ministration and his disappointment at not having found what might be expected in the capital of Christendom.

LECTURER AT THE UNIVERSITY OF WITTENBERG

Staupitz recognized the talents of the young monk and directed him into studies at the university that might prepare him to teach. In

33

1512 Luther became a doctor of theology. Staupitz held a professorship at the newly founded University of Wittenberg, a position he found a burden along with his administrative duties as provincial vicar of his order. He appointed Luther to take his place at the university.

One of the legends in Luther lore is that the Bible was unknown in his day either by clergy or laity. On the contrary, study of the Bible was required in the Augustinian monasteries, and Luther's first course in the University of Wittenberg was on the Psalms. We now know that Luther had studied the Scriptures in the Erfurt monastery and that he had a good acquaintance with them long before he began to teach. In 1513—1514 his lectures were on the Psalms, in 1515 to 1516 on the Epistle to the Romans, in 1516 on the Epistle to the Galatians, and in 1517 on the Epistle to the Hebrews.

RIGHTEOUSNESS BY FAITH

Controversy reigns among scholars as to the exact time when Luther came to his discovery that the righteousness of God with which he had been so deeply concerned was not a forbidding attribute of God but a gift of God to the man who believes, so that the righteous live by faith. It would be natural to suppose that the "breakthrough" might come as he was preparing his lectures on the Epistle to the Romans in 1515—1516. But there is ground to believe that Luther had already caught something of the meaning of righteousness by faith in his work on the Psalms a few years earlier. While it is impossible to date this event, it is clear that the discovery of the Gospel as "the power of God for salvation to everyone who has faith" and of the "righteousness of God" as a righteousness given by God to the believer for the sake of Jesus Christ is the climax of the spiritual struggles Luther had experienced for a decade. All his intense efforts to merit the love of God by the works which the penitential system of the church had prescribed had proved vain. He could not attain the conviction that he had done enough, although he had tested all the ways of the medieval sacramental system — confession, penance, absolution, celibacy, poverty, obedience, ordination, pilgrimage. God still seemed a wrathful face. He interpreted the royal passages of the Psalms as descriptions of Christ. This led him to understand the work of Christ as opposed to his own works. Christ became the face of God — a loving face, the face of

34

One who sacrificed Himself for us. Forgiveness of sins became a reality in Christ, in whom alone was salvation. It was God's work — man received a free gift, in faith. But even the forgiven man could not meet the demands of the Law. Judged by the righteous will of God he was still a sinner, but accounted righteous (*simul justus et peccator*). Faith in Christ — God's sacrifice for sin and the source of man's spiritual life — placed the believer in God's favor as one justified, or accounted righteous.

For a while Luther was fascinated by certain aspects of mysticism. He even prepared editions of *Theologia Germanica,* or *German Theology,* and praised the mystic John Tauler. But this interest was soon overwhelmed by his new reading of Scripture, where Christ is the Key to its interpretation. Here was a new standard by which to judge theology and the church.

Luther had become convinced that the truth of the Christian faith was to be found in Scripture and not in the traditional philosophy adopted by the church. The great attempt of Thomas Aquinas had been to fit the truths of revelation into forms of rational thought — forms that were a heritage from Plato and Aristotle. Luther knew especially the writings of scholastic theologians like William of Occam and Gabriel Biel who, following their master Duns Scotus, differed from Aquinas in their emphasis on the will of God and the will of man. But Luther felt that none of the philosophers understood the Gospel as a revelation known by faith and not resting on rational arguments drawn from various experiences in the physical world. It had become clear to him that the grace of God is a gift, through Christ, and that all the acts of man's will could neither earn that grace nor be done without grace, if they were to be called good deeds at all. How far Luther had gone in his thinking may be seen from a set of theses, or propositions, for debate that he drew up at the university in 1517. They are less famous than the 95 Theses drawn up later that year, but they reveal positions Luther had attained and from which he could go on to attack abuses in the church.

Theses Against Scholastic Theology

"Compared with the study of theology the whole of Aristotle is as darkness is to light," Luther contended, and "it is a wrong thing

35

to say a man cannot become a theologian without Aristotle." For the philosophers talked as if man had a free will and could of himself love God and His law and choose to do the right. This Luther denied, emphasizing the connection between the grace of God and good works. No work is good unless it is done out of a good heart, and without the grace of God no man can even will, much less do, a work good in God's sight. "The sole means of obtaining grace is the eternal election and predestination of God." So faith looks to a work of God, not to works of man, and the will to do the law of God can come only "by the Child who has been born to us" (Is. 9:6). The grace which God gives "is never present in such a way that it is inactive, but it is a living, active, and operative spirit," the source of all good deeds. "The grace of God is given for the purpose of directing the will" so "that we not only will what God wills but also ought to will whatever God wills." "He who is outside the grace of God sins incessantly" in whatever he does because his center is self rather than God.

This is the heart of Luther's theology. Thomas Aquinas had tried to describe the nature of God as essentially the goodness of Being, and all goodness is related to Him. Created by God, man is good; and though he sinned, man can be helped by the sacraments of the church to do good. Grace is imparted to man in the sacraments, and by virtue of this infused power man fulfills the law of God, does good deeds, and merits salvation. In the tradition of Scotus, Luther questions whether God can be known as rationally as Thomas Aquinas supposed. We know only His will toward us, and this has been revealed in Scripture. We can study the world, which we perceive by our senses, and reason about it. But the will of God is not apprehended by our senses. It is known only through faith, and "in vain does one fashion a logic of faith." In Christ we find a revelation of God's dealing with man, and it must be accepted if we are to be accounted righteous. "We do not become righteous by doing righteous deeds, but having been made righteous we do righteous deeds."

Such an interpretation of the grace of God necessarily places the center of gravity of Christianity in the Scriptures. Man can neither know God nor do His will without finding the revelation of God's grace in Scripture. Luther believed that this was the message of the church, and so he could conclude the theses by asserting: "In all we wanted to say, we have said nothing that is not in agreement with the Catholic Church and the teachers of the church." But he held that the philosophers and theologians had been led astray by trying to make Christian knowledge conform to the traditions of Greek philosophy. Because they had interpreted human nature in terms of that philosophy rather than in terms of the Biblical revelation, they had developed doctrines and practices in the church alien to Christian truth.

The theses against scholastic theology were theoretical and academic and therefore attracted little attention. But a few months later, in October 1517, Luther drew up another set of propositions that hit squarely at one of the most popular practices of the day. This time he attacked the errors of the system of penances, and the result was the crumbling of one of the pillars supporting the whole medieval sacramental and hierarchical church.

The 95 Theses Against Indulgences

In the early church confession and absolution were the means by which the sinner received the benefits of the redemption in Christ. At first the forgiveness of sins was associated with Baptism, after which the recipient was not to commit sin. But could there be forgiveness after the "washing of regeneration"? Experience soon convinced the church that forgiveness must be repetitive. To forestall indifference to the seriousness of the promise implicit in forgiveness, confession would have to be followed by deeds confirming the penitent's earnestness. This might be a deed of charity, a work of discipline, or a gift, any of which would be required before the absolution and would constitute a satisfaction for the temporal consequence of the sin — only God could take away the guilt of the sin. In the development of the practice a distinction was made between mortal and venial sins, and a whole classification of sins resulted each of which had its proper penalty. When the practice became a sacrament enjoined on all members of the church, the priest in the parish and the bishop and the pope in more important cases claimed that they were God's vicars in assessing transgressions and imposing penalties. It was taught that confession and contrition could not be altogether complete and that some penalties would carry over into purgatory. In fact the hierarchy held the keys of the kingdom of God. They could close the Kingdom to high or low, and the pope could excommunicate kings or emperors and close the doors of churches under ban. Since absolution was necessary for the sacraments, the church had the power to withold the means of grace from any dissident member, high or low.

Another side of the matter was the translation of penalties into money payments. Not only venial sins could be pardoned by appropriate gifts but even mortal sins had their price. The church could take from its treasury of good deeds built up by the works of saints who had earned more than needed for their own salvation and add them to the donations of the penitent who wanted to care for the penalties of purgatory for himself or dear ones. Here was an enterprise of immense commercial gain for the medieval church. Its funds and lands and treasures made the church the single richest institution throughout Europe. The pope acted as an international banker, and his or his bishops' transactions influenced the course of monarchs of the emerging nations. When the penitent found it inconvenient to meet an imposed penalty in the form of pilgrimage or prayers, he could secure an indulgence, which allowed him to pay in cash instead.

Once started, the system of indulgences could be used for other purposes. By the purchase of an indulgence the individual would receive credit on his score of penalties, shortening his stay in purgatory. Through the sale of such indulgences the pope in 1500 — a jubilee year — found a way of financing the erection of St. Peter's. But princes and bishops might cooperate in the distribution of indulgences and agree on the division of income for their own purposes.

Luther's prince had used the system to raise money for the University of Wittenberg. This had brought protests from Luther. In 1517 the archbishopric of Mainz was for sale. Albert of Hohenzollern bought it for 10,000 ducats, which he had to borrow. The pope allowed him to sell indulgences in his three bishoprics, half of the proceeds to be retained by the young archbishop, the other half to go to the building fund of St. Peter's. Tetzel, a Dominican monk, was in charge of the operation. He proclaimed the indulgence as effecting the forgiveness of sins and the liberation of friends from purgatory. It was this brazen abuse of a sacrament of the church that drove Luther to issue another set of theses — the 95, which on Oct. 31, 1517, he nailed on the door of the Castle Church in Wittenberg as on a bulletin board, inviting discussion and debate.

In the theses Luther expressed his belief that the pope was uninformed of what was going on. "Christians are to be taught that if the pope knew the exactions of the indulgence preachers, he would rather that the Basilica of St. Peter were burned to ashes than built up with the skin, flesh, and bones of his sheep" (Thesis 50). But the prevailing practice was hurting the pope. "This unbridled preaching of indulgences makes it difficult even for learned men to rescue the reverence which is due the pope from slander or from the shrewd questions of the laity" (81). People were slyly asking why the pope, if he had power to release from purgatory because of money, did not do it from love. And if souls are redeemed by the prayers bought for them, why does the pope still go on as if they were not redeemed? Why doesn't the pope with his enormous wealth build St. Peter's out of his own wealth? Why do other and former indulgences have to give way to the jubilee indulgence if each is efficacious? So it is apparent that the people suspected the motives back of the indulgence traffic.

But Luther was concerned more about the glory of God than the reputation of the pope. In fact the pope can only remit penalties imposed by canon law or for violations of papal decrees. He can declare that God has forgiven the guilt of a repentant sinner, which any priest can do after confession. But he has no power from God to impose penalties in His name, nor has he any jurisdiction over souls in purgatory. He may only pray for them. "Any truly repentant Christian has a right to full remission of penalty and guilt, even without indulgence letters" (36). "Any true Christian, whether living or dead, participates in all the blessings of Christ and the church" (57). If only people knew it, the treasures of the church available to the believer are not the merits of the saints but "the grace of God" (56—62). "If indulgences, which are a very insignificant thing, are celebrated with one bell, one procession, and one ceremony, then the Gospel, which is the very greatest thing, should be preached with a hundred bells, a hundred processions, and a hundred ceremonies." (55)

39

The only adequate explanation of the rapidity of the spread of these propositions throughout Europe, everywhere raising discussion, approval, or opposition, is that Luther had touched a sensitive nerve in the ecclesiastical body of his day. In the parish the indulgence could be of interest to every parishioner, and both mendicant monks and local priests were engaged in hearing the confessions that the indulgence demanded. On higher levels the participation of bishops and orders was involved, and even princely treasuries would feel the consequences of the devaluation of indulgences, though secular rulers would not be unhappy if fewer of their coins would go to faraway Rome. But most of all, the extent of the papal power was questioned. Did the pope have the power to proclaim indulgences? Whence came this power? It was only a step to skepticism about the papacy itself. Luther had already created doubts and was soon to take the full step and challenge the grounds on which the papacy was exercising its power.

The theses were immediately printed and soon appeared in the cities, the universities, and the parishes throughout Europe. It has been estimated that within the next two years no less than a quarter of a million copies of Luther's writings in German were distributed in the church. The monk of Wittenberg had called for an academic debate — he created a controversy in which all of both church and state participated.

In his own university, order, and principality Luther received sympathetic treatment. Frederick, the ruler of Saxony, surnamed the Wise, was proud of the publicity given his university, and though cautious about being drawn into the battle demanded that Luther be treated fairly. A powerful help was given Luther when in 1518 Philip Melanchthon joined the Wittenberg faculty. Staupitz, his vicar, requested Luther to expound his views further at the order meeting in Heidelberg in April 1518. In a series of theses at Heidelberg Luther drew a distinction between a theology of glory and a theology of the cross and contended that "true theology and recognition of God are in the crucified Christ" (Thesis 20), whereas scholasticism seeks a "theology of glory." In Rome opposition was immediate. The Curia had received complaints from the archbishop of Mainz and the

Dominicans, and in June and August of 1518 it charged Luther with heresy. Luther went to work on an elaboration of the theses, published a treatise on *Explanations of the Disputation on the Value of the Indulgences,* and sent a copy to Pope Leo X, to whom the work was dedicated. The book was hardly apt to conciliate the pope, especially since the author recalled that popes had erred and since they at no time had jurisdiction over the Eastern Church. In August Luther was summoned to Rome, but his prince demanded that any hearing be on German soil. So Cardinal Cajetan came to Augsburg. He was unsuccessful in persuading Luther to recant, and Luther proceeded to ask that a council be called to consider the issues he had raised. Another attempt by the Curia to quiet the Wittenberg monk, this time undertaken by Carl von Miltitz early in 1519, was no more fruitful.

IMPERIAL POLITICS

At this juncture Emperor Maximilian died. The election of a successor became the most important matter in the chancelleries of Europe and in the Curia at Rome. The pope had fears concerning the election of either of the two contenders, Francis I of France, or Charles V of Spain and Burgundy, for both had designs on the control of Italy. One of the electors was Frederick the Wise, whom the pope dared not antagonize by harsh action against Luther. So for the time being Luther was left free. In June and July he came to the rescue of Andreas Karlstadt, his colleague at Wittenberg, who was holding a series of debates with John Eck of Leipzig on the questions Luther had asked. Luther's entrance into the fray was significant because he now publicly questioned the infallibility of councils, one of which had burned John Huss at Constance, not far from Leipzig. Having attacked both the papal system and the councils, Luther was clearly maintaining the sufficiency of Scripture as the final authority, an authority not dependent on a hierarchical institution but available to every believer as a member of the priesthood of all believers.

Denounced as a heretic in Rome, applauded by diverse groups with different motives for a change in the current order of things, and deeply concerned with the needs of the common Christians in

41

the parishes, Luther turned to a defense of his stand and to a program of reform in a stream of lectures, sermons, pamphlets, and books that made the year 1520 memorable.

TREATISE ON GOOD WORKS

A Treatise on Good Works rejected the notion that by his devaluation of good deeds Luther was destroying the basis of Christian morality. A good tree brings forth good fruit — Luther was concerned about the true goodness of the heart. They are false prophets "who through manifold good works (as they call them) want to win the will of God and purchase for themselves His grace as though He were a peddler or day laborer who will not give His grace and mercy without pay" (Section X). "If everyone had faith, we would no longer need any law, but each one would of himself at all times do good works, as his confidence in God would sufficiently instruct him" (XIV). "We never read that the Holy Spirit was given to anyone when he did works, but always when men have heard the Gospel of Christ and the mercy of God" (XVII). From a consideration of the First Commandment, which commands the greatest work of all — faith — Luther goes on to apply this principle of receiving health through faith and exercising all of one's love in the area of the other Commandments — life with one's neighbor. The treatise was originally planned as a sermon to the congregation in Wittenberg, where Luther served as supply pastor, but it grew into a long work, and when printed in May 1520 it served to bring the thought of Luther to the common man throughout the church.

THE PAPACY AT ROME

The attacks on the papacy had aroused its defenders — after the Leipzig debate. The extravagance of these papal defenders and their criticisms of Luther led him to clearer, more vigorous statements of his doubts that Rome was truly the head of the church. In June appeared his treatise on *The Papacy at Rome* in which he contended "for but two things. First: I will not suffer any man to establish new articles of faith and to abuse all other Christians in the world and slander and brand them as heretics, apostates, and unbelievers simply because they are not under the pope. Second: All that the pope decrees and does I will receive on this condition: that I first test it

42

by the Holy Scriptures." If this is not granted, "he shall be to me neither pope nor Christian."

AN OPEN LETTER TO THE CHRISTIAN NOBILITY

That a break with Rome would be more than a personal affair was hinted at in another passage. "Moreover, I would be truly glad if kings, princes, and all the nobles would take hold and turn the knaves from Rome out of the country and keep the appointments to bishoprics and benefices out of their hands." This became the theme of *An Open Letter to the Christian Nobility of the German Nation Concerning the Reform of the Christian Estate* published in August. Charles V had been elected emperor in June. Luther hoped for better times since "God has given us a noble youth to be our head." The letter is a trumpet call to break down the walls of the Romanists, three of which are enumerated, namely, the Romanist claims that the temporal power is subordinate to the spiritual, that only the pope can explain Scripture, and that only the pope can call a council. The secular princes should call a council to discuss the abuses of the Curia in its multiform levies on the churches of their territories. The church in Germany should be independent and manage its own affairs. The orders should be reformed and monks be allowed to marry. Subservience to the pope should cease and his presumed authority over the emperor be denied. He should no longer be a secular lord. The princes should look to the care of the poor and of the schools. Saints' days and canonizations should be abolished. Here in fact was a declaration of German independence from the Roman Curia and a program of radical reform of the clergy, the churches, and the laws of the land.

"THE BABYLONIAN CAPTIVITY"

To answer critics who had assailed his teachings and to give his friends a full, comprehensive statement of his position, Luther brought out in October — three years after the 95 Theses — *The Babylonian Captivity of the Church*. This was a careful analysis of the seven sacraments that had become the foundation of the medieval church. In analyzing them he exposed the errors and inventions of the church. The seven he reduced to two. "It has seemed best to restrict the name of sacrament to such promises as have signs attached to them. The remainder, not being bound to signs, are bare promises. Hence there are, strictly speaking, but two sacraments in the church of God — Baptism and Bread; for only in these two do we find both the divinely instituted sign and the promise of forgiveness of sins." In this treatise Luther brought together much of what he had previously written in shorter tracts on subjects related to the sacraments.

This work meant a complete break with the theology of the medieval church, making Luther's return to that church quite impossible. Indeed Eck was arriving in Germany with the bull of excommunication.

Treatise on Christian Liberty

The repeated efforts of the Curial representative von Miltitz to bring about a reconciliation proved futile, but one result was the tract *The Freedom of a Christian,* which Luther sent to Pope Leo as a token of the kind of writing he preferred over polemics. Although written after his condemnation by Rome had been pronounced, Luther made no mention of it. His interest was in the relationship of the Christian to God and to his neighbor. "A Christian is a perfectly free lord of all, subject to none. A Christian is a perfectly dutiful servant of all, subject to all." The Christian, as the tract elaborates, has all freely from Christ, in faith, and in turn gives himself freely, in love, to his neighbor. "He ought to think: Although I am an unworthy and condemned man, my God has given me in Christ all the riches of righteousness and salvation without any merit on my part, out of pure, free mercy, so that from now on I need nothing except faith which believes all this is true. Why should I not therefore freely, joyfully, with all my heart, and with an eager will do all things which I know are pleasing and acceptable to such a Father who has overwhelmed me with His inestimable riches? I will therefore give myself as a Christ to my neighbor, just as Christ offered Himself to me; I will do nothing in this life except what I see is necessary, profitable, and salutary to my neighbor, since through faith I have an abundance of all good things in Christ." It is also necessary to have some forms of ceremonies and regulations, not that men "should be made righteous or gain merit by them, but that they might thus be kept from doing evil and might more easily be instructed to the righteousness of faith." In the midst of the storm clouds surrounding

44

Luther he could quietly and gracefully pen this devotional classic of Christendom.

THE BREAK WITH ROME

In Rome Leo X had on October 10 issued a bull, or decree, threatening the excommunication of Luther. It gave Luther 60 days to recant. On December 10 Luther gathered a group of friends, proceeded to a city gate of Wittenberg, and burned a copy of the papal document along with books of papal decrees and canon law. The pope's sentence had suggested that the writings of the heretic should be burned. This was Luther's reply. The actual excommunication was formulated in Rome early in January 1521 and was brought to Germany by Eck. In April it was to be presented to a meeting of the imperial diet at Worms where, according to custom, the excommunication would be followed by the ban of the empire, making it unlawful for anyone to give food, shelter, or assistance to the fugitive. Frederick the Wise insisted that Luther be heard and condemned on Scriptural grounds. He gave Luther a promise of safe-conduct to Worms and succeeded in getting him an opportunity to appear before the emperor himself. It was here that Luther dared tell the highest official of the empire: "Unless I am convicted by Scripture and plain reason — I do not accept the authority of popes and councils, for they have contradicted each other — my conscience is captive to the Word of God, I cannot and I will not recant anything, for to go against conscience is neither right nor safe. God help me. Amen."

Despite his heroic stand Luther was convicted and put under the ban. Charles V, a pious Catholic, pledged himself to rid his domains of the heresy promulgated by Luther and his adherents. Yet Luther still had the protection and help of his prince, Elector Frederick. From Worms Luther was spirited away and brought to Frederick's castle at Wartburg. Here for the moment he was secure, and while enemies abroad raged at his writings, Luther could go on with the reformation of the Western Church. Both pope and emperor were to find that forces far beyond their power to control had been released.

IV

DEMARCATION OF REFORM

To protest against error and evils is not an infrequent part of man's story. But only to a few has it been given to build up a better structure on the ruins of what has been torn down. Had Luther's task been only to discern and criticize the unscriptural teachings and practices of the church, his name might soon have been forgotten. His great constructive deeds, however, proved of permanent worth to the church and affected its future course and character.

THE GERMAN BIBLE

In the enforced quiet of the Wartburg Castle Luther turned to study, prayer, and writing. Among the results was the translation of the Bible into German, one of his great achievements.

There were Bibles in Germany before Luther. We have already noted Luther's study and use of the Bible in the Erfurt monastery and at the University of Wittenberg. His order enjoined earnest study of the Scriptures. One of the rooms in the medieval monasteries was a *scriptorium,* or writing room, where monks copied manuscripts before the days of printing. The translation that Jerome had made around the beginning of the fifth century had become the common one (Vulgate) in Europe, and it was copied in every part of Western Christendom. It has been estimated that probably 26,000 copies were in use during the 15th century. They would be found mostly in churches, monasteries, and universities. When printing was invented, the first printed book was Gutenberg's Bible around 1452. Before the end of the century there were over 100 editions of the printed Latin Bible. Translation into German had also begun, so that 14 translations into High German and 4 into Low German had appeared by 1500. The complete Bible was expensive, but many separate parts of the Bible were available both in Latin and German. They were included in his-

47

tory books, which reproduced the historical portions of both Testaments. Or they could be in service books that provided in handy form the readings from Scripture used in the Mass, especially the Gospels and Epistles. The Psalter was a favorite part of the Bible. It was widely used in whole or in selections of psalms — daily in the hour services — and Latin and German printings were quite common.

So the Bible was not unknown in the church. But only the educated could read the Latin versions, and the German ones were mechanical and often inaccurate. The people had been taught that their true teacher was the church — only the church could be sure of the meaning of Scripture. Any study of the Bible was secondary and reserved for monk or scholar. Furthermore, the Vulgate was the authorized version, which was to be preferred over vernacular versions, whose accuracy might be doubted. To the hierarchy the Albigensian heresy had seemed to have been prompted by laymen who had read the Bible, and the church had expressed fear that lay reading would lead to misunderstanding and wrong beliefs. But the Bible was included in monastic and university education, and knowledge of it was widely extended.

Luther had steeped himself in Bible study as he prepared for his lectures on the Psalms, Romans, Galatians — all before 1517. He had become interested in the Hebrew original of the seven penitential psalms. Around 1510 he had studied Reuchlin's Hebrew grammar. In 1512 he made Reuchlin's Hebrew text of these psalms the basis of his own treatise — his first attempt at a popular translation. In 1516 Luther secured a copy of the first Hebrew Psalter published in Germany. Through all these years he was perfecting himself in the original language of the Old Testament.

About the same time that he began his study of Greek, Erasmus' epoch-making Greek New Testament appeared in 1516, printed in Basel, and before the end of the year Luther was using it in his lectures on Romans. Melanchthon, the Greek scholar of his generation, came to Wittenberg in 1518, and immediately Luther availed himself of his friend's mastery of the Greek language.

Luther's search for the true meaning of Scripture by close attention to the original languages in which it had been transmitted is parallel in time to his discovery of an authority superior to that of the hierarchy and the church. As he became increasingly aware of the nature of the Gospel, he became correspondingly bolder in challenging what he was sure were false teachings. By the time he faced the spiritual and secular authorities at the Diet of Worms in April 1521 he could ask to be convinced only by the Scriptures that he was wrong. Here he stood. In the light of what he had learned by the help of the best scholarship of his age he could not do otherwise.

But if the church was to be purified of its errors, Luther knew that the common people must learn what he had learned in the Bible. His immediate task must be to give them a German translation that truly interprets the original meaning of the Old and the New Testament in a language that everyone can understand. Between Christmas 1521 and Easter 1522 he produced the New Testament in German — in the words of Hans Lietzmann "a miracle of God performed for the German race." Luther had grown up in a home that knew the language of peasants and small-town folk. He had enjoyed the privilege of good schools in Magdeburg and Erfurt. Various errands had taken him to different parts of his country. Choosing the Middle High German of the court of Saxony, he moulded a language which by its clarity, force, and color became the instrument of a great literature.

The publication of the New Testament in September 1522 was an immediate success. Before the end of the year another edition was necessary. Between 1522 and 1546, the year of Luther's death, 21 different editions were printed in Wittenberg alone. Reprints were made in many places — almost 100 different editions have been counted from 1522 to 1546. The copies of the September Testament (as it was called) ran into the hundreds of thousands. Revisions were constantly made by Luther, especially in 1527 and 1530.

Meanwhile work progressed on the translation of the Old Testament. In order to satisfy the demand, the Old Testament was issued in parts as each section was completed. The first part, the Pentateuch, came out in 1523. The books from Joshua to Esther comprised the second part, published in 1524. The third part — Job, the Psalms, Proverbs, and Ecclesiastes — also was printed in 1524. But the prophetical books took longer — until 1532. When the apocryphal books were completed, the whole Bible came out in 1534 in one volume. Meanwhile revisions had been going on, with Melanchthon, Spalatin, and

49

other Wittenberg friends cooperating. Luther never felt fully satisfied. Until his death he kept revising, correcting, refining.

Besides the translation Luther provided prefaces for practically all the books, for groups of books, and for each of the Testaments. In these the people found the core of his teaching and thereby received an education in the Bible. Not only was the language new and direct but the interpretation was a break with the past. Luther had gradually discarded the traditional fourfold interpretation of Scripture — the literal, the allegorical, the moral, the anagogical (prophetic) — and insisted on the simple, literal sense of what was written. He could and did revert at times to the other uses, but the basic meaning was in the literal sense, which any reader should be able to understand. This was the supreme authority for the Christian. Therefore he should be clear and sure about its meaning. Here the church heard the Word of God, received the promise given to faith, and experienced the fellowship of the Spirit. The translation of the Bible was Luther's restoration of the cornerstone of the church of Christ.

LITURGICAL REFORMS

While Luther was absorbed in the translation of the New Testament at the Wartburg, events were taking place in Wittenberg that would compel him to determine in which direction reform should not go. There Dr. Andreas Karlstadt, a colleague at the university, started putting into practice what he thought were consequences of the new teachings. He advocated the marriage of monks and encouraged them to leave their monasteries. He opposed all ritual in the worship of the congregation, including vestments of clergy, the use of statuary or pictures, and even music. Preaching and worship were to be in the German language. Similar developments took place in neighboring Zwickau and Allstedt under a former student of Luther, Thomas Müntzer, who composed a German service with German hymns. Later, however, he introduced apocalyptic ideas and even advocated secular power to suppress opposition to his radical proposals. So threatening were these fanatical movements that Luther took it on himself to leave the Wartburg, return to Wittenberg, and preach against the ill-considered reforms of Karlstadt. The boundary lines of change beyond which Luther would not go now began to appear. At the same time he had to suggest the kind of structure that should truly reflect the Gospel on which the church was founded.

In 1523 Luther issued a German-language ritual for baptism, omitting acts that he felt did not belong in an evangelical sacrament. He did retain the ancient ceremony of exorcism, or renunciation of the devil. Later in the same year he recommended an evangelical revision of the Mass — a most important proposal because hitherto the Mass had been the principal observance of the Christian congregation and embodied the teaching of the church. The Mass had come to be considered a sacrifice which the priest renewed on each altar as an offering to God for the merit of the believers. The very saying of the Mass was effective before God and therefore the presence of the congregation was not necessary. Hence the practice of private masses developed, for through them the person who gave a gift for having masses said could earn grace for himself or for those he named. This custom Luther utterly opposed. But he saw in the other parts of the Mass a chance for the education and worship of the congregation, wherefore he urged the retention of the elements that did not suggest sacrifice. The Lord's Supper was a gift to the congregation — not a good deed of the worshiper. The *Formula Missae* of 1523 indicates how conservative Luther was in retaining the historic forms of congregational worship. Because of its influence we list the recommendations of the Formula:

The Introit — The customary psalm verses for the day are to be used, but it would be better to use the whole psalm rather than parts of it.

Kyrie — The various melodies for the seasons of the church year should be retained.

Gloria — The bishop decides when it is to be omitted.

Collects — These should be used, but one of them is sufficient.

Epistle and Gospel — These should continue, but the use of candles and incense at the reading of the Gospel is optional.

Gradual and Hallelujah — The bishop may decide, but the selection should be proper and not too long.

Nicene Creed — May be sung, if the bishop so decides.

Sermon — This should be in German. It may come before the Introit.

51

Any of the above items may be changed, for none of them are commanded by God. In the following items Luther made the greatest change, eliminating from the service any mention of sacrifice by the priest. This left the following rubrics:

Preparation of the bread and wine — the wine may be mixed with water.

Preface, with passages proper for the day.

Words of Institution, continuing the prayer form of the Preface. These may be said or sung.

Sanctus, with the elevation of the host during the Benedictus. This may be sung by the choir.

The Lord's Prayer.

Pax, "The Peace of the Lord be with you."

The Distribution — both bread and wine. During the distribution the choir sings the Agnus Dei.

A Collect (Communion psalm) may be sung and short prayers said.

The Benediction.

Though willing to root out every vestige of false doctrine, Luther was averse to radical changes in historic forms of worship. The preaching should be in the vernacular — and this, according to Luther, was the heart of every assembly of Christians — but the ancient forms of prayer and praise were in Latin, and he knew how difficult it was to translate these. Especially the parts carried by the choir, he felt, could be learned in Latin. But his instinct for popular participation inclined him in the direction of more German. He wanted the congregation to sing. Therefore German hymns must be provided. When he failed to prevail on others to write hymns, he began to do so himself. The publication in 1524 of his little book of *Eight Hymns* initiated a long and noble history of hymn writing in which some of his own contributions were to be memorable. "A Mighty Fortress" first appeared in a Wittenberg hymnbook of 1528.

The *Formula Missae* was not meant as a new law. Luther expressly opposed making liturgical practices rigid and unalterable. He even encouraged a variety of forms, though urging that they be improvements and not mere novelties. In 1525 he outlined a form of *German Mass* for congregations that did not have the resources for a more formal worship. It emphasized German singing and the sermon. The service was constructed thus:

Song or psalm.

A threefold Kyrie.

Collect, Epistle, German hymn as Gradual, Gospel.

Creed — a German versification of the Creed.

Sermon.

Exhortation to Communion.

Words of Institution, German hymns during distribution.

Collect. Benedicamus. The Aaronic Benediction.

That such an order was experimental, Luther himself was aware, and he did not want it officially adopted. He defended sections of the Latin service, especially where music was involved. Years later Latin was still used in his own Wittenberg church. German preaching and German hymns Luther insisted on; also that the chief service should be a Communion service with the congregation receiving both bread and wine. Beyond this he was willing to allow freedom in the use of the ancient liturgy.

THE PEASANT REBELLION

Events were already showing that forces being unleashed by Luther's defiance of the papal power would go farther than Luther himself. Thomas Müntzer and Andreas Karlstadt were but two of many who saw in a religious reform an opportunity for social and political changes. The peasants of Germany and Switzerland found in Luther's preaching encouragement for their demands on their feudal lords. In some circles the yearning for economic improvement was mixed with a martial temper of the Old Testament against the foes of God's people, and the coming of the millennium was to right both religious and economic wrongs. Luther witnessed with dismay the unwarranted use of his teachings. He had not advocated rebellion against the constituted authorities of the state. Rather, as in his treatise of 1523 *On Secular Authority,* he recognized the necessity of law and order and found in Scripture a God-given place for authority — else society would disintegrate. Part of his resentment against the hierarchy was due to his conviction that bishops and pope had usurped functions that belonged to the secular government. He himself had disobeyed the imperial authority, but only on the ground that there are times when God rather than men must be obeyed. He based his stand on Scripture, whereas Müntzer and his followers were advocating a following of "Spirit." They would establish an earthly kingdom of God by force. This Luther would not condone. He saw a divine retribution on the rebellious spirits when they were crushed by the authorities at Mühlhausen in 1525. Nor would he allow his cause to be identified with the revolt of the peasants in southern Germany and northern Switzerland, though many of their demands were just. His writings against them betray a certain fearfulness of the way economic demands were clothed in religious forms, revealing a harshness that disappointed those who saw in the revolt a misguided multitude of simple and earnest workers.

Luther was not a social reformer and despite his peasant ancestry hardly understood the plight of the lower classes. When we speak of the demarcation of reform we must acknowledge Luther's limitations. He was intent on a reform of the church as a bearer of the Gospel. When he and those who spoke in his name gave rise to expectations of the downtrodden peasants, we might, from a modern point of view, wish for a wider sympathy and constructive action on their part. But to do this is to ask for more than any thinker or leader of that age was able to give, least of all the very spiritual leaders whom Luther challenged. Neither church nor university men had any other answers. Had Luther entrusted his cause to the rebellious masses, it would have perished with the revolt and the revolt not have been helped by it. That Luther was not interested in the political intrigues of the knightly class is shown by his coolness toward the plans of Franz von Sickingen and others to win power for themselves against the empire.

ANABAPTISM

How difficult it was to see a clear path ahead is shown by another development in the ferment of the times — that of Anabaptism. The Peasants' Revolt was a social-political movement. But among both lower and higher classes lived an age-old tendency to question the sacraments of the church and its organization. Instead of child baptism

54

there should be for true believers a baptism of the Spirit. There was no need of priests or ritual or altars. Believers could come together in small groups for Bible reading, meditation, and prayer. Something of this we have already found in the Albigensian period, and it was to reappear in Bohemia among the Taborites. In some places it would take the form of rejection of military service or indeed of the whole apparatus of the secular government. Followers of Menno Simons in the Netherlands showed no interest in the state. Conrad Grebel of Switzerland revealed that this was not a lower-class phenomenon. In the breakup of the 16th century there was no clarity on the relationship of church and state and no agreement on what were the limits of the authority of either one.

Luther could not distinguish clearly between the various currents — no one could. But in general he held to his Scriptural authority. He opposed the Anabaptists, who thought there was a guidance of the Spirit apart from the Word. "Heavenly prophets" he called them and devoted a long treatise against their interpretation of the Lord's Supper. He decried their spiritualism, which was not bound by the Word, and insisted that the words of the institution of the Supper must be taken seriously. The reform Luther sponsored was something other than what they sought, and Luther separated himself from a reformation which has been called "radical." His was "conservative."

RELATIONSHIP TO ZWINGLI

A practical application of this principle and of great historic importance was Luther's relationship to Zwingli, the Swiss reformer. Philip, prince of Hesse, had political reasons for bringing together the friends of reform in Germany and Switzerland. Zwingli had been the leader in Zurich, which in 1523 declared itself for the new order. With Luther he had shared interest in the humanist movement — both appreciated the works of Erasmus. Though not a part of the Anabaptist groups, Zwingli had no great interest in child Baptism, and in the interpretation of the Lord's Supper he leaned to a view of a memorial feast. He had accepted a Dutch writer's view that the words "This is My body" meant "This signifies My body." Hoping to reconcile the two centers, Wittenberg and Zurich, Philip arranged a conference in his territory at Marburg between Luther, Melanchthon, Zwingli, Oecolampadius, and others in 1529. Luther suspected Zwingli of Anabaptist and spiritualistic sympathies, probably more than was justified. Although agreement was reached on 14 out of 15 points, the breach was widened by Marburg.

Luther was not happy over the background of the conference. He did not relish being used for political purposes of princes. At Marburg the difficulty of defining one's position in the welter of contemporary currents was evident. But on one point Luther was immovable. The Scriptural "is" cannot be changed. The Lord's word was, "This *is* My body." The conference did not achieve its purpose. Luther's opposition to Zwingli was not lessened by the further career of the Swiss leader, who adopted military measures in his cause and fell in battle in 1531. He had, however, won a number of the Swiss cities to the evangelical program, and their adherence was not affected by his death. They gradually distinguished between the more cautious reformers and the radical views of the Anabaptists, rejecting the latter as heretical. But the lines drawn at Marburg between the Zwinglians and the Lutherans have continued through four centuries into our own time.

DEBATE WITH ERASMUS

On yet another front Luther found himself in opposition to a school of thought he had earlier favored. The scholar Erasmus had taught him to seek the Greek source of the New Testament. And Luther applauded his satirical writings aimed at the weaknesses of the clergy and the papal church. But Erasmus was a child of the Renaissance who followed a classical view of the freedom of the human will. Luther had been persuaded by his Biblical study that man has no freedom in his relationship to God. Rather he is in bondage until he is made free by the grace of God through His Word. On this point Luther broke with Erasmus. In 1525 he wrote one of his most profound treatises entitled *On the Bondage of the Will* in reply to a work of Erasmus on the freedom of the will. Henceforth Luther could not count on the favor of those who were more interested in man's ability to seek God than in Luther's utter dependence on God's grace. But among his followers there were those who, like Melanchthon, were influenced by Erasmus and who would in the coming years continue the debate.

Visitation in the Parishes

While the leaders of reform were engaged in clarifying their positions on theological questions, very important issues in the parishes demanded attention. The followers of Karlstadt had disrupted the traditional forms of worship. Those with Anabaptist leanings questioned the sacraments, which were at the heart of medieval devotion. Confession and absolution by the priesthood was challenged by Luther's doctrine of the right of every Christian to confess to a fellow Christian and be forgiven. Monks left monasteries without making provision for the maintenance of their property or for their functions as teachers in schools. In the main the parish priests were slow to change their allegiance to their bishops — the preachers of the new doctrine came rather from the ranks of the monasteries. But parishioners were restless and bewildered. The bishops had exercised a certain discipline, and the ecclesiastical courts had regulated marriage laws. Now these courts were spurned. The new preachers needed supervision, support, and education. Who would take the place of the officials of the old order?

In his own territory each prince exercised governmental powers. Society was still feudal in character, and on their estates the nobles ruled over their lands and the people. Luther had already turned to them in his *Open Letter to the German Nobility*, calling on them to assume responsibilities that the "spiritual estate" (the hierarchy) had wrongly assumed and unjustly discharged. For several years the Elector John, who had ruled Saxony after his brother Frederick died in 1525, had been importuned to undertake a comprehensive reordering of conditions in his province. Finally in 1527 a "visitation" was begun. In place of the bishop a team of four—two jurists, two theologians — was appointed by the elector to go from parish to parish. They were to make an inventory of church property, examine the clergy, and give instructions as to the conduct of the pastor and the congregation. Provision should be made for the salary of the clergy. The schools should be regulated in regard to teachers and to curriculum. Melanchthon drew up the instructions for the visitation; Luther wrote a preface to the articles. Here was a model later followed in other territories.

Church and Secular Rulers

Thus was set in motion the administration of the churches after the break with Rome. Luther's *Open Letter* was a call for the independence

57

of Germany from a tyrannical government in Italy. He could see no reason why, in this independent nation, all the functions of the church could not be carried out at home. He would like to have seen each community church elect its own pastor and regulate its affairs. But in the 16th century there was no separation of church and state. Since nominally all the people of a city or region were Christian, Luther could speak of "Christian temporal rulers." There were no other officials to whom to turn, and Luther suggested that they take over the duties of the "spiritual rulers" formerly appointed by Rome. Whereas the Roman Church had secured its wealth and power from tithes, fees, and gifts, which made it a stronger power than the secular rulers, the reformers, in returning these sources of income to the government, stripped the churches of their material resources. In the feudal system the lord had maintained chapels and clergy on his own lands — the tendency now was to take back all church property as his own. In the cities the councils took over monastic and parish properties. In this way the church became dependent on the secular power.

It was an emergency situation to which the reformers had to resort for want of any other authority to establish order. The seed was sown for state control of the church and would bear undesirable fruit. Yet Luther believed in the power of the Word to make the "principal members" of the congregation — the secular rulers — obedient to the dictates of the Gospel.

THE "LOCI" AND THE CATECHISMS

Among the duties of the visitors was the investigation of the faith of the preachers. In a time of turmoil and controversy how should one determine the true Gospel that the church was set to proclaim? As one of the visitors, Melanchthon was best prepared to give an answer. Already in 1521 he had published a little textbook on the theology taught by the Church of the Reformation. Because it treated each doctrine as a separate topic or place, it was called Loci (places). But in time various questions were raised as to the interpretation of Biblical teachings. In his prefaces to the German Bible Luther gave clear statements. Questions on predestination and the freedom of the will, however, were still debated. Even during the visitation Melanchthon and the Lutheran pastor Johann Agricola could not agree on the relationship of the Law to the teaching of the Gospel, and Luther had to intervene.

58

The need in the churches led Luther to compose two of his most effective and educative works — the Small and the Large Catechism. In the earlier schools there had been emphasis on the Creed, the Commandments, and the Lord's Prayer. Often these were taught from charts in the schoolroom. Around these subjects Luther wrote an elaborate treatise on the main teachings of the church. He hoped thereby to contribute to the raising of the level of lay knowledge, which the visitation revealed to be deplorably low. The materials of the Catechisms he had already worked on in sermons and treatises, but he added to the traditional topics the parts on the two sacraments, Baptism and the Lord's Supper, as well as a section on confession and absolution and a table of duties. The two Catechisms were produced about the same time, 1528—1529, the shorter one intended for the housefather who should be responsible for the religious literacy of his household. Before the father of the family could do so, he himself would first have to learn from the pastor. In the preface to the Small Catechism Luther therefore exhorted the parish pastor to consider it a primary duty to instruct his people. What Luther himself found in the parishes may not be an exaggerated account of the situation the reformers generally encountered. "Although the people are supposed to be Christian, are baptized, and receive the Holy Sacrament, they do not know the Lord's Prayer, the Creed, or the Ten Commandments, they live as if they were pigs and irrational beasts, and now that the Gospel has been restored they have mastered the fine art of abusing liberty."

Not only the laity was illiterate and superstitious. A pressing need was for pastors who knew the heart of the Gospel and the needs of the people. Luther pleaded with the princes and cities to improve the schools where the youth could learn the elements of both learning and religion. He urged instruction in music in order to carry on the liturgical service, and he himself led in teaching the congregation to sing. The Creed could be learned also by singing it! His translation of the Bible and his Catechism were illustrated by the foremost artists of the day — Hans Holbein and Lucas Cranach. To help the pastors, Luther issued collections of sermons based on the pericopes, or lessons of the church year. Although radically reducing the number of festivals and omitting many of the saints' days, Luther kept the church year with its traditional festivals. While not enjoining confession, he did include a form in the

Catechism for congregational confession and absolution. His forms for baptism and marriage established an evangelical ministry in the vernacular that bound the family to the church. By his own marriage Luther set the example of an evangelical parsonage. Everywhere he was concerned about the common man. The Gospel had to do with the individual in his daily task, and the church was to nourish faith so that it would express itself in all the routine of daily life. The great error of the medieval church was its emphasis on the theology of glory — the glory of outward splendor, high rank, material wealth. The Gospel was a Gospel of the cross that each Christian had to bear in his own way.

From Worms to Augsburg

Thus for a decade the reform movement in Germany was able to carry on. That the Edict of Worms, outlawing and excommunicating Luther, was not carried out was due to a political conjunction in the imperial affairs none could have foreseen. Yet the threat hung over the entire realm all these years and eventually would have to be met. This the friends of reform knew. Therefore sporadic attempts were made to bring together the forces that opposed the old order. But alliances were complicated by imperial ambitions, by the Peasants' War, and by the lack of agreement at Marburg. Also it was not agreed what exactly was the faith that was to be defended. In Brandenburg and Nürnberg a series of articles had been drawn up about 1525 known as the Ansbach Articles which, it was hoped, would define the main doctrines concerned in the reform of church and state. Before the debate at Marburg leaders in Nürnberg and Saxony had formulated in 1529 another list in the so-called Schwabach Articles. The Marburg conference failed to unify the German and Swiss reformers, but it tended to consolidate the Lutherans so that they realized they would have to stand together when the imperial diet should finally call them to account for their actions.

The Augsburg Confession — Augustana

The summons to a diet where the religious question might be discussed and decided came from Emperor Charles in January 1530. The princes and cities were to be at Augsburg in April. Realizing the importance of the coming diet the Lutherans prepared their case. They

60

knew they could not join with the Swiss cities nor with some of the cities of southwestern Germany, who made their own defense. Elector John of Saxony asked the Wittenberg theologians to draw up a statement describing the changes that had been made in teaching and practice. The articles of faith were already at hand in the Schwabach Articles. To these was added a list of the abuses the reformers wanted corrected, a list drawn up by Melanchthon and adopted at Torgau, hence called the Torgau Articles. A preface was written, also by Melanchthon, and the document was presented to and read before the diet June 25, 1530. From the place of the diet the document received the name Augsburg Confession, or in Latin *Confessio Augustana*. (Augsburg had been founded by the Romans in the time of Caesar Augustus.) Outlawed by the Edict of Worms, Luther could not come to Augsburg. But he stayed at the nearby Coburg Castle and kept in close touch with the theologians and Saxon officials at the diet. His letters and writings of these days, including an exposition of Psalm 119, reveal his distrust of human power but inconquerable faith in his Lord.

Melanchthon was intent on showing that what had happened since Worms was not heretical. In the church were grievous abuses that needed reform, and the Church of Rome should be as anxious as the reformers to see these wrongs corrected. In giving the wine in the Sacrament the reformers were following the original institution. The marriage of priests was also permitted in early centuries. The abuse of masses had brought about the evangelical teaching that the Mass was no work of merit but a sacramental gift of Christ — private masses as a source of income for the church were rejected. The reformers explained their stand on confession, fasting, marriage laws, monasticism, and the power of the bishops. "Nothing has been received among us, in doctrine or in ceremonies, that is contrary to Scripture or to the church catholic" was the conclusion of the part of the document on abuses. Also in the first part, on doctrine, it was held that "there is nothing here that departs from the Scriptures or the catholic church or the church of Rome, in so far as the ancient church is known to us from its writers." The articles of faith dealt with God, original sin, the Son of God, justification, the ministry of the church, the new obedience, the church, Baptism, the Lord's Supper, confession, repentance, the use of the sacraments, ecclesiastical order, ecclesiastical rites, civil affairs, the return of Christ for judgment, free will, the cause of sin, faith and good works, and the cult of saints.

Luther felt that Melanchthon treaded softly, and it was clear that the latter was emphasizing the agreement in doctrine with traditional teachings. At the same time he was warding off suspicion that the Lutherans were in sympathy with the excesses of the "enthusiasts" or of those who used religious doctrine as an excuse for rebellion. Though relatively brief and sketchy, the articles of the Confession became the charter of the Church of the Lutheran Reformation and for centuries to come would be the standard around which a reformed part of Christendom gathered. The Roman theologians at Augsburg replied with a Confutation, and Melanchthon in turn responded with a defense, or Apology, of the Augsburg Confession. The foundation for Lutheran theology was thereby laid at Augsburg.

Before his death Luther composed a series of doctrinal articles called the Smalcald Articles (1537). In the Augsburg Confession, the Apology, the Smalcald Articles, and the Small and Large Catechisms the Church of the Lutheran Reformation in Germany had a wealth of material which along with Melanchthon's *Loci* and Luther's voluminous writings made it a theologically conscious community. It was necessary for this church to know where it stood, for it had rejected a tradition which in many cases was no longer understood, and it had parted company with a highly organized and powerful hierarchical organization that had, in the eyes of the people, equated itself with the kingdom of God on earth.

V

BREAKUP OF CHURCH AND STATE

When Charles V became emperor in 1519, he was under the spell of the first Charles, or Charlemagne, that Europe could be one and in partnership with a pope holding sway over a universal church. That dream had persisted through seven centuries and had been a controlling factor in the Christianizing and civilizing of all the European lands. But while the papacy had gathered strength and since the days of Gregory VII had extended its power into every corner of Europe, the empire had vainly tried to exercise sovereignty over lands that were intent on becoming independent nations. Not only were the rulers of England, France, and other emerging nations warding off the encroachments of a shadowy empire but they resented also the interference of the papal agents in their domains. The cities of Italy, of the Hanseatic League, of Germany and Switzerland were demanding freedom from imperial taxes and levies of troops. The empire could have no existence apart from national powers; hence it was associated with one or another of the royal houses of Europe. In the 13th century the honor had gone to the Hapsburgs of southeastern Europe, and the fourth Charles had regulated the election of emperor in the Golden Bull of 1356. But the seven electors were always subject to pressures at the time of change of emperor. In 1519, by various forms of bribery, Charles V, who in 1516 had become king of Spain, won the election over Francis of France. For the next 35 years he tried to maintain the illusion of one empire, one church.

PROBLEMS OF THE EMPIRE

The 19-year-old youth was heir to half the civilized world of his time. His father's father, head of the Hapsburg dominion, had been emperor. His mother's parents, Ferdinand and Isabella, ruled Spain, Naples, Sicily, Sardinia, and vast territories in America. His

63

parents had held the provinces of the Netherlands and Burgundy. But such an inheritance also meant involvement in practically all the affairs of Europe with the result that at every step he would be met by some alliance or other of his opponents. Although the emperor nominally was protector of the church, the pope distrusted the universal pretensions of the empire, and in trying to keep Charles out of Italy the pope time and again turned to France, Charles' perpetual foe. The German princes wanted no restrictions on their power and had a long list of complaints against both pope and emperor. Only by giving promises to them would the Germans allow Charles the imperial name. He had to pledge not to employ foreign troops without the consent of the electors. No diet was to be held outside Germany. The offices of the court were to be filled with Germans. He was to honor old customs, duties, and privileges. German as well as Latin was to be the court language. The sovereignty of the princes was to be confirmed and an imperial court established. An imperial chamber of electors was to rule with Charles. And of great significance in the religious situation was the provision that no one should be outlawed without trial.

Such was the emperor before whom Luther appeared at Worms in 1521 and from whom Elector Frederick of Saxony was willing to shield Luther. Charles was devout and determined to restore the unity of the church. He was urged on by the pope, Hadrian VI, who demanded the enforcement of the Edict of Worms against Luther. But Charles was not free to act as he wished. The imperial chamber refused to put down evangelical truth without a free and general council, which should be called within a year. When the papal legate objected, the chamber presented him with a list of over a hundred grievances of the German states against the papacy. These *Gravamina* give us a picture of the issues at stake. They include indulgences and dispensations; marriage laws and other legal abuses; bans and interdicts; papal levies in the form of annates and incorporations and new tithes; the extravagances of festivals and pilgrimages; the conduct of priests and monks. Until these conditions were corrected the German princes were unready to have the edict enforced.

No sooner had Charles become king of Spain than he had to put down a rebellion there. He had made an alliance with the pope to drive the French out of Italy — with England's Henry VIII to help him against France. The war which the emperor began against France was to last intermittently for 200 years. He could never be sure which of his enemies, or even friends, might be in secret alliance with France. At first Charles was successful and drove the French out of Italy, took the French king prisoner, and made him cede not only Italy but also his holdings in southwestern Netherlands and Burgundy. But Francis, out of prison, renewed the war and joined the new pope, Clement VII, in driving the Spanish troops of Charles out of Italy.

FORMATION OF PROTESTANT ALLIANCES

Meanwhile the papal legate had succeeded in stemming the spread of reform in the dominions of Ferdinand of Austria, the brother of Charles, and of the dukes of Bavaria. Catholic princes formed the League of Dessau in 1525, and Protestant princes countered in 1526 with the League of Torgau. Hereby the empire was divided and a fateful schism appeared in German history. Leaders of the Dessau group were Duke George of Saxony, the elector of Mainz, the elector of Brandenburg, and the duke of Brunswick. Their aim was to crush Lutheranism. The Torgau alliance was made up of the Saxon elector, Margrave Philip of Hesse, five north-German princes, and the city of Magdeburg. Political considerations were mixed with religious aims, as had been done in all previous centuries. In this situation the emperor could not execute the Worms decision. Instead at the Diet of Spires in 1526 he could only recognize reality and allow the policy of *cuius regio eius religio* — whose the territory, his the religion — in other words, the religion of a province was that of its ruler. For the first time the Lutherans had some legal rights on which to depend in making reforms. It also meant a control of the church by the secular authority, though this was equally true of both opposing ecclesiastical forces.

Charles had to grant this freedom of action to the Protestants in Germany in order to get aid against his enemies in Italy. In the course of the war Rome itself was invaded and sacked in 1527, bringing to an end the Renaissance in the city by scattering its writers and artists. France was decisively defeated. In the peace of 1529 the emperor allowed the pope to keep his possessions; he himself took

65

Naples. Now, finally, Charles was crowned emperor by the pope, a decade after his election, and could feel triumphant over his enemies.

Even so, the emperor was not strong enough to put an end to the Lutheran movement, for he was not ready to start a civil war. The Diet of Spires in 1529 resolved that each territory should carry out the decision of Worms by itself, and no new reforms should be permitted even in places where the Reformation had established itself. Five princes and fourteen cities presented a *protest* against the policy of deciding religious questions by a majority — from this the term *Protestant* was applied to the reforming party.

The shadows of another enemy hovered over the eastern provinces of the empire and influenced the decisions of Charles, namely, the Turks. Under Solyman II (Suleiman) the Turks had reached Hungary. The king of Bohemia and Hungary lost his life in the Battle of Mohacs in 1526, whereupon Ferdinand of Austria became ruler of these countries as well. In Hungary he was opposed by a native patriot, John Zapolya, whom the Turks established as their vassal. When in 1529 the Turks met defeat at Vienna, the empire enjoyed a temporary breathing spell.

At the Diet of Augsburg in 1530 the emperor hoped to come to some settlement of the religious dispute. Requested to put their case in writing, the Lutherans under Melanchthon's leadership presented their *Confessio Augustana*. But the effort at reconciliation failed, and the diet adjourned in the conviction that force would be necessary to suppress the Protestants. On their side the Lutherans sought to prepare their defense. They formed the Smalcald League and by the end of 1531 counted on 9 princes, 11 cities, and an army of 12,000. Again Charles, in need of united help against the Turks, would not venture into civil war. At the Diet of Nürnberg in 1532 he promised that no action would be taken against the Lutherans and justified the promise on the grounds that a council of the church should be called where the religious problem could be solved. It was to take 13 years before the council finally was agreed upon — meanwhile the Reformation enjoyed a significant advance.

ATTEMPTS AT A COUNCIL

For the present the emperor pinned his hopes on a council. Such a council would have to be called by the head of the church, and

66

the pope's political problems were inextricably tangled up with his religious purposes. Charles had other concerns than the papal demands for extirpation of heresy. He was busy in Spain and with explorations in the New World. He had gathered 80,000 troops after the Diet of Nürnberg and forced Solyman II back into Asia, but he was plagued by Turkish forays in the Mediterranean. Also the Netherlands were again causing him trouble, and France was always suspect. In 1536 Charles and Francis were again at war — this time Pope Paul III secured a truce, and the booty — the province of Savoy — was divided between the contenders. Pope Paul also negotiated a settlement by which Hungary was to go to Ferdinand of Austria on Zapolya's death. Ferdinand was intent on eliminating Protestants from his possessions, but in view of the Turkish threat on his eastern borders he could not alienate the Smalcald League. The league, moreover, was ready to ally itself with Francis. To strengthen their position the members of the league made another attempt to bring together the theologians. Martin Bucer, the Strasbourg reformer, and Melanchthon finally reached an agreement, or concordat, at Wittenberg in 1536 in which the varying theories of the Lord's Supper were seemingly reconciled. But defining the presence of the body of Christ as sacramental did not resolve the real differences, and before long the question was opened again.

Pope Clement VII had tried to get Charles and Francis to agree on a time and place for the much-desired council, but failed. Paul III got so far as to send out in June 1536 a call for a council that was to meet at Mantua in May 1537. This was later postponed to May 1538. Only the exiled bishop of Uppsala appeared. Obviously no council could be held while France and empire were at war. But by this time there were other objections to the kind of council envisioned by the pope and the emperor.

LUTHERANS AND A COUNCIL

The papal bull of 1536 calling for a council put the Lutherans on the defensive. For years Luther had demanded a council which in the tradition of the ecumenical councils could define the true faith and reform the abuses in the church. The elector had been on legal ground in defending Luther since he had not been properly heard —

only a free and open council could debate religious issues. A political diet had no proper jurisdiction in matters of conscience. The emperor had recognized the validity of this argument. Repeatedly he urged the pope to set his house in order. But where should a council be held? Who should attend? How were decisions to be reached? These were questions widely debated in the Curia and chancelleries. The Germans insisted that a council should be held in Germany. The pope preferred Italy. France would not sanction an imperial city and rejected Mantua. At length Trent was chosen as being within German bounds. Naturally the pope looked on a council as under his leadership, and proper delegates would be the bishops of the church. The canonists agreed that princes should attend, though not allowed to vote. It became increasingly apparent that there would be no "free" council at which Lutherans would have a chance to debate reforms in doctrine or practice. The projected gathering would convene in the name of Rome and would judge the Protestants according to standards established by Rome.

Luther had already challenged the pope as the primate of Christendom. He would not submit to his decision on the truth of the church and the Gospel. Elector John Frederick interpreted attendance at the council as an agreement to accept the council's judgment. He asked the Wittenberg theologians to answer the call and justify absence on the part of the members of the Smalcald League. He and Philip, the leaders of the league, opposed attendance. The result was a vote of the league not to accept the invitation — and two documents, one by Luther, one by Melanchthon. Luther prepared a series of articles distinguishing between what might be debated and what the reformers could not give up. "This article concerning the Mass will be the decisive issue in the council," Luther wrote. On this point he believed the papists and "we are and remain eternally divided and opposed to one another." Luther was vehement in his judgment on the papacy. "The pope is the real Antichrist who has raised himself over and set himself against Christ, for the pope will not permit Christians to be saved except by his own power, which amounts to nothing since it is neither established nor commanded by God." Luther's so-called Smalcald Articles were subscribed to by a number of the theologians but not officially adopted by the league. Melanch-

68

thon's *Treatise on the Power and Primacy of the Pope* was, however, officially adopted as a sort of supplement to the Augsburg Confession. It is a calm rejection of the threefold claims of the papacy — that the pope by divine right is above all bishops and pastors, that he has authority over both spiritual and secular rulers, and that it is necessary for salvation to believe that the pope is Christ's vicar on earth. In 1538—1539 Luther developed more completely his ideas in his treatise *On the Councils and the Churches,* despairing of any reformation under the pope, who would not allow a diminution of his prerogatives. In this treatise Luther gave a full description of the nature of the church as he believed Scripture defined it.

Thus in 1537 the issue of the council served to separate more clearly the Church of the Reformation from the medieval church. Indeed Luther asserted in the Smalcald Articles that "we ourselves need no such a council, for by God's grace our churches have now been so enlightened and supplied with the pure Word and the right use of the sacraments, with an understanding of the various callings of life, and with true works, that we do not ask for a council for our own sake, and we have no reason to hope or expect that a council would improve our conditions."

The policy of the emperor had to be adjusted continually. He wanted to bring the Lutherans back to the church — if possible, without war. He hoped a council would bring agreement, if the pope would cooperate. He needed help against France in the west and the Turks in the east and in the Mediterranean. He had to be concerned at all times about his subjects in Spain and the Netherlands, while constantly seeking the unity of the empire.

Hoping to facilitate the conciliation of the Lutherans, Charles arranged private conferences in 1540 between theologians on both sides but found no Lutherans willing to bind themselves in advance to respect a council controlled by the pope. He and the pope finally agreed on Trent as the place for the council, and a date in 1543 was set. But France had now allied itself with the Turks and Francis with his large army was set to regain power in northern Italy. The pope did not dare to declare himself for Charles against the French. So the council was again postponed and the emperor could not promise the Lutherans any early settlement of their grievances. Meanwhile the

69

Saxon elector had won control over Brunswick and introduced reform measures. Cologne too seemed on the point of joining the Reformation forces.

THE VICTORY OF CHARLES AND THE INTERIM

By diplomacy and force Charles improved his position by 1544. A victory over the French gave him the opportunity to bind the French king to aid him against both the Turks and the Protestants and to support the council. The Lutheran movement in Cologne was stopped by the deposition of Herman, the archbishop who had been friendly to it. In 1545 the council opened at Trent.

The Lutheran cause seemed precarious. It had been winning ground during the truce granted reluctantly by the annual diets and the emperor, but the Smalcald League was not unified. One of its leaders, Philip of Hesse, had been involved in the scandal of a bigamous marriage. Even Luther was brought into it through a violation of the secrecy of the confessional. Philip was crippled as a leader and realized his dependence on the emperor's favor. In February 1546 Luther died. Although sickness had weakened him in his later years, he had remained the symbol of the Reformation. His going left the field open for theological differences, and his strong, clear voice no longer rallied divided followers.

At the Diet of Regensburg in 1546 Charles' attitude toward the Lutherans hardened. He refused the request of the Germans for a national council and demanded that the religious reforms be referred to the council now assembling at Trent. A treaty with the pope brought a promise of troops and money. Preparations for attack had been under way, and before the Smalcald League was fully aware of the danger, Charles had overwhelmed their forces. Both Philip of Hesse and the Elector John Frederick were taken prisoner. Duke Maurice of Saxony had joined Ferdinand of Austria in the war — the duke was rewarded by the transfer of the elector's title from the defeated John. Since Wittenberg University remained Lutheran, a rival Saxon institution was established at Jena.

Despite his victories in the Smalcald War, the emperor was still beset with frustration. The pope was suspicious of Charles' plans, and Charles was opposed to decisions of the council which would make agreement with the Lutherans impossible. Furthermore, an epidemic caused the council to move from Trent to Bologna, away from German into Italian domain. Exasperated with the papal procedures, the emperor attempted a settlement on his own at the Diet of Augsburg in 1548. The Interim, as the name denotes, was a temporary measure, but its purpose was to allay the religious controversy that was splitting the empire. It proposed measures of reform of clergy, education, and church through visitation and provincial synods. While the cup in Communion and the marriage of priests were conceded to the Protestants, the definition of dogmatic points and the retention of most of the customary ceremonies and festivals made the plan unacceptable. In fact neither party was satisfied. The Romanists objected to a secular authority's interference in religious matters. The Protestants saw no fundamental change in the matters they considered essential. But the emperor was adamant. With the aid of Spanish troops the Interim was imposed wherever he had power. Some of the imperial cities gave in and dismissed their evangelical preachers. Others of the theologians resigned. Martin Bucer, the Strasbourg theologian, eventually found his way to England where he played a part in the reformation under Edward VI. Saxony and Württemberg resisted. Over 400 pastors gave up their positions rather than accept the new order. An attempt on the part of the Lutheran princes to have the theologians distinguish what could and could not be conceded resulted in late 1548 in the Leipzig Interim, which only revealed the differences among them. Melanchthon seemed too compromising and lost influence. Matthias Flacius became the leader of the conservatives. Though unsuccessful, the Augsburg Interim was another example of the contemporary opinion that the secular power had a responsibility to seek unity in religious matters. There was no difference between Charles' protectorate over the church and the influence which the Protestant princes felt it incumbent on themselves to exert in order to secure peace in their provinces.

While the council was in Bologna, Paul III died in 1549. The new pope, Julius III, yielded to the emperor and returned the council to Trent. The Germans were to be made to attend and to submit to decisions when reached. In 1552 the Protestants were allowed to state their case. They demanded a free and thorough discussion of the articles in dispute and a ratification of the legal decisions already made in

71

their favor. The Saxon and Württemberg theologians presented separate statements. But the council would not dispute with those who were already adjudged heretics and who would not in advance bind themselves to future resolutions. Charles saw that it was hopeless to expect agreement to be reached by a papal council.

LUTHERAN VICTORIES AT PASSAU AND AUGSBURG

In the Smalcald War the emperor had not thought it worth while to press the siege of the northern German cities. Even within the conquered territories the Interim had kept alive the flame of rebellion. In 1550 Albert of Prussia, John Albert of Mecklenburg, and Hans of Küstrin (Kostrzyn) formed an alliance to defend Protestantism. The Elector Maurice, who had helped defeat the Smalcald League, was disillusioned by the emperor's failure to release the elector's father-in-law Philip, who was still a prisoner. Maurice joined the alliance, which was successful in signing a treaty with France whereby the French king, now Henry II, would be given imperial cities in Charles' territory and an offer of the imperial crown in exchange for help to the alliance. The show of force was sufficient to frighten Charles, who released John Frederick and Philip and approved a declaration in 1552 that the peace of the empire was not to be broken for matters of conscience in religious issues. This agreement at Passau between Maurice and Ferdinand of Austria and other princes signaled a weariness on every hand and a desire for peace. A band of neutrals sought to extricate themselves from the ceaseless strife. Charles would accept the declaration only until the next diet. But there was a yearning on both sides for an end to what seemed a hopeless struggle that only complicated all other political purposes.

The Peace of Augsburg (1555) therefore marks a significant date in Western history. It was a compromise dictated by the realities of the situation. It did not solve all questions, but it established a new principle according to which further settlements would be made. The unity of Europe was a fiction both in church and empire, and the peace of 1555 recognized the fact. Instead of imposing the fiction, the rulers allowed Catholics and Protestants to live together under certain conditions. Where Evangelicals had established themselves, their reforms, their possessions, and their freedom were allowed. While these rights

72

were restricted to those who accepted the Augsburg Confession, the same privileges were soon won also by Calvinists, especially in the Palatinate. But it was still believed that there could not be more than one religion in any territory. The minority in any principality therefore had the choice of submission to the majority or to emigrate. Only in the cities it was thought, could two religious cults coexist. While the treaty described conditions then current, the future was uncertain. Efforts should be continued to attain unity. No further expropriation of church property should be allowed. Roman bishops should not exercise any jurisdiction over evangelical territories. If a bishop became Lutheran, he could no longer enjoy his privileges or property. In the course of events the provisions of the Peace of Augsburg tended to consolidate the Lutheran and Catholic territories, the minorities in each disappearing. Germany was thus divided between the two, and the seeds of further conflict were present. Freedom of religion was not yet achieved for individuals apart from their political situation. On both sides the medieval tradition of one state, one religion persisted, but the significant change was the admission that an external unity could not be enforced on all Christians. Church and state had broken up into churches and states.

THE FAILURE OF CHARLES' POLICIES

Charles knew himself defeated. Born at the opening of the century, he had lived through a turbulent half century full of change. With all his resources and dedicated to the traditional faith he, if any emperor, was in a position to uphold the medieval church. He was as concerned about its unity as any of the popes of his period, even prodding them to reform. No one could have given greater support to the conciliar movement. Yet he failed. It is a biased view which lays the blame on the ambitions of German princes. They were themselves moved by forces under them. The uprising of the peasants, the demands of the cities, the thoughts of the humanists, the faith of the Evangelicals, who had rediscovered the power of the Gospel — these were impelling movements which broke up old traditions, the feudal system, the pretensions of temporal, and spiritual monopolies. France, England, Spain, Portugal, Austria, Bohemia, Hungary, the Swiss cities and cantons, the Italian cities, the trade centers from Novgorod to

73

the Netherlands were transforming themselves into new powers which no antiquated notion of a universal Roman empire and church could contain. Religious faith was one of the elements in this upsurge of the human spirit. It demanded a freedom which sometimes was won at the sacrifice of self, sometimes was able to create new agencies in defiance of old authorities. Luther had become the spokesman for this spirit, and in German cities and territories the Lutheran Church of the Reformation took form. At Augsburg — 25 years after the confession at a former diet — it won the right to take its place as a form of the Christian church on earth even if some hoped it was but a temporary right.

In 1555 Charles abdicated the Netherlands to his son Philip II and in the following year the Spanish possessions. The administration of the empire he turned over in 1556 to his brother Ferdinand, king of Austria. He retired to a monastery and died two years later.

VI

FORMING THE CHURCH ANEW — IN GERMANY

The Germany of Luther's time was a collection of some 300 different authorities — vestiges of a rapidly disintegrating feudal system. Some territories were considerable in area, such as Saxony, Hesse, and Württemberg, and ruled by dukes who could force the emperor to their terms. Many were small counties, or even estates, where counts vied with one another to increase their lands and possessions. A great part of the people were peasants, some enjoying relative freedom, but most were pawns of their overlords and subject to heavy taxes or duties. Occasionally their unrest broke into open rebellion, as in the Peasants' War, but mostly they lacked leadership or means and at best got only temporary relief in a system where they depended on the manor for tools and living.

German and Swiss Cities

Of increasing importance were the cities situated along rivers or at crossroads of travel. A rising class of burghers, or townsmen, was growing wealthy in commerce. Its leaders demanded privileges and freedom for the city council, or *Rat,* from the hereditary princes in whose area they were situated. About 65 of the cities had charters direct from the empire, the majority being in southern Germany and Switzerland. These cities were organized as corporations closely knit politically, socially, and culturally. Religiously they were as one, but council and bishop were often in conflict over material matters, for in many ways the church and the council were rivals in business. The ruling class was aristocratic, suppressing a lower level of people among whom a revolutionary spirit could easily be inflamed. In northern Germany and around the Baltic a chain of strong commercial centers had developed out of the Hanseatic League. Merchants circulated freely and exchanged goods at the yearly markets from Novgorod to the Netherlands. Printed material also flowed along these channels. Sons of merchants went back to Prague or Leipzig for their university study. Colonies of Germans were strong in Poland and Scandinavia.

Equal in extent were the travels of the clergy. Missions to and from Rome were commonplace. The provincial meetings of the monastic orders brought the friars and monks together regularly, and their tours of begging covered the land. The universities were arms of the church — thousands of monks and sons of nobility wandered around in the university world of Paris, Bologna, Salerno, Oxford, Cambridge, Prague, Louvain, Leipzig, Erfurt, and Tübingen.

A chronicler of the time tells us that Luther's 95 Theses were circulated throughout Germany in two weeks and within four weeks had covered almost all of Christendom. Allowing for partisan exaggeration, we may still believe that Luther's words were soon the main topic of discussion all over Europe.

Within a few years reformed congregations were established in Wittenberg, Nürnberg, and Strasbourg. Among the first in reform were the Hanseatic cities: Magdeburg 1524, Stralsund 1525, Celle 1526, Goslar 1528, Brunswick (Braunschweig) 1529, Göttingen 1529, Hamburg 1529, Lübeck 1530, Rostock 1531, Greifswald 1531, and Hanover 1532. In these commercial communities the initiative came not from the patrician families, who were often allied through relatives with the ecclesiastical leaders, but from the guilds of merchants and the populace, who saw in the religious movement a chance to protest against their economic disadvantages.

In upper Germany and Switzerland the cities had been influenced by humanism and the newer spirit of the Italian Renaissance. The city councils had obtained large freedom from imperial control and considered their cities almost independent. Often when disorder followed the coming of the new preaching they arranged for debates and then decided the policy of the city. They had already won the right to appoint preachers in the main churches and could therefore vote to adopt the Reformation cause regardless of the local bishop. Basel in 1521 declared itself free from the bishop in temporal things and after 1529 was spiritually autonomous. Baden held a disputation in 1526 in which Oecolampadius of Basel and John Eck took part. Here the Roman party won, and some of the Swiss cantons never left the papal church. But in 1528 Wolfgang Capito and Martin Bucer were among the victorious Protestant debaters in Bern, and the city suspended Roman rites. Strasbourg abolished the Mass in 1529, and Augsburg resolved on reform in 1533.

LUTHERAN PREACHERS

But where did the preachers of the reform come from? The rapid spread of Lutheran teaching after 1517 can be explained only by the universal desire for reform and the conviction that the practices of the church were in conflict with its real message and purpose. Many of the "new" preachers were former monks. The orders themselves had grown up in protest against the low spiritual condition in the churches. We have seen how even in earlier centuries Cluny was the monastic center of reform. The Franciscan and Dominican were reform movements. It is not surprising then that so many of the Lutheran preachers came from the monasteries rather than the parishes. The desire for marriage was no stronger than in former centuries, and so it was not the prime reason for leaving the celibate life. When, however, Luther placed a new emphasis on vocation and gave to every calling in life a sacred meaning, he undermined the doctrine that a monk's life was more spiritual than a householder's. Marriage of the clergy was a result, hardly a cause, for reformation preaching, and the emptying of the monasteries came as a consequence of teaching a Gospel of faith in place of one where good works merited special spiritual status.

Wittenberg became a source of evangelical preachers. The little town of 3,000 people soon found itself doubled in population as students were attracted to it from all parts of Europe. Many of these returned to their native cities or homelands and carried with them reports of the theology taught there as well as treatises and books printed in reform centers. Luther's interpretation of the priesthood of believers led many to sense their own responsibility in city council, in manor house, and in town schools, and to view the church otherwise than in the traditional observance of rites and customs.

Of critical importance was the attitude of the princes in the major territories. Luther had powerful support in the tolerant attitude of his own territorial lord, Elector Frederick the Wise. Though cautious in his relationship to the emperor, Frederick demanded a free and impartial judgment of Luther. Since this was never realized, the elector provided the Reformer with freedom until the elector's death in 1525.

77

The same policy was pursued by Frederick's successor, John the Constant, who died in 1532, and by Elector John Frederick the Magnanimous, who lived but a year longer than Luther. Thus Luther had the continuous protection of the temporal ruler, and we have seen how the prince cooperated with the reformers in the visitations begun in 1527.

BUGENHAGEN

In the transition from the old to the new the name of Johann Bugenhagen occupies a prominent place. A native of Pomerania in northeast Germany, Bugenhagen had been impressed by the spirit of humanism, especially by Erasmus. He studied in Münster, then came back to Pomerania, where he became acquainted with Luther's writing. He went to Wittenberg and soon won the confidence of Luther and Melanchthon for his ability in the interpretation of Scripture. But his great talent was in the field of organization. In 1522 he became city pastor of Wittenberg, then superintendent of the region, and for a decade was called to different places to reorganize the church. He was the author of a series of church ordinances that became models for Lutheranism in Germany and elsewhere. Hamburg, Lübeck, and the province of Pomerania were scenes of his activity, and Lutheran church administration dates from Bugenhagen's ordinances in these places.

Bugenhagen had participated in the Saxon visitation. He made such visitations essential in the reformed territories, recommending that they be made regularly every four or five years. A superintendent replaced the bishop. The city council or the prince of the territory had a voice in the election since the territory or city was thought of as a unit — a Christian community. The superintendent ordained the pastors of the congregations. Schools were enjoined for the training of the clergy, but weekly lectures in Latin should be open also to the laity. Preaching received a central place in Bugenhagen's ordinances, for the instruction of the laity in the Catechism and in Scripture was the most important duty of the church. The Augustana and the Apology were the norms for doctrine. The pastor was to preach, teach, and give pastoral care — he should not be burdened with extraneous things. The city council or the provincial prince should set up a common treasury for the promotion of schools, the payment of pastors' salaries, and the care of the poor — even of the aged monks left in the monasteries.

Since the temporal authorities took over the property of the churches and monasteries, they should use the income for the common welfare. The church no longer had an independent treasury, but deacons were to be appointed as representatives of the Christian community and be given the means of aiding those in need. The community thus became responsible for the charitable work formerly assumed by the parish and the monasteries. The church was to concentrate on preaching, worship, and education. Although a host of difficulties prevented the full realization of Bugenhagen's regulations, the Lutheran communities had received a program of organization that was to be of influence for generations to come. Characteristic of all his ordinances was a spirit of freedom and flexibility. He recognized differences in various regions and avoided a legalistic tone. The newly adopted forms should be adopted for their value in creating order — not because they were divinely ordained. Only the Word must prevail.

PHILIP OF HESSE

Of more political than spiritual significance was the role of Philip of Hesse. He had been impressed by Luther at Worms and was versed in the writings of the Reformer. Actuated as Frederick the Wise had been by a desire for the prestige of a university, Philip founded Marburg. After 1526 his province of Hesse was counted as Lutheran, and Philip assumed the judisdiction of a bishop. He was earnestly interested in keeping the Swiss and German movements together, though the colloquy at Marburg in 1529 proved the impossibility of reconciling the views of Luther and Zwingli on the Lord's Supper. Still he persisted, for he realized the importance of a common front against the imperial aim of destroying Lutheranism. He found a capable ally in Bucer, who had led the reform movement in Strasbourg, giving it an ordinance in 1534—1535. The closest the Swiss and Lutheran parties came to each other was in the Wittenberg Concordat of 1536, though it proved ineffective. In 1538 Philip commissioned Bucer to reorganize the church in Hesse. Significant decisions of the synod which met that year were the introduction of confirmation and the provision for the appointment of an elder lay member to assist the pastor in church discipline. The ordering of confirmation instruction laid the foundation for a school system. Philip's bigamous marriage hurt both his political and his religious standing, and his imprisonment ended his prestige, but his loyalty to the Reformation did contribute to the establishment of reform in his principality.

EAST PRUSSIA

More consequential than could have been foreseen at the time was the winning of East Prussia for the evangelical cause. The military order of the Teutonic Knights had gained control of Prussia, Christianizing the pagan people in the 13th century. But the knights were bitterly opposed by Poland and Lithuania, their neighbors, and in 1521 Poland conquered West Prussia. East Prussia was made a vassal of Poland and given as a dukedom to Albert of Brandenburg, the last grand master of the order. He was a nephew of the king of Poland, who stoutly resisted reform in his own realm but allowed Duke Albert freedom to introduce a full Lutheran order in East Prussia. Albert had been converted by Andreas Osiander to the Lutheran faith in 1522 in Nürnberg and had visited Luther in 1523 and 1524. Luther sent able German preachers to Albert in Königsberg, including Paul Speratus, the hymn writer. Unique was the appointment of two bishops, both of whom served as evangelical bishops and thus retained episcopal jurisdiction in church matters. German was used in worship in Königsberg before it was introduced in Wittenberg. Visitation took place as early as 1525. In fact East Prussia was the first evangelical province of Germany.

BRENZ

Hanover joined the Lutheran cause in 1533, Leignitz and Brieg of Schleswig in 1534. A most important addition came in 1534 when the province of Württemberg was won. Duke Ulrick had regained Württemberg from the Austrian Hapsburgs by the help of Philip of Hesse. Though at first Zwinglian in sympathy, on his return to power he called on Johann Brenz to help organize his land as Lutheran. What Bugenhagen meant for northern Germany, Brenz accomplished in the south. In 1526 he had provided Swabia-Halle with an ordinance. His catechism of 1529 had a wide circulation. He helped Andreas Osiander organize Nürnberg, but his chief monument was the reformation in Württemberg, from Stuttgart as center. Tübingen was made into an evangelical university in 1537—1538. Opposed to the Interim, Brenz had to flee to Basel, where he wrote his commentary on Isaiah. After

80

the Peace of Passau he returned and ministered to the church in Stutt-gart. Throughout his career he was dubious of conciliation with the Swiss and remained a true disciple of Luther, defending his concept of the Lord's Supper. He was the author of the Ordinance and Confession of Württemberg in 1559. This ordinance first made the institution of "visitors" permanent by constituting them as a sort of *Kirchenrat*, or council. Both theological and economic concerns were represented among the visitors — they and the superintendent acted together, sub-ject to the approval of the ducal council. This arrangement was later copied in other territories, including Saxony.

That part of Saxony which had been ruled by Duke George had remained Roman through the years after Worms, but on the death of the duke in 1539 it turned evangelical, including Leipzig University. The arbitrary regulation of the churches by the succeeding princes, however, evoked Luther's apprehension. Duke Henry, who was faithful to the emperor, was driven out of Brunswick in 1542 by the Smalcald League, and an evangelical church was established. The same year Joachim of Brandenburg died. He had been a staunch Catholic, but one of his sons, Margrave John, openly favored the reformers, while the other, Elector Joachim II, was tolerant of them.

THE DEFENSE OF ROME — THE JESUITS

Nothing suggests the low estate of the churches in Germany at the time of Luther's 95 Theses so much as the fact that for 25 years thereafter the papacy and hierarchy reacted so feebly and irresolutely. The conflicting interests of kings and emperor and popes revealed how deeply entangled the affairs of church and governments were. Even the common danger of the Turks in the east failed to unite those who pro-fessed loyalty to the Church of Rome. To attribute the success of the reform movement to the political ambitions of German princes is to disregard the tremendous popular enthusiasm for church reform and to overlook the fact that the movement was stopped only by the military power of other princes who took the side of Rome. Wherever the Haps-burgs held power, as in Spain and Austria, repressive measures stemmed the evangelical tide. The Parlement of France was opposed to further reform than their Gallican program had already won from the papacy. Italy itself was saved less by the pope than by two allies who at this time entered the contest with striking results.

81

In 1540 a papal bull authorized the Jesuit Order, organized by Ignatius Loyola. This Spanish-born "spiritual Don Quixote" had a remarkable career of warfare, travel, and acquaintance with romantic, mystical, philosophical, and theological literature before his life's purpose became clear. He was in Paris in 1528 when a church council condemned Lutheranism. With six disciples he bound himself in 1534 by oath to serve the church either converting Saracens in Jerusalem or contending with heretics in Rome. He won Pope Paul III to his plans, and in 1541 the former "company of Jesus" became the "Society of Jesus" with Loyola as general. The following year the papacy received its second ally when the methods of the Spanish Inquisition were introduced with its examination and execution of heretics and censure of the press. The society and the Inquisition had as their objects the upholding of the supremacy of the pope, the suppression of heresy, and the strengthening of the authority of the church over the world. Through the strategy of the Jesuits and the use of the Inquisition the Lutheran movement in Italy and Spain was crushed within a decade.

At the same time the plans for a church council finally materialized. But when the meeting at Trent was convened, it was not for the reform of the church so much as for the defense of the papal church. It was too late for a free and general discussion in which both sides could be heard and an agreement reached. New forms had taken shape in the Western churches. The council and the Counter-Reformation could at best cleanse and revise the traditions of the Roman churches. With the help of still loyal governments Rome could end the further conquests of the evangelical movement and try to win back areas already lost. Neither the evangelical nor the Roman churches had won independence from the state. Each church depended on temporal authority to guarantee its organization and rites. Whereas in earlier centuries one church had claimed universal sovereignty under the protection of one imperial head, now a variety of forms of church organization sought the same kind of protection under a local or national authority.

THE SWISS REFORMATION — CALVIN

That the reform movement would take many different forms was clear from the beginning. Conditions varied from place to place, but of greater consequence was the right of conscience, which Luther so dramatically defended at Worms. Moving the center of ecclesiastical gravity from Roman tradition to the Gospel as proclaimed in Scripture changed the nature of Christian faith from loyalty to a human institution to loyalty to a Christ revealed in the Word. But this also opened up the possibility of a variety of interpretations, with differences among the Evangelicals. We have seen how Luther had to define his position over against Anabaptists and Spiritualists. The Marburg Colloquy revealed basic differences between Luther and Zwingli. This resulted in a division between the Swiss and the German Reformation, with some of the southern German cities, such as Strasbourg and Augsburg, leaning toward Zwingli. Zwingli's death in 1531 seriously affected the further advance of his cause and produced a division in the Swiss cantons, the forest cantons remaining traditional, the cities — Zurich, Basel, Bern — adopting the Reformed faith.

Meanwhile a new evangelical center developed in Geneva, where John Calvin first arrived in 1536. Only 27 years old, this brilliant doctor of law had studied at Paris, Orleans, and Bourges, and had come into contact with a churchly humanism then strong in France. With other scholarly friends he hoped for a reformation within the church, collaborating with a cousin in a French translation of the Bible. Influenced by Lutheran writers, he soon moved closer to an evangelical position. Anti-Protestant reaction in France, however, drove him and others out of the country. Calvin fled to Basel where in 1536 he issued a classic defense of the evangelical reform, the *Institutes of the Christian Religion*. When he came to Geneva, the city was in the midst of a transition from the old to the new. The reformers were William Farel and Peter Viret, who had come from Bern, a city with which Geneva was in alliance against the domination of Savoy. Farel persuaded Calvin to join in the reform program as lecturer, preacher, and organizer. Calvin prepared a confession of faith and articles on government of the church. However, the rigor of the discipline that he enjoined met with popular disapproval, and both Farel and Calvin were banished in 1538.

From Geneva Calvin went to Strasbourg. This was then a center of religion and culture. Representatives of Roman Catholicism, humanism, Zwinglianism, Lutheranism, Anabaptism, and Spiritualism all mingled here as refugees came from France, Holland, and England. Calvin was pastor of the French refugees. Bucer was the leading spirit of the city, assiduously striving to reconcile opposing Evangelicals. Calvin could observe the activities of this remarkable churchman. Bucer contended for an independence of church and state, but for cooperation between them. The preachers met regularly in assembly; church discipline was exercised by elders. In his theology Bucer stressed the glory of God, the doctrine of predestination, and verbal inspiration. He departed from Luther's concept of the ubiquity of Christ in the Sacrament of the Altar and believed that only to the faithful is Christ present as God and man. Calvin was impressed by the participation of the congregation in the Strasbourg liturgy and in the singing. In 1539 he published his own Psalmbook with the aid of Clement Marot, the psalm composer. Jacob Sturm was then in Strasbourg establishing his famous *gymnasium*. Calvin served as professor, lecturing and writing. A treatise of 1540 explained his teaching on the Lord's Supper — Christ is in heaven and His presence is spiritual, the Holy Spirit conveying the power of Christ's body to believers. His *Institutes* he published in a second Latin edition in 1539, which he issued in a French translation in 1541 and created a new French language of religion. The cardinal features of the *Institutes,* a masterpiece of evangelical doctrine, are the articles on justification by faith, verbal inspiration, the will of God, and predestination. Man is to contribute to the glory of God by a holy life in the world. The secular power is to be advised by the spiritual and to serve its purposes.

In 1541 Calvin returned to Geneva and organized the churches and pastors as well as the city government along evangelical lines. Holidays were abolished along with all "signs of idolatry" — crucifixes, stained-glass windows, candles, flowers. In the worship service the sermon was central. Hymn singing was restricted to the Psalms. The Sabbath was strictly observed. While a distinction existed between the various civil councils on the one hand and the consistory — made up of preachers and 12 laymen, and the preachers, called the venerable company — on the other, the civic administration was subordinate to the ecclesiastical. Adultery, blasphemy, and witchcraft were major crimes, and the execution of Servetus as a heretic was urged by Calvin.

From Geneva Calvin's influence spread through refugees and writings to France, Scotland, England, and the Netherlands. Along the Rhine, in the Palatinate, Lutheranism and Calvinism met and mingled.

In 1544 it seemed as if the Palatinate might become Lutheran. The *German Mass,* the chalice, and the marriage of priests were introduced in the electoral and upper districts. Frederick III of the Palatinate vainly tried again to unite the Protestants. In 1563 his territory became Calvinistic, adopting the Heidelberg Catechism.

LIMITS OF GERMAN REFORMATION

When in 1555 the Peace of Augsburg recognized the adherents of the Augsburg Confession, the limits of Lutheranism in Germany were quite clear. The strongholds were in the northern and central parts. Zwinglian and Calvinistic churches confronted it in the south and west, while France, Catholic Switzerland, Austria, and Bavaria surrounded it on the south and southeast. It was in the north and east that the evangelical message was to find acceptance and to result in new forms of church organization.

VII

FORMING THE CHURCH ANEW — BEYOND GERMANY

BOHEMIA

Bohemia had attempted a reformation a century before Luther, but the martyrdom of John Huss was all the Council of Constance could effect. The cup became the symbol of the Utraquists, who defied the Roman hierarchy after Huss' death, contenting themselves with a consistory without a bishop ordained by Rome. But in 1467 another branch — the Brethren — formed their own church, electing bishops by lot. Among the Utraquists at Prague were those who gladly followed the challenge of Luther and found in him a champion when he addressed to them a letter in 1523 urging them to choose their own bishop, regardless of Rome. In their desire for a regular bishop German settlers in Bohemia joined the Utraquists and established contacts with Wittenberg theologians, who furnished guidance and ordination through German superintendents. But Bohemia was under Ferdinand, the Hapsburg Austrian who joined his brother Charles V in the Smalcald offensive. He was determined to bring the Utraquists back to Rome — the Brethren he pitilessly persecuted in despair of their return.

A Prague Interim of 1549 was no more successful than that of Augsburg, but it united the Lutherans and the conservative Utraquists in the demand that the century-old compact by which they were tolerated by Rome though separated from it be respected. Augusta, the bishop of the Brethren, suffered persecution and a 16-year imprisonment. On his release, despite earlier personal acquaintance with Luther, he turned toward Calvin and Geneva. In 1575 Maximilian II asked for a statement of faith from his dissident subjects. The Utraquists and the Brethren could not agree on the *Augustana;* instead they drew up the *Confessio Bohemica,* which they presented at a diet. The emperor wanted the consent of the estates for the election of his son Rudolf as king of Bohemia. The price he had to pay for unity was toleration of the different religious parties, and for 60 years a truce obtained, less by the wish of the king than by the strength of the Protestants. For by the end of the century the nobles and burghers of Bohemia and Moravia were predominantly evangelical.

AUSTRIA

While Charles was emperor, Austria in 1524 forbade the sale and reading of Lutheran literature, and martyrdoms took place in 1524 and 1527. The Turkish threat always prevented action against the Lutherans, who increased rapidly. Ferdinand I, successor of Charles as emperor, doubted the policy of repression and was lenient toward the Protestants, who in a few decades constituted a majority of the population both of peasants and of nobility. Since the king and the kingdom were legally Roman Catholic, the Lutherans could not organize congregations or invade the rights of the hierarchy.

HUNGARY

In Hungary, ironically, the Protestants had greater freedom. There most of the country was under the Turks, who in the decisive battle of Mohács in 1526 had wiped out the nobility. Lutheran teaching had spread among the German settlers in Hungary and also to the Slovaks in the north, the Slovenes in the south, and the Magyars in between. Humanism had prepared the way and kindled resentment against conditions in the church. Peasants protested against both secular and spiritual leaders. In the cities the Germans in the councils introduced reforms and called evangelical pastors, many of whom had received their education in Germany. In the 12th century Saxons from the middle Rhine and Moselle valley had settled in Transylvania, the eastern part of Hungary. John Honter became the reformer of this region. He printed Luther's Small Catechism in his own printery. In 1543 he prepared a program of reformation for Kronstadt and a church ordinance in 1547. As a vassal state of the Turks, Transylvania paid tribute but had relative freedom, and its Magyar rulers tolerated not only Lutherans and Calvinists but also Socinians from Poland and the Orthodox from Rumania. Buda, a former German city on an ancient Roman site, was the official residence of the Turkish governor and also had a German court under Margrave George, who favored the Lutherans. In Pressburg,

88

where a remnant of the old faith and state remained, the Evangelicals were tolerated in the suburbs of the city. As a rule the Germans and Slavs were Lutherans, the Magyars Calvinists. Magyar was the official language, but pastors used also Hungarian, Slovak, and Latin. Hungary was not entirely freed from the Turkish rule until 1699.

Farther south in Carniola Primus Truber made Laibach a center for Lutheran preaching until he was forced to flee persecution by a Roman bishop and an Austrian prince. But in Nürnberg and Württemberg, where he found refuge, he pursued a remarkable career in giving his people a Slovenian religious literature. Between 1550 and his death in 1586 he provided them with the New Testament, the Psalms, a catechism, a postil — even the Formula of Concord and a church ordinance — all issued from Tübingen. At the same time he was collaborating with Stephen Consul in a printing establishment at Urach, in Württemberg, in publishing Croatian works. The project was subsidized by Hans von Ungnad, an Austrian official who had resigned his post rather than carry out government suppression of the Evangelicals, and from Urach he directed efforts to spread the true faith in Carniola, Croatia, and Serbia. One catechism was even aimed at the Turks and printed in Cyrillic letters. Another colleague of Truber was George Dalmatin, who completed a translation of the Bible into Slovenian in 1584 and produced a hymnbook and prayer book. But the Counter-Reformation was to wipe out most of these gains and ironically the Nürnberg-made type of the new languages was to be captured in the Thirty Years' War and made to serve anti-evangelical propaganda from Rome. In Lutheran history the name of Matthias Flacius the "Illyrican" reminds us of evangelical concepts in southeastern Europe, for this redoubtable champion of strict doctrine was a native of these regions.

POLAND

Poland, through its connection with Lithuania on the east, had long known that the Orthodox Church, which was not bound to Rome, gave both bread and wine in the Sacrament and did not demand celibacy of all its clergy. From the west had come the persecuted Brethren of Bohemia, whose simple life and organization impressed the Poles. The Roman Church was deeply entrenched in the country. It controlled large estates. Its clergy came from wealthy, aristocratic families. But

89

a tradition of tolerance existed even before Lutheran and Calvinistic teachings reached the land. Lutheranism spread rapidly among the German citizens of the towns and the nobility of old Poland, and they engaged evangelical preachers. Polish students went to Wittenberg and came back as leaders. Sigismund II Augustus became king in 1548. Himself a humanist with a large library, he made no move against the magnates who favored reform. In Lithuania the Radziwill family was the leader of a Calvinist movement and built a large stone church in Vilna. The clergy were encouraged in further studies, and a school was established in Radziegow. In Poland the Gorka family was Lutheran. Three sons attended Wittenberg, and close contact was established with the leaders in East Prussia. The Calvinists produced a great theologian, John Laski, who came back to Poland after an eventful ministry in the Netherlands, London, and Frankfurt, and organized his people in a Calvinist synod. A Socinian "Polish Brethren" group shared in the general religious freedom.

RIGA

Northward along the Baltic was the region which the Teutonic Knights had ruled until their power was broken by Poland. Catholic bishops had their seats in Riga, Pilten, Pernau, and Dorpat. Half-Christianized peasants inhabited rude villages. German tradesmen were influential in the few, small cities. Johann Lohmüller, a councilman in Riga, was in correspondence with Luther as early as 1522 — there was preaching of Lutheran doctrine in his church a year earlier. Luther replied by letter in 1523, and in the following year dedicated a Psalm exposition to "the dear friends in Christ in Riga and Livonia." He reminded the council of its threefold responsibility — support of the pastor, ordering of instruction of children, care of the poor. He wrote again in 1525, emphasizing the importance of concord in the congregation and of congregational worship. In 1527 Dr. John Briesemann from Prussia was brought in, on Lohmüller's proposal, to help arrange the order of worship. Two years later he drew up a church ordinance that was generally accepted in Livonia. The ordinance was printed in Rostock in 1530, along with a *Sankböklin* of 54 hymns, including Luther's "A Mighty Fortress." The songs were probably collected by the Lutheran preacher Andreas Knöpken, a pupil of Bugenhagen, who had first preached in Riga.

LATVIA, ESTONIA

The new order in Riga became the example followed farther north as Lutheran preaching reached Latvia and Estonia, together then called Livonia. Briesemann's liturgy was translated into Lettish for the use of pastors. Luther's Catechism was printed in the Lettish language in Wittenberg in 1535, along with a "Platt deutsch" (Low German) text. The Livonia to which Luther wrote included Reval, the capital of Estonia, and Dorpat (Tartu). There was evangelical preaching in Reval in 1517, and in 1524 the city council named John Lange as evangelical pastor. The unity of this region was soon broken as Poland, Denmark, and Sweden fought for its possession. In 1561 Sweden and Denmark took over the northern section, Estonia going to Sweden. Poland received the major part, eventually including Riga. What happened to the evangelical churches in these lands depended on the policies of their overlords.

DENMARK

The Union of Kalmar (1397), bringing Denmark, Sweden, and Norway under one king, proved unbearable, though in effect for over a century. To preserve his power the king had to make concessions to both prelates and nobles of all the countries. Intrigue was constant. Early in the 16th century the Swedish nobles revolted, and their leader Sten Sture was condemned by both the Danish and the Swedish archbishop. Christian II was king of Denmark and of the union. His rule was unpopular in Sweden. At home he was confiscating the indulgence income for his own use while persuading the pope to place the ban on the Swedish Sture. When the archbishopric of Lund became vacant, he opposed the pope's candidate — a cardinal who already held three bishoprics — and appeased the pope by an annual money payment. He felt the reform movement might be useful. Through his uncle, Elector Frederick, he negotiated with Wittenberg, which sent Martin Reinhart and then Karlstadt to Copenhagen, though with little result. The Carmelite monk Paulus Heliae proved more influential. He had been a humanist and interested in reform of the church, but when he discerned that a break with the old church might result, he became its defender. He turned on the king when it became apparent that Christian II was most concerned about keeping church money from going to Rome and curtailing the wealth and power of the bishops. But the king's attempt to break the resistance of Sweden by murdering the leaders in the "Stockholm Bloodbath" cost him his crown. His own council forced him into exile in 1523. He fled to Saxony, spent some time in Wittenberg, and was present at Augsburg in 1530, where he swore fealty to the old faith and was promised help by the emperor to regain his throne. A vain attempt at invasion of Norway led to his imprisonment by Frederick, the new king. Christian represents a combination of the old and the new. His laws indicated a desire for economic and religious reform, but his methods were inconsistent with his purposes.

The Danish nobles who in 1523 elected Frederick I king wanted a national church independent, as the French, from the papacy. Some like Mogens Gjoe were religiously convinced by Lutheranism, others saw in the transfer of church property a gain for themselves. The burghers in the cities were favorable to the reform. Frederick was ready to protect the preaching of the Gospel. His daughter was married to Albert of Brandenburg, who made Prussia Lutheran. His son Christian was duke of Schleswig-Holstein, where he brought Lutheran theologians to preach and teach and through the Haderslev Ordinance of 1528 made his land the first Lutheran province in the North.

The spiritual leader of the Danish Reformation was Hans Tausen. He entered a Johannite convent in Antvorskov, to which he returned after studies and a period of lectureship at Rostock. In 1521 he became professor of theology at Copenhagen but left after the king's flight and spent two years at Wittenberg with Luther, 1522—1524. On his homecoming to Antvorskov he preached a Lutheran sermon in Holy Week 1525, for which his prior put him in a dungeon. When the prior sent him to the prior at Viborg (Finland), it was the prior instead of Tausen who changed his stand. In Viborg both the mayor and the people heard his preaching gladly and joined in the singing of Danish hymns. Around him was a band of helpers, including his brother-in-law Jorgen Sadolin who had studied in Wittenberg, the rector of the cathedral school and the first evangelical head of the school. A seminary was established for the training of pastors. Tausen also enjoyed the protection of Frederick, who in 1526 named him as chaplain.

The king's stand at the Diet of Odense in 1526 revealed his sympathy for the new order. When criticized for his position, he defended the preaching of the Gospel. He won the friendship of the new arch-bishop of Lund, and his council agreed that henceforth the confirmation of bishops should be sought from Lund, not Rome, with the usual fee going to the royal treasury. Furthermore, nobles should have the right to buy back property acquired by the church. At the Diet of Odense the following year the prelates received further setbacks. The new bishops of Odense and Roskilde paid their fees to the king. In 1529 Tausen was called to Copenhagen as pastor of the St. Nicholas Church. In 1530 he joined other evangelical pastors in the disputation between the old and the new teachings at the Copenhagen Diet. The "Forty-Three Articles" presented at the time are comparable to the Augsburg Confession of the same year. As at Augsburg, the Romanists replied in a "Confutation" and evoked a counter "Apology." When the citizens started breaking altars in the church of Our Lady, the king ordered it closed. Tausen's *Postil* meant much for the education of the evangelical clergy, and his hymnbook had lasting influence. After 1541 he worked vigorously as bishop for the betterment of his diocese of Ribe.

Meanwhile across the sound, in Malmö, Claus Mortensen, a priest, and Hans Olafsen, a monk, were initiating popular reforms. They had visited Haderslev to study the program of Schleswig-Holstein and returned in 1528. The Malmö *Salmebogen* of that year was the first Danish hymnal, for which they had translated German hymns. They also prepared an order of worship, assisted by helpers they had called in. One of these was Frans Vormorsen from Antwerp. Olaf Chrysosto-mus, who had taught at the University of Copenhagen and became the new rector of the school in Malmö, was evangelical in spirit. Also in Malmö, after 1532, was Christian Pedersen. In his humanistic period he had published among other writings, Saxo's *Chronicle*. He became a disciple of Luther and in 1529 produced a Danish translation of the New Testament. An earlier translation had been printed in 1524 by Hans Mikkelson, then mayor of Malmö, who had followed Christian to Wittenberg and studied there under Luther.

After the death of Frederick the 1533 Diet of Copenhagen seemed to threaten the reform measures. The bishops succeeded in postponing the election of Christian III, whom they did not want. They secured an acknowledgment of their jurisdiction in spiritual matters and silenced Tausen, who was to be prohibited from teaching or writing and confined to his diocese. It was a temporary victory. After a civil war, Christian entered Copenhagen in 1536, supported by the populace. The bishops were imprisoned until they pledged not to oppose the new ordinance — one bishop remained in prison until his death. At the Diet of 1536 the bishops were found guilty of fomenting civil war and were deposed. In their place new evangelical superintendents (later called bishops) were named. The income of the former bishops was to go to the royal treasury, which would support the churches. The nobility could regulate worship on their estates, recovering properties which had been given for masses for the dead. Monasteries would remain for the present, but begging was not permitted. The tithes, which were to continue, would be divided between the parish priest, the church, the schools, and the officials. At a meeting in Odense a commission drew up an ordinance which Luther approved. It was published in Latin in 1537 and in Danish in 1539. Bugenhagen was called to supervise the introduction of the new ordinance and to reform the university. He anointed the king and ordained the new bishops. Outstanding among the seven was the bishop of Sjelland, Peder Palladius, a Wittenberg master of arts and doctor, a translator of Luther, and an acknowledged literary master, as witnessed by his *Visitation Book*.

After 1536 the Danish Church developed in much the same manner as the churches in Germany, though the bishops were recognized as spiritual leaders and, more than in Germany, kept the church from becoming a department of the state. In the absence of consistories or synods the bishops held their place by force of character and faithfulness to their duties, though aided by a royal respect for their office.

NORWAY AND ICELAND

Norway's dependence on Denmark and the Hanseatic League stood in the way of its growth. Quarrels among the ruling class and the effects of the Black Death further reduced it to a secondary role in the Scandinavian Union. The course of the reform followed closely that of Denmark. Frederick I permitted Lutheran preaching in Bergen, a Hanseatic city, around 1525. When Denmark adopted its new ordinance, its provisions were applied also in Norway — the old bishops were deposed and new superintendents elected, the church's property was confiscated, and the clergy made dependent on state grants. Danish superintendents, teachers, and officials brought in the Danish liturgy, Bible, and hymnals. Popular resistance was limited to revolts against the removal of images and relics from the churches. It would require years to change the religious instruction of the nation, but the foundation was laid in these years for a close relationship between Lutheranism in Norway and Denmark.

Similarly Iceland received the new forms of church life from Denmark. The two Roman bishops were forcibly removed from office. One was deported to Denmark, the other was executed in Holar in 1550. An Icelandic New Testament was printed in Copenhagen in 1540. The deepening of a religious consciousness consonant with the new teaching belongs in Iceland, as in Denmark and Norway, to a later period.

SWEDEN

In Sweden too the disintegration of the traditional Roman power was related to political events. The hated Danish rule, which had culminated in the Stockholm Massacre, called forth a popular uprising among nobility and a strong independent peasantry. In 1523 Gustavus Vasa emerged as the leader and was elected king after he had driven the Danes out of Sweden. Intent on building up a strong monarchy, the king had to settle accounts with the hierarchy that often had been in collusion with the Danish crown. The church owned almost half the wealth of the country, and men like Bishop Brask of Linköping wielded both secular and spiritual power. Gustavus found help in another direction.

Olavus Petri, after studies in the monastic school of his home city Örebro and at Uppsala, had gone to Leipzig and then Wittenberg. He seems to have been in Wittenberg at the time of the 95 Theses, for he received his bachelor's degree there in 1516 and his master's in 1518. His later writings show the influence of Luther's teaching of grace, the Bible, and the place of the vernacular. He had learned of Luther's challenge of the supremacy of the papacy, and, like Luther, Olavus came to consider it nonessential to the unity of the church. On his return to Sweden he became chancellor to Matthias the bishop of Strengnäs, and a close friend of the archdeacon, Laurentius Andreae, who also had studied abroad and had witnessed the conflict of pope and secular authorities. The bishop was among the victims of the massacre, but Olavus stayed on and soon attracted attention by his sermons against the Mass, the monks, confession, and the worship of the saints. After his coronation in Strengnäs, Gustavus took Laurentius along to Stockholm as his chancellor and there installed Olavus as pastor of the city church and secretary of the city council. Half the townsmen were Germans, and a German pastor preached to them.

In late 1523 relations with the papacy ceased. Christ, Gustavus asserted, was the supreme pontiff. Taxes were levied on the churches, and troops were quartered in monasteries. Bishop Brask tried to resist, but in vain. The king encouraged Lutheran preaching and literature, even commanding a New Testament translation. The character of the reformation in Sweden was determined to a great extent by the varied literature produced by Olavus. An Useful Teaching, or book of catechetical instruction, appeared in 1526, and a New Testament in Swedish the same year — Laurentius Andreae cooperated in the latter. The whole Bible was completed in 1541. The Reply to Twelve Questions was Olavus' response to a request from the king for a statement from both the Roman and the Lutheran teachers. It and a treatise Concerning the Word show an acquaintance with events and literature from Nürnberg and the writings of Osiander. Olavus' Mass in Swedish was influenced also by a Nürnberg form, via Rostock, and a Swedish Hymn Book of 1530 bore resemblance to a Low-German collection. In 1529 Olavus published the first Protestant Manual — a handbook containing orders for worship and pastoral acts. His productions also included homiletical, legal, and historical writings. Following his theory that the church must be reformed by the education of clergy and people, Olavus made available a body of material that gave an intellectual and liturgical basis for such education.

The progress of the royal program was impeded by a series of rebellions both in the north and in the south, but by the time of the Diet of Västeras in 1527 Gustavus had established his supremacy. The changes in liturgy were cautious, but the control over the church was complete. Bishop Brask left the country. Evangelical bishops replaced the conservative ones as vacancies occurred. A brother of Olavus, Laurentius Petri, was named the new archbishop — the former one had fled — and he officiated at the marriage of the king to a German Protestant princess in 1531. Five years later a convocation of the church was held at Uppsala. It decreed that pastors should preach only the Holy Gospel, read the service in Swedish at all cathedral churches and wherever else possible, and that pastoral acts should follow the provisions of the *Manual*.

The relations of king and reformers were often strained in the following years. Olavus did not hesitate to criticize Gustavus and his excessive measures. Olavus and Laurentius were even threatened with death sentences. For a period of years the king brought in German counselors and set *ordinarii* over the dioceses. But the bishops succeeded in retaining their offices, and the Germans returned home. The diet of Västeras in 1544 went beyond the 1527 program, and slowly the people adopted the teachings of their leaders. After 1543 Olavus resumed his preaching in Stockholm and the supervision of the school. He opposed the Interim and the Council of Trent, and neither found favor in Sweden. Both Olavus and Laurentius died in 1552, the king in 1560. During their lifetime Sweden had passed from a Danish and Roman dependency to an independent nation with a firmly established evangelical church.

FINLAND

The reform in Finland, a province of Sweden, stood in close relationship to that of the Swedish Church. Through his lieutenants Gustavus insured for the royal treasury the income of such church property as he believed was beyond the needs of the church. Martin Skytte, the bishop of Abo (Turku) from 1528 to 1550, was a former Dominican monk from Sigtuna. A humanist and a moderate Romanist, he encouraged young men to go to Wittenberg to study, with the result that several of them became the leaders of the evangelical reform in Finland. Foremost among them was Michael Agricola, who earned a recommendation from Luther himself. During his Wittenberg years from 1536 to 1539 Agricola started work on a Finnish New Testament and a prayer book. After a period as rector of Abo high school and coadjutor to Skytte, he became the bishop's successor. Gustavus delayed his consecration, for he was considering the abolition of the episcopate, but Agricola was finally confirmed and consecrated in 1554. The king employed him also on secular errands. On his way home from a commission in Moscow he died in 1557. Agricola contributed not only a New Testament — printed in Stockholm and pub-

97

lished in 1548 — but also a Finnish order of worship and a handbook of pastoral acts and began a collection of Finnish hymns. A bulky prayer book that contained also miscellaneous secular information was probably his most widely read book. Lutheran in his teaching, he also displayed interest in mysticism, in the early pagan religion of his homeland, and in the spiritualism of Schwenkfeld. His theology was a blend of humanism and the evangelical faith, tolerant of both the old practices and the various expressions of the new.

When Agricola was made bishop of Abo, a second diocese was established at Viborg (Viipuri) near the Russian border. This city had relationships with Reval and early received Lutheran impulses. A native of Viborg, Paul Juusten, who also had been at Wittenberg in 1543—1546 through Bishop Skytte's patronage, was made rector of the cathedral school at Abo and in 1554 the first bishop of Viborg, later transferring to Abo. As author of a catechism and a manual in Finnish for the clergy, through his visitations, and through efforts for the education of the clergy Juusten rendered his native church enduring service. In 1573 he convoked the first synod since Roman times, meeting with the pastors of the Abo diocese. What Olavus Petri and Laurentius Andreae did for the spiritual nurture of the people of Sweden during the transition from a Roman to an evangelical community, Agricola and Juusten accomplished in Finland.

VIII

RECONSTRUCTION IN THE CHURCH OF ROME

Despairing of changes in the policies of the papacy the reformers had repeatedly called for a council that might reorder the life of the church. The emperor realized that the forces of reform could not be suppressed by bans of excommunication or even by military force. He continually urged the papacy to arrange for a council that would allow the abuses to be debated and, if possible, corrected. But the popes were not anxious to lose any of their power or prestige. Nor would they admit that a council could exercise supremacy over the chair of St. Peter. When therefore the Council of Trent convened in December 1545, it was under the leadership of the papal legates and terms agreeable to Paul III, who had set up a commission of cardinals to advise him on needed reforms. Their report in 1538 confirmed every charge the reformers had made but was not made public because of the conditions it admitted.

Only when the political situation in Germany threatened a complete break did the pope join Charles V in the calling of the council. It was too late, however, to win the dissidents. Only the faithful would come. The voting was limited to bishops and heads of orders. No proxies were allowed, and the majority would be Italian churchmen. The business was to be governed by the proposals of the papal legates. So what had been demanded — a free, open, general council for the consideration of the condition of the church — became a closed gathering of Roman prelates engaged in the defense of the traditions of their church.

THE COUNCIL OF TRENT

Yet the Council of Trent marked the beginning of a new era in the papal church. The Lutheran movement had forced the Church of Rome to self-reform. Addressing itself to those doctrines and abuses which had been the targets of the reformers, the council adopted a state-

99

ment of faith and a program of reforms that effectively stayed the course of rebellion. It set in motion instruments of defense that in another generation everywhere jeopardized the existence of the reformed churches. From this moment the Lutherans and Calvinists had to face the combined forces of conciliar measures, the Jesuits, the Inquisition, the Index, and a revived papal leadership.

Although the council first met in 1545 and finally adjourned in 1563, the assembly actually was in session hardly one third of that period. Its 25 sessions extended from 1545 to 1546, 1551 to 1552, and 1562 to 1563. When controversy broke out as to the priority of discussion on doctrine or of reform, it was decided that the two should be treated concurrently. Definition of faith and measures of reform thus emerged in parallel lists.

TRENT: FIRST ASSEMBLY

The doctrinal decrees reveal the council's concern with the questions raised by Luther. The source of religious truth was declared to be Scripture and tradition, and the church alone was able to expound Scripture. The Apocrypha were included in the canon; the Vulgate was the official text; no printing of Scripture should be allowed without the consent of the bishop. Original sin was interpreted as a consequent taint of the Fall — it inclined the soul to sin but was not itself sin. Justification begins in God's prevenient grace with which man is free to cooperate or which he can reject, though he is conditioned already by that grace. It is more than an imputation of righteousness — it is an infusion of sanctification, for faith cannot be without love and hope. Only a special revelation can give a person complete assurance of salvation. The traditional system of seven sacraments was reaffirmed — three imprint an indelible character and are not repeatable: baptism, confirmation, holy orders. Though operating through the repetition of outward acts, the sacraments have their validity by virtue of Christ's institution.

Such were the doctrinal decisions of the first assembly. The reforms adopted called on bishops and clergy to reside in their localities and to preach regularly. But pardoners were not to preach, and in a later session the institution of pardoners was abolished. Bishops were not only to conduct visitations in their dioceses but also to supervise the monks and nuns of their area.

TRENT: SECOND ASSEMBLY

Despite the emperor's protest the council moved to Bologna, ostensibly because of a plague. Charles was in the midst of the Smalcald War and was to try his hand at conciliation in the Interim when he saw that the council was only widening the breach with his Lutheran subjects. But the Interim was unsuccessful. Charles was confronted by an alliance of Lutherans and France. The new pope, Julius III, was not greatly interested in the council but went along with the emperor's desire for action. The results of the second assembly were meager, though the canons on the Eucharist, penance, and extreme unction touched on central points of doctrine. The traditional doctrine of transubstantiation was reaffirmed, and thus the adoration of the elements was justified since Christ was present in the Sacrament both before and after reception. Confession of sins and absolution were enjoined on the participant.

TRENT: THIRD ASSEMBLY

Ten years elapsed between the second and third assemblies. During this decade the Peace of Passau and of Augsburg marked the rupture in western Europe. All hope of conciliation was gone. Paul IV, in his brief tenure from 1555 to 1559, showed his uncompromising spirit. Passionately orthodox and devoted to the primacy of his office, he preferred to rely on a commission of cardinals of his own appointment to effect reforms. He did create a new climate of austerity in Rome and of strict discipline beyond. To him the Jesuits and the Inquisition seemed the best means of dealing with the heretics. But his successor, Pius IV (1559—1565), found it expedient to accede to the demands of rulers in countries still loyal to Rome to complete the work of Trent. So in 1562 the council convened again. Its goal was now to regroup its forces for the reconquest of what had been lost. It was completely dominated by the papal aims of Paul IV to make the pope supreme in the church.

Opposing parties in the council vied for control. The eastern lands — Austria, Bohemia, Hungary — wanted concessions for the use

101

of the cup in the territory where the legacy of Huss still lived. They were seconded by France, which also was ready to grant marriage to the clergy. Spain was resolutely opposed to these concessions. It wanted a recognition of the principle that bishops held power by divine appointment, not by papal endowment, and that Christ demanded their residence in their dioceses — the pope could not alter this injunction. The French moreover had a program of reform that would drastically reduce the resources of the papacy. Early in 1563 there was a period when the council seemed bent on collapse. The pope did not relieve the tension by appointing at this juncture one youth of 11, another of 18, as cardinals. But the naming of Cardinal Morone as papal legate saved the cause. For this able diplomat repaired to Innsbruck to win over Emperor Ferdinand, who was open to compromise if his son Maximilian was promised election as king of the Romans. Both the Spaniards and the imperialists were promised that their demands would be cared for after the adjournment of the council — by the pope. Thereby the papal purpose was saved, as it was by the resolution that all the decisions of the council should be confirmed by the pope. In the final rush to adjourn many important matters again were referred to Rome. More clearly than ever before the pope had established himself as the supreme ruler of the church. The council, which had been called to reform the papacy, ended in elevating it to a new height of power.

The decisions of the third assembly, though a victory for the pope, signified important changes in the hierarchical church. The abolition of the indulgence seller was a positive reform. Communion in both kinds was declared not to be a divine obligation but an issue which the church — that is, the pope — could decide; Christ was wholly present in either bread or wine. The Mass was held to be propitiatory; it could be celebrated in honor of saints and be of avail for both the living and the dead; communicants, though desirable, were not essential; only Latin might be used. The necessity of the hierarchy was asserted, and the pope could both appoint replacements of bishops and create new bishoprics. Some steps were taken in the direction of papal power over secular princes, but in general the Curia had to be satisfied with minor concessions by the rulers of loyal states. The use of indulgences was defended, except when evil gains were involved.

102

Attention was called to abuses in the practices connected with images and relics, but the invocation of saints and prayers for those in purgatory were upheld. Probably the most important decisions were those having to do with the establishment of schools for the education of youth, especially of the clergy. Seminaries were to be provided in every diocese except where a university was available — a measure destined to raise the level of the church more than any other, especially when it was implemented by the Jesuits.

The revision of the breviary and of the missal, together with other unfinished business, was referred to the pope. In January 1564 he confirmed the decrees and canons of Trent. Later in the year he issued a summary of the faith in a creed which gave the church a standard of faith and practice. Almost half a century after Luther the Church of Rome presented another face to the peoples of Europe. It had met the attacks of the reformers and forged a system of doctrine authoritative in every diocese and order. It had established an organization which with the help of the Jesuits, the Index, and the Inquisition now proceeded to eliminate the Protestants wherever possible.

THE SOCIETY OF JESUS

The decisions of the council were translated into action by the most remarkable army ever at the disposal of a spiritual institution — the Jesuits. Authorized by the pope shortly before the first assembly of Trent, the Society of Jesus was forged by Ignatius Loyola into a highly disciplined and intensely purposeful weapon of the hierarchical church. It demanded unquestioning obedience to the pope at a time when the pope was designing a church wherein he would have supreme power. The result was the undoing by Loyola of much of the work of Luther and Calvin.

Borrowing principles of his *Spiritual Exercises* from earlier rules of the Brethren of the Common Life in 15th-century Netherlands, Loyola imparted a Spanish fanaticism to the training and conditioning of his followers. Four weeks of meditations led the novice into a system that fitted him for absolute obedience to Christ and the Church of Rome. The order had but a single superior to whom members yielded themselves "to be ruled as if they were a corpse." Under the general was a general congregation and provincial congregations —

103

the only check on the superior was a group of consultors. It was a military army that went out to conquer and reconquer for the Roman concept of the church of Christ. The weapons were not material — teaching, preaching, hearing of confessions.

The original band consisted of 10 members. The mere mention of the places of activity of some of these suggests how rapidly and extensively the influence of the society spread. Lefevre worked in the Netherlands and in Germany. Lainez was in Parma, Venice, Padua, Brescia, Piacenza, and participated at Trent. Rodriguez labored in Portugal, Salmeron in Verona and Modena. Le Jay traveled to Bavaria, Austria, Bohemia, Moravia, and Hungary; Francis Xavier journeyed to Portugal, India, Japan, and China. The order was originally held to 60 members, but this restriction was soon removed, and disciples multiplied wherever the Jesuits went. They preached against heresy, especially Lutheranism, burned heretical books, and taught the decrees of Trent. They followed explorers to the new worlds of the East and West — their missionaries were soon in India, the Congo, Brazil, and Abyssinia.

JESUIT SCHOOLS

One of the early converts in the Netherlands was Peter Canisius. Sent to Vienna after demonstrating his talents for controversy at Cologne, he became dean of the theological faculty at the university in 1551. His series of catechisms counteracted Luther's Small and Large Catechisms. He persuaded King Ferdinand to adopt a policy that the Jesuits sought to have adopted wherever they worked — purge Lutherans and Calvinists from all places of influence in the government. When Canisius was later made a saint, his beatification described him as "apostle of Germany, second only to St. Boniface." And this because from his center in Vienna he aided in the suppression of the Evangelicals in Bavaria, Austria, and Bohemia, and in such cities as Würzburg, Passau, Bamberg, Münster, Paderborn, Fulda, Salzburg, and Augsburg.

Foremost among the accomplishments of the Jesuits was the establishment of schools. Loyola understood the significance of preparing the men who would win Europe back to Rome. Canisius was but one who used this means. Not only did he gradually assume control over the university but he also set up colleges in Prague,

Hungary, and Moravia. Beside the theological colleges were schools for the sons of the nobility, who soon would rule their inherited estates in the interest of the church. In the same year that the Jesuits acquired the University of Vienna they gained Cologne, from which branch colleges spread to Coblenz, Mainz, Speyer, and Würz-burg. The University of Ingolstadt fell to them in 1556, and colleges followed in Munich, Dillingen, Augsburg, Innsbruck, and Tyrolean Hall. At first Polish youth were drawn to Vienna — among them the later patron saint of Poland, Stanislas Kostka — but before long there were Jesuit schools in Plotzk, Braunsberg, Vilna, and Posen, and under Stephen Batory the number of Jesuits in Poland exceeded 300 in a dozen colleges and missions.

Nor was Loyola satisfied with the power he could exercise over old universities and in native schools. At Rome he established in 1550 the Collegium Romanum, which grew to over 2,000 students in the next 35 years. A special Collegium Germanicum was set up in Rome for the training of missionaries to Protestant Germany. The emissaries were welcomed everywhere by princes and bishops struggling to hold their land against the Evangelicals. By their grammar and secondary schools as well as their universities the papal forces built up a new generation that learned its doctrine from the decisions of Trent. Also a new type of bishops, reformed by the council, inspired the respect of the populace. The older orders looked jealously to their own position in Spain and France, but a college was established by the Jesuits at Lyons in 1563. By the time of Loyola's death in 1556 the company of 10 in 1540 had grown to 13 provinces with over 1,500 members. All Europe felt their power.

THE INQUISITION

The same pope who established the Jesuit Order summoned another institution to his support — the Inquisition. It was not the first time that the papacy had asked the secular powers to enforce the decisions of spiritual courts. The Third Lateran Council had invoked this partnership against the Cathari in the 12th century. Innocent III had renewed the policy at the Lateran Council of 1215, and the death penalty for heresy had gone into the legal code of Emperor Frederick II. Spain had used the system effectively against Moors and Jews. The church found and examined the heretics (hence the term Inquisition — inquired into), passed sentence, then turned over the guilty to the government for execution. The first inquisitor general in Spain, Thomas de Torquemada, had over 2,000 persons burned. Cardinal Caraffa, papal nuncio to Spain, had been impressed by the effectiveness of the system and recommended it to Paul III, who was beginning to take repressive action against the Protestants. In 1542, supported by Loyola among others, the pope organized the Roman Inquisition. A commission of six cardinals and an inquisitor general was given power over all other agencies or offices in the church. Caraffa laid down four rules: punish even on suspicion; show no regard for persons in high position; demand most severe penalties for those seeking shelter of persons in power; and pay particular attention to Calvinists.

The results were indeed conclusive. The vicar-general of the Capuchins, Bernardino Ochino, and a prior of the Augustinians, Pietro Vermigli, who accepted the Reformed faith, were forced to flee. The University of Modena was closed. The bishop of Bergamo was deposed from his see. Caraffa became pope in 1555, as Paul IV, and intensified the examinations, especially after the peace of 1557, which gave Spain power in Milan and Naples. On his death in 1559 the people of Rome burned the office and records of the Inquisition in venting their resentment against its methods. But Paul's successor, Pius IV, aided by the archbishop of Milan, Charles Borromeo, extended the Inquisition, and to his credit was the massacre of 2,000 Waldensians in Calabria in 1562. Another inquisitor general became pope — Pius V. Among his victims was a noted humanist scholar of Florence, Pietro Carnesecchi, who was beheaded, and a 70-year-old professor, Aonio Paleario, who was strangled. Fires burned regularly in Rome and in Spain, where Lutheranism had won friends in Seville, Toledo, Valladolid, and Saragossa. Italy and Spain were burned clean of all heresy, though in the process some of the best of its people perished. Conformity was purchased at the expense of sterility, and the church saw no inconsistency in making saints of popes and Jesuits who in the name of Christ had pitilessly tortured and exterminated thousands whose only crime was their search for a purer faith in the same Christ.

The Council of Trent, the Jesuits, the Inquisition — the armory of the Roman Church in its reaction to the reformers in Germany and

Switzerland — were directed by a line of able popes in the years after the Peace of Augsburg. To this period belong constructive measures in the improvement of the worship and organization of the church, as well as programs aimed at the destruction of all nonconformity.

INDEX AND CATECHISM

In its hurried adjournment the council left unfinished business in the hands of the pope — Pius IV. He relied on the able leadership of his nephew, Carlo Borromeo, who was made a cardinal and an archbishop in 1560 and placed in charge of papal affairs in Rome and at Trent. One of the referred items was the Index — a list of books prohibited to the faithful. Pius V in 1571 made the keeping as well as the reading of prohibited books a cause for excommunication. Bible translations were subject to episcopal veto, and all books had to pass through the hands of censors before publication. One concession allowed nonreligious books of heretics to be read if they had been found harmless to believers. A second task referred by the council resulted in a papal summary of its doctrinal decisions for the use of pastors. The Roman Church has never issued a catechism for universal use, partly because of the excellence of such books as those of Canisius in Austria and Auger in France. The Roman Catechism of Trent did, however, constitute an authoritative doctrinal statement for all the clergy of the Roman obedience.

THE REVISED BREVIARY AND MISSAL

The revision of the breviary was not finished until the administration of Pius V (1566—1572). Cardinal Quinones had revised this series of forms for the daily, or hour, observances in 1535. But he had omitted much and reduced a sung service to a recitation, and so criticism led to its recall. Instead the Tridentine commission began a revision that was completed in 1568 and ordered the supplanting of all other forms that had been in use less than 200 years. The same commission prepared a revision of the missal. Long sequences and some elaborate ceremonies were omitted, but five sequences (hymns) and the use of candles, ashes, and palms were retained. The prayers and rites of the canon were regulated, but the essential character of the Mass as a sacrifice was left unchanged.

107

The decisions of Trent concerning synods and visitations were carried out by Borromeo, archbishop of Milan, in a manner that was widely emulated. Pius V had other notable assistants in discharging the duties laid on him by the council — St. Philip Neri in Rome; Canisius in Germany and Austria; Possevino and Charles, cardinal of Lorraine, in France; Juan de Avila in Spain; Alesandro Sauli in Corsica. The provisions for residency of bishops and priests in their dioceses and parishes were enforced, as were the regulations for monks and nuns to keep to their houses.

CONVERSION BY FORCE

Pius followed with interest the intrigues of Catholic princes and lords to gain by persecution what could not be won by persuasion. When the duke of Alva put to death over 18,000 people during a 6-year period in his Council of Blood in the Netherlands, the pope sent him a jewelled cap and a sword. He was aware of and in sympathy with the plots against the life of Queen Elizabeth of England, as was his successor, Gregory XIII, whose secretary wrote that her murder "would be no sin."

Gregory is best known for his reform of the calendar, "the Gregorian," in 1582. But he was directly involved in the restoring of Europe to the old faith. He is reported to have spent 2 million ducats on the education of youth, mostly through liberal endowments to the schools of the Jesuits. The society now numbered over 6,000 members in 21 provinces with 110 houses. No less than his predecessor, Gregory rejoiced over the massacre of heretics. When 10,000 Huguenots were killed on St. Batholomew's Day 1572 in Paris — and other massacres in the provinces decimated the Calvinists — the pope celebrated the victory with a *Te Deum* and the striking of a medal. By such means France was brought back to the fold, and Sixtus V, Gregory's successor, could hail a Huguenot turned Roman as King Henry IV. He had less success in England where storms shattered the Spanish Armada and the dream of a Roman restoration, or in Sweden where the Polish Sigismund and his legate Possevino were trying to impose the royal faith on a Lutheran nation. In the realm of scholarship he gave his name to a Sistine revision of the Latin Bible, a title he was, however, to share with his successor Clement VIII.

108

A Clement (the VII) was pope when the Lutherans were summoned to Augsburg in 1530. Clement VIII (1592—1605) closed the century. The intervening years had seen a revolution in the religious, political, and economic life of Europe. The reforms in the Roman hierarchy were of enduring significance. Clement VIII published the results of Trent in the new books of the church and revised the Sistine Vulgate in an edition of 1592, known as the Clementine. This critically improved edition gave the church its standard text for centuries. And the last decades of the century saw a doctrinal exposition of the Tridentine faith that served all the defenders of Rome against their Protestant critics. For Robert Bellarmine, a foremost scholar and teacher, came from Louvain to Rome and for 12 years (1576—1588) lectured at the Jesuit Collegium Romanum. His 4-volume work on *Disputations on the Controversies Concerning the Christian Faith* systematically presented the doctrines of the church in a manner that Protestant theologians had to meet. The fact that the Bellarmine orthodox Roman theology had no more room for divergent opinions than the Roman theology at the opening of the century was proclaimed by the burning of Giordano Bruno in the year 1600.

It was indeed a formidable, well-organized, highly self-conscious Roman Church which the generation that followed Luther had to face in its struggle for survival. In that struggle it had to fashion its own constitution and make clear its own concept of the church of Christ on earth.

IX

THE CONSTITUTION OF THE LUTHERAN CHURCH

Opposing the age-old hierarchical Church of Rome on fundamental points of doctrine and organization was the fateful task of Luther. The necessary consequence for the followers of the reformers was to build a new organization and to restate the message of the church of Christ. Theologians were to play a very significant part, but since the refashioning of the church involved the vast property and power of the medieval bishoprics and monasteries as well as the maintenance of education and public order, the participation of the magistrates was inevitable. The Lutheran Church that gradually took shape was the result of interaction and cooperation between theological teachers and administrators on the one hand and princes and city leaders on the other. By the end of the century the new forms were quite firmly fixed.

MELANCHTHON

Second only to Luther in the reconstruction of the church stood Philip Melanchthon. Related on his mother's side to the great Hebrew scholar Reuchlin and drawn through his education to Erasmus, the foremost humanist of the day, Melanchthon became a classical scholar of great distinction. Reuchlin recommended him to the new university at Wittenberg as professor of Greek and Hebrew. His inaugural address was on the reform of the education of youth. Melanchthon's Biblical learning and humanistic spirit earned him the admiration of Luther, who proved himself a loyal friend through the many years they labored together at Wittenberg. Melanchthon was the careful, cautious scholar. He lacked Luther's depth and emotional power and personal experience of faith. Yet he agreed with Luther's concept of the Word as the final authority and tried to explain the contents of faith in clear and convincing style. In 1521 he produced the first theological

111

textbook of the Reformation, the *Loci Communes,* or General Topics, of theology. As the events around him revealed the various ways the released power of reformation might go, Melanchthon became apprehensive. The Zwickau prophets and the Peasants' War caused him to stress the necessity of order and of obedience to government. He was hopeful that a reform in the papal church would heal the divisions already evident, and even at Augsburg in 1530, when he drew up the Confession and the Apology, he thought in terms of reconciliation and restoration of unity.

The differences that had developed between the Swiss and the Germans on the Lord's Supper, resulting in the failure of the Marburg conference, made Melanchthon fearful of the Protestant ability to oppose Rome. After the Diet at Augsburg, when it was certain that there would be no return to Rome, Melanchthon persisted in a course of exploration of possible agreement with Bucer and the cities of southern Germany. To remove differences, he was willing to soften the language of the Augsburg Confession, which he treated almost as a personal document. In 1540 he published an edition of the Confession that came to be known as *Augustana Variata* because of expressions varying from the original. Most important was his change in Article X, which in 1530 read: "It is taught among us that the true body and blood of Christ are really present in the Supper of our Lord under the form of bread and wine and are there distributed and received." In 1540 the sentence was changed thus: "Of the Lord's Supper they teach that, together with the bread and wine, the body and blood of Christ are truly tendered to those that eat in the Lord's Supper."

But Melanchthon was as unsuccessful in attaining unity with the followers of Zwingli and Calvin as with Rome. When the emperor in the Augsburg Interim of 1548 attempted to force a show of compromise by requiring outward compliance with traditional practices, Melanchthon yielded in the Leipzig Interim to an extent that cost him his place of leadership after Luther's death. His own inclination toward conservatism made it possible for him to counsel a retention of traditional forms both to friends in England and France and to his followers in Germany. But the result in Germany was a cleavage between those who saw differences in Melanchthon from Luther, the true leader, and after the Interim serious controversies arose between "original" Lu-

112

therans (Gnesio-Lutherans) and Philippists. The last decade of his life was filled with bitter debates that the irenic Melanchthon disliked. The issues were to continue to divide the theologians after his death and to find authoritative settlement first in 1580 in the Book of Concord.

Scholars are still divided as to the real position of Melanchthon on many points because it is hard to distinguish between his own thought and his official statements as spokesman of the Lutherans. Quite clearly he diverged from Luther's position on the Lord's Supper, though here the difference was on the manner of the Real Presence and not its actuality. More than Luther he was ready to give tradition a place beside Scripture as authority, though not going so far as Trent to give it an equal place. Unlike Luther, too, he would keep more of the traditional view of natural law and the proper functions of human reason.

While Luther held God's law and revelation in a certain tension, allowing each a vital relationship to man, Melanchthon remained at heart a humanist interested in man's ability to reason about revelation. The image of God in man consisted in a capacity to know God and His will, though what that will does for man and demands of him can be known only by faith in Christ through the Spirit. Following Luther, Melanchthon could balance elements of his thought that his followers could not, and some of the charges against him probably should more justly be directed toward Melanchthon's disciples. His interpretation of justification is Lutheran, and he therefore opposed Osiander, who wanted to posit in man the presence of Christ as the prerequisite for God's forgiveness of sins. Melanchthon, like Luther, saw no merit whatever in man — all was of God's grace. Yet in Luther faith was a more living, active, all-embracing force while Melanchthon tended to interpret it as intellectual assent to the truth. In his scholarly spirit Melanchthon smoothed out the rugged, rough places of Luther's teaching, but in so doing lost something of its revolutionary power.

Melanchthon's function was that of schoolteacher of the Reformation. Despite his deficiencies he rendered incalculable service at a critical period in the history of the church. His was the pen that framed the Augustana and the Apology, which gave the new movement a solid ground to stand on in the battle with the old. His textbook of theology, in many and enlarged editions, became the school theology of generations of pastors and teachers. His methods became standard in the schools of Germany and beyond, and his reforms reshaped universities—Wittenberg, Leipzig, Tübingen, Greifswald, Rostock, Heidelberg, Marburg, Königsberg. His interest in the natural sciences gave them new importance, and his devotion to Aristotle was lifelong. It is impossible to conceive of the Reformation without Luther, but it is hard to imagine how the spiritual power of his teaching would have been conserved and channeled into permanent and fructifying streams of influence without the mental clarity of Melanchthon.

CORPUS DOCTRINAE

The Peace of Augsburg in 1555 guaranteed legal toleration for the Lutheran churches, which were identified by their adherence to the Augsburg Confession of 1530. But in the 25 years that had elapsed many questions had arisen to which theologians gave different answers. Who was to decide on the right answer? As long as Luther lived, his personal authority could be appealed to, but after his death controversy arose as to what he would have held. Especially troublesome were the issues raised by the emperor's attempt in the Interim to effect a temporary compromise. Lutherans had to decide how far they could yield and on what points. While the Roman Church was consolidating its power during and after the Council of Trent, the teachers and leaders of the reforming churches were drawn into conflicting parties. Melanchthon died in 1560, and a second generation came on the scene. Thus in the quarter century following the Peace of Augsburg the churches of the Augsburg Confession gradually reached sufficient agreement to embody their teachings in a commonly accepted document called the Formula of Concord, included in the Book of Concord. Since the Book of Concord has served as the basic theological foundation of the Lutheran Church during the succeeding centuries, we need to notice the particular problems to which it offered the solution. Doctrinally we may call the Book of Concord the constitution of these churches.

Because the empire recognized only the Lutheran churches and not those following Zwingli or Calvin, the territories claiming legal recognition had to give proof that they were Lutheran. Thus began the practice of a territorial *corpus doctrinae,* or body of teachings which the ruler and church leaders of a political unit would draw up as their standard. Usually this would include the Augsburg Confession and the

114

Apology together with writings of Luther or Melanchthon. While satisfying local requirements, the practice did nothing to unite the churches of various provinces or cities — indeed, it increased the differences by creating a number of standards. The rulers were concerned, for they needed to present a unified front to the the emperor and wanted to avoid internal conflicts among their subjects. It is altogether natural to find them involved in these matters. Their faith was the legal basis for the Augsburg decision that allowed their territories freedom in religion. It was to the interest of the ruler that there be agreement among the people, for the only course open to the dissenter was emigration. And only by cooperation could the princes hope to make secure their present strength and privileges. When therefore we find them taking leadership in the religious disputes, it is because of political necessity as well as by virtue of their own membership in the church. If in this respect we find little difference between Roman Catholic and Lutheran involvement of secular government in church affairs, it is due to the organization of society at that time, when no settlement of religious problems could be effected without such participation.

The Lutheran rulers who played a part in the organization of the evangelical church were principally Duke Christopher of Württemberg, Count William of Hesse, Duke Julius of Brunswick, Duke Louis of Württemberg, Elector August of Saxony, Elector John George of Brandenburg, Elector Louis of the Palatinate, and Count George Ernst of Henneberg. The theologians on whom fell the burden of bringing together the various factions were Jacob Andreae, Martin Chemnitz, and Nikolaus Selneccer.

POINTS OF CONTROVERSY

Especially three theological questions had begun to agitate the leaders of the various territorial churches. They were connected with the great issues which Luther had raised in his criticism of the papal church and medieval theology. One was a cluster of questions about justification. We have seen how this was at the heart of Luther's teaching — man is justified, or declared righteous, not by any merit or works of his own but by the work of Christ whose grace he receives in faith. Out of this statement such questions as these emerged: Is man fallen in sin totally corrupt? Can he do anything of his own will to come to faith? When God declares a believer righteous, is it because of his

115

faith or even because Christ already dwells within him? Do good works play any part in justification? Is the Christian still under the Law? All these points somehow relate to the central doctrine of justification. A second significant source of difference was the doctrine of the Lord's Supper. The Lutherans rejected the Roman theory of the Supper as a sacrifice and of a change of bread and wine into the body and blood of Christ, but they also refused to endorse the Zwinglian idea of the Supper as a memorial feast with no real presence of Christ. This led to questions of *how* Christ is present in the Supper and to a renewed study of the old problem of the relationship of the divine and human natures in Christ. The third of our groupings of controversial points had to do with "adiaphora," or indifferent things, especially the question of ceremonies and usages that had been raised by the Interim.

The peril of division among the Lutheran churches was evident as parties began to form and to attack one another. One party was led by Matthias Flacius and assumed to speak for Luther. It was called the "old" or "original" (Gnesio) Lutheran group. Another followed the spirit of Melanchthon, though claiming to be no less Lutheran. It was given the name "Philippist." The parties did not agree on all matters among themselves, but in general they were unified enough not to cause serious ruptures. Sometimes their quarrels had to be stopped by the authorities. Indeed it was the secular rulers who were most intent on finding a basis of unity.

Steps Toward Concord

Christopher of Württemberg was one of the princes earnestly seeking unity. He was the more concerned as he saw his neighbor, Frederick of the Palatinate, going over to Calvinism. He commissioned the theologian Jacob Andreae to draw up a statement of the points dividing the churches. This Andreae did in "Five Points" — Justification, Good Works, Free Will, Adiaphora, the Lord's Supper. Julius of Brunswick endorsed the efforts of Christopher, and Andreae was sent around to win interest for a common declaration of faith. By May 1570 he had gained widespread support for a consensus that would contain the ancient ecumenical creeds, the Augustana, the Apology, the Smalcald Articles, and Luther's Catechisms. But Saxony, whose Wittenberg faculty had developed in a "Philippistic" direction, ob-

116

jected to the theory of the Lord's Supper that Johann Brenz had elaborated in Württemberg. According to his teaching the two natures of Christ are so united in the one Person that the human nature as well as the divine is present in the Sacrament. Using the Latin word for everywhere, *ubiquitas,* his explanation asserts the ubiquity of Christ's human nature. The Philippists, on the contrary, wanted to explain Christ's presence by the exercise of Christ's will to be wherever He promised.

In 1572 Andreae elaborated his "Five Points" into "Six Sermons" in which he tried to state the questions in controversy and give what he felt were the Lutheran solutions. He sought and gained the approval of other respected theologians, such as Selneccer, Chemnitz, David Chytraeus of Rostock, Joachim Westphal of Hamburg, and Johann Wigand of Königsberg. These conferences and negotiations had the generous support of Duke Julius of Brunswick, who spent some 50,000 taler on the project. On his suggestion Andreae reformulated his sermons into a series of theses called the Swabian Concord of 1575. Chemnitz secured the cooperation and suggestions of the Saxons, who after 1573 had deposed the Philippist theologians. The resultant revision was designated the Swabian-Saxon Concord of 1575.

Meanwhile another effort at unity had been started by George Ernst of Henneberg, Louis of Württemberg, and Karl of Baden. Their theologians had worked out a program in the Maulbronn Formula of 1576. In Saxony elector August, on Andreae's advice, referred both the Swabian-Saxon Concord and the Maulbronn Formula to a conference of theologians at Torgau in April and May 1576, from which came the Torgau Book. Andreae drew up a digest of the report for the guidance of the elector — this book later became the "Epitome" of the Formula of Concord. So confident was August of Andreae's ability that he borrowed him from Württemberg to reform his own churches and schools. The Torgau Book was sent to leaders and theological faculties for approbation and suggestions. When replies were in, Andreae, Selneccer, and Chemnitz met in March 1577 at Bergen Cloister for a final revision. There the "Bergen Book" became the Formula of Concord. A synod had been proposed to receive the document for general acceptance, but it was decided instead to circulate it among the signatories of the Augs-

117

burg Confession for their subscription. Over 8,000 names were secured — rulers, councilmen, preachers, teachers.

THE FORMULA OF CONCORD

The importance of the Formula of Concord in the future history of the church justifies a brief summary of the contents of its 12 articles. A reference to the nature of the dispute will indicate the relevance of each article to the problems with which the churches were contending.

Article I refuted the argument of Flacius that sin is of the essence and substance of fallen man's nature. Rather, the Formula held, the Christian faith in the creation, redemption, sanctification, and resurrection of man points to a human nature which even after the fall into sin is a creature of God. Sin affected all that nature but did not change it into an evil nature.

Article II dealt with arguments about the role of the human will in conversion. Amsdorf and Flacius, criticizing Melanchthon who described the will as passive, claimed that the will resists God in conversion. They termed Melanchthon's view synergistic, that is, that he made man active in his own conversion. The Formula affirmed that only the Spirit of God working through the means of grace can change man, but this change is not a creation of a new human faculty but a turning of the will, which after conversion can cooperate with the Spirit in doing the will of God.

Article III was occasioned by the teaching of Andreas Osiander in Königsberg that in justifying the believer God looked on the Christ indwelling in him. Osiander was opposed by most of the theologians because he seemed to want to find a cause for God's forgiving act in man himself. The Formula affirmed that there is no such cause in man, either in his own or in any incipient new nature, but justification depends entirely on grace, unmerited even by faith.

Article IV sought to settle a controversy as to the proper consideration of good works. A statement by Georg Major that good works are necessary to salvation had been challenged by Amsdorf, Flacius, and Nikolaus Gallus. Amsdorf had gone to the other extreme by saying that good works are injurious to salvation. The Formula rejected both statements. It wanted to rule out the subject of good works in treating of justification. It emphasized the various meanings of the word "neces-

118

sary"; good works are not a requisite for justification since God freely forgives the sinner, but, as Melanchthon had taught, good works are God's will for the forgiven sinner in his new obedience. They are not the observance of a law but the spontaneous activity of the new man.

Article V. The question of the role of the Law was raised early by Johann Agricola, who criticized Melanchthon's stressing of the preaching of the Law in the Visitation Articles of 1527. Agricola thought Law was not to be stressed since the Gospel alone called forth the obedience and righteous life of the hearer. Luther was unhappy about Agricola's continued criticism and termed him and others like him "antinomian." Luther saw the necessity of teaching the Law even to the forgiven sinner, though its primary purpose was to lead the sinner to repentance and to make possible a social order. The Formula stressed the importance of distinguishing between Law and Gospel as fundamental in preaching. One was not to be preached without the other — the Law to reveal sin, the Gospel to offer forgiveness. In a broad sense the Gospel includes Law.

Article VI treated of the relevance of the Law for the believer. Some of Luther's followers in emphasizing the spontaneity of the new life in Christ seemed to the Gnesio-Lutherans to suggest a life of the spirit apart from the Word. Luther, and even more Melanchthon, spoke of a "third use" of the Law, that is, the regulation of the life of the believer who despite his justification never fully attains to the doing of God's will. The Formula defended the role of the Law since it is God's will for all men, but distinguished between obedience as a result of conversion and obedience as a bringing forth of the fruits of the Spirit.

Articles VII and VIII were the outcome of the debates on the nature of Christ's presence in the Holy Supper. Against the Roman doctrine of the sacrifice of the Mass, Luther and Lutheran theologians had steadfastly denied any change of substance in the bread and the wine, but insisted on the literal interpretation of Christ's words "This is My body," "This is My blood." They opposed Calvin's interpretation that the body of Christ is not on the altar but in heaven, to which the believer rises in Communion. Likewise they were unsatisfied with a "spiritual" presence, an interpretation they called "Crypto-Calvinistic." The Formula of Concord followed the doctrine of Luther, rejecting the theories of transubstantiation and sacrifice and the practice of withholding the cup. Though holding to a bodily rather than a spiritual presence of Christ, the Formula denied any Capernaitic idea (eating of flesh or drinking of blood). It went beyond Calvin too in teaching that even the unworthy participate — to judgment — in receiving the body and blood of Christ in the Sacrament. The worthy — those who believe — receive Him for growth in grace.

The insistence on the real presence of Christ was commonly accepted by Lutherans. But differences of explanation of the body had been formulated by Brenz and Melanchthon, the former going back to the definition of Chalcedon in 451 and arguing that the attributes of the divine and human natures are in communion with each other through the unity of the person of Christ. Even in His earthly ministry Christ possessed the qualities of the Son of God, though in humility He did not exercise them in the same manner as He does after His ascension. Now in His glory He still possesses the properties of His human nature. By virtue of the unity of His person Christ can be everywhere present and thus fulfill His promise of being at His table.

Article IX gave no final answer to the question whether Christ's descent into hell was a part of His humiliation, the final act of His suffering for mankind, or the first step of His triumph, a victory over hell and death. The Formula declared no one could give the answer, but the descent into hell should be proclaimed as the expression of the fullness of the redemption won by Christ.

Article X referred to the divisions caused by various interpretations of what were "adiaphora," or indifferent matters, in the church, especially after the Interim. The Formula gave to the church the right to establish ceremonies and practices neither commanded nor prohibited by the Word of God but which should be judged by their intentions and motives. If concessions were made in the name of peace but at the cost of witness to the truth of the Word, they should be resisted even at the risk of persecution. Churches should not condemn one another on the basis of external rites, that is, such as do not affect the true proclamation of the Gospel.

Two concluding articles looked beyond the Lutheran churches in order to warn of errors. Article XI was aimed at Calvinism. It denied that God had predestined any to damnation. The will of God is that all men should be saved. The true use of the doctrine of predestination

120

lies in its assurance that our salvation is not our work but the result of God's purpose and action in Christ. Article XII described "sects and factions . . . which never accepted the Augsburg Confession," naming Anabaptists, Schwenkfelders, New Arians (Unitarians), and Anti-Trinitarians.

THE BOOK OF CONCORD

The Formula had accepted as the basic confession of the Lutherans the three Ecumenical Creeds, the Augsburg Confession, the Apology, the Smalcald Articles, and the Catechisms of Luther. With the Formula these were now brought together in one volume as the Book of Concord and published in a German text in June 1580, the 50th anniversary of the Augsburg Confession. A Latin text followed in 1584, written by Lukas Osiander and corrected first by Selneccer and then by Chemnitz. The introduction to the Formula became the introduction for the whole book. An appendix containing a series of quotations from the Fathers was designed to show the connection between the Concordia and the theology of the early church.

ACCEPTANCE OF THE BOOK OF CONCORD

Not all the territories that subscribed to the 1530 confession set their names to the document of 1580. A new generation had come on the scene, and new alignments had been created in the crowded years. While the Formula united many Lutheran provinces and cities, it alienated those who favored reconciliation with the Calvinists. The Palatinate had gone over to Calvinism in 1563 and adopted the Heidelberg Catechism as its standard. Some of the Lutheran areas, for instance Nürnberg and Brunswick, desired no new declaration, believing the Augustana and the Catechisms to be sufficient.

Outside Germany Lutheran countries were not at first concerned. The arguments had been among German theologians, and the Formula was a solution for them. Denmark and Norway had adopted an ordinance in 1537 that made the Gospel the basis of preaching—in 1574 the Augsburg Confession was recognized as a confessional norm. The Church Law of 1683 specified the Scriptures, the three Ecumenical Symbols, the Augustana, and the Small Catechism as the confessional standard. At the Council of Uppsala in 1593 Sweden adopted the Augustana and the three Ecumenical Symbols and in the Church Law of

121

1686 bound all inhabitants to the Scriptures, the three ancient creeds, and the Augustana as this was "explained in the so-called Book of Concord." Both in Sweden and in Finland the orthodox party had urged the adoption of the Formula, and in practice the Book of Concord had been considered the norm for preaching since the Manual of 1614. A royal decree in 1663, adopted by the Diet in 1664, prepared the way for the church law regarding the Book of Concord.

As the Roman Church had its decrees and canons of Trent, so the Lutherans had their standard of teaching. The nature and scope of the norm had been determined by the religious discussions of the years since 1517. The authors of the Formula emphasized that the document answered the questions that had been raised among the reformers. It was proof of the fact that they had not departed from what was declared at the Diet of Augsburg. The Augsburg Confession defined the differences between the Lutherans and the papal church. The Book of Concord set forth the statement of agreement within the Lutheran Church.

FROM REFORM TO UNIFORMITY

[[W]]hile the theologians were seeking to resolve the conflicts in doctrine and to establish standards of Christian faith, life in the churches was being standardized according to the new norms of worship, church organization, and discipline.

EVANGELICAL WORSHIP SERVICES

The medieval Mass had been a Holy Communion service with a sermon, if there was one, before the service. Luther had kept a great part of the Mass in his proposed "Form of Mass" of 1523, but in his *German Mass* of 1526 he brought the sermon into the service. The consequence was an order of Communion service though there might be no Communion. A Roman Mass can be held even if there is no other communicant than the priest. This the Lutheran service did not permit — if there were no communicants the minister could not partake of the bread and wine. But the Lutheran churches, in the main, kept the form of the Communion service even if there were no communicants, omitting those sections or rubrics which pertained to the distribution. Since most of the services were without Communion, we might say that the Lutheran service retained the form of the medieval Mass but substituted the sermon for the "canon of the Mass," that is, the Roman Communion rubrics. So widely accepted was this form of the main Lutheran worship service that a brief explanation of each of the main rubrics seems justified. The Lutheran services were adopted by the various cities, territories, or countries and printed in what were called *Agenda.* In the following we refer mostly to the rubrics common in these Agenda but mention also divergences.

The Roman Mass opened with a private confession of the priest — this was kept as a private prayer by the Lutheran minister, or more

123

often, changed into a congregational confession and absolution. The penitential nature of this confession was emphasized — in some Agenda — by the recitation of the Ten Commandments and by the minister's words of retaining of sins where the confession did not seem serious enough to merit the words of absolution. In some cases a German hymn opened the service, the minister then saying, "In the name of the Father and of the Son and of the Holy Ghost," and the congregation responding with "Amen" or "Our help is in the name of the Lord" and "Who made heaven and earth."

The Introit composed of Scripture verses was the opening of the Roman Mass as far as the congregation was concerned. This the Lutheran service retained as a choir song, even keeping the verses in Latin. Gradually the Latin gave way to German, and the Introit was sung in German by the choir or the minister.

The threefold Kyrie, "Lord, have mercy on us," was retained in Greek or German. On festival days it was expanded into a ninefold version.

The Gloria in Excelsis by the minister remained but the congregational part, "On earth peace," etc., was soon replaced by a German hymn — usually either Luther's "All Praise and Honor," or Decius' "All Glory Be to God on High." In some places the Gloria was sung only on festival days.

The medieval collects with a preceding salutation were kept, sometimes sung in Latin, more often in German translation. A German series by Veit Dietrich attained widespread use.

As in the Roman order, the Epistle was sung in Latin but soon gave way to singing or reading in German.

Between the Epistle and Gospel the Gradual verses with Hallelujah were transformed into a hymn, considered the chief hymn of the day. Even some of the old Sequences (songs following the Hallelujah) were allowed, so that a choice was possible between a hymn, a sequence, or a seasonal Scripture verse ("tract" — in Lent). Choir and congregation joined in the singing.

At this point the baptism of children might take place or the Litany be sung.

The Gospel was often read from the pulpit, followed by the Creed. The Creed, the Nicene, was sung either in Latin or German,

124

but Luther's creedal hymn, "We All Believe," often took its place or followed it. In many places the Apostles' Creed became the ordinary form, the Nicene being reserved for festivals. Instead of the Gospel lesson parts of the Catechism might be read.

Sometimes the sermon followed the Gospel, sometimes it came after the Creed. If it came after the Gospel, it would be preceded by a congregational hymn, a general prayer, and the Lord's Prayer. Then the Creed would be thought of as the introduction to the Communion. If the sermon followed the Creed, it would take on the character of a Communion exhortation and end in a series of prayers, including a prayer for the forgiveness of sins.

The pulpit was the location of this part of the service, from the reading of the Gospel through Creed and sermon and prayers up to the Communion.

When there was Communion, the communicants came forward into the chancel — the men toward the south, the women toward the north (the altar faced east). For a while the ancient Preface was retained but soon disappeared, and in its place the minister addressed a brief exhortation. In parts of southern Germany the common confession and absolution were combined with this exhortation.

The Sanctus and Hosanna remained from the medieval Mass and were often sung in Latin. They were placed, following, after the Verba, or Words of Institution. During the singing of the Sanctus the minister read a threefold prayer: for the government, for the ministry of the Word, and for Christian unity. Almost without exception Lutherans obeyed the counsel of Luther to omit all elements of the ancient prayer of consecration of the elements.

Instead of a consecration the reading of the Words of Institution became central in the Sacrament. These words were the essential proclamation of the Gospel that Christ died so that our sins might be forgiven. While the presence of Christ was thought of as connected with these words, that presence was not in the elements outside of their use. The Lutheran doctrine stressed that outside the distribution there was no Sacrament and thus rejected the notion of a "reservation" of the Sacrament. But respect for the elements led to disposition of unused wine by pouring it into the ground or by preserving it until the next Communion or by using it in the visitation of the sick. Unleavened bread was usual. The elevation of the host, even the use of bells, was not uncommon, but the making of the sign of the cross was omitted in the Communion service though it remained in the baptismal formula.

After the Verba the Lord's Prayer was sung in German by the congregation, and the Agnus Dei, "the Lamb of God," during or after the distribution. Other German hymns might also be sung during the Communion. Usually the ministers distributed first to men, then to women, but sometimes to youth first. The elements would be tendered with some phrase containing the words, "the body and blood of Christ." When differences with Calvinists were stressed, this would be changed to "the true body and blood."

Generally Communion concluded with the singing of a collect, sometimes the Nunc Dimittis, and a benediction, ordinarily in the Aaronic form.

MUSIC IN WORSHIP

The Lutheran worship service was thus a cautious retention of the centuries-old form in Western Christendom. The difference between the Lutheran and the Calvinistic attitude was evident especially in the use of music in the church. Gregorian music retained its place in the Lutheran services, whereas it was rejected in the Calvinistic tradition. It was continued in the singing of the lessons, the collects, and the Verba by the minister, and in those parts where the choir or the choir and minister participated, as in the Introit and Gloria Patri, the Kyrie, the Gloria in Excelsis, the Gradual with Hallelujah, the Credo, the Preface and the Sanctus, the Hosanna and Benedictus, and the Agnus Dei. The ability to sing these parts, often in Latin, depended on the presence of musically trained school youth. The tendency toward making the sermon central, the increasing use of German hymns, and the absence of musical leadership all contributed to a gradual decline in the amount of Gregorian music in the service. Longest retained were the singing of the Collect, the Our Father, and the Verba.

Meanwhile a new type of music was being heard. Polyphonic singing, as distinguished from the one-note recitation of the Gregorian tunes, introduced part singing. Its popularity in the church was associated with the name of Giovanni Palestrina. Luther had enjoyed polyphonic singing, and one of his close friends and colleagues, Johann Walther, founded the first evangelical cantors' society in 1535. The disappearance of the monastery schools was followed by the cultivation of music at the courts of the princes or in the homes of the nobility. Here the use of instruments and especially of the organ was cultivated. Choirs continued the pre-Reformation custom of singing at weddings, funerals, and festival occasions.

Polyphonic singing found its way into Lutheran services through such leaders as Jerome and Michael Praetorius in Hamburg. Foremost among those who brought influences from the Italian school into evangelical circles was Heinrich Schütz. The development of complex compositions and instrumental participation in the worship service reduced the participation of the congregation, and its singing suffered. But on the gain side was the flowering of the evangelical choir song into the cantata, which included solo, arias, choir, and orchestra, and reached its maturity in the works of Johann Sebastian Bach.

The organ too had made its way into the service despite opposition — in the Roman Church even by Thomas Aquinas. Zwingli and Karlstadt had denied the organ any part in the liturgy, and even Luther was less than sure about its use. Yet the Wittenberg organ held its place. At first the Lutheran practice followed the traditional method of allowing the organ to alternate with minister and choir — not accompanying either of these or the congregation. Thus the organ would play before the Introit, Kyrie, Gloria in Excelsis, and Agnus Dei, and would alternate with the congregation in hymn verses. Its unchallenged place was in the playing of preludes, either before the service or before the hymns, giving the congregation its pitch. The Thomas School at Leipzig and J. S. Bach carried artistic organ playing to its height. Eventually the organ came to accompany the singing of the congregation but in a simpler manner than in compositions.

Matins and Vespers

In one area of worship and music the Reformation failed to carry forward earlier forms, namely, the hour services. Only in isolated instances were they attempted, as in some schools. But two of the services did survive — Matins and Vespers — for congregational use. They consisted of psalms, Scripture lessons, hymns, and collects. While daily observance was possible in large city churches, the daily use was usually reserved for schools, and Sunday observance was all that remained of them in country parishes.

127

The Matins and Vespers helped preserve some earlier liturgical material, such as the Canticles — the Benedictus and Te Deum at Matins, the Magnificat and the Nunc Dimittis at Vespers. The use of the Psalms was encouraged — Psalms 1 to 109 being prescribed for Matins, 110 to 150 for Vespers. New Testament readings were listed for Matins, Old Testament for Vespers. Preaching was sometimes included in these services. Often the Catechism was the source of themes for sermons, and in the country catechization held a prominent place. Hymn singing was usual.

Matins and Vespers, where not observed daily, were common on Wednesdays and Fridays — on the latter day the Litany was sung. On Sundays at various hours Matins preceded and Vespers followed the chief, or Communion, service.

THE SERMON

In the century following the Lutheran reforms the order of worship followed the pattern here outlined. Only in the territories adjoining Calvinistic territory did the altar service change markedly. There the worship was less formal, as in Württemberg, Alsace, and Baden. But everywhere the tendency was toward a didactic service. The sermons were long — the hourglass on the pulpit was supposed to regulate the time, but parishioners complained that the preacher often turned the glass and went on. In the first decades the preaching was exegetical and Biblical. As the theological controversies grew, the content of the sermons became more dogmatic and all too often concentrated on theological disputes. The learned clergy built up their sermons with many divisions and subdivisions and exhibited their skill in festival and especially funeral sermons. In the broad ranks the preachers devoted much time to catechetical preaching or catechetical instruction. The learning of Luther's Catechism was a prime duty, and its questions and answers had to be memorized — even sung or repeated at altar stairs by youth asking and answering each other. In Norway Peter Dass cast the whole of Luther's Catechism into verse.

PARISH LIFE AND THE PASTOR

We should not overestimate the literary or cultural or moral life of the average 16th- and 17th-century parish. Peasant life was rude.

128

Even in the cities the masses lived on a low economic level. The parish visitation reports uniformly complained of swearing, immorality, and intoxication. In medieval times the Mass had been considered a magical rite, pilgrimages brought merit, and the priest's requirements in confession could earn forgiveness. The removal of these checks on the average person, even in a time of proclamation of the free grace of God, did not make for sanctification of the community. There were voices that declared the reverse. We have already noted the question raised by the first visitations in Saxony as to the preaching of the Law, which was heard more and more. It is characteristic of the period of orthodoxy that an Old Testament legalism pervaded the churches.

The pastor could not compel private confession, but he could disbar from Communion. And if offenses were great, he could call on the consistory as an arm of the government to take a hand. In teaching the commandments he could point out and judge and decry the sins of his community. His hope of improving the moral tone of his parish was in teaching the Catechism — the summary of the Christian faith. So we find the Catechism combined with preaching, confession, and Communion. In some countries the recalcitrants were placed in stocks outside the church or made to sit in a prominent place in the church to be seen by all. And at the height of the period it was possible, because of communal assent, to force out of the thief, the adulterer, or the swindler public confession before the congregation.

For more than the prestige of the clergy was needed. The early years found the pastor in a difficult position. Only the favored few could attend the university for their education. The ordinary candidate for the ministry read theology with an older pastor, then took the examination under the superintendents. With the goods of the medieval churches and monasteries passing to city councils and territorial princes and estates of nobles went also the privilege of calling pastors. Subservience to the calling authorities was a natural result, for the pastor's very existence and chances of promotion depended on their goodwill. The lot of the rural pastor was especially hard, burdened as he often was with several parishes and suffering from irregular income. The death of a pastor left a widow — if a younger parson was willing to marry her, the parsonage was his and the parish was least inconvenienced. This practice became a general one. Despite it all the evangelical parsonage developed into the cultural center of the community. From there gradually came leaders in church and state.

A Sunday in Norway

More than Germany, the Scandinavian countries kept a strict Sabbath. Sunday markets after worship were not unusual in many German territories, but commerce had less occasion in the rural regions of Sweden and Norway to use Sunday for its purposes. A description of a Sunday in Norway affords evidence of the discipline the Lutheran Church succeeded in imposing on its people. As the congregation assembled, the sacristan noted the names of those in attendance. The men were seated on the right, the women on the left, all according to social status. The pastor came from the parsonage, dressed in a long, black gown and a white, ruffled collar about his neck. While the people stood in front of the chancel he led them in a confession of sins and declared absolution. The churching of recent mothers followed. The sacristan led in the singing of hymns, reading a verse and the people then singing it, for there were no hymnbooks. He then read an opening prayer, whereupon the minister sang the liturgy. He now was clad in white. The hour-long sermon was divided between a homily and an explanation of a part of the Catechism. Nodding heads brought a rap on the head from the stick of a watchman. After prayer sinners were brought in to confess their misdeeds. A collection for the poor was received. There might be a marriage and baptisms. Then followed Communion. On leaving the church the people might see someone in the stocks. The Sabbath morning experience was long and varied, but it touched the everyday life of the community, and through its weekly repetition the people of Scandinavia learned a respect for authority that endured for a long time.

Organization of the Swedish Church

The success of the Swedish Church was unique in upholding the rights of the church against the encroachments of secular powers — nobles, cities, the royal crown. The first Lutheran archbishop, Laurentius Petri, was able in 1571 to have his Ordinance, ready a decade earlier, adopted by the government. It was the fruit of his 40 years of service in the evangelical cause. He was opposed to the subordination of the church, as in Germany, and succeeded in preserving the historic episcopate. The king's consent was needed, but pastors and laity could still elect their bishop, and parishes had a voice in calling their pastor as well as in governing their community by a small number of elected wardens. The duties of the bishops were carefully outlined. They were to hold yearly visitations, to ordain candidates after strict examinations, and to care for their pastors and congregations. The archbishop set an example by his own attention to the needs of the church. He arranged for associate pastors in larger parishes. He was concerned about books for the preachers, Bible translation, and devotional books. He regulated the dress of the clergy: cassock and cloak for daily wear, alb and chasuble for the altar service. The Ordinance prescribed how the *högmessa* (High Mass) was to be conducted. The Verba were to be read. Elevation of the host was allowed, but not adoration. Wine remaining should be used in a subsequent Communion. The presence of Christ was affirmed, but no explanation was given of the mode of His presence — the Swedish theologians were not happy over some of the German Christological speculations. Communion was received in a kneeling position. Latin could be used in the Kyrie and Gradual, in the Creed on festival days, as also in the Sequences. Altar appointments were preserved. Statuary and paintings also kept their places in the churches, though new (Biblical) scenes were painted over older themes in the ceilings and on the walls. The new scenes were often rendered in concepts common folk had of the Biblical events.

All in all the Swedish Ordinance of 1571—1572 laid the foundation for a liturgical church that was to have permanent significance. The bishops retained administrative power in their dioceses, and an educated clergy soon became a dominant force in the national life. Their attempt in 1593 to establish a national convocation independent of the king could not be attained. But for the following generation a line of strong bishops and archbishops including such names as Peter Kenicius, Laurentius Paulus Gothus, Johan Rudbeck, Haquin Spegel, and Jesper Swedberg provided the church with spiritual leadership of a high order. Kenicius' *Theological Compendium,* based on the work of a Württemberg professor, Matthew Haffenreffer, was used for two centuries in the education of theologians in Sweden.

Laurentius Gothus in Strengnäs, author of a prodigious *Ethica Christiana*, raised education to a new level. Johan Rudbeck, after service in Finland and Estonia, made his diocese of Västeras a model of episcopal administration. Spegel at Uppsala and Swedberg at Skara enriched the Swedish Church through their preaching and hymn writing.

THE CHURCH IN FINLAND

The Finnish Church, also under Swedish administration, enjoyed strong episcopal leadership. Eric Sorolainen and Isaac Rothovius, bishops of Abo, worked diligently to improve the instruction of the clergy through postils, Bible translations, and translation of Swedish books. The University of Abo was founded in 1640. Another bishop of Abo, the elder John Gezelius, organized the church in Estonia and Livonia, where the University of Dorpat was founded in 1632. Gezelius' son and grandson also became bishops of Abo, all three distinguishing themselves for efforts toward improvement of clergy and people. In the 17th century Peter Bang was the foremost incumbent of the younger bishopric at Viborg on the Russian border.

The leaders in the Scandinavian churches had studied at the German universities. They brought back influences of the German professors, and strife among the strict orthodox, the moderates, and the more liberal echoed in all these lands. Those accused of being friendly to Calvinism were labelled "Synergists," and followers of Georg Calixtus († 1656) were suspected of heresy. But throughout the century strict orthodoxy was in the ascendancy.

ORTHODOX THEOLOGY

In the German universities the Book of Concord had become the standard of right teaching. The argument had not finally settled all controversy, for differences still developed, as in the doctrine of the two natures of Christ. The University of Tübingen taught that Christ possessed in His ministry the power of the divine but concealed it, while the University of Giessen held to a renunciation of these powers while Christ was on earth. The main concern of the theologians, however, was to elaborate more fully the teaching of the Reformation. Melanchthon's *Loci* was replaced by the more comprehensive compendium of Hutter († 1616). But the most complete statement of Lutheran doctrine was formulated by Johann Gerhard († 1637) of the University of Jena.

The first generation of Lutheran theologians had concentrated on interpretation of the Bible, emphasizing its central teachings. But in the century following the Formula of Concord the aim was to erect a full-blown system of Christian thought not unlike the *Summa* of Thomas Aquinas. Luther had thrown out Aristotle as a guide for Christian thought, but the followers of Melanchthon had brought the Greek philosophy back again, for they imitated the method of philosophy in reasoning out the meaning of each article of faith, distinguishing between all possible aspects. Melanchthon's *Loci* was a work of a couple hundred pages of comment on what were considered essential topics. Gerhard's *Loci,* completed in 1622, covered in a Leipzig republication of 1855 over 4,000 pages of small Latin print. The nine volumes were divided into 31 chapters, beginning with a consideration of Sacred Scripture and the attributes of the Trinity and ending with a chapter on "Eternal Life." In between, every facet of Christian thought and speculation was studied — angels, providence, the image of God, original sin, actual sin, Law, Gospel, good works, sacraments, the church, death, resurrection, the final judgment. A whole volume was devoted to marriage, another was divided between the ministry of the church and the rule of government.

Chemnitz († 1586) had devoted his great work on theology to a defense of the Lutheran teachings against the decisions of the Council of Trent. Gerhard's *Loci* also was an apologetic, or defense, against contrary teachings of Rome, Geneva, the Socinians, and the Spiritualists, but its purpose was rather to establish the evangelical faith on its own foundation. This set an example for other dogmaticians until the result was a sort of philosophy of religion. The last in the line of great dogmatics, the work of David Hollazius († 1713), referred in its title to "Universal Theology." In his system God was considered the "final object of theology," and man was the "subject." Faith was so finely analyzed that the work of God was dissected into an order or process which the Spirit was supposed to follow: the "call" through the church, illumination of the hearer, conversion, regeneration, justification, mystical union, new life, preservation, and glorification. The place of justification in this series indicates how great was the distance from Luther's original preaching.

133

In this elaboration and philosophizing of the faith the intellectual had taken precedence over the emotional factors, and a rationalization of Christian experience had made God Himself an object of study rather than a creative source of life. In the course of the movement the Bible tended to become less the energizing Gospel and more an arsenal of prooftexts for the particular system it served. Gerhard gives evidence of religious feeling and included prayers and hymns in his treatment, but the theological system of Johannes Andreas Quenstedt († 1688), a masterpiece of logic, lacks the warmth of faith which its author possessed and which found expression in his life and teaching. Calixtus departed from the *Loci* method and tried to analyze the contents of faith under one leading concept. For him the goal of theology was eternal bliss, and all the component parts of doctrine were subsumed under this idea. Man was the subject of salvation, which God brought to him through Christ in justification by faith. In his attempt to make theology a practical discipline Calixtus softened the differences between the churches, wanting to distinguish between fundamental and nonfundamental doctrines in their relationships to one another. This was looked on as treason by Abraham Calovius († 1686), who opposed any reconciliation with Calvinism. Calixtus was professor at the University of Helmstedt, and his name and that of his university became synonymous with "unionism." While his attitude was considered compromising, his analytical method was imitated and later systems of dogmatics were built up on some one fundamental aspect of the faith. The writings of these theologians spread throughout Lutheran lands, and positions taken on them determined the character of teaching not only in the universities but also in the pulpits and schools. In America the system of Johann W. Baier of Jena († 1695) was to prove significant by its use under C. F. W. Walther at St. Louis.

Devotional Literature

For all their ponderous worth these classic systems of doctrine remained intellectual possessions of the schools. More often than not they were the armament of rival theological movements. They affected the climate on theological heights, but they did not reach down into valleys of lay thinking and feeling. Gerhard's dogmatic production was read by professors and students, his devotional books by the broad

134

masses. His *Sacred Meditations* appeared in 1606. About the same time (1606—1610) the four books of Johann Arndt's *True Christianity* came out. Luther's Catechism, with prayers and postils, served as popular devotional material. Popular interest continued in such works as Tauler's *German Theology* and above all in Thomas a Kempis' *Imitation of Christ*. Evangelical counterparts to medieval meditations on preparation for Communion and for death were also much in use. But Arndt's *True Christianity* and *Garden of Paradise* attained greatest popularity in all Lutheran countries. The dry atmosphere of scholastic theology was tempered by misty emotionalism of a direct appeal to a daily living of the faith and by the clouds of mysticism that had their source in Bernhard of Clairvaux, Bonaventura, and the sentimentalism of the wounds of Christ. The price of Bibles was still prohibitive for the ordinary individual, so prayer books, sermon collections, and devotional books became the daily bread of earnest Christians.

HYMNODY

In addition there were the hymn collections, which are a remarkable phase of evangelical worship and devotion. In the 16th century the songbook of the Bohemian Brethren antedated Luther and may have had something to do with the Wittenberg *Gesangbüchlein* of 1524, to which he wrote an introduction. But after that date a steady stream of hymnbooks flowed forth from far-separated fountains. Wittenberg printers brought out collections in 1526 and 1528. Breslau, Nürnberg, and Rostock produced their own about the same time, Riga in 1530. Luther's "A Mighty Fortress" was first published in a Leipzig book of 1529. Musical notes soon appeared. By the time of Luther's death Valentin Bapst of Leipzig had produced the most comprehensive collection — 124 songs by Luther, Hans Sachs, Spengler, Huber, Speratus, Agricola.

In Sweden the Uppsala Hymnal of 1572 was enlarged in 1621 and was most popular until the revision of 1695 was adopted for use throughout the country. Hans Tausen had begun the use of Danish hymns, but the hymnbook of Hans Thomisson of 1659 prevailed until the hymnody of Bishop Thomas Kingo († 1703) gave the church a religious poetry that has lived on until the present day. Kingo's collection attained unusual favor in Norway — 85 of his hymns were

135

in the official hymnbook of 1697. The rector of the Abo school, Jacob Finno, published the first Finnish hymnal about 1583. Over 200 hymns were included in a revision by Henrik Hemming, 1611—1614. Bishop Gezelius the elder sponsored a new book in 1668. The official collection of 1701 paralleled the Swedish Hymnbook of 1695 but contained native Finnish hymns. In Iceland the first hymnbook was a translation of 35 hymns by the bishop of Skalholt, Martin Einarson, in 1555. The hymns were mostly German, half of them by Luther. Translations from the Danish were added in 1558 by Bishop Gisli Jonsson. Icelandic authors were represented in the hymnals of Bishop Gudbrandur Thorlaksson, published in 1589 and 1619, a collection of over 300 hymns, some with musical notes. His Gradual, with hymns and melodies, dates from 1594. Bishop Gisli Thorlaksson of the Tholar diocese published a hymnal in 1671. The first Hungarian book was a translation of Bapst's Leipzig Hymnal of 1545 — the work of John Honter and Valentin Wagner.

Only a small number of hymns were actually used in the service, and sometimes these were fixed. Saxony in 1624 forbade the use of any other than Luther's hymns. The hymnbooks were no more in general circulation than the Bible — the service hymns were learned by rote in the schools. But the writing of hymns was a means of religious expression, and where possible the reading and singing of hymns was a private devotional exercise. Over a thousand hymns are known from the 16th century. Gradually the best of them found their way into the hymnals that were officially adopted. The hymns of Decius, Nicolai, Heermann, Rist, Rinkart, and — greatest of all — Paul Gerhardt († 1676) became a permanent treasure of Lutherans everywhere and by translation a heritage of Christendom. Examples of these hymnists, found in contemporary collections, include the following:

Decius: "All Glory Be to God on High," "O Lamb of God Most Holy";

Nicolai: "Wake, Awake, for Night Is Flying," "How Brightly Beams the Morning Star";

Heermann: "O God, Eternal Source";

Rist: "O Living Bread from Heaven";

Rinkart: "Now Thank We All Our God."

136

Gerhardt, a staunch disciple of orthodoxy, refuted the theory that interest in doctrine meant a lack of emotional warmth, and out of the misery of the Thirty Years' War he could hold high the hope of spiritual victory.

> Love caused Thine incarnation,
> Love brought Thee down to me;
> Thy thirst for my salvation
> Procured me liberty.
> O love beyond all telling
> That led Thee to embrace,
> In love all love excelling,
> Our lost and fallen race.

This in itself was a summary of the evangelical faith, and while borrowing imagery from Bernhard of Clairvaux, he could respond to this love in his own language as he contemplated the "Sacred Head Now Wounded":

> What language shall I borrow
> To thank Thee, dearest Friend,
> In this Thy dying sorrow,
> Thy pity without end?
> Oh, make me Thine forever!
> And should I fainting be,
> Lord, let me never, never,
> Outlive my love to Thee.

In the sure confidence of a personal trust in Christ he could voice the duty that orthodoxy demanded be fulfilled in the daily life of the believer:

> Put thou thy trust in God,
> In duty's path go on;
> Walk in His strength with faith and hope,
> So shall thy work be done.
>
> Commit thou all thy griefs
> And ways into His hands,
> To His sure truth and tender care
> Who earth and heaven commands.

STATES AND CHURCHES

In worship, in doctrine, in discipline the line of development in each of the Lutheran areas shows an approach to uniformity, the characteristic of the 17th century. In the background was a parallel movement in the political life of Europe. But it was no longer a universal

137

unity in one church or one state. Rather it was a drawing together into smaller, integral units challenging absorption by others. The empire had given way to a collection of national states — France, Spain, England, Scotland, the Netherlands, Austria, Denmark, Sweden — each jealous of its sovereignty and ready to wage war for its independence. The Catholic Church under Rome had broken up into various parts — Lutheran, Calvinistic, Roman, Bohemian, Socinian. Each had been on the defensive and was ready to take offensive action. Only isolated voices were heard urging better relations between Christians.

In this milieu the churches everywhere were subordinated to the governments of their countries, and ecclesiastical affairs were inextricably entangled with political interests. In the countries where the Roman papacy still exerted power an alliance between rulers and Jesuits determined the direction of policy. In Reformed lands the religious and political parties made common cause against oppression. In Lutheran territories the princes and cities and kings demanded allegiance of clergy and people in order to strengthen and safeguard a still-precarious independence. These tendencies were already present before the Thirty Years' War, but the terrible trials of these years increased the drive toward an absolutism in the state that reached its height by the end of the 17th century. After 1660 the king of Denmark controlled the appointments, the administration, and the finances of the churches in his realm. The king of Sweden in 1693 assumed a similar sovereignty in his land, though in all the Scandinavian lands the law still was above the crown. The practice in German lands of placing ecclesiastical affairs in the hands of a consistory led to a similar supremacy of the state, for the final word lay with the political members, one of whose number was often chairman.

That we are confronted here not by a consequence of Lutheran reforms but by a powerful movement toward the formation of independent and absolute states will become evident as we seek to trace the role of force in the story of Europe, a force that created a new array of nations and a new attitude toward all religions.

XI

THE APPEAL TO ARMS

To Lutherans in Germany the Peace of Augsburg gave a certain legal status — a concession of an emperor too weak to suppress the new, yet too loyal to the old but to hope for its ultimate victory. To Calvinists and other Protestants the peace had promised nothing. Yet where they were strong they might, as in Switzerland and in certain German provinces, compel toleration.

From Geneva the followers of Calvin had carried their faith into France, the Netherlands, and Scotland. Their influence was felt in Scandinavia and Germany. On the eastern borderlands they were strong — in Bohemia, Poland, Hungary, Transylvania. Despite the efforts of a few to bring Lutherans and Calvinists together in the tradition of Melanchthon and Bucer, the gap widened with time. Often was heard the embittered cry of Lutherans that they were more inclined to agree with Rome than with Geneva. But Rome was in no mood to yield to any dissenters and for the century after Augsburg attempted by persuasion, intrigue, and force to win back those who had left. Its strongest arm was the Jesuit Order, whose program was to control the policies of governments and thereby gradually crush the Protestants. Since the principle of Augsburg was the determination of religion by the ruler of the territory, the history of the following period was affected by the faith of the rulers. The churches — their doctrine, worship, discipline — became subordinated to the attempts of political rulers to defend their power against the rulers of opposing territories and churches.

THE HUGUENOTS IN FRANCE

In France Lutheranism quickly gave way before the rapid spread of Calvinism, whose adherents bore the name of Huguenots. Between 1555 and 1558 they acquired over 2,000 churches. In 1558 the Synod of Paris adopted a confession of faith drawn up by Calvin. The provincial synod gave strength to the national council, and everywhere an active laity dominated the presbyterian organization. Its confession of faith, regular ministry, and strict discipline made the French Calvinist church a contender for supremacy in the nation. But the French peasantry was staunchly Roman, and the Protestant nobles were opposed by a determined aristocracy led by the house of Guise. The Guise were prepared to go to any length to keep France united and under the Roman papacy, even to plotting with Spain, the traditional foe. During this period in France as everywhere else it was deemed impossible to have more than one religion in the state — Protestants as well as Romanists were convinced that the unity of a people demanded unity in faith. At first the French monarchy, recognizing the strength of the Huguenots, allowed a defined toleration. In 1562 the Huguenots were permitted freedom of public worship on estates and in places outside walled towns and in private gatherings in cities. But even this provision was opposed by the Guise party and by the Jesuits, who had been welcomed in 1562. For the next 36 years France was to witness no less than eight wars between Huguenots and Catholics.

In 1572 the massacre of St. Bartholomew's Day cost the Huguenots over 10,000 lives in Paris, the loss of their leaders, and resulted in their expulsion to the south. The attempt of the monarchy to give some freedom to the Protestants was consistently thwarted by the Catholic party, which wanted one faith, one law, one king. An observer estimated that by 1580 the Huguenots had lost 70 percent of their people, mostly by forcible reconversion. The party led by the duke of Guise became so strong that even the king was subordinated to its policies and bargained for the support of the Huguenots by making concessions to them. The evil effects of the national divisions led a mediating group called the Politique to seek a unity that would leave room for the Huguenots. But the Guise party was stirred to extreme action by the possibility of Henry of Navarre, a Calvinist, succeeding to the throne. Henry, however, turned Catholic. The Spanish ally of the Guise was turned back, and in the year that Philip II died (1598) the French monarchy issued the Edict of Nantes — a victory for the Politique party. The Huguenots were given full civil rights in courts, schools, and public office. Private worship was permitted in any place, and public services could be held in designated places, for instance, on the estates of some

3,000 nobles. Freedom of church assemblies was guaranteed, and the Huguenots were given control of 200 fortified towns.

France remained a Catholic country, but for the next 87 years its unity was made possible only by a recognition of the rights of a minority it could not crush. For all its allegiance to Rome, the French monarchy developed into an absolute rule that declared its right derived not from Rome but from the Divine Ruler, and within half a century a French cardinal would become an instrument for preserving Lutheranism in Germany.

CALVINISM IN HOLLAND AND SCOTLAND

France, despite its Catholicism, was a perpetual foe of Catholic Spain, and on its northern borders the Spanish were trying to maintain their hold in the Netherlands. Charles V had enjoyed the fidelity of its people, but his successor, Philip II, alienated the Dutch by making the country subservient to Spanish interests — taxation for Spanish needs, quartering of Spanish troops, appointments of Spanish officials. An independent spiritual life with roots in medieval mysticism had been nurtured by the Brethren of the Common Life and the humanism of Erasmus. Anabaptism early won many recruits, and the Lutherans counted their first martyrs in Holland. After 1560 Calvinism had a rapid growth. Its condoning of resistance made it an ally of the movement toward independence. In 1563 the Synod of Antwerp adopted the Belgic Confession.

Leadership in the long and bitter rebellion against Spain came from the house of Orange, whose William the Silent turned from Catholicism first to Lutheranism, then Calvinism. He would have preferred a toleration of all faiths, even to a division of the nation among them. For not even in Holland could the ideal of one territory, one faith be rejected. But when the Dutch Republic was proclaimed in 1581, it was on the basis of Catholicism in the south and Calvinism in the north. While the Flemish provinces followed Roman exclusiveness, Holland allowed a freedom that made it a refuge for exiles of all faiths — sometimes a stopping place to other lands, as in the case of the English Pilgrims on their way to America. Even Calvinism lost its unity, and after the Synod of Dort in 1619 Arminianism was separated from the orthodox stem. At the expense of Spain the Dutch had become a great maritime nation able before long to lend support to

England, Scotland, and Sweden in a final challenge to the Spanish and Austrian supporters of Rome's supremacy.

Anti-Roman, anti-England, anti-France factors had impelled Scotland on a Protestant path. Under John Knox this country exhibited a rare unity characterized by a strict Presbyterianism. Its relations with Geneva were close, and in 1566 it adopted the Second Helvetic Confession as its declaration of faith. Its struggles were rather with England and episcopacy than with continental parties. But Scots were in Protestant armies; and a Scotsman, John Dury, was to play a part in the story of attempted reconciliation between Protestants.

It was on the eastern borders of European civilization and of the Western Church that the final struggle of the papacy to retain its place had its beginnings. There the house of Hapsburg arose as the imperial defender and restorer of the faith. What Charles V and Philip II of Spain could not accomplish, their successor in the Austrian branch of the family hoped to achieve. A sort of prelude was played in Poland and Bohemia before Ferdinand II took over the main role.

COUNTER-REFORMATION IN POLAND

In Poland the tolerant Sigismund II Augustus had allowed the Protestants freedom of worship. Although unable to agree among themselves, they had presented their declaration of faith in the Consensus Sandomir of 1570, and in 1572 the nobles had compelled the sovereign, through the *Pax Dissidentium* (Peace of the Dissenters), to give equal protection to Catholics and Protestants. The successor of Sigismund, Duke Henry of Anjou, soon left Poland to become Henry III of France, where he became embroiled in the Huguenot wars. Stephen Bathory had been a Lutheran in Transylvania, but he married a sister of Sigismund and became a Catholic ruler in Poland. Though tolerant, he fell under the influence of the Jesuits. Favored by the queen and king, the Jesuits were able to establish their schools in every part of the kingdom, including Lutheran Latvia, which had become a part of Poland in 1569.

Bathory's successor, Sigismund III (reigned 1587—1632), was a son of John III of Sweden. He had been reared a strict Catholic by his mother, and his zeal for the restoration of the papal church was such as to earn him the title "King of the Jesuits." He challenged the right of his uncle Charles IX, father of Gustavus Adolphus, to the throne of Sweden, but was decisively defeated in 1598 on Swedish soil. His rule in Poland meant the end of Protestantism there, for he excluded Protestants from public office, restored churches to the bishops, and placed education in the hands of the Jesuits, who in 1600 had almost 500 members in Poland in 17 different centers outside Warsaw. The Peace of 1572 was violated, and after 1608 Poland became a Catholic nation with few rights for Protestants.

IN BOHEMIA

Almost simultaneously the tide was turning in Bohemia. There the Utraquists and the Brethren had maintained ancient privileges, and Lutherans and Calvinists had established themselves under the tolerant rule of Maximilian II. This Austrian prince had long been friendly toward the new reforms. He was even suspected of being heretical, and a pope had wanted his father to disinherit him. In 1562 he promised his father that he would remain a faithful Catholic and was thereupon elected king of Bohemia and Hungary. In 1564 he became Holy Roman emperor, showing tolerance toward both Protestants and Jesuits. In 1575 he promised not to interfere with the religious activities of the Protestants in Bohemia, and on his death his son Rudolf did the same. But the father had already in fact turned in another direction. Hoping for the throne of Spain for himself and the crown of Poland for one of his sons, he allowed his lieutenants to persecute the dissenters. With the succession of his son Rudolf II on Maximilian's death in 1576 the principle of Austrian toleration ended both at home and in the imperial territories. Bohemia endured the misrule of Rudolf and gained in 1609 a charter of religious liberty from his brother Matthias, who deprived the incompetent Rudolf of his possessions. But the actions of Austria indicated all too clearly what lay ahead, and Bohemia was in revolt when the Emperor Matthias died in 1619.

IN AUSTRIAN LANDS

Ferdinand II's name is central in the crucial first decades of the 17th century when the supreme effort was made to force religious unity upon Europe. When he became emperor in 1619, he was duke of Styria, Carinthia, and Carniola, the eastern districts, and there set in motion the elimination of Protestantism. A determined Catholic brought up by Jesuits, he conceived of his mission as a champion of imperial policy and the Roman faith. In 1597 he had promised the pope that Catholicism would be restored. The following year he began the systematic expulsion of Protestant preachers, the closing of their schools, the prohibition of worship, and giving the laity the choice of conversion or exile. Ferdinand boasted in 1609 that he had converted over 40,000 persons. His territory was again Catholic.

In Austria Ferdinand had taken over when Rudolf II was declared incompetent. There Rudolf had already forbidden Protestant worship in 1578. The crown lands were forcibly converted. Only Catholics could exercise the right of citizenship. Education was restricted to the Jesuit schools and the university placed under strict provision. Canisius' Catechism alone was permitted. The Protestant nobles offered some resistance, but by 1628 Austria, which a half century earlier was largely Protestant, had returned to Rome.

IN GERMANY

The reversion of the Hapsburg territories to Rome was aided by a line of dukes in Bavaria who followed similar policies. A Jesuit college had been founded in Munich in 1559. The order was given the universities of Dillingen and Innsbruck, and it virtually controlled the school at Ingolstadt. The Index was introduced in 1561. Duke Albert had received from the pope financial privileges that made him independent of the nobility, and using the rule of Augsburg enjoined Protestantism in his extensive domain. In 1587 Wolf Dietrich became archbishop of Salzburg. He gave his people the choice of conforming or exile, the majority choosing the latter. Thus when Maximilian I became duke in 1597, he was in a position to give powerful support to the policy of Ferdinand when he became emperor.

Meanwhile Protestantism was suffering serious losses elsewhere in Germany. Trier, Osnabrück, Eichstadt, Augsburg, and Passau were restored to their bishoprics. In Fulda an abbot who was a convert to Rome achieved supremacy almost single-handed. The elector of Mainz drove out pastors and replaced them with priests. Bishop Julius of Würzburg was in authority after 1573. He expelled 170 Lutheran pastors and claimed to have regained 100,000 converts. Schools and universities

144

owed much to his reforms. The bishop and elector of Cologne, relying on Jesuits, brought back to Rome by 1600 such centers as Freising, Hildesheim, Münster, and Aachen.

PROTESTANT DISUNION

When in 1619 the election of an emperor took place on the death of Matthias, three of the electors were Protestant. Frederick III of the Palatinate was a Calvinist. His province had turned from Catholicism in 1546, but in the bitter strife between Lutherans and Calvinists the latter emerged victorious and in 1563 adopted the Heidelberg Catechism, a moderately Calvinistic confession. Elector Frederick IV became fearful of the advances of the Austrian and Bavarian leaders and of the Catholic League that Maximilian of Bavaria had organized in 1609. He attempted a counterleague of Protestants, but since Saxony refused to join, it became mainly a Calvinist alliance.

Brandenburg was an important fortress of Lutheranism but in 1614 its ruler, Elector John Sigismund, turned Calvinist. He changed the religious status of his territory and adopted a policy of toleration of dissent.

Only John George of Saxony was Lutheran and also elector. He was looked upon as a leader of the Lutheran cause, for his land was stronger than Hesse, Württemberg, and Anhalt to the south, or Brunswick, Mecklenburg, and Holstein to the north. But he was averse to change and was content to live by the Augsburg arrangements. Respect for the law of the empire was fundamental with him, and so he would follow a properly elected Catholic emperor. If he could hold Saxony to its usual course, he would not consider it his duty to defend Lutheranism elsewhere. His fondness for drink made him hard to deal with, but the emperor could count on his loyalty to the imperial constitution.

BEGINNING OF THIRTY YEARS' WAR

As Protestants everywhere feared, Ferdinand, who had been elected king of Bohemia in 1617, was chosen emperor in 1619. Bohemia was ripe for revolt against the Hapsburgs, and rather than accept the new ruler the Protestants of Prague threw his deputies out of the council windows. Instead of Ferdinand they invited the Calvinist elector of the Palatinate, Frederick V, to be their king. Their revolt began the Thirty

Years' War in which all of Europe was to become involved before the religious question was settled.

Bohemia was no match for the emperor, who called in Maximilian, the duke of Bavaria. Under the able administration of its duke, Bavaria had grown strong and prosperous, and its resources were available to the general of its army, Count Tilly. This "monk in armor" had originally planned to become a Jesuit but decided to offer a more military devotion to his patroness, the Virgin. At Prague he crushed the rebellious forces, and Elector Frederick fled to Holland unsupported by the Protestant princes he had hoped to associate with himself.

The elector of Saxony not only had refused aid but himself joined in the attack on Bohemia. He had been bribed by the emperor with a promise of a part of Bohemian Lusatia. On his part Ferdinand acted unconstitutionally by placing Frederick, an elector, under the ban of the empire and transferring the Palatinate, his electorate, to Maximilian as payment for his services. Frederick thus lost his kingdom of Bohemia, his domains on the Rhine, and his electoral title. For the Protestants it meant the end of the power of the Bohemian nobles and the complete Romanization of the kingdom. All the aid the Saxon elector could win was some protection for the Lutherans in Silesia. As for the Palatinate, an area adjoining Bavaria was given to the new elector, who proceeded to replace Protestant pastors by Catholic priests.

The deposed Frederick was a son-in-law of King James of England. Not much help, however, could be secured from the English Parliament. But the Dutch were at war with Spain, seeking their independence, and they saw a further threat to themselves when the Hapsburg emperor acquired lands on the Rhine. They therefore gave refuge to what forces Frederick had collected under the German military adventurer, Count Ernst Mansfeld, and Christian of Brunswick. The king of Denmark, Christian IV, too, feared for the safety of his duchy of Holstein, especially after Tilly had led his army northward. Most potent of the enemies of imperial expansion was France, Spain's traditional enemy. In almost constant war with Spain, France now hoped for a Dutch victory over Spanish masters in the Netherlands, and it feared that Spanish troops in Italy might gain access to the Rhineland. Though a Catholic country, France was ready to wage war against other Catholic lands — Spain and Austria — for European hegemony. The real power behind the French Louis XIII after 1624 was Cardinal de Richelieu, whose fear of Spain was shared by Pope Urban VIII. Thus it was possible for Catholic France to ally itself with Dutch Protestants, the Danish Lutheran king, the Calvinist Brandenburg elector, as well as Protestant England. But the leadership of Christian IV proved weak and fruitless before the onslaught of Tilly, and the appearance of a new Catholic general, Count Wallenstein, who had become — on his own terms — the military leader of Duke Maximilian. Christian was driven back to his islands and by the treaty of Lübeck in 1629 forced to renounce his German claims. The Catholic armies now had extended their sway to the shores of the Baltic.

THE EDICT OF RESTITUTION

At "the peak of the Catholic tide" Ferdinand issued in 1629 the Edict of Restitution. By it the Calvinists were to have no legal rights, all lands acquired by the Protestants since the Peace of Passau in 1552 would go back to the Roman Church, and the emperor's will was to transcend any previous legal decisions. Ferdinand meant to establish himself as emperor and ruler of a Catholic Europe as defined before the Peace of Augsburg. The power to enforce his decree lay in Wallenstein's army.

But at last the Hapsburg dynasty had overplayed itself. Even the Catholic princes feared the arrogant Wallenstein and his marauding troops who lived off the plunder of lands they traversed. The princes concerned with the constitution of the empire resisted Ferdinand's reckless violation of their rights. It was a bad time for the Hapsburg to ask that his son be declared his successor, and even the dismissal of Wallenstein failed to win this goal. The Edict of Restitution, however, had proved effective enough to rouse the Protestants to active opposition. Hope for their cause now depended on the North — the king of Sweden.

GUSTAVUS ADOLPHUS

In the century since Gustavus Vasa inaugurated a new era Sweden had extended its power beyond Finland by winning new lands at the expense of Russia. On the breakup of the Teutonic Knights, Sweden had gained Estonia in 1561. The war with Poland over Sigismund's claim to the Swedish crown moved from Sweden to the shores of the Baltic. Gustavus had secured from Russia all the lands along the Gulf

147

of Finland, but in the contest with Poland he met the resistance of Protestant burghers of Riga and Danzig, who saw their commerce threatened. The Swedish king was a brother-in-law of the elector of Brandenburg who, technically a vassal of Poland for a part of his Prussian possessions, was unwilling to become embroiled in a war between a Protestant relation and a Catholic overlord. Yet Gustavus, with reluctant aid from Denmark, held his own and was more than a match for Wallenstein in the port city of Stralsund.

In 1630, at the low point of Protestant power in Europe, Gustavus Adolphus decided to enter the German scene. He was undoubtedly concerned over Sweden's power in the Baltic. And it is equally certain that he believed it to be his duty to challenge the seeming supremacy of the Catholic Hapsburgs. Neither Brandenburg nor Saxony's elector welcomed him, but the Protestant populace saw in him a last hope for survival. Ironically his coming was facilitated by Richelieu, who had arranged a truce between him and Sigismund and who furnished subsidies for his attack on the foe of France. He came too late to prevent Tilly's destruction of Magdeburg, but that fearful catastrophe finally brought Frederick William of Brandenburg and John George of Saxony to his side. At Breitenfeld, a few miles from Leipzig, the military genius of the Swedish army overcame the great Tilly in September 1631. The Protestant cause was saved.

From Breitenfeld Gustavus moved south in a triumphant march, spending the winter at Mainz. In the spring he entered Bavaria and would have gone on to Vienna after the death of Tilly at the battle of Lech, but the frantic emperor recalled Wallenstein, and at Lützen the "deliverer" from Sweden lost his own life in November 1632. The Swedish army carried on under Chancellor Axel Oxenstierna until his defeat at Nordlingen in 1634. Wallenstein was assassinated and the command of the Catholic armies passed to the young heirs of Austria and Spain. Despite the general desire for peace and the projected peace at Prague in 1635, which would have restored the situation of 1627, the war went on for more than a decade.

DEVASTATION OF GERMANY

In the last phase of the Thirty Years' War Richelieu used Swedish, Dutch, and German armies to defeat the plans of Austria to retain its possessions along the Rhine. The devastation of Germany, Bohemia, and Austria was indescribable. For two decades cities were plundered, the countrysides ravaged, populations scattered; tens of thousands died of plague, hunger, and wounds of war. By and large the economy was wrecked; moral life deteriorated; schools were closed, churches burned, and the care of the sick and the poor was nonexistent. The distress of the nation became proverbial, though careful research discounts much of contemporary exaggeration. Yet the evil effects were immeasurable, and the progress of Germany was seriously retarded.

It is difficult to assess the religious character of wars of religion. Although there were pastors who labored heroically to minister to decimated congregations — also religious books and hymns date from this period — war is not religious, and every church suffered. The mixture of political and religious motives in the rulers cannot be accurately estimated. At times Lutherans fought Lutherans under Catholic rulers; at other times Catholic leaders and generals easily transferred to the Protestant side. The exemplary discipline of the Swedish army did not survive Gustavus, but a mercenary spirit permeated all the military forces. Political rulers were never sure of their generals, who might easily be bribed.

PEACE AND THE NEW EUROPE

Only one permanent gain came out of the eventual peace. Men everywhere perceived that religion was not a proper object of warfare. The Treaty of Westphalia (1648) finally gave legal recognition to Calvinism. It allowed Protestants to retain all they held Jan. 1, 1624. They had wanted to return to the status of 1618, but a compromise was accepted, for it meant the rejection of the Edict of Restitution. In Hapsburg lands the Catholics had rights to all their gains. These were the religious terms, and in some cases it meant emigration for thousands of persons who wanted religious freedom. For as far as the Catholic lands of Bohemia, Hungary, Austria, Bavaria, and Poland were concerned, the principle of one land, one faith prevailed. How far the principle could survive in Protestant lands the future would reveal. But this much had been won — no power, religious or political, could claim the right to enforce one faith on all of Europe.

149

After 30 years of huge expense the various contenders tried to compensate for their losses in the peace treaty. Sweden was given the western half of Pomerania and the bishoprics of Bremen and Verden — thus the control of the German shore of the Baltic. France acquired Metz, Toul, Verdun, and a great part of Alsace, as well as a foothold in Italy. The Palatinate, the occasion of the start of the war, was divided, Maximilian retaining the eastern half and the elector's title, Frederick receiving the region around Heidelberg and the title of an elector — eighth in number and lowest in rank. Brandenburg gained four bishoprics and eastern Pomerania, the nucleus of a future Prussia. Indeed, Brandenburg and Austria alone remained strong territories among the 300 fragments into which Germany had been broken. The princes, moreover, were given the right of forming alliances between themselves or with foreign powers. The Swiss and Dutch republics were recognized as independent and sovereign nations. A new Europe was emerging. The Hapsburg power in Spain was broken, while the Austrian branch grew into an eastern European empire. The new maritime nations of England, Holland, and Sweden entered the stage of history. Under Louis XIV France was to set the example of absolute monarchy until challenged by the rise of new classes grown rich by commerce and industry. Papal influence ceased in international politics. In the new nations religion would have to contend with new movements in philosophy, science, politics, and economics. Modern Europe dates from the end of the wars of religion.

Lutheran Lands

The settlement after the war prefigured the limits of the Lutheran Church. The Roman Church prevailed in the south, where Austria and Bavaria would block its advance, and on the west the power of France forbade its expansion. After the revocation of the Edict of Nantes in 1685 and the expulsion of several hundred thousand Huguenots, France was again Roman Catholic. The Swiss Cantons and the Netherlands were divided between the Calvinists and the Catholics. England developed its own forms of Protestantism in which after Archbishop Cranmer's time Lutheran influence was slight. Central Germany and Scandinavia remained the hearth of the Church of the Lutheran Reformation, though divided into fragmentary units. For a brief period Sweden maintained its role as a European power, enlarging its domain at the expense of Denmark, which lost its three provinces in southern Sweden, and of Norway, which gave up a border province to the victorious neighbor. And for a while Lutheranism followed the Swedish conquests around the Baltic: Estonia, Latvia, and Courland were taken from Poland; Karelia, Ingria, and Keksholm were acquired from Russia. But the meteoric career of Charles XII ended in disaster, and Sweden lost its Baltic possessions. The Russian absolutism of Peter the Great — even in his control of the church — and the Roman Catholicism of Poland left little room for Protestantism. Only in the Prussian territory regained from Sweden and expanded by the partition of Poland did Lutheranism find protection.

At the beginning of the 18th century the Lutheran church found itself established in Scandinavia and northern and central Germany. With Calvinism it had won equal rights with the Church of Rome; but unlike Rome, neither the Reformed nor the Lutherans had a single capital. As yet they depended on secular authority for external power — no less than the Roman dioceses. All that bound the Lutherans together was a common faith expressed in a simple manner in Luther's Catechism and more fully in the Book of Concord. In Denmark, Norway, Sweden-Finland, and in all the German territories secular authorities regulated the church by comprehensive ordinances that spelled out the worship, education, discipline, and pastoral care of the congregations. Orthodoxy was rigid, but it achieved a definiteness and singleness of purpose that helped preserve the church in perilous days.

XII

THE UNIVERSAL PRIESTHOOD

The relationship of faith in Christ and the good works of the believer was at the heart of Luther's struggle. He was convinced from Scripture that the sinner could be restored to the position of a child of God only by the grace of God apart from any merit of his deeds. No less was he sure that the faith which brought the forgiveness of sins was a source of new life. Engrafting the believer into the tree of life would produce the fruits of true righteousness.

FAITH AND SANCTIFICATION

Already during Luther's lifetime the question arose as to the place of good works in the plan of redemption. Some of his followers, as we have noted, placed all emphasis on faith and wanted none on Law and on good works a Christian should do. Grace alone was the watchword. It soon became apparent that the common man needed guidance in the ordering of his daily endeavor. For this the commandments of the Law were the guide — hence the teaching of the "third use of the Law" after the first use of declaring the will of God and the second of driving the penitent to Christ. The deeds of the Law, however, had nothing to do with man's justification. They belonged to the realm of sanctification — the living of a holy life because of the forgiveness received in Christ.

The devastation of the Thirty Years' War was spiritual as well as physical. In congregations the contrast between orthodoxy as it was taught and the actual spiritual condition of the people deeply disturbed earnest souls, both clerical and lay. Faithful preachers strongly criticized the formal devotions of the church member whose life was a denial of his faith. Drunkenness, sexual license, material greed, ever-present vices, were multiplied by the breakup of family and community relationships while armies ravaged the countryside. Congregations were leaderless, pastors poorly educated, schools closed or deteriorated. The scholastic debates in the universities were of little interest or edification to the average layman.

DEVOTIONAL LITERATURE

A source of comfort was found by many spiritually concerned people in a type of literature outside the orthodox dogmatics. Long before the Reformation a mystical literature had flourished whose content reflected the writings of Augustine, Bernhard of Clairvaux, Johannes Tauler, Thomas a Kempis, and other medieval German and Dutch authors. This literature found its way even into Lutheran circles, especially through popular prayer books and books of devotion. Johann Arndt, a Lutheran pastor in Germany, in the first decade of the 17th century combined this stress on a mystical union with Christ and the Lutheran teaching in his *Four Books on True Christianity*. This book spread rapidly, was soon translated into other languages, and profoundly influenced the evangelical churches. It called for a practical Christianity — the *true* faith as opposed to mere assent to a system of articles of faith.

Other Lutheran manuals of devotion expressed a similar purpose of deepening spiritual life within the framework of the confessions of the church, such as Lütkemann's *Foretaste of the Divine Bliss,* Christian Scriver's *Treasury of the Soul* and *Gotthold's Devotions,* and Heinrich Mueller's *The Kiss of Heavenly Love.* In the same category belong books produced by Puritan writers in England, whose works circulated in translation among Lutherans as well as Calvinists. Lewis Bayly's *Practice of Piety* and Richard Baxter's *Saints' Everlasting Rest* were to be found in all Lutheran countries. Something of Jesuit disciplines also crossed confessional borders, carrying with it Spanish mystical strains and the rigorous discipline of self in the training of the soul. Such an influence was revealed for instance in the writings of the Danish pastor Holger Rosenkrantz. Like Arndt, he blended his orthodoxy with Jesuitical literature, stressing sanctification and the fruits of faith as well as faith and the forgiveness of sins.

SPENER

Philipp Jacob Spener (1635—1705) had been affected early in his life by Arndt's *True Christianity* and the writings of Baxter. Following his studies at the University of Strasbourg he visited Geneva where the discipline of the Calvinist congregation impressed him greatly. At Frankfort he became senior pastor in 1666 and attempted to raise the level of congregational life in the Lutheran churches. Tradition held his sermons to the pericopes, but he would begin with a practical exhortation based on passages related to the text of the day. Every Sunday afternoon he held Catechism exposition not only for children and servants, which was customary, but also for adults. Confirmation had fallen into disuse because by many it was considered Roman, but Spener's practice of aiming his catechetical instruction at the conversion of the youth, who were to profess their faith before the congregation and receive its intercession, led to a renewal of the confirmation rite in many churches. Frankfort itself was not friendly to the program, and the orthodox preachers were quick to point out that it was not possible to know who were sincere in their confirmation profession.

Of greater importance was Spener's practice of arranging small gatherings of interested members for the reading of the Bible and doctrinal literature and for discussion of the religious life. "Collegia pietatis" these gatherings were called, or piety groups, and the name "Pietists" was soon applied to those who attended. Such were not without precedent, but the name of Spener gave them widespread publicity. For in 1675 he published a book that made him famous and started a movement that was to spread throughout the Lutheran Church. It was the *Pia desideria* (Devout Desires). In this Spener voiced his criticism of the low estate of the church. He called for better preaching, improved education and discipline of pastors, less polemics, and more edifying sermons. He appealed to the spiritual priesthood of believers, calling on the laity to witness to the faith by the quality of their lives. He believed the teaching of smaller groups would get closer to the people and their needs, thus defending his conventicles. In short, Spener desired an emphasis on sanctification that would balance the orthodox teaching of justification.

Few could deny Spener's charges. The orthodox leaders themselves recognized the sterility of much of the polemical preaching and formal catechetical instruction. At Wittenberg exegetical study of the Bible had given way to polemics, and sermons were artificial in their elaboration of a theme. It was immediately clear that the Pietists were

155

attacking the clergy, at least a great part of them. And when the followers of Spener went beyond him in attacking popular amusements, such as opera, dancing, and card playing, it was not difficult for those on the defensive to show the weaknesses of the critics. The Pietists did presume to judge between "converted" and "unconverted" pastors and laymen. Some would not receive Communion at the hands of the "unworthy" pastor but wanted a separate celebration of the Sacrament. Leadership in the congregation passed from the constituted clergy to laymen, often to women. In the conventicles emotions were given free reign and often led to extravagances. The reading of mystical writers awakened distrust of the organized church and made the distinction between Lutheran and Reformed seem less important. So suspicious did the authorities of both church and government become of separatism and divisions that in many districts private religious gatherings were forbidden and exile was threatened for those who forsook the regular services and attendance at confession and Communion. Such was the outcome in Hanover, Bavaria, Stuttgart, Bremen, and Nürnberg.

FRANCKE

Never popular in his pastorates, Spener nevertheless exerted profound influence through his personal friendships, a huge correspondence, and able followers. In Dresden and Berlin he found men who carried his ideas still farther and even saved them from consequences he himself came to fear. His most successful disciple was August Hermann Francke (1663—1727), who had come under Spener's spell as a student and who was a member of Bible study groups while a teacher at Leipzig. Francke himself had experienced a sudden conversion — he made this a model of Christian experience. Conversion, further, seemed to him a prerequisite of theological leadership, more important than the objective study of theology. Philosophy, even dogmatics, was secondary to Bible study, prayer, and an exemplary life. Naturally those accused by Francke of not having been converted as he had been resented the charge, and the close association of the converted seemed to many a pharisaical exclusivism. Accordingly Francke incurred the hostility of the orthodox leader, the younger Johann Carpzov at Leipzig, and was forced to leave first Leipzig, then Erfurt. But through Spener he found a place at Halle, and this he made a great center of Pietism.

156

At Glaucha, near Halle, Francke demonstrated his powers as preacher and spiritual advisor. Sin and grace was his constant theme in sermons, catechization, prayer services, and private confession. Content was more important to him than form — what he sought was conversion and edification. At the university in Halle he defended himself and like-minded colleagues, such as Joachim Lange, Joachim Breithaupt, and Johann Rambach, against orthodox opponents. They were opposed to any separation from the church, but Francke had to dissociate himself from radicals like the physician and lay theologian Johann Konrad Dippel, who went from criticism of the church to advocacy of separation from it. Francke was not an "enthusiast," but often among his adherents were men and women — and sometimes children — who saw visions and were bent on radical ventures. The breakdown of class distinctions in the conventicles also bothered the conservatives. To the orthodox it seemed that the extreme emphasis on conversion and individual experience meant a decline in the significance of the church and the clergy. Christianity became a private matter; the church a collection of like-minded people with common religious experiences. The aversion to the world so characteristic of many pietists looked like a renunciation of learning and culture, a disregard of beauty in nature and art, and a denial of responsibility for a social and economic order. Introspection, the keeping of diaries, and interest in emotional satisfaction all looked like the emergence of a new type of personality.

Francke, full of confidence and unconcerned about opposition, showed the fruits of his faith in the institutions he founded at Halle. A lover of children, he gathered together orphans and established a "Waisenhaus" (home for orphans) that became a model for other places and countries. It grew to large dimensions, and Francke established schools for the hundreds who came. They were to work as well as study, and the pedagogy of Halle had widespread imitation. An apothecary shop and a printing press were ornaments of the establishment. Students assisted in instruction, for which they received their meals. On graduation they went to the far corners of the world bearing the Gospel in the form they had learned it at Halle. At his death Francke had 2,200 children, 183 teachers, and 250 assistants. And the work depended entirely on voluntary support. The priesthood of believers had found expression — here the laity were not objects of the ministry of the church but active subjects in it.

The spread of the pietistic movement in the first half of the 18th century bears witness not only to the inherent energy of its members but also to its relationship to the orthodoxy then dominant in the churches of the Reformation. Many princes were attracted to Spener and Francke, for they saw the need of improved conditions in their churches and schools and preferred Spener's and Francke's programs to the theological controversies that divided the people. The elector of Brandenburg, now king of Prussia and himself a Calvinist, kept a protecting hand over the pietistic center at Halle. The Saxon king forbade the Wittenberg theologians to criticize the Pietists.

In the Swabian cities, the Palatinate, Alsace, and Baden Pietism met resolute resistance. Hanover not only issued edicts against conventicles and itinerant preachers but excluded pietistic hymns from its hymnal of 1740. Among the universities the strongholds of orthodoxy — Rostock, Strasbourg, Wittenberg — were averse to the forces of Halle, but Giessen, Kiel, Tübingen, and at length Leipzig were favorable to the new methods.

Württemberg proved to be good soil for Pietism, and here it took on a churchly character, opposing separatistic temptations. Johann Hedinger's preaching, hymn writing, and pastoral theology gave strength to a renewal of congregational life. But the name of Johann Albrecht Bengel towers over all others. He exercised influence as a consistorial member at Stuttgart, but it was as a Bible theologian that he was to mean most both for his contemporaries and for later generations. Whereas orthodoxy was prone to use the Bible as an arsenal of proof-texts, Bengel saw the New Testament as a whole, a revelation in which each part was to be considered. His *Gnomon* became a standard of Biblical interpretation. A keen student of his times, he foresaw political changes and a growth of naturalism and scepticism. His study of the Book of Revelation convinced him that the millennium would come in 1837. While his prediction did not materialize, his exposition of the book left abiding results. The world of his day did come to an end, but in the following age his Biblical interpretation was to help men of a new age.

158

Frederick IV of Denmark, though himself loose in life and morals, welcomed friends of the movement. Through his court preacher, R. J. Lütkens, the king not only gave status to pietistic preachers in the churches of Denmark and Schleswig but also had his name associated with the beginning of overseas missions by the Lutheran Church, for from Halle he secured the pioneer missionaries to the Danish possessions in India. To his reign also belongs the beginning of missionary work in Norwegian Lappland through the Pietist Thomas von Westen. In far-off Greenland a mission was established by Hans Egede and his sons, though this Norwegian pastor counted himself rather among the orthodox. In Denmark itself leaders in state and church were themselves Pietists or friendly to them. An orphan home modeled after Halle cared for children but also served as a center for the printing of Bibles, hymnbooks, and devotional materials. Pietist interest in education contributed to the establishment of hundreds of new schools — though it was not possible to reach the goal of a school in every parish — to facilitate the reading of religious literature by all.

The fact that pastors were at the head of the movement — Lütkens at court, Enevold Ewald at the orphan school, Broder Brorson in Schleswig-Holstein as leader of the missionary institute — kept the fruits in the church, making for better parish ministration, catechization, and preaching, and for the moment warding off the separatistic tendencies of Pietism. Many of the leaders had been in the circle of the crown prince, an avowed Pietist who in 1730 became King Christian VI. He was married to the daughter of a German Pietist prince, and the royal family supported the cause on many fronts. The conventicles were looked on with disfavor because of their divisive results. In 1732 and again in 1741 decrees were issued which permitted them only under the leadership of pastors. Confirmation, which presupposed the ability to read, was made a regular practice.

In two areas we find names of enduring significance. One was that of Eric Pontoppidan, court preacher in Copenhagen and later bishop of Bergen in Norway. His exposition of Luther's Small Catechism, entitled *Truth unto Righteousness,* proved to be for many generations a national reader in Denmark and Norway. It combined Law and Gospel, orthodoxy and Pietism in a manner that left a profound influence, especially on national character in Norway. Something of the same kind of proclamation had already been effective in the diocese of Oslo where Bishop Hersleb had built and renovated churches, supervised schools, hospitals, and the keeping of records, and introduced confirmation. Although Norway was still a part of Denmark and Norwegian students had to study in Copenhagen, national stirrings were beginning. The pietistic emphasis on individual experience, coupled with a new interest in history, nature, and education, revealed itself in the patriotic poetry of J. N. Brun, the widening of horizons by Pontoppidan, and the opening of the borders to other churches. Bishop Hersleb, for instance, distributed 10,000 copies of devotional treatises of English origin in homes of his diocese. His preaching and Pontoppidan's *Pastoral Theology* set the fashion for the work of the pastor.

Comparable to Pontoppidan's influence was that of a hymn writer, Hans Adolf Brorson, bishop of Ribe. A lyric poet, he sang of the inner experiences of the believer in a way that made him the classic hymnist of Danish-Norwegian Christendom. His Christmas hymns for children were among the best beloved.

> Thy little ones, dear Lord, are we,
> And come Thy lowly bed to see;
> Enlighten every soul and mind,
> That we the way to Thee may find.
>
> O draw us wholly to Thee, Lord.
> Do Thou to us Thy grace accord,
> True faith and love to us impart.
> That we may hold Thee in our heart.

But his vision also went beyond the toil and grief of earth.

> Behold a host like mountains bright!
> Lo! who are these, arrayed in white,
> A glorious band, with palms in hand
> Around the throne of light?
> Lo, these are they who overcame
> Great tribulation in His name.
> And with His blood the Lamb of God
> Hath washed away their shame.
> Before God's face they sing and pray,
> Their voices blend with angels' lay.
> And all conspire, a joyous choir,
> To laud Him night and day.

160

No less than 90 of Brorson's compositions found a place in Pontoppidan's hymnbook of 1740. Many have been translated into other
languages and have found their way into hymnbooks of other lands.

Through Denmark Pietism reached Iceland. The orthodoxy of
a bishop of Skalholt, Brynjolfur Sveinsson († 1675), had blended with
a mystic strain that nourished itself on his valuable collection of ancient
sagas. Hallgrimur Pjeturson († 1674) deeply influenced the piety of
the Icelandic church by his more than 50 Passion hymns and his
translations of Kingo's and other Danish devotional works. Arndt
too had become a part of Icelandic reading. Another bishop of Skalholt,
Jon Vidalin († 1720), made a notable contribution to Iceland when
he wrote for the pastors in their own language a postil after the
fashion of Gerhard's *Gospel Harmony*. A Danish bishop, Ludvig
Harboe, introduced confirmation into Iceland, and Pontoppidan's Catechism was widely used.

SWEDEN AND FINLAND

Pietism in Sweden followed a unique course. Although Spener's
royal acquaintances and well-wishers included Queen Ulrika Eleonora
of Sweden, a most violent anti-Pietist affected the early policy of the
government toward the innovators. The previous king, Charles XI,
had placed the Hamburg pastor J. F. Mayer over the churches of
the Swedish territory in northern Germany. Mayer was able to per-
suade the king to forbid all conventicles, and it was not until Francke
personally visited Charles XII on his Russian campaign that the government saw Pietism in a more favorable light. Yet Pietism got
through the walls raised against it by the leaders of church and state.

Over a dozen Swedish students were at Halle in 1694, among
them Nils Grubb, who later made his parish in Umea a Pietist center.
The tone of the opposition he encountered may be guessed by the
accusation of one of his critics who bewailed "the damnable new
birth which they now have begun to proclaim." The German congregation in Karlskrona offered another port of entry. A Västeras
teacher, Jonas Salan, published a colleague's translation of Francke's
Guide to True Christianity, which further provoked the pastor in
Hamburg. In Stockholm a group of laymen, among them government
officials, were meeting with returning Halle students and on Wednes-
day and Friday evenings engaged in Bible study, prayer, hymn singing,

161

and discussion of the spiritual life. They were in correspondence with Francke, who assured them that he wanted no new doctrine but only that the true doctrine should express itself in good works. Elias Wolker, a leading spirit, wrote a pamphlet on the "Priesthood of Believers." Included in the group were pastors: Andreas Hilleström from Karlskrona; George Conradi, the German pastor in Stockholm; and the Kiellin brothers, Carl and Samuel, from Finland. An important event was the production in 1717 of a songbook, *The Songs of Moses and the Lamb*. George Lybecker and Jonas Rothof, both government officials, contributed about two thirds of the collection; the remainder consisted of translations from the Halle hymnbook, namely, J. A. Freylinghausen's *Geistliches Gesangbuch*. In the songbook the Swedish groups everywhere had a common treasury and a symbol of those who had joined the company of the converted.

But the revival in Sweden was to receive new force from an unusual direction. After the defeat of Charles XII at Poltova, more than 30,000 Swedish prisoners were quartered in Russia, mainly in Siberia. Children of orthodoxy, these lonely exiles sought comfort in religion. A consistory in Moscow supervised church activities in the various camps. In Siberia a Pietist, Josiah Cederhielm, served as leader. In Tobolsk the prisoners built their own church. Correspondence was carried on with Francke, whose writings along with Arndt's were eagerly read. In Tobolsk a school was organized and attracted even Russian youth. When finally in 1724 the last prisoner had been released, it was found that hardly 5,000 had survived to return home. Among them were ardent Pietists who carried the message of faith active in works back to their parishes.

The collapse of Charles XII's imperial dream caused great changes in the government. The estates assumed control, and as one of them the clergy gained influence. They regained some of their older privileges in the election of parish pastors and bishops, though they were unable to eliminate all supervision of ecclesiastical matters by the state. In their assertion that the church leaders derived their power direct from God they met Pietist critics of the episcopacy who spoke of "natural law" and rights of individuals and congregations. Here as in other countries Pietists were willing to make alliance with governments in their opposition to orthodoxy. As yet the latter was in

162

domination. A statement in the statutes of government in this period reveals a fundamental motive in the position of the orthodox bishops and clergy. "Unity in religion," it was declared from the side of the state, "and in the correct form of worship is the most eminent and powerful foundation of a legal, harmonious, and enduring government." To the Swedish Lutheran no less than to the French Catholic of the 17th century it was inconceivable that a nation could survive if differences in faith were allowed.

When the Pietists threatened the unity of the church, orthodoxy called on the government to forbid private gatherings. In 1726 the Conventicle Act that made such gatherings for religious purposes unlawful was passed, and for a century Swedish church life was held to conventional forms. The conservative party could not silence men like Eric Tollstadius, the leading pietist pastor in the capital, but through the bishops of the dioceses it was able to retain a uniformity of practice that drove the movement underground except where a bishop such as Andrew Rydelius in Lund was sympathetic and tolerant. For there were, even among the leaders, those who desired some of the changes for which Pietism was clamoring.

Finnish as well as Swedish soldiers had followed Charles XII to his victories and his defeats. They too, returning from Russia, called for a more spiritual life in the congregations. Both before and during the Baltic Wars the literature on which Pietism throve had been read in Finnish homes — Arndt, Spener, Scriver. Finland was in the path of the armies and the countryside suffered severely. In the rebuilding after the war the structure of orthodoxy proved an enduring foundation. The bishops — three in the Gezelius family — were true to the orthodox tradition but interested in a Bible commentary on which all of them worked. In the cataclysm of war laymen had to be put into vacant parishes, but this exercise of the universal priesthood was unfortunate because these men were ill prepared for the ministry and hard to move after the war. As early as 1688 Lars Ulstadius had made a public attack on the church, and Peter Schaefer followed in his path. But the leaders maintained their position, and the Conventicle Act of 1726 applied to Finland as well as Sweden. An orthodox bishop, Daniel Juslenius of Borga (Porvoo), where the bishopric of Viborg had been moved, combined his theology with a new interest in philology

163

and history and created a new nationalistic feeling in the people. In its early phases Pietism in Finland blended with orthodoxy to produce a milder form of conservatism.

EASTERN EUROPE

While under the Swedish government, the churches of Estonia and Latvia felt the force of orthodoxy as maintained by the Swedish bishops. But Ernest Glück, awakened by Spener's writings, enjoyed the encouragement of the sympathetic general superintendent Johann Fischer in translating the Bible into Lettish by 1689 and the support of the Swedish government in its publication. An Estonian translation was made about the same time, but it was not until 1715 that an Estonian New Testament was printed and the entire Bible in 1739. Meanwhile Charles XII had met defeat, and Estonia and Latvia were brought under Russian rule. Peter the Great allowed the churches many privileges as he put them under the control of a governor in Moscow. Indeed Pietism had greater freedom than under Swedish orthodoxy. In 1736 a former student of Francke, Jacob Benjamin Fischer, was the general superintendent of Latvia. Literature and schoolteachers from Halle contributed to the development of the religious life in the Baltic provinces as the ties with Sweden were broken.

In Poland, Bohemia, and Hungary the Hapsburgs were engaged in eradicating all Lutheranism in the period of the spread of Pietism. But on the edge of their domains, fronting Turkish-held territories, Slovaks and Magyars kept in touch with centers of the evangelical world. John Burius was ministering around Pressburg (Bratislava). His son was in contact with Jena and Halle. The eminent historian and geographer Mattias Bel had been a student at Halle. He and the Slovak superintendent Daniel Krman made available for the Slovak Lutherans an edition of the Bohemian Brethren-sponsored Kralice Bible that was used until the present century. Pastor Elias Milec was the author of pietistic literature in his native Slovak language. A name of honor in this region was that of the Magyar nobleman Georg Bárány who had studied at Halle and was ordained in 1711. His ministry extended to Germans and Magyars, Lutherans and Reformed. His educational interests brought the rite of confirmation and Halle pedagogy to Hungarian churches.

164

It was from this corner of the European world that the Pietism of Spener and Francke was to be challenged and both orthodoxy and Pietism were to be influenced. In Silesia, which had escaped the fate of Bohemia and Hungary by being transferred to Saxony, a colony of Bohemian Brethren found a refuge on the estate of Nikolaus Ludwig Zinzendorf (1700—1760). Zinzendorf was of a Lutheran family in Dresden and educated at Halle. Unlike Francke, he did not stress the necessity of penitence but rejoiced in a personal love of Jesus, which for him was the supreme teaching of Scripture. He thought of this love as actually being present in all churches whatever their other differences, and to bring them together was for him a consuming ambition. The colony of Herrnhut was to be the center of a worldwide community. From it he himself would go in all directions, even to America, and his diaspora emissaries would go, two by two, wherever they could awaken faith in the beloved Jesus. Lutherans, Reformed, Brethren — all were in Herrnhut, and the Moravian, or Herrnhut, congregation was to include them all. The peculiar preaching of Zinzendorf's disciples followed his concentration on the wounds of Christ, the blood of the Lamb, and the redemption of the world. During his lifetime Zinzendorf sent out over 200 missionaries. Their influence was felt far and near.

A cofounder, Christian David, left Herrnhut for Latvia and Estonia where he spent the year 1730. The diaspora teams worked especially among peasants, in their language, raising up lay leaders. A Swedish Pietist was along at the beginning of Herrnhut and introduced the diaspora workers to friends in Stockholm. A congregation of Brethren was soon established in Abo, Finland. Zinzendorf visited Copenhagen and Stockholm. At first received with interest, on a second visit the attitude had changed. For again the phantom of separatism appeared to those in authority. Expelled from Saxony, Zinzendorf was made a Moravian bishop in Berlin in 1737. Bengel in Württemberg counselled against his plans, and in Hanover he was forbidden. In 1748 Zinzendorf visited German immigrants in America, where Muhlenberg publicly denied him the name of Lutheran.

The movement eventuated in a new church of the "Unity of the Brethren" with representative congregations both in Europe and in

America. The administration of the church owed much to a former Lutheran, Bishop August Spangenberg. The message of the Brethren found expression in a voluminous literature and in hymns, some of which have endured, especially:

> Jesus, Thy blood and righteousness
> My beauty are, my glorious dress;
> Midst flaming worlds, in these arrayed,
> With joy shall I lift up my head.

and

> Jesus, still lead on,
> Till our rest be won.
> And although the way be cheerless,
> We will follow, calm and fearless;
> Guide us by Thy hand,
> To our fatherland.

The emotional extravagances of the movement burst into full flower in Herrnhut, causing a reaction that threatened its survival. A more sober Zinzendorf salvaged his plans, but the dream of a new church of the Lamb throughout the earth had vanished.

Radical Pietism

Pietism had in fact stirred into life other latent forces that confused the church in its judgment of the program of Spener and Francke. Not only Arndt had been read but also Gottfried Arnold's new interpretation of church history. Arnold revived an interest in Boehme, Weigel, and other mystics for whom the inner light was normative in religious experience. Johann Konrad Dippel, a disciple of Arnold, combined an interest in the healing of the soul with his profession of bodily healing. When Dippel came to Sweden in 1726, ground had already been prepared for him. Another Arnold devotee, Peter Schaefer, a Finnish teacher, had been initiated into the secrets of mystical experience by Ulstadius in Abo. Schaefer visited Halle, then Gottfried Arnold in Quedlinburg, then Pennsylvania, where he got to know the Quakers. Returning to Finland in 1707, he soon landed in prison but was allowed to correspond with a large number of friends and led them to the same wells from which he had drunk.

Dippel was first welcomed by his followers when he came to Stockholm as a physician to attend the king. His pietism, however, was of a radical kind. He had moved from orthodoxy to a denial of it, also rejecting the clergy and the regnant theology. He taught that with the help of Jesus, the Great Physician, man can of his own power change his life. The love of God made atonement unnecessary. In short, Dippel had reached the state of a rationalist. The Stockholm Pietists therefore turned away from him. Although his influence remained, he was exiled and proceeded to bring the "bright light of the Gospel of Jesus Christ" to other parts. To Arnold the church had at first ceased to be important, but he later returned to minister in a parish. To Dippel and his followers the church had become a Babel and an obstacle to faith. The Pietists had wanted to reform the church. The radicals had no interest in it. Rather they enjoyed the experience of the "inner word" and "inner light." They borrowed from Madame Guyon in France, Gerhard Tersteegen in Germany, and John Bunyan in England. Doomsday was not far off, and so they waited for the apocalyptic coming of the Kingdom. Some of their groups resorted to communal living.

It is not surprising that these heralds of the end of the church should provoke the authorities to action. The Swedish government sent one after another into exile — the two Finnish brothers and mystics Jacob and Erik Eriksson, the student Eric Molin, the gifted Sven Rosen. The Danish government strengthened its prohibition of conventicles by a decree of 1741. In its defense of the existing order the leaders of church and state saw no great difference between the moderate and radical Pietists. Since the latter were not inclined to organize new churches, action was directed against individuals. The Herrnhut representatives succeeded in establishing congregations of Brethren who were variously treated, depending on the tolerance of authorities. But among the Pietists themselves fluidity prevailed. A leader of the movement in Finland, Abraham Achrenius, moved from a mellowed orthodoxy to the radicalism of Ulstadius, Dippel, and Rosen, and was led by the Ericsson brothers to oppose the church. Disillusioned, he sought fellowship with the Herrnhuters but ended as a pastor of a parish. In exile for his radical views, Rosen joined the Herrnhuters and as a diaspora worker died among the Moravians in Pennsylvania.

In Moscow the reports of excesses in Herrnhut cost Zinzendorf's wife entrance to the court. Alexander I was not unfriendly to the Pietists, but Russia would not allow free churches in the occupied provinces. By the time of Zinzendorf's death the movement had lost momentum in Lutheran lands, and the radical element of Pietism had drifted away from the church to new ideas of the times. But the orthodoxy of a previous century was also gone. In indirect ways the currents started by Spener had penetrated all Lutheran lands and produced results in theology and practice not yet exhausted.

FRUITS OF PIETISM

Willingly or unwillingly the leaders of the churches in Lutheran lands had conceded the validity of much of pietistic criticism. It had pointed to the unworthy character of many of the pastors and the uninspired routine of their labors. It had ridiculed the custom of placing men in vacant parishes who would marry the widow of the predecessor in order to "conserve" the parsonage, or take a bride selected by the "patron" of the congregation on whom the support of the pastor depended. It had asked for better pastoral care, better sermons, better teaching in the parish schools. It had demanded a Christian activity as a sign of Christian life. And in varying measure these criticisms and demands had been met. In Württemberg, in Sweden, in Denmark there had been new emphasis on parish visitation, confirmation instruction, and education of the ministry. In Halle, Tübingen, and Leipzig a new interest in the Bible had been awakened.

While theology had hardened into the logical system of Quenstedt, men like Lange, Chr. Pfaff, and Bengel had restored biblical exegesis to its rightful place in theological study. The extent of devotional material in the hands of the laity was amazing, and the study of Scripture had been central in the conventicles. The consciousness of the meaning of prayer, discipline, and spiritual growth had been deepened by the self-analysis of the awakened, and an order of salvation was being proclaimed. The institutions at Halle had been imitated elsewhere and the missionary spirit introduced into orthodox thinking. Ziegenbalg in India, Mühlenberg in Pennsylvania, Egede in Greenland, as well as Thomas von Westen in Lappland were all basing their instruction on the Catechism, but a new earnestness had come with Pietism, and the good deeds of faith were not considered separable from justification.

Many and salutary as the fruits were, it must be admitted that Pietism's intense concentration on the religious experience of the individual meant a contraction of the interpretation of the Word of God. The spiritual experience was often expressed in terms of intimacy with the loving Savior whose blessings were personally appropriated. Luther's teaching of a "hidden God" *(Deus absconditus)* who cannot be known but whose awfulness inspires humility and ineffable reverence was lost in pietistic self-analysis. Along with this attitude went a withdrawal from and condemnation of the "world." The salvation of one's own soul was so paramount that Pietism had no understanding of the salvation of the world for which Christ died. The gap between the church and the world, caused by the development of a secular culture and state, was widened by the withdrawal of Pietist conventicles into their own associations as they waited for the end of the world.

The Western world, which orthodoxy had tried to hold together by encompassing all the estates of society within a religious system, thus fell apart. The new theories of the state, grounding human government on natural law apart from theology, gave man the right to order secular affairs by his own reason. The churches would be left to their own devices. And since the religious experiences of Pietists cut across confessional lines, a fellowship of Christians of various confessions was possible. In state and church a new spirit of toleration was growing — to have profound effects on both.

XIII

NEW IDEAS OF MAN AND SOCIETY

The struggles between churches and nations that filled so much of the history of the 16th and early 17th centuries caused thoughtful men to ponder the question of the relationship of religion to government. Was it right to demand uniformity in faith, and were states justified in waging war to determine religious matters?

Jacob Acontius, an Italian who belonged to the Dutch Reformed Church, had advocated in a work of 1565 that a distinction be made between the principal doctrines necessary for salvation and those which were secondary and not basic enough to divide Christians. This distinction was taken over by an English writer, Richard Baxter, whose writings were read throughout Protestant Europe. A French author concerned himself with the problem that arose when the king was of one faith, the people of another. Who was to decide? The anonymous author became famous through his work *Against Tyrants*. In it he argued that the power to decide lies fundamentally with the people, whose relationship to the king is one of contract. Individuals might not resist the government but officials could resist the king. Herein lay a theory of great consequence, for it challenged the right of kings to rule their subjects as they pleased. Later it would be put into practice in the Netherlands and Scotland.

NEW POLITICAL THEORIES

From a different direction the absolutism of royalty was challenged. Roman Catholic thinkers too held that the king's power came not from God but from the people. The Jesuit theologians Robert Bellarmine and Francisco Suarez claimed that the kings were set to meet the needs of the people, whose rights were based on natural law. But they claimed further that kings were under the pope, who alone held his sovereignty from God. Kings dealt with secular affairs but were responsible to

171

a higher power than the people. The Calvinist theologians also considered the state responsible in a religious sense, not to the pope but directly to God.

The idea of a secular power independent of the church was to grow in France, where a succession of religious wars ravaged the nation. Jean Bodin was not sure whence the state derived its power to rule, but he was sure that only that government which was strong enough to rule deserved the name of a sovereign state. The government might reside in the king, estates, or a popular body; but whatever its form, it must dominate all other bodies within it, even the church. As a matter of national policy a state should tolerate religious differences.

In Johannes Althusius the separation of state from religion was complete, except that the natural law on which the independence of the state rested was interpreted as the Second Table of the Commandments. The people as a whole were the source of authority. The ruler was responsible as under a contract, and lower magistrates might resist the king. Most famous of the political thinkers who wrestled with the problem of church and state was Hugo Grotius. Although he too found the base of government, both national and international, in a law of nature known by all men, that law was from God. As scientists were studying the workings of the laws of nature in other realms, he wanted to make law, national and international, an exact science. Laws and governments must be just, and rulers and people were subject to justice. While Grotius, himself a Christian, thought of justice in religious terms, the development of the idea was to be in the direction of a justice determined by human reason apart from God. Here was the beginning of the modern state, which members of society set up for their own interest and security and which makes laws — "a mortal God" (Hobbes).

Through Samuel von Pufendorf these ideas were introduced into Germany and applied to the church by him and his followers, especially Christian Thomasius. Political theory was to concern itself with earthly matters, apart from theology, which taught about a heavenly life. Lutheran theologians called this a pagan method, for it cut the connection between the demands of God and the demands of society. More than this, it placed the state over the church, for the state was to supervise the religious organizations of its people if they were of different faiths and govern for them if all were of one faith. In theory the church had

172

the right to formulate its belief and order its worship, but in practice the government through its appointment of church officials could exercise control of religion.

New Ideas of Church Unity

The church was so weakened by its own divisions that it could not resist the growing secularization of the state. Georg Calixtus, a professor at the University of Helmstedt, had studied in France, England, and the Netherlands and had been impressed by the new ideas being proclaimed. As against the claims of orthodoxy, Calixtus held that the unity of all churches could be attained if agreement were required only on the main articles of the creed. He thought that these had been clearly determined in the first five centuries of the Christian era and therefore advocated a return to the theology of this age. Instead of defending a system of doctrine, he advocated an analytical method that would consider theology as material for investigation. His irenic spirit was welcomed by the universities, which were tired of theological strife, and his disciples soon filled chairs in many of the schools. He was not interested in parish life or common people but hoped to win the aristocratic leaders back to religion. They were attracted by his tolerance, but it only deepened their own indifference or weakened their faith in the church. Indeed in many cases it stimulated a return to Rome, which could claim to hold the theology of the early centuries. August of Saxony, John Frederick of Hanover, and Anton Ulrich of Brunswick were among the prominent converts to Rome, and in Sweden even the daughter of Gustavus Adolphus, Queen Christina, renounced her faith and throne and moved to Italy. The conversion of rulers met with great popular antagonism, indicating that orthodoxy had shaped the beliefs of the people.

Political motives mixed with the religious, but the idea of a reconciliation between the Protestants and Rome still lived on. In 1645 the king of Poland and the Calvinist elector of Saxony arranged for a colloquy at Thorn, though without results. Among the educated the views of Calixtus that the differences between the churches were not significant made for a spirit that decried animosity. Preachers were cautioned to cease attacks on each other's faith. Among those who refused to bow to the ruler's demands was Paul Gerhardt, who was deposed from office.

173

In their defense of orthodoxy the leaders realized that they were against the spirit of the times and sometimes went to extremes in resisting the teachings of the opposition. Erdmann Neumeister, the pastor of Hamburg, was so bitter in his anti-Calvinism that the *Rat* had to quiet him. Abraham Calovius, professor at Wittenberg, made theology almost synonymous with the Confessions and Luther equal with revelation. Valentin Loescher, professor at Leipzig and superintendent at Dresden, in his religious journal — the first — attacked both the disciples of Calixtus and Spener but was driven to a seeming defense of even "godless" preachers provided they were "orthodox." Loescher became opposition leader to the plan of the Prussian Prince Frederick II to unite the Evangelicals in Brandenburg. This plan of making religion subservient to the government followed ideas taught in France, whose thought and manners were imitated in Berlin. The orthodox were fighting a losing battle not only because of new ideas. The revocation of the Edict of Nantes (1685) caused over 300,000 French Protestants to emigrate in the next 15 years. By 1700 some 25,000 had been welcomed in Brandenburg. With the defection of the Saxon ruler, the elector of Brandenburg and king of Prussia — a Calvinist — was looked on as the titular head of German Protestantism. Orthodoxy was giving way to a spirit deeply affected by the teachings of Spener and Zinzendorf, Calixtus and Pufendorf.

A NEW PHILOSOPHY

But more threatening than these forces within the evangelical churches was a new movement of thought that would undermine the church itself, if not religion. About the time the Thirty Years' War broke out René Descartes had a vision that was to influence all European thinking. He had received a Jesuit education and became a brilliant mathematician. Impressed by the certainty and definiteness of the method of mathematics he came to believe that its way was the way to demonstrate truth. The night of Nov. 10, 1619, he was entranced by the idea that all knowledge could be expressed in the terms of relationship used in algebra and geometry. Indeed to think in these terms was the glory of the mind — "I think, therefore I am." He exempted from this formula the idea of God, thought itself, and the idea of extension — the property of bodies. These were comprehended by direct intuition. They were pure ideas, not objects of empirical reality. Outside of these,

174

however, all ideas were to be known by the mind in practical experience of the senses. This knowledge was in terms of mathematical proof, and only that which was so verifiable was truth.

Descartes made doubt a principle — everything was to be doubted until the mind had satisfied itself of its truth. The mind would therefore construct its own universe. He separated the mind from the body — the mind knows, the body is known. While he conceded the necessary existence of God, the result of his philosophy was to make the human mind determine the nature of God. His followers divided into two groups. One went on to construct a universe of the mind, another went in the direction of making the material universe a substitute for God. In French materialism the mind was lost; in English spiritualism the body was lost. Man became a machine even though he reflected on its movements. In his reflection on himself man became psychological, and a new science of self-consciousness made man the center of all truth. If there is an order or goal in the life of man, he himself discovers it and even creates it. Using Descartes' own method, it was natural that man would deny his innate ideas. Since God and the mind could not be proved, they did not exist except in the minds of some. Others, such as Baruch Spinoza, identified God with the order found by the mind, while John Locke defended himself against the charge of atheism by claiming that if the idea of God was innate, there could be no atheists.

A New Theology

For theology the new philosophy created serious problems. The Christian doctrine of revelation was challenged. Reason was enthroned as the source of knowledge. To begin with, the break was softened by a traditional respect for Scripture, and Descartes had excluded the idea of God from man's determination of truth. The philosopher Leibniz sought to reconcile theology and philosophy. A theistic view was necessary for an absolute world view. Christianity was the purest religion, the world the best possible. The differences between the churches were less important than that which all religion taught, namely, love to God. The function of reason was to prove that revelation is of God. Baron Christian von Wolff, a contemporary of Francke at Halle, was of kindred mind to Leibniz. Convinced of the superiority of the new mathematical and scientific method, he wanted to apply it to those articles

175

of religion which were clearly known by reason. He distinguished between these and the truth that was given man by revelation, but even the latter could not be opposed to man's reason.

While Wolff had been driven from Halle by the Pietists, they had in reality prepared the way for his teaching. For by their criticism of dogma and the church, their concentration on the feelings of the individual, and their use of the Bible the Pietists had made room for a subjective, psychological ("practical"), view of Christianity. Wolff was a devout man. He hoped to prove the reasonableness of Christianity in the spirit of Locke, but no one could control the current toward rationalism once the old beliefs were weakened. Johann Semler (1725 to 1791), also a Halle professor, judged all dogmas as speculative. He turned his attention to the study of the Bible and history. The Bible was like any other book and to be investigated by reason, which was interested in the formation of the Biblical canon but not in miracles or prophecies. He distinguished between a personal religion that each man freely formed for himself and a public religion that the government could regulate for the sake of good order and decent conduct. Johann Mosheim set himself to write an objective history of the church; Johann Ernesti and Johann Michaelis made the New and Old Testaments their study. Each sought a better understanding of Christianity and the Bible but was drawn more to the human elements than to the idea of revelation.

On such a basis the church could hardly endure, and the philosopher Lessing set an example for the learned to turn away from theology to literature, art, and philosophy. His satire made the conservative pastor Johan Goeze of Hamburg ridiculous in cultural circles. Truth, according to Lessing, cannot rest on temporary events of history. It must be based on the eternal verities of reason. Sin, grace, inspiration, revelation, atonement, miracles — all were derided. The Christian religion was something different from the religion of Christ, whose teachings had at least a historic, at most a moral importance.

In France rationalism was made popular by the writings of Rousseau and Voltaire. The naturalism of the one and the skepticism of the other were widely diffused in literature and in cultural circles. Rationalism in England took on the form of deism. There was a supreme being but not a personal God, and the universe operated on laws which could be discovered by man, as Newton had found the law of gravity, Galileo and Kepler and Brahe the laws governing the planets and stars. In Germany the movement emphasized the idealistic more that the materialistic side, and a strong religious heritage colored the writings of Herder, the poetry of Schiller and Goethe, and the philosophy of Kant. Kant subjected the mind to a penetrating analysis, attempting to show its powers and its limitations. His ethical integrity posited a religious imperative to duty which man could not escape, but his religon was confined within the limits of pure reason.

Low Estate of Church

The intellectual revolution made the latter half of the 18th century a period of confusion and religious decline. The training of the clergy suffered, a large part receiving little university training. The dominant interest in economics, agriculture, and commerce made the pastor's position one of community leadership in secular affairs and public health. In the rural regions the pastor was subject to the demands of a people less and less interested in church and sacraments. The festive rites were turned into social events — baptisms, confirmations, marriages, burials being transferred from the sanctuary to the homes. There was much ado about instruction but little preparation of teachers, though the name of Pestalozzi emerges in this period. For all the talk about reason the times show an astounding interest in the secrecies of societies, especially Masonry. The liturgical life of the church was at a low ebb. In general the cultured class looked condescendingly on the ministry. A rising interest in philanthropic programs — the care of the sick, the poor, and the prisoners — ran parallel to rather than through the churches. Indifference marked the age as much as tolerance, and government regulation of the church was taken for granted. But even this had its limits, as the attempts of Frederick of Prussia to enforce either union or conformity in Brandenburg demonstrated.

Rationalism and Biblical Faith

The gradual adoption of reason as authoritative was considered an enlightening of man in his search for truth and gave to the movement the name of the Enlightenment in contrast to the enlightening that orthodoxy had attributed to the Holy Spirit. In reaction to the new fashion of thought, theologians such as Wolff and Semler conceded the place of reason, and the term "neology" was applied to this school. But as the more radical teachers discarded much of traditional theology, like Hermann Reimarus, author of the *Wolfenbütler Fragmente,* conservative teachers advanced the claims of revelation in matters beyond reason. The term "supranaturalists" describes men who insisted that the Scriptures brought to mankind what the mind of man could not contrive and urge that there is a truth above the natural with which reason can deal. Gottlob Storr († 1805) at Tübingen and Franz Reinhard († 1812) at Wittenberg and Dresden denied that the Bible could be dissected into the essential and the nonessential. In Württemberg a pupil of Bengel, F. C. Oetinger († 1782), interpreted the Bible from the viewpoint of redemption, and J. J. Hess († 1828) of Zurich indicated the unique purpose of Scripture. They were later followed by teachers who renewed faith in revelation.

The trend of the times, however, was in the direction of a complete rationalism that felt itself competent to decide what in Scripture conformed to man's estimate of reasonableness. And the temptation of theology was to yield to the distinction between the natural and the supernatural, thus falling victim to the dominance of the natural. Theologians such as Johann Roehr († 1848), H. E. Gottlob Paulus († 1851), and Julius Wegscheider († 1849) made of Christianity a "natural" religion even though they used the Bible and spoke of God, virtue, and immortality.

Underneath the superficiality, the materialism, and the skepticism of the age of reason there were, however, currents of Biblical faith and true religion. These were fed by persistent traditions of orthodox reliance on the Word of God, by earnest love for a crucified and risen Christ — the center of the pietistic message — and even by the unconquerable confidence of the Moravians in the missionary strength of a communion of believers. In the study of the Bible and devotional literature, in the use of prayer books and hymnals, a faith lived on that asked for no endorsement by philosophy or cultured aristocracy. As the churches became tools of secular governments and societies of likeminded individuals, the church was still being confessed by men and women who found enlightenment and strength in obedience to the call of God in Word and Sacrament.

178

From Wolff's lectures at Halle Danish students brought the ideas of the Enlightenment back to Denmark. Some of them had already been spread in broader circles by writings of Pontoppidan. His interest in nature, with its proofs of design only a provident God could have created, had opened the eyes of many to the mysteries of the world around them. With Leibniz and Wolff he held to a God-given revelation, but reason too was a gift whereby to appreciate what was revealed. Students at the University of Copenhagen heard the same message from Rosenstand-Goiske. The atonement was necessary, he held, because of the distance between the ideal and the actual.

A common trait in all these influential thinkers was their belief that they were combatting the atheistic tendency of deism. They were using the arms of reason against those whose reason had driven them to unbelief. This was the case also of the most popular of Scandinavian writers — Ludvig Holberg (1684—1754). Of a long line of ministers in Norway-Denmark and trained in theology, Holberg turned to poetry, drama, and history at the University of Copenhagen, and through his writings did what kings had been unable to do — united Scandinavia, with bonds of interest and admiration. True to his inheritance, he countered attempts by friends in Paris to lead him back to Rome, but his mild rationalism and openness to the world made him critical of Pietism and its aversion to the theater. He never doubted the existence of God, but the historical study of the Bible caused doubts as to its uniqueness. Pierre Bayle's *Dictionary* had a great attraction for him. He fought for tolerance but was unwilling to extend it to those who threatened the power of the state. He both represented and helped create the intellectual climate of his day in Denmark. That spirit was evident also in Ove Guldberg, who rose to power in the government. A Pietist in his youth, Guldberg followed Goiske. His spiritual temper appeared in the books he wrote for the crown prince — one on "Natural Religion," another on "Revealed Religion" — and in a hymnbook of 1778 that included hymns of Klopstock.

The effect of the new movement on the life of the church can be traced in the careers of N. E. Balle and Christian Bastholm. Balle was a supranaturalist who hoped to retain the old in adopting the new. His doctrinal textbook of 1791 followed an orthodox outline, but the major emphasis was on the moral virtues. Likewise his *Evangelical Christian Hymnbook* of 1798 managed to leave out all mention of the devil, of judgment, or of Christ as God — the First Article of the Creed supplied most themes.

Bastholm, the most admired preacher of his generation and author of a textbook on preaching, expressed himself in 1785 on the nature of worship in a proposed *Liturgy*. The service should be short, interesting, moving. Material from the Old Testament or confessional dogmatics should be omitted. Only hymns of praise ought to be sung. The Lord's Supper should not be a part of the service but a separate action, and in rural districts a sermon could be replaced by catechization. Bastholm shared the notion that only city pastors needed a university education. In the country they should busy themselves with agriculture, medicine, and the economy of the people. In fact the main need of the church was to educate the common people in their role. Bastholm's *Liturgy* never materialized, for Balle succeeded in having it rejected. Balle, bishop of Seeland after a professorship at Copenhagen, became the champion of a Biblical Christianity. His textbook replaced Pontoppidan, and his sermons won support among the people if not among the "moderns."

Church attendance declined generally, and the closing decade of the 18th century was one of spiritual poverty. While the status of the clergy fell, their efforts in the economic improvement of the land must be acknowledged. It may seem strange that they should teach their parishioners how to raise potatoes, vaccinate against smallpox, and care for their livestock, but the foundation of Danish prosperity was being laid. In 1788 the peasants won freedom, and in 1792 Denmark became the first nation to forbid slavery in its colonies. Seminaries for teachers were established in Schleswig in 1781 and a decade later in Copenhagen, thereby raising the standards of the people's schools. Nor were evidences of a deeper religious interest lacking. Not only did the people follow Balle in rejecting the excesses of the Enlightenment in the proposed *Agenda*, or *Liturgy*, but in Schleswig the congregations rebelled against the rationalism of J. G. Adler's *Agenda* of 1796.

After the French Revolution the government forbade the bitter attacks that had been common in pamphlet form against the church and the clergy. The tolerant attitude of the authorities had permitted a Herrnhut colony to become settled in Christiansfeld, and its emissaries carried encouragement to scattered groups of faithful in all parts of Denmark. A laymen's revival, led by Peter Lauersen and Peder Frandsen, finally forced the government to give back to them Pontoppidan and Kingo in place of Balle's books. A new century would see new springs of spiritual life welling forth.

IN NORWAY AND ICELAND

The political union of Norway and Denmark was matched by similar religious developments, though Norway's distance from the centers of rationalism saved it from the more radical tendencies. The positive elements of the Enlightenment served Norway in promoting its own self-consciousness. Foremost among its representatives were bishops. John Ernest Gunnerus, bishop of Trondheim, born in Norway, educated at Jena, and teacher at Copenhagen, was Wolffian in his desire to defend Christianity. Natural religion and morality were inadequate to meet human sin. The atonement was necessary, as was a revelation of God beyond the ability of reason. The Swedish naturalist Carl von Linné had inspired in him an interest in nature, an interest he cultivated on his visitation tours into northern Norway and which made him a pioneer in the botany and zoology of that region. His cultural leadership was evident also in the organization in 1760 of a literary-scientific society in Trondheim.

Peder Hansen, bishop of Kristiansand, went beyond Gunnerus and followed closely in the steps of Bastholm. Neither miracles nor the Bible itself impressed reason, but the teachings of Jesus had an immediate effect. The Old Testament had no religious value; the New Testament was written in accommodation to the cultural level of its times. The sacraments had meaning only for the untutored. Hansen represented the length to which the movement went in Norway. Nordahl Brun, bishop of Bergen, remained more orthodox, though he attempted to explain miracles in accord with reason. The period was marked by an increasing attention to education and the care of the sick, especially by Hansen. Bishop Gunnerus agitated for a university in Norway, but the time was not yet ripe.

Interest in native history, flora, and fauna characterized the church also in Iceland. The two bishop Jonssons, Finnur the father and Hannes the son, explored the origins, the language, and the history of Iceland. The history of the Icelandic Church by the father became fundamental. A jurist, Magnus Stephensen, succeeded despite opposition to get a new hymnbook in the spirit of the Enlightenment adopted in 1801, and Balle's text in doctrine was introduced. In 1802 both of the old bishoprics were merged into one and moved to Reykjavik.

IN SWEDEN

The 17th century had been one of martial glory for Sweden — in the 18th its heroes were intellectual. More than in any other Lutheran land the Church of the Reformation was able to maintain its freedom and develop in a way that conserved old as well as adapted new qualities.

Olof von Dalin served as a Swedish Holberg, though more religiously conservative. His *Swedish Argus* of 1732—1734 introduced through translation the currents then predominant in England and France. In literary circles his satire of both orthodox and pietistic characteristics set a tone, but his supranaturalism saved him from the excesses of French rationalism. He found a means of expressing his tolerance and latitudinarianism in his influential work, *History of Sweden.*

An even greater influence was Emanuel Swedenborg. Son of the orthodox but tolerant Bishop Jesper Svedberg of Skara, Emanuel developed interests in many directions. In England he studied Newton, empiricism, and mysticism; in Germany, Wolff and rationalism. His scientific inquiries extended to geology, neurology, and cosmology. He drew from mystical wells as diverse as Herrnhut, Dippel, the Kabala, and Boehme. The Bible remained central in his thought, which spiraled upward from a natural to a spiritual and a divine height, using allegory and "correspondence" to win the contents of *True Religion,* published in London in 1772. His spirit penetrated into a hidden world of angels and visions which he described in his *Arcana coelestia,* purporting to be the concealed truth in Genesis and Exodus. The resultant new rationalistic-mystic religion denied such fundamental doctrines as the Trinity and the Atonement, but did include a final judgment and eternal life in which the ethical life of man found its justification. Swedenborg had no part in the founding of the Church of the New Jerusalem organized by his admirers in London, but his keen insight into the work-

182

ings of the mind, with a strong moral and mystical emphasis, left a deep impression on several generations of pastors in Sweden.

Science had a strong hold on Swedish intellectuals. At Uppsala Anders Celsius and Samuel Klingenstierna made the faculty famous, putting theology in the background. In defense Nils Wallerius of the theological faculty sought to use the new philosophy in proof of the articles of religion. Celsius the astronomer was a skeptic, but the chemists Bergman and Scheele were personally devout. The admiration even of theological students centered, however, on another scientist, the botanist Carl von Linné. He came from an orthodox parsonage where his thought had been shaped by the Bible, Arndt, Scriver, Haffenreffer, and Pontoppidan. The latter led the way by the light of nature to the light of Scripture. Even when he left theology for botany and medicine Linné held to a faith in revelation. God was hidden, but He could be followed in His works, and like Swedenborg, Linné felt his call was to make God known. It was God's majesty rather than His forgiving love that seemed central to Linné, and a certain fear of the "nemesis" of wrong followed him. Holberg's moralism was reflected in Linné's emphasis on right action in order to avoid God's punishment. God's providence impressed him in his study of nature, which was more empirical than speculative. He read the Bible constantly and was faithful in worship. His influence on students was profound. He served the ministry especially by aiding orthodox ministers to use the knowledge of nature in the service of God. He raised up a host of students of nature, but in Sweden these beheld a glory of God in creation rather than an idolization of the reason of the beholder.

The period between Charles XII († 1718) and Gustavus III (crowned 1771) was one in which the estates rather than the king ruled. As an estate of the realm the clergy were involved in the politics of the contending parties, and their fortunes rose or fell with their party. The strength of the bishops saved the church from the subservience the German churches suffered under their governments. Voltaire had followers in Sweden, and caricature of the church went beyond Holberg and Dalin. But when Sweden in 1766 passed the first European ordinance for the freedom of the press there was a reservation against antireligious literature.

In 1757 a far-reaching redistribution of lands caused great changes

183

in the parish life, and the corruption of party politics made 1760 a low point in social morality. Nor did the accession of the French-inclined Gustavus III mean aid to the church. There was a growing feeling for the need of more beauty in architecture and worship, vestments, and clerical dress. But it was an aesthetic rather than a religious interest, and freely discarded old altars, fonts, reredoes, and spires, and white-washed pictured church walls. In 1781 a Tolerance Edict that theo-retically announced religious freedom practically restricted it to for-eigners in Sweden, who were excluded from public office. Herrnhut congregations were permitted, but not their organization into a national body. The orthodox church party, headed by several members of the gifted Benzelius family in the archbishopric of Uppsala, was able to guard what it considered the rights of the church in the face of the opposition of secular and rationalistic groups. As in Germany and Den-mark, the literary circles fostered skepticism or a vague deism, but the majority of the population were in rural parishes where a different spirit prevailed.

Even in Stockholm the pietistic preaching of Anders Rutstrom and Peter Murbeck drew crowds. But throughout the mass of Christian people the spiritual guide was the postil of Anders Nohrborg. After only a few years of ministry in Stockholm Nohrborg died in 1767 at the age of 42. But he left a collection of sermons that were read for the next century. Following an "order of salvation," an orthodox pro-gram, but filling it with pietistic ardor, Nohrborg produced a book of spiritual instruction and edification that did more to keep faith alive than any neological defense. In Gothenburg his *ordo salutis* became the basis of the psychological teaching of Henric Schartau. Likewise the works of Michael Fant and Sven Baelter conserved Lutheran teaching by acknowledging some of the newer interests and exhibiting pietistic warmth. Herrnhut emotionalism found expression also in the newer poets of Sweden — Hedvig Nordenflycht and Bengt Lidner — while something of Rousseau found echo in Oxenstierna. A group of hymnists introduced the note of God's revelation in nature: Samuel Ödmann, F. M. Franzén, and Johan Olof Wallin — names of importance in the next generation.

The conflicts within the church may be traced in the efforts to secure a revision of the official books which in Sweden, unlike Germany, were adopted for the whole nation. Bishop Jacob Serenius, an advocate of improved instruction and the first to introduce confirmation in his diocese of Strängnäs wanted a translation of the Bible in more modern language. A commission was set up in 1773, but its progress was very slow. He found less interest in a revision of the Catechism than in that of a new hymnbook. Proposals were ready in 1793 when the Swedish Church celebrated the bicentennial of the Uppsala Decree, but diverse judgments prevented any adoption. The king's desire for a handbook in the style of Bastholm was not met.

Indicative of the meeting of the old and the new was the career of Anders Knös. The Uppsala theological faculty had been disturbed by his doctoral dissertation on natural and revealed religion. But Knös was a Biblical Pietist of the Arndt type. At first he had been attracted to the Herrnhut preaching but was repelled by Zinzendorf's excesses and later found himself at home with Württemberg piety and practice. This was evident in his *Institutions of Practical Theology* of 1768. When criticized by the orthodox, he fell back on a Biblical defense. Yet he gave to justification a nonorthodox interpretation, stressing what happens in man rather than God's act of forgiveness. As dean of Skara, Knös exerted deep influence on his pastors, and he must be reckoned as a leader in a return to the study of the Bible and of Luther. His relationship to Württemberg suggests an important connection between the Lutheran character of the church there to that of Sweden.

In Finland

Finland, like Norway, felt fewer effects of the rationalistic factors of the Enlightenment. A new interest in nature characterized all the Scandinavian countries. Johan Brovallius, bishop of Abo from 1749 to 1755, was an admirer of Newton and Linné and knew the writings of Bacon and Wolff. Before becoming bishop he was a professor of physics and divided his attention between Finnish flora and a new translation of the Bible. Karl Mennander, who proceeded Brovallius in the bishopric of Abo, was also a follower of Linné and sponsored a series of doctoral dissertations in natural history. Besides his concern for the health of his people he explored folk poetry and wrote a history of ecclesiastical councils in Finland. Jacob Riif gained recognition in church building, and Michael Topelius became known as a mural

185

painter. Organs multiplied but old altars and sculptures disappeared. The pastors in Finland, as elsewhere, were leaders in welfare programs of their communities and as owners of land gave time to economic and health conditions of the peasantry. Henrik Gabriel Porthan, an Abo professor and cultural leader, edited the first Finnish newspaper in 1771. Parsonages were the centers of learning, and a good standard of living was common among the higher clergy, who were often found with officials and the military in the membership of lodges, the first of which was established in Finland in 1756. As in Sweden, Pietist groups maintained themselves. Nohrborg was widely read. In Abo a Herrnhut congregation provided a base for the later revivals of Henry Renquist, in whose library was the English writer Arthur Dent's *True Conversion.*

Of great future significance was the religious interest latent among the laity and fanned into flame by popular leaders. Such leaders included women: Lisa Ericsdotter, who also read Dent and excited ecstatic groups in the year of the Lisbon earthquake (1755), and Anna Rogel, a friend of church and clergy. Often these Finnish revivals crossed over into northern Sweden. Bang-Karin carried on in the Härnosand region of Sweden with visions and impulses of the spirit. Characteristic of the revivals in Finland was their lay leadership that lived on Biblical and devotional literature and was little affected by the currents of speculation in higher intellectual altitudes.

XIV

MISSION AND MIGRATION

The charge sometimes made that in the 16th, 17th, and 18th centuries the Church of the Reformation showed no interest in missions is no longer considered valid, for the Reformation itself was a tremendous mission effort opposed by formidable forces. Not only did it mean a reinterpretation of the work of the church but in many regions it brought a deepened sense of the Christian faith to people whose conversion from paganism had been very superficial. Nor should it be forgotten that in the 16th century knowledge about the people of the earth was still limited. A survey of the continents by Philipp Nicolai in 1599 actually seemed to imply that the message of Christ had penetrated everywhere. The missionary journeys of the Jesuits, who had reached India, Japan, China, and the new world, were known. In Asia they found remnants of older Christian communities which seemed to confirm the idea that the apostles had fulfilled the commission of bringing the Word to all countries.

Roman Catholic and Protestant Missions

That the Jesuits rather than the Evangelicals should have carried the message of Christ to newly found continents has an obvious explanation. Fighting for their very existence, the followers of Luther and Calvin had neither men nor means for exploration of foreign lands. Furthermore, the discovery of new continents came before the Reformation, and the hemispheres were divided by the pope between Spain and Portugal. Their sailors, soldiers, and missionaries ruled the new lands and guarded them against encroachments by either political or spiritual rivals.

The Reformation took place in the interior of Europe, in countries without sea power or hemmed in by Catholic powers. But as England and Holland challenged the Spanish fleets and gained supremacy, a new era dawned, and their churches were soon sending ministers all over the earth. Denmark and Sweden joined them in the newly won lands. Once the way was open, the Evangelicals engaged in mission work no less than the emissaries of Rome.

In those years governments were involved in missions. Jesuit missionaries followed Portuguese sailors and Spanish and French soldiers. In the evangelical countries the administration of the churches was in the hands of government officials — a missionary project would have to be a state undertaking. Since the king felt a responsibility for the church, he became interested in the expansion of the church when his domain expanded. And so the early Lutheran missions were a church-state venture.

SWEDISH MISSIONS — LAPPLAND — ON THE DELAWARE

In Sweden Gustavus Vasa already before 1560 had been interested in work among the Lapps, and his successors laid the obligation on Swedish pastors along the coast of the Baltic to make regular visits to these nomads. During the rule of Gustavus Adolphus the archbishop of Uppsala made a visitation tour to the northlands and directed the dean at Pitea to provide literature and schools as well as worship for the Lapps. The first Lapp books were ready in 1619, and a school at Lycksela in 1632 became the center for the mission. Norway too had an interest in Lappland, and a pietist-inspired pastor, Thomas von Westen, became known as the apostle to the Lapps. Through men whom he won for church work, a school that he founded, and his own three missionary journeys he gained wide attention for Lappland. Sweden intensified its efforts. Pehr Fjellstrom, son and grandson of Lapp missionary pastors, gave the Lapps a literary language and in 1755 a New Testament in that language. He was aided by Pehr Högstrom, who in 1742 became the first rector in Gällivare. Similar activity went on around the borders of Finland under the direction of the bishops of Abo (Turku) and Borga (Porvoo) as land was won from the Russians. We are justified in considering the missions among Lapps and Finns as the Christianization of regions hitherto pagan. And while the governments had political reason for their concern, it is to their credit that ecclesiastical matters were an integral part of their programs.

How natural a part the church played is exemplified in the first Lutheran venture into the New World. Through their relationships with the Dutch the Swedish rulers gained access to the Western seas. When the Swedish colony was settled on the banks of the Delaware in 1638, clergymen came along. Most of them returned after a short stay, only one remaining after the colony fell to the Dutch of New Amsterdam in 1655. Johan Campanius, who was there from 1643 to 1648, took time to learn the language of the Indians around the Delaware and made a translation of Luther's Small Catechism into their language, though it did not appear in print until 1696 in Stockholm. When William Penn became the owner of Pennsylvania in 1682, there were about a thousand Lutherans in the Swedish congregations. For another hundred years the Church of Sweden, under the bishop of Skara, supplied these emigrants with pastors, Bibles, hymnbooks, and catechisms.

The churches in Philadelphia and Wilmington still stand as witnesses of the ordered, orthodox faith maintained under the rules of the Church of Sweden until the change of language and customs brought them into the Episcopal Church shortly after the Revolution. "Our priest," the governor wrote back to the Swedish chancellery in the 1640s, "is vested with a chasuble and differs in all manners from the sects surrounding us." A century later the Swedish High Mass was still being intoned when Henry Melchior Mühlenberg, another Lutheran missionary, came to this province. Names of pastors such as Campanius, Rudman, Björk, Acrelius, and Wrangel belong in the story of evangelical missions.

LUTHERAN MIGRATION TO NORTH AMERICA

While the Church of Sweden was sending ministers to the church on the Delaware, the Lutheran consistory at Amsterdam was receiving communications from Lutherans on the Hudson. The Church of Holland was Calvinistic, and no other church had legal sanction. But the Dutch were becoming a world power. For purposes of industry and trade they welcomed artisans of other countries and winked at the existence of non-Reformed religious groups. In Amsterdam alone were some 35,000 Lutherans, and the Dutch East India and West India companies enrolled many of them in their ventures. Thus Lutherans were among their colonists on the Hudson, in Manhattan, and in Albany. In 1649 some of the leaders petitioned the Amsterdam Lutheran consistory for a pastor. When, however, Johannes Gutwasser, a Saxon theological student, was willing to go to America and was ordained by the Amsterdam consistory, the Dutch in Manhattan refused to allow him to conduct services. The colony was even more intolerant than the mother country.

Not until the English took over the Dutch power in New York in 1664 could Lutheran pastors gain entrance. When the Amsterdam church found a new candidate, it is indicative of the international situation of the time that he was a Lutheran pastor driven out of Upper Hungary by the Turks and that he numbered among the people organizing the congregations in New York and Albany in 1668 German, Dutch, Danish, Frisian, Norwegian, Swedish, and Polish nationalities. After 1688 Holland no longer felt obligated to supply the American churches. In 1701 they were served by Pastor Andrew Rudman of the Swedish Delaware church. In 1703 he ordained at a service in Philadelphia a German Pietist student, Justus Falckner, for the New York Lutherans.

There were Germans in Pennsylvania and New York who had left the desolated regions of their mother country after the Thirty Years' War. The ravages of the French along the Rhine drove many out of the Palatinate. They fled to the New World via London, where the German court preachers and Queen Anne sought to help them. In 1709 over 10,000 encamped in England, hoping for transportation. One group was given lands around Newburgh on the Hudson where their pastor Joshua von Kocherthal accompanied them. After Kocherthal's death Justus Falckner ministered to them, but the leader of the Hudson Valley Lutherans was William Berkenmeyer, a theological student from Hamburg and ordained by the Amsterdam pastors. He was assisted by Michael Knoll of Holstein, whom the Lutherans in London ordained, and John August Wolf, sent by the Hamburg consistory. These men represented an orthodoxy dominant in northern Germany and gave to the New York congregations a clear Lutheran identity in their confused religious environment.

Before long the stream of German immigration turned to Pennsylvania. Many came from New York, others from Europe. Of the Palatinate exiles the English government directed some to North Carolina, and many of these went on into Virginia. Though without spiritual guidance from Europe, these early colonists often possessed gifted leaders. Anthony Jacob Henkel had been court preacher in Saxony but left the country in 1717 when Duke Maurice became Roman Catholic. Himself founder of congregations near Philadelphia, he became the ancestor of a line of Lutheran pastors who ministered in Virginia, North Carolina, Kentucky, Indiana, and Missouri. Their printing plant in New Market, Virginia, became a center for the publishing of orthodox Lutheran literature, even the Book of Concord. The John Caspar Stoevers — father and son — were untiring missionaries in the middle colonies where by mid-18th century dwelt over a hundred thousand Germans.

Lutherans from the Palatinate found homes also in South Carolina. A colony from Württemberg settled in Virginia. In Georgia a renowned group founded the Ebenezer community near Savannah. This was the colony of Salzburgers driven from their homes in Bavaria in 1731 because of persecution by a Catholic archbishop. Their plight attracted the attention of Europe, and the English General Oglethorpe gave them a home in his Georgia possessions. By 1741 their numbers exceeded a thousand. Two pastors from Halle served them, John M. Boltzius and Israel C. Gronau. With help from Europe they maintained their congregations until the colony was dispersed by the tensions of the Revolutionary War.

Most influential of the emigrant pastors or missionaries from Europe was Henry Melchior Mühlenberg. In their desolation German Lutherans in Pennsylvania had written to Halle for help. Francke and the court preacher in London, Frederick Ziegenhagen, at length responded by sending Mühlenberg, who was known to Francke and trusted by him since his days at Halle. Born in Hanover and well educated at Zellerfeld and Göttingen, he had taught at Francke orphanages and had been interested in mission fields. He came to Philadelphia in 1742 at a critical time, for Zinzendorf had preceded him by a year and was setting himself up as supervisor of Lutherans in the colony. Mühlenberg, mildy pietistic but orthodox in his faith, soon established himself as the leader, greatly aided by the close cooperation of the Lutherans in the region. Organization of congregations in eastern Pennsylvania, Maryland, and New Jersey followed rapidly. Doc-

191

trinal teaching was based on the confessional writings of the church, and a liturgical order of service was gradually made uniform. In 1748 a conference of pastors was realized, together with lay representatives of the united congregations, and six ministers joined in ordaining a theological student — following an examination that Francke thought too severe. In these early years Mühlenberg and his associates regularly reported to Halle and considered themselves responsible to European church authorities.

Among the most lasting of Mühlenberg's achievements was the formulation of a congregational constitution in 1762 for St. Michael's of Philadelphia. The constitution became a model for the free Lutheran churches in America. There was no precedent in European Lutheranism where congregations were a part of the state system, but Mühlenberg had learned of independent structures in Amsterdam, New York, and in Georgia Lutheran congregations. He also had the counsel of the Swedish churches, which had long experience in colonial America. A church council of 14 trustees (for life), 6 elders, and 6 deacons (3-year term) was elected by the congregation, the pastors being included among the trustees. This council governed the congregation: the trustees holding and caring for the property; the elders being responsible for pure doctrine, sound discipline, finances, and the supervision of the school; the deacons assisting the pastor at services, maintaining orderly worship, and visiting the sick. A pastor was nominated by the council — after a trial sermon — and was elected by a two-thirds vote of the council and the congregation, or he might be recommended by a European consistory. In 1760 the previous conferences of the united congregations developed into the Evangelical Lutheran Ministerium in North America. In 1792 a revised constitution restricted the title to Pennsylvania and gave the right of vote to lay delegates. By 1771 there were 81 congregations under Mühlenberg's supervision. In 1787 a hymnbook was provided for the congregations. The accepted liturgy was enjoined. The New York Ministerium came into being in 1786. A North Carolina Synod was organized in 1803, and two synods, the Maryland and Virginia and the Tennessee, date from 1820.

Mühlenberg's motto *Ecclesia plantanda* had been realized and an autonomous Lutheran Church organized under his guidance. He was on good terms with Episcopalians and Reformed but never deviated from his course of establishing a self-conscious Lutheranism in the New World. Through him a blending of orthodoxy and Pietism gave character to the new church, repelling the extravagences of Zinzendorf. Only after Mühlenberg's death did the influence of the Enlightenment and the rationalism of Europe appear in the American synods.

Danish Missions in India and West Indies

While Sweden and Germany were aiding, in different ways, to establish evangelical churches on the continent of North America, Denmark was writing a unique chapter in missions elsewhere. In London a German court preacher was instrumental in gaining government support for German emigrants. In Copenhagen another German preacher at court acted as an intermediate in a missionary cause. King Frederick IV of Denmark was concerned about his colony in India, and though the trading company was less interested, the king asked court pastor Julius Lütkens to find men willing to serve Tranquebar, that faraway place on the southeast coast of India. This had been Danish territory since 1624. The company had its chaplains, as customary, but, as also customary, they served the military and officials for a 3-year term, then returned home. The king wanted missionaries to the native populations. Lütkens, a friend of Francke, wrote to fellow pastors in Berlin for nominations since no one in Denmark seemed available. The Berlin pastors nominated Batholomew Ziegenbalg and Heinrich Plütschau, who met with Francke's endorsement. They were ordained in Copenhagen, and in July, 1706, they landed at Tranquebar. The Zion Lutheran Church was already in the colony for the use of Europeans, from whom the missionaries received little help, often active opposition. But Ziegenbalg gave himself to the study of the Tamil language and soon produced a dictionary and a grammar, enabling him to translate the New Testament, the Catechism, hymns, and a service book. A church building named Jerusalem was erected in 1715 with gifts from Europe wherever the Halle reports were read. On a visit to Württemberg in 1715 Ziegenbalg received collections for the mission. The Danish king proved his continuing interest by establishing an annual grant and setting up a board in Copenhagen to cooperate with Halle in the program.

Because of the careful preparation of catechumens for membership, growth was slow. At the time of Ziegenbalg's death in 1719 there were some 250 Christians. A pietistic emphasis on Bible study, prayer, and personal experience was followed. Almost all the missionaries came from Halle. Benjamin Schultz continued the literary work of Ziegenbalg, finishing the Bible translation and also translating the Bible into Hindustani and Telugu. Native pastors were ordained after 1741, and the congregations grew more rapidly. Johann P. Fabricius spent half a century in India, part of the time in Madras, whither the influence of the mission had spread. Fruits of his ministry were a hymnbook and a revision of the Bible translation.

Most famous of the missionaries was the gifted Christian F. Schwartz. He was trained at Halle and spent 48 years in India. He mastered the language of the Tamil people and knew their religions and customs. The English made him chaplain in Trichinopoly. He served their church but retained his status as a Lutheran pastor. The Indian rajah trusted him even to the point of sharing power with him. He won the respect of everyone he associated with. Churches were built and schools organized both for the English and the natives. In time the Tranquebar mission was merged with the English, extending its connections north to Calcutta, east to Ceylon, and south to the tip of India. Rationalism dried up the source of missionaries from Europe, and the Danish board lost interest. The Society for the Propagation of Christian Knowledge of England had given generous support through many decades and gradually took over the control of the Tranquebar field. In 1845 the Danish government sold its property to England. The following year the Copenhagen board turned over the mission property to the Leipzig Missionary Society. When the Church of Sweden later joined the society on the field, there grew up the modern Tamil Evangelical Lutheran Church, thus preserving a bond with the original Tranquebar mission.

The Copenhagen Mission Board also was a sponsor of Thomas von Westen's work among the Lapps and of the Egede mission in Greenland. Again it was a combination of orthodoxy and Pietism that assumed responsibilities for the carrying of the Gospel to foreign lands. Nor should the foundation of the church in the Danish West Indies be overlooked, where at St. Thomas the Frederick Lutheran Church dates from 1666 — a church still in existence.

Mission and migration characterize the history of the Lutherans on the eastern borders of Europe. Here the vicissitudes of war and politics constantly affected the peoples' religious institutions as well as their welfare and survival. The changing currents swirled around the foundations of Austria, Prussia, and Russia; and in their wake names of territories and populations emerged and disappeared along with their churches.

From Alpine regions of Carniola, Carinthia, and Styria the Hapsburg power had extended east, north, and west. In 1526 it had inherited Hungary, but most of this was soon taken from it by the Turks in the days of Luther.

Hungary, like ancient Gaul, was divided into three parts, after the Turkish victory of 1526. The conquered territory was ruled from Buda, and the evangelical churches were allowed considerable freedom in local parishes but forbidden wider relationships. Only the western section remained under Austrian rule. Here the measures of the Counter-Reformation were enforced. Transylvania in the east maintained relative independence, its Magyar princes accepting vassalage under the Turks. The tolerance of this island in Islam was widely known and refugees came from persecuted areas. Lutherans, Calvinists, Socinians, Orthodox, and Roman Catholics managed to live peaceably together. The Magyars were predominant in Hungary and by and large had adopted Calvinism. Despite some losses to the Reformed and the Unitarians the Siebenburg Lutherans held their own. Delegates from 20 chapters — each presided over by a dean — met regularly in a synod. Their orthodoxy made these Lutherans suspicious of Pietists and Moravians, but their own reasonableness tempered their aversion to rationalism.

Changes followed when by 1700 the Turks were finally driven out. Roman bishops and Jesuits looked on the reclaimed territory as a return to pre-Turkish conditions and everywhere harrassed the Evangelicals. Church buildings were forcibly retaken, pastors driven out and exiled, and pressure put on the people to renounce their Protestant faith. As Austrian authorities took over, the Evangelicals defended themselves by referring to treaties and agreements but got little attention, for the emperor in Vienna was under Jesuit domination. The exile of some pastors who were finally made galley slaves in the Mediterranean excited general European resentment. But even rebellion was fruitless, for the leaders were charged with treason. Only the need of settlers for the new lands led the authorities to grant religious privileges to those who came. Immigrants from Württemberg, Hesse, and the Palatinate — some fleeing from other persecutors — settled around Fünfkirchen, making this fertile region a "Swabian Turkey." But even here, and in Transylvania whither a group of Salzburgers took refuge in 1734, the Roman Church held religious freedom to a minimum, granting only a certain number of buildings and pastors and making all of them subservient to Roman episcopal visitation.

AUSTRIA

The Hapsburg power had also stretched northward. Bohemia, Moravia, and Silesia were unwilling subjects ever since the Brethren, the followers of Huss, had fought for a century against the claims of Rome before their cause was endorsed by Luther. Both nobles and people embraced the evangelical doctrine. Vienna could not but recognize their strength as they presented a common front in the Bohemian Confession of 1575. But with the Hapsburg dedication to the Counter-Reformation a new era began. Compelled by the agreement of 1609, the emperors reluctantly tolerated the dissidents until the rebellion in Prague gave Ferdinand an occasion to quell the reforms. The result was the beginning of the Thirty Years' War. The troops of Wallenstein successfully resisted Gustavus Adolphus, and the Peace of Westphalia left the Catholics victorious. Czechs and Germans endured all the force of government oppression of their faith. In 1706 another Swedish king, Charles XII, at a moment of success wrung concessions at Altranstädt for the Silesian Lutherans, who enjoyed enough freedom to maintain their church life. Many from Bohemia and Moravia emigrated south toward the Balkans, north into Brandenburg and Saxony. One group was received in Herrnhut, Saxony, and made famous by Zinzendorf. Another became the nucleus of the Bethlehem Church in Berlin under Pastor Johann Jänicke.

After 200 years the government at Vienna began to realize the futility of its aim to exterminate Protestantism. The climate of the

Enlightenment had nourished also a new spirit of tolerance. In 1781 Emperor Joseph II issued an edict that is a milestone in the life of eastern Europe. It gave joy and hope to all the Evangelicals in Austria-Hungary even though toleration was hedged by restrictions. The Church of Rome retained its old privileges as the church of the state. But Lutherans, Calvinists, and Orthodox were now permitted to build prayer chapels — without towers, bells, or entrances onto a main thoroughfare. Private schools were permitted at the expense of those desiring them. State records were still in the hands of the parish priest of the Roman Church and Roman bishops were to supervise the evangelical clergy. The Evangelicals were to declare their faith publicly by registering with the authorities.

Within two months 73,000 registered in Austria, and the number doubled by the time the lists were closed in 1789. Moravian Brethren registered as Lutherans (the Brethren were not given legal status by the edict). In Bohemia they declared themselves mostly as Calvinists. Calvinists of the Helvetic Confession in Bohemia were more than three times as numerous as the Lutherans, numbering 70,000 souls as compared with 20,000 Lutherans. Upper Silesia had about an equal number of German and Polish Lutherans, around 40,000. Separate organizations divided Lutherans and Calvinists, though before the edict they had much in common as persecuted groups. The emperor appointed seven superintendents — four for the Lutherans, three for the Reformed. Seniors with supervision of some 20 congregations were assistants to the superintendents. In Vienna and Upper Austria the congregations were mainly German, in Bohemia they were Czech, in Moravia and Silesia half were Polish, half Czech and German. The Jesus Christ Church in Teschen, with a capacity of 8,000, became the center of Lutheran work in Austria; after 1867 its school furnished leaders for administration and teachers for parishes throughout the land.

Because of its frontier position Hungary had enjoyed much greater freedom than Austria and counted over 5 million Evangelicals — half of the population. The Edict of 1781 did not therefore cause as drastic a change in policy as in Austria, but it did give a legal foundation not hitherto conceded. The organization of the churches, however, met with delay and dissension, for in Hungary nationalism had created distinctions between Magyars, who were in the main Calvinists, and

197

Slovaks, Slovenes, and Germans. Separate synods combined religious and cultural interests and created tensions between Hungarians, Slavs and Germans.

PRUSSIA

In somewhat the fashion that Austria had added country to country and set itself up as an exponent of Roman Catholicism, the province of Prussia was enlarging itself and emerging as a leader in Protestantism. Saxony had been the staunch defender of Luther and orthodox Lutheranism, but when August II, the Saxon elector, became a Roman Catholic and accepted the Polish throne in 1697, his influence as a Lutheran leader was lost. The elector of Brandenburg gradually acquired surrounding provinces — in the west, lands on the Rhine; in the east, Prussia; in the north, Pomerania — and established the Hohenzollern family on a throne, first at Königsberg, then at Berlin. The Hohenzollerns were Calvinists and welcomed immigrants of other countries to the new Prussian possessions — 25,000 Huguenots came between 1685 to 1700. Mennonites found work in the Baltic coastal areas. Frederick I, the ambitious elector and first Prussian king, had even envisioned a union of England and Holland with German Lutherans but could effect neither this nor a smaller union of Lutherans and other Protestants in his own realm. Among the recipients of royal favor was Francke at Halle, whose institutions received state aid. In all the new territories provision of clergy and church services was carefully observed. The court at Potsdam imitated the more luxurious one at Versailles, and French influence showed itself in the progress of the Enlightenment and rationalism in the German capital. Frederick II became king in 1740 and enlarged Prussia by taking Silesia from Austria and receiving a part of Poland when it was divided between Austria and Russia. By the time of his death in 1786 he had won the title "The Great" and made Prussia the leading Protestant power on the Continent.

POLAND

To the north and east lay a region that tried in vain to preserve identity and independence and whose fate affected the destiny of large numbers of Lutherans. Poland had become a name for a degree of unity that characterized the relations of northern Slavic tribes on the border of the East and the West. Lithuanians and Poles were ruled by magnates who treated their peasants on their vast estates as serfs. The Orthodox Church of Russia opposed the claims of the Roman Catholic Church but lost some of its sees in the Ukraine to Rome. Calvinism was widely accepted, but Lutherans, Bohemian Brethren, and Socinians had been welcomed and a charter of privileges accorded the signers of the Sandomir Consensus of 1570. The son of John III of Sweden became through marriage the first of the Vasa kings in Poland, and while his kinsman Gustavus Adolphus was fighting for the Lutheran faith, Sigismund III was helping the Jesuits make Poland as Roman as the Hapsburgs were making Austria. Their victory was only partial and transient. Orthodox Russia, Protestant Prussia, and Catholic Austria first broke off edges of the country and then in three steps partitioned it among themselves. Prussia got Silesia and Posen (the dukedom of Prussia), Austria took Galicia and Cracow, Russia annexed the kingdom of Poland, with the czar assuming the crown. By the time the Napoleonic wars were over and the Congress of Vienna arranged boundaries in Europe, Russia had taken Finland in 1809, thus completing her conquest of all the Lutheran Baltic lands.

Galicia, the Austrian part of the division, contained Lutheran settlements made up mostly of German immigrants from the Palatinate. As Vienna established ecclesiastical supervision after 1792 over the evangelical churches, it created an additional Lutheran seniorate for Galicia and newly acquired Bukovina, formerly under the Turks. This district existed for a century and the theological faculty at Czernovtsy trained pastors for congregations in Rumania and Siebenbürgen as well as for its own field until the advent of communism extinguished the church here.

In the Polish lands that fell to Prussia the German state church made arrangements for schools and churches. A provincial consistory of Posen operated under the Berlin authorities. Even the plan for a Prussian Union applied to the new territory despite opposition that led some to emigrate.

RUSSIAN LANDS

Quite different was the fate of the churches under Russian rule. After an initial attempt by Russia to govern the Protestants through a common consistory in Warsaw, the supervision was moved to Petrograd. Czar Nicholas gave the Reformed and the Lutherans each a consistory, though around 1865 the Reformed counted less than 10,000, the Lutherans over 235,000, of whom 90 percent were Germans. The naming of superintendents and lay presidents was reserved for the czar, who did not hesitate to intervene in spiritual matters as was his wont in his own Orthodox Church. The large number of Germans in Russian Poland was due to immigration, for the Russians invited and induced artisans for the growing industrial centers and farmers for open lands. But as a rule the Germans lived in closed communities, and except in older city congregations there was little assimilation with the Poles. The rising nationalism widened the gap. Germans who often were government officials were looked on as agents of the hated Russians. Their own schools kept the German youth from Polish contacts. In a subtle way Polish nationalism was identified with Roman Catholicism — if there were conversions, they would more often be to the Reformed persuasion. Polish Lutheranism came to be associated with the Germans, and its fate was intertwined with them. In the old East Prussia the Masurian Poles did combine with Lutheran immigrants from the Baltic countries, but here a Lithuanian nationalism dominated.

With Peter the Great Russia started its advance toward the west. A large number of Germans had been drawn to Moscow already in the previous century, and they had their own community outside the Kremlin, where Protestant services were allowed. Peter's founding of a new capital was in a region where Finnish Lutheran churches had long been organized. When the Swedish power was broken, Latvia and Estonia passed from the control of Sweden to that of Moscow. A well-regulated church life followed the Swedish pattern, and Peter was willing to let them continue to exercise a relative autonomy. Consistories in Reval, Narva, Dorpat, Pernau, Riga, Pilten, and Mitau supervised the schools and churches in the two countries, and in Courland, which Catherine II added to her realm about the time she helped herself to a part of Poland. These Baltic provinces added a couple of million people — most of them Lutheran — to the czars' lands. In addition a large number of German immigrants had come in Peter's time to build up St. Petersburg and its trade, and another large immigration in Catherine's reign settled on the banks of the Volga to till the vacant fields.

Study at foreign universities was restricted. Instead the University of Dorpat in Latvia became the cultural center. From it the government drew trained professional men and the churches their pastors. The faculty were Germans of high intellectual caliber, and Dorpat students enjoyed good training. Balts were employed too by the Russians in ecclesiastical posts in Poland, their Western manners making them popular also at court. The churches were mostly rural, for the population was composed of peasants and cities were few. Parishes were large, pastors overworked. The orthodoxy which the provinces had learned from Sweden had been influenced by Pietism. The German settlements within Russia stood in only a loose relationship with Germany, mainly with the consistory in Hamburg. They were often without pastors or served by lay teachers. An attempt was made in Peter's time to bring all the Lutheran churches under one administration and a common liturgy, but this was resisted by the Estonians and Latvians, who cherished old traditions. In the 19th century the czars gradually turned away from the West and a policy of Russification developed. By 1832, when other consistories had been added in Odessa and in Saratov on the Volga, the czar proclaimed a law for the Evangelical Lutheran Church in Russia by which all the consistories were placed under a Supreme Consistory whose president was appointed by the czar and whose four other members — two clerical, two lay — were nominated by the consistories, now defined as six: Estonia, Latvia, Courland, the island of Osel, Moscow (including the Volga church), and St. Petersburg (including the Ukraine). The churches of Estonia and Latvia thus lost their autonomy. The Orthodox Church was the state church governed by the czar with the assistance of a Holy Synod of 12 members.

A Missionary Church

Our survey of missions and migration has swung full circle from Lappland on the one side of the Baltic to the Russian provinces on the other side. It discloses a ceaseless expansion toward the frontiers of the age and a Christian witness by the Lutheran countries to other lands and peoples. Sweden and Norwegian emissaries carried the Gospel to Lapps and Finns, to Greenland, and to the Delaware River in America. The Danish government together with Halle missionaries began the Protestant movement in missions on the east coast of India. German consistories followed with prayer and men the mounting emigration

201

to the eastern shores of North America. On the changing, troubled eastern border of Europe Lutheran churches arose in migrations and movements of people in Slovenia, Slovakia, Hungary, Austria, Bohemia, Moravia, Silesia, and Poland. Older churches and new ones found themselves under Russian autocracy. Despite the difficulties on all these fronts, the Lutheran doctrines of sin and grace, Law and Gospel, Word and Sacrament were planted in all these regions. Some feared that the revolutions of the time in the beliefs of man and in the structures of society meant the end of Christianity. The result, however, was quite the contrary. The Church of the Lutheran Reformation was spreading seed that would bear rich fruit in many climates.

XV

THE QUEST FOR FREEDOM

The close of the 18th century marked the beginning of a new period in the history of Western civilization. A century that had seen the rise of French culture to dominance in Europe ended with the French Revolution. This great explosion overthrew old political dynasties and the secular power of the Roman Church and initiated an age of democracy. It had been preceded by the Revolution of the American Colonies, which also proclaimed a government of, by, and for the people. In Europe the dream soon turned into the dictatorship of Napoleon, who shook the continent, but after him France again asserted in 1830, 1848, and 1870 a popular sovereignty that had repercussions in all of western Europe. The new idea of the state as a secular power left open the question who was to possess its power. The age of royal absolutism as well as of church dominion was gone. A dying aristocracy tried to hold power that a rising middle class in the cities was taking from it. All the while a muttering could be heard in the new class of industrial workers. In their name a third revolution in the next century was to proclaim in Russia the might of an organized proletariat, which again would fall into the grip of a dictatorship.

PHILOSOPHICAL SPECULATION

No less revolutionary was the cultural transformation. The deism of England gave way to skepticism and after Darwin to an explanation of man and society in purely secular and materialistic terms. Yet the common sense of England saved it from the naturalism of French literature. Rousseau's man of nature found expression in a French realism that denied the reality of Christian theology and ethics. Germany showed its deep-seated religious heritage by an idealistic view of life that preserved religious terms. At first the leaders of thought celebrated their independence from the church by turning from Hebrew to classical forms of philosophy and art. Here more than in supernatural Christianity, they thought, reason found freedom. The infinite power of man displaced the will of God, and in himself man could create new heavens and a new earth. In the poetry of Klopstock life was still related to God, but idealism tended to make God a spirit within the world, and Spinoza's pantheism became the religion of many.

On the whole, however, German thinkers did not go so far as to lose their souls in the world soul. Fichte and Lessing maintained a distinction between man and God. Love was the goal of life toward which the Spirit of God guided mankind. Schelling too gave importance to history as well as philosophy. But for Hegel the Ideal was absolute. All of human experience was seen as a movement from a thesis to its antithesis and final culmination in a synthesis. Sin, evil, forgiveness, revelation — all of religious experience — were swallowed up in the world mind which was God. Against this philosophical speculation even the poets rebelled. Goethe and Schiller saw reality in human individuals. The glory of life was in the variety and riches of human personality. These they portrayed with brilliance, and their pictures of life were full of feeling. But there was little room for religious truth — truth lay in what men felt and imagined. Here and now man found his satisfaction, and for the cultured the churches were unnecessary.

Another thinker created still more difficulties for the church. Immanuel Kant, the keenest intellect of his age, analyzed the mind of man. He found it so constructed that it could pass judgment only on what the senses reported. Pure reason knows only the phenomena we perceive. Yet this cannot be all. There is a realm of practical life where a voice from beyond us — or in us — tells us what we must do and how we are to behave toward our fellowmen. Reason can tell us nothing of God; but our duty, our recognition of God and of the dignity and immortality of the soul are real. In the field of ethics religion therefore has something to teach man. We are reminded of the distinction Descartes drew when he said he could be certain only of what he could count and measure. Kant too gave reason the function of understanding the world the scientist discovers. While theologians were grateful that Descartes and Kant allowed religion a place in the realm of human conduct, both are nevertheless responsible for the modern idea that religion lies outside the scope of reason. They helped relegate religion to the mystical intuition of the individual.

204

Philosophy, no more than politics and literature, thus had no responsibility to the church. It was even a question whether there was any necessary connection between religion and the church. For the idealists and romanticists religion was absorbed in philosophy and literature. At best the Bible, as in the case of Herder, could give some ethical guidance. But revelation was not uniquely Christian, for all of human experience revealed something of the upward struggle of man toward a future fulfillment of humanity on earth. Schleiermacher protested this dethronement of religion. Himself an example of high intellectual attainment and urbane manners, he addressed the cultured despisers of religion. He bade them examine their own deepest consciousness where they would find mirrored the truth of God. But so general and vague were the objects in this consciousness that little of the doctrines of the church remained in the mirror. His effort was the last to relate Christian theology to the new independent spirit of the intellectual class. Culture pursued its secular path until at the end of the century Schopenhauer and Nietzsche openly denounced all religion. The forces of culture joined with the dark shadows of the masses under Marx, himself an interpreter of Hegel, to banish God from man's thought and life.

While these philosophical battles were being waged in the high places of the universities, scholars were examining the Bible as any other human book. They studied its origin and languages and customs, casting much new light on its meaning. But they began to question the date and authorship of individual books, the relationship of the Old to the New Testament, the establishment of the canon. Freed from traditional views of the meaning and the authority of Scripture, they stressed its human side. They questioned the relationship of Jesus and Paul and the relative value of the Gospel of John. Ferdinand C. Baur inaugurated at Tübingen a new interpretation of Jesus, seeing the New Testament documents as a creation of the early church. Even more sensational was the *Life of Jesus* by another Tübingen professor, David F. Strauss, a biography that made of the historical Jesus a mythical miracle worker and divine being. Some of the critical Biblical scholars, like Johann Semler, were themselves professed Christians and thought they were serving the church. In reality they were reinterpreting Scripture in the light of the rationalism of the day, discovering proofs for their Hegelian doctrines in the controversies and agreements of the early church or like Schleiermacher, finding their own self-consciousness corroborated in the consciousness of Jesus. They read God's revelation in the mirror of their own depths and reflected their own ideas in the explanation of it

THE PRUSSIAN UNION

To the religious dilemma of the Church of the Reformation in Germany was added the ambiguous situation in which the organized churches found themselves, not the least in Prussia. The relationship of church to governments produced strange results as governments changed. Saxony, the defender of Luther, was still a strong Lutheran province, but its king was Roman Catholic. The rulers in Prussia had a long Calvinist tradition, yet Prussia was now becoming the centralizing power in a new German Empire. It had long been tolerant of both Lutherans and Reformed under a common administration. The king, Frederick William III, in the year of the 300th anniversary of the Reformation on his own authority proclaimed a union of the two churches. He did not merge them or change their confessions, but he wanted them considered as one communion, and he hoped they might celebrate the Sacrament together. He looked on himself as a liturgical scholar and prepared an Agenda, or order of worship, which he tried to impose on the union in 1821. In the face of opposition the Agenda was allowed as an alternative form. As Prussia incorporated other territories in Pomerania and Westphalia, he tried in 1830 to bring their churches into the union. But the confessional Lutheran Church now had the strength to resist. Instead a general superintendent, with separate consistories for each communion, was allowed the provinces. For a while these superintendents bore the title of bishop, and the Prussian superintendent was archbishop. When Frederick William IV tried to expand the episcopal system rather than allow greater freedom through lay representation in synods, the only result was the placing of the superintendents directly under the king, thus increasing his power over the churches.

OPPOSITION TO UNION

Nassau, Rhine-Bavaria, and Baden followed the example of Prussia. While the respective confessions were acknowledged, they lost their normative value in the declaration that the Bible alone was to be the basis of teaching and preaching. On the other hand the union called forth strong protests and a determination on the part of convinced Lutherans not to allow the loss of their identity. As a commemoration of 1517 Claus Harms of Kiel in 1817 issued 95 theses containing a ringing denunciation of the rationalism that pervaded Lutheran churches. When Silesian Lutherans began to organize an independent church, the government would not give it legal standing but looked on it as a sect. In 1841, however, they were allowed to organize as the Evangelical Lutheran Church in Prussia, with Breslau as center. The role of the pastor in the new independent church soon became an issue that resulted in a division and a new synod called Immanuel. One dissident group chose to emigrate to America under Pastor John Grabau and to form with him the Buffalo Synod. Meanwhile in Saxony a large and well-organized group expressed protest against a unionistic spirit by following their pastor, Martin Stephan, to the state of Missouri in 1839. Other Saxon congregations sympathized with Pastor Friedrich Brunn in Nassau, who with his congregation left the state church in 1877 and helped establish the Synod of the Evangelical Lutheran Free Church of Saxony and Other States. The synod included congregations from Rhenish Prussia, Hanover, and Pomerania. In 1908 it merged with the Hermannsburg Free Church.

The war with Denmark in 1864 brought Schleswig-Holstein under Prussian dominion, and after the war with Austria Hanover, Electoral Hesse, Nassau, and Frankfort were added to Prussia. Hanover firmly resisted becoming a part of the church union. Leaders such as Ludwig A. Petri and Karl J. Spitta gave depth to the Lutheran consciousness of the province, the former through administrative measures, the latter through his sermons and hymns. Within the Prussian Union many Lutherans were dissatisfied with the vague creedal stand of their church government. In Pomerania Theodor Kliefoth wielded great power as a strong confessional administrator. In Prussia the jurist F. J. Stahl and the journalist E. W. Hengstenberg argued for a clear distinction between church and secular government and for finding the church's identity in its confessions. Hengstenberg's *Evangelische Zeitung* openly opposed the attitude of the secular press of Berlin.

While Prussia was consolidating a new Germany in the north, the southern provinces kept their ancient independence until 1870. From this quarter the new awakening of Lutheranism would receive significant leadership. Württemberg had treasured its heritage from the days of Johann Brenz, Jakob Andreae, Johann Valentine Andreae, and Johann Albrecht Bengel. It had developed a strong, Biblically oriented, pietistic character. Bengel's mediating stand between strict orthodoxy and separatistic Pietism had given a certain tolerance to rationalistic influences. These had found expression in a hymnbook of 1791 and a liturgy of 1809, when exorcism and the mention of the devil were omitted, as well as the words of institution in Baptism. Some Pietists reacted vigorously against such changes and emigrated to Russia and America rather than conform. However, the rationalistic spirit was never radical and showed itself rather in the improving of schools and congregational life. The renewed use of Epistles as well as Gospels in the lessons showed an interest in liturgical worship, which had been abbreviated in Württemberg. Enrichment of the hymnbook came through Albert Knapp and Philip Hiller in the hymnal of 1842. *The Life of Jesus* by the Tübingen scholar David F. Strauss parted the confessional Lutherans from the nominal Pietists, and from this event came — as elsewhere — a tendency to consider the confessional Lutherans the true exponents of Christianity. In Württemberg the kings showed no great interest in confessions but did deal fairly with the Roman Church, allowing it a theological faculty at Tübingen. The Evangelicals strove in vain for a voice in the government of the church. Despite the revolutionary spirit abroad, the king was afraid to grant lay participation. Even the leading Pietists were no friends of democracy. Not until 1869 did a synod come into existence.

One of the leaders in the Württemberg church was to prove highly influential. This was Johann T. Beck who turned to the Bible as the center of a theological system. Not the confessional writings but the Scriptures as the Word of God were his concern. Here he found the kingdom of God as a central theme. Both justification and sanctification could be treated fully from this point of view. A new Biblical theology thus came into being, with wide influence in the Lutheran Church. Especially impressive was his theory that only when Christ is in us can we understand Scripture.

Even more than Württemberg, the province of Bavaria was to become a stronghold of confessional Lutheranism. At the University of Erlangen a group that included Gottlieb C. A. Harless, Johann C. K. von Hofmann, Johann Höfling, and Franz H. R. von Frank built up a theology on the basis of the Confessions. Theology, they maintained, was not completed in the 16th century but could be developed in the light of later study. Bavaria was heavily Catholic, and the Lutherans had to defend themselves against Rome rather than a union. They tended to give weight to the experience of the individual, following Schleiermacher, and sought an inner certitude as well as an assurance of the objective validity of the creed. Through the *Zeitschrift für Protestantismus und Kirche* the school attained wide influence. Near Nürnberg, at Neuendettelsau, Wilhelm Loehe developed a deeper understanding of the life of the Lutheran congregation as he made it a center of liturgical renewal and practical service. His efforts extended to America, where he sent a large number of ministers to work among German immigrants. Opposed to a secular *summus episcopus,* Loehe wanted the pastor to act as local bishop of the parish, and the congregation should have the right to exclude from the sacraments those not in accord with the teaching of the church. Loehe's evaluation of ordination as a transmission of an apostolic succession of teaching was not shared by Harless and Höfling, who placed greater stress on the congregation, from which they derived the ministry. These men, like C. F. W. Walther in America who at one time was in association with Loehe, gave the laity a larger place than the seemingly "high church" Loehe, Stahl, and Kliefoth.

LAY MOVEMENTS

Throughout the century a new force was finding its way into the churches and vitally affecting their nature. To begin with, it came from England and Switzerland in the form of voluntary societies whose members hoped to further the cause of the kingdom of God. Earliest were the Society for the Propagation of Christian Knowledge and the Society for the Propagation of the Gospel in Foreign Parts, English societies reaching back to the beginning of the 18th century and pioneers in the spread of literature and the support of foreign missions. The

209

London Missionary Society, started in 1795, was the organ of the Congregational Church; the Church Missionary Society, organized in 1799, was the agent of the Church of England. The Religious Tract Society, the British Bible Society, and the Wesleyan Missionary Society appeared between 1799 and 1814. Similar groups soon sprang up in Germany. In Berlin the Moravian preacher Johann Jaenicke established in 1800 an independent Institute of Missions. The Basel Missionary Society combined Lutherans and Reformed who began by supporting the Church Missionary Society. A confessional Lutheran Berlin Missionary Society dates from 1824. Another Lutheran society arose in Dresden in 1836 — in 1840 it took over part of the Danish India Mission from the Church Missionary Society. On the initiative of Pastor Louis Harms a society was organized in his parish in Hermannsburg, and Johannes Gossner founded a society in Berlin, bearing his name.

Out of the same interest for evangelization and ministry came the Inner Mission movement. Industrialization was shifting population from rural regions to cities. Crowded living conditions, poverty, sickness, and juvenile delinquency were accompaniments of the new social order. Neither state nor church seemed ready to meet the pressing needs of working classes who were without roots in the community. Few new churches were built, and clergy were neither sufficient nor well trained. In this situation individual Christians rallied volunteers to create new agencies. Johann H. Wichern made the "Rauhes Haus" in Hamburg, begun in 1833, a training center for workers in many cities. Three years later Theodor Fliedner founded Kaiserswerth whose deaconesses, working among children, the sick, and unmarried mothers, made this home a model for scores in and outside Germany. Adolf Stöcker went beyond his Berlin City Mission and founded a Christian Social Workers party. Friedrich Naumann, a disciple and colleague of Stöcker, tried vainly to bring church and laboring class closer together, leaving the church to devote himself to socialist politics. The Blumhardts, father and son, turned Bad Boll, a health resort, into a center for spiritual well-being for multitudes who sought their counsel. Württemberg had its own Bible Society, as did Prussia.

All of these voluntary groups tended to bring the Lutherans and the Reformed together, awakening the concern of conservatives. At first they opposed the movement because of dislike both of unionism and of the lay leadership. Loehe was able to build an Inner Mission of his own on strictly Lutheran principles, but this was rarely possible. Therefore, because of the desperate need of the population, Lutherans gradually joined the Reformed in joint endeavors and gave their sincere support. Yet where possible they preferred their own organization. Thus in rivalry with the Gustav Adolf Society for aid to German Protestants outside Germany, the confessional Lutherans built up their own "chests of God." In certain cases the official church assumed responsibility for new work. The consistory of Hanover provided some men for the Lutherans in America and for a long period supported congregations in Capetown, Africa. But in the main the consistories were satisfied to carry on routine duties, unaware that the Inner Mission was itself a protest against the rigidity and clerical dominance of the church-state arrangement.

RITSCHLIAN THEOLOGY

In the context of the time the theology of Albrecht Ritschl seems both a cause and an effect. Disavowing interest in the mystical and supernatural nature of Christianity and finding in Christ a worthy model of righteousness rather than a divine Redeemer from sin, he concentrated on a social and ethical kingdom of God that Jesus came to establish as God's will for mankind. This was, in a way, his answer to the difficult questions raised by Julius Wellhausen and others in regard to the nature of the Scriptural record. The *teachings* of Jesus were clear. His church was to bring in the ethics of God's love. Willing obedience to Christ was the mark of the Christian in changing this world rather than waiting for an eschatological event. The confessional Lutherans sensed here an abridgement of the Gospel. But for a generation that was anxious for help in a bewildering world and not satisfied with religious controversy the Ritschlian program seemed to offer hope and guidance.

On the other hand this program was inadequate. The Lutherans, who were seeking a clearer definition of what the church of Christ really is, saw that once the state had thrown off its guise of protector the church would need a foundation of its own. If religion was not to be dissipated in a general mood of philanthropy, it needed a Gospel rooted in the truth of God as revealed to man. The kingdom of God was more than an optimistic secular society. Therefore they clung to the Confessions of the church. As it was, Western civilization was following an illusion of progress while itself progressing on a path that brought it to the brink of disaster — the World War of 1914—1918. Romanticism and realism had created no ideal world of humanity.

How closely knit the countries of Lutheranism had become and how common their problems were is apparent as we trace the story of the Scandinavian churches in the 19th century.

THE DANISH CHURCH

As in Germany so in Denmark a divergence soon appeared between those who were led by romantic literature to an idealistic view of man and those who saw in Kant and Fichte a challenge to a sterner ethical life. The writings of Henrik Steffens and Adam Gottlob Oehlenschläger reflected Schelling's unity of man and nature, while the official theology of Henrik C. Clausen was a rational explanation of man's duty in a world governed by God's providence. P. E. Muller at the university and Jakob Mynster, the bishop, found a firmer faith through the study of the Bible. But a deep stream of Pietism ran through the Danish Church, nourished by older Spener traditions as well as by the Moravian center at Christiansfeld. Pastors cooperated in the revivals that flared up in different sections of the country. But the laity were the real force. They resisted the effort of the church to impose new hymnbooks and worship forms they considered rationalistic. There was also a long-standing contact with England. An English pastor, Ebenezer Henderson, was along at the founding of the Danish Bible Society in 1814, and English friends cooperated in the new start of the Danish Missionary Society in 1821.

But something of all these elements — romanticism, rationalism, biblicism, pietism, activism — merged in the many-sided leader who put his stamp on Christianity in Denmark, Nikolai F. Grundtvig. His romantic trait inspired his great interest in Denmark's heathen past and its Christian destiny. He had a consuming passion for education, and the Danish folk schools were the result. He could join with Pietists in the criticism of the church, though his interest in fellowship contrasted with their separatistic individualism. Central in his thinking was the Sacrament of Baptism and the Apostles' Creed, which had been

212

repeated down through the generations as the true succession of the church. The Creed and the Lord's Prayer he considered living words of Jesus which, rather than the Bible, held the communion of saints together and which opened up the meaning of the Bible. Grundtvig's hymns cover the Three Articles of the Creed, the First Article interpreted by the Second and the Third. At first Grundtvig challenged Clausen's party to leave the church because of its rationalism. Then he wanted freedom for his followers to leave. He was finally satisfied if they were allowed to stay in the church as a party. But Grundtvig's ideas in some degree influenced all the church in Denmark.

The mildly rationalistic administration of the Danish Church had to bear not only Grundtvig's attacks but also those of Sören Kierkegaard. His proclamation, however, was of a different kind. Rooted in Moravian Pietism and struggling for clarity in his wrestling with Hegelian philosophy and Biblical faith, Kierkegaard aimed his darts at a worldly Christianity that seemed to deny the truth of Jesus Christ. In fact he was opposing the whole system of philosophic idealism while making a leap of faith into a kind of purity of life and thinking beyond the ability of the unlearned layman. Hence his criticisms led to no great changes although his denunciation of the bearers of ecclesiastical power found ready acceptance among the critics of the church. Rather than reforming the church, Kierkegaard inspired Vilhelm Beck and others to found an Inner Mission which overshadowed the official organization. Kierkegaard's large literary production, however, has had a profound effect on the thought of individual Christian thinkers in many lands.

In Denmark, as in Germany, the church had been unable to cope with a mobile population. In Copenhagen there were fifty to sixty thousand people to a parish. The slums were being filled by laborers who called religion capitalistic. The loss of Schleswig-Holstein embittered the nation. Economic conditions were unfavorable. In the half century after 1858 over 100,000 Danes emigrated to Utah alone. Both Grundtvig and Beck were more successful in the regions of the small farmers. A separate Inner Mission Society worked in the capital, but with less emphasis on personal conversion than Beck demanded. In Copenhagen the mission operated hospitals, a deaconess institute, Magdalene Home, hospices, a seamen's mission, and incorporated the program of the YMCA and YWCA into its work.

213

Bishop Mynster, who had been the object of Kierkegaard's attack, was succeeded by Hans L. Martensen. As a former professor of theology he had exerted definite influence on a theological generation by his works on dogmatics and ethics. He continued a mediating tradition, accepting much of Grundtvig except his view of the sacraments and hoping to keep the intellectual class in the church. In the seventies and eighties the cultured class was avidly following the lectures of Georg Brandes who introduced the naturalism of French realists and the atheistic philosophy of Feuerbach and Nietzsche into the North. In the face of such opposition the church leaders of the "Center" were unwilling to concede the demand of the Pietists for "pure" congregations. They were helped by the establishment of the Church Fund, a voluntary effort to build small chapels in thickly populated sections instead of large, expensive edifices.

The remarkable achievement of the Danish Church was to keep all these movements within a common framework. Grundtvig's followers did not separate, nor did Beck's Inner Mission. The sacraments came to have a unifying force, and the hymns of Grundtvig found place in the Danish hymnbook. Synods did not govern the church, which by the constitution of 1849 was still assured economic support by the state, but probably nowhere in the Lutheran churches did laymen have so much to do with church affairs as did the followers of Grundtvig and the members of the Inner Mission in Denmark. No great emphasis was placed on confessionalism, but all three parties considered themselves faithful to an orthodoxy that had been deeply colored by pietistic experience. As state and church parted company, there were among church people differences of belief as to the true nature of the church among men. On the island of Bornholm Pastor Peter Trandberg in 1863 protested the loose discipline of the congregations, but his followers were unwilling to form a separate church.

The Church in Sweden

The Napoleonic wars brought change to all the Scandinavian countries. Denmark lost Norway, which gained its own government but was related to Sweden through a personal union with the Swedish royal house. Sweden in turn lost Finland when Russia gained suzerainty and placed it with the Baltic countries under a governor in Moscow.

A French prince became king of Sweden, and his house of Bernadotte soon identified itself with the Swedish people. The constitution of 1809 reasserted the Lutheran faith as the faith of king and nation, though freedom of religion was extended, especially through a greater freedom of the press.

Neither rationalism nor romanticism made deep inroads on the religious temper of Sweden in the first half of the century. Erik Gustaf Geijer and Esaias Tegnér represented the highest level of Swedish thought and letters. Both had learned of Kant and Fichte, and Tegnér, who became a bishop, was a follower of Herder and De Wette. Archbishop Henry Reuterdahl was a disciple of Schleiermacher. The new church books that were authorized — a catechism in 1810, an Agenda, or handbook, in 1811, and a hymnbook of 1819 — bore marks of supranaturalistic thinking. Exorcism was omitted in baptism, as was the sign of the cross. Confirmation was given a fixed formula. And voices were raised against some of the hymns of Ödmann, Astrom, and even of J. O. Wallin, who was recognized as Sweden's "David of the North." But in general there still was interest in the church on the part of the educated classes. Even current literature, such as the poetry of Atterbom, Stagnelius, and Almquist, breathed a religious spirit. Not a few among the clergy retained interest in Böhme, Knös, and Swedenborg. The church welcomed the visits of John Paterson and E. Henderson from the British Isles. A Swedish Bible Society was begun in 1810, and tract and Bible distribution became general.

Yet the strength of the church lay in a widespread revivalism that carried on in various forms in different parts of the country. In central and southern Sweden popular revival preachers attracted the ordinary parishioners in large numbers. J. O. Hoof and Pehr Nyman preached a gospel with heavy emphasis on judgment of the unrepentant. Peter Sellergren had roots in Arndt, but Martin Landahl echoed more of Nohrborg. The deplorable extent of drunkenness made temperance an element in their preaching. In some regions a dormant Moravian tradition came to life. But more generally the harvest was one of seeds sown by older Swedish devotional books. The temperance movement received high ecclesiastical leadership under Peter Wieselgren, pastor in Hälsingborg, later dean in Gothenburg. Robert Baird, an American, had given the movement strong impetus by his visit in 1836.

Unusual was the ministry of Henric Schartau, dean at Lund. He too represented both Moravian and Swedish Pietism but was opposed to all conventicles, even to organizations within the parish, and concentrated on an integral congregational life. Far ahead of the times in the psychological understanding of religion, he led his followers by oral and written teaching along a carefully marked out "order" of salvation. The strictness of both his thought and practice gradually gave character to the ministry of great parts of Sweden. Other Pietistic leaders in Smaland and Skane were protagonists of a church freed from state control. The Free Church of Scotland was their model. Since this was hardly in prospect, they hoped for renewed life in the traditional parish system.

A more militant revivalism grew up in northern Sweden. Luther, Nohrborg, Pontoppidan, as well as the Bible were authoritative for the "readers," as they were called in Norrland. They were dissatisfied with the new church books, for these seemed too rational. Irrationalism in fact characterized some of the groups, one of which under Eric Jansen migrated to America. Ecstaticism and speaking in tongues was not uncommon. Lars Laestadius among the Lapps and Per Brandell in Norrland guided the revival movement in a churchly course. From Norrland the lay preacher Carl Olof Rosenius came to Stockholm. Here he met George Scott, a Methodist preacher from Scotland whom Samuel Owen, an English industrialist, had sent to Stockholm to minister to his English workers in Sweden. Scott extended his work to include not only the distribution of tracts and Bibles but also temperance activity. By making Rosenius editor of *Missions Tidning* he gave Swedish laymen a place of leadership among the many revival groups that found kinship through this journal. Scott also had a hand in getting even the official church authorities interested in founding the Swedish Mission Society in 1835, but not until 1873 did the church itself assume the direction of an overseas program. Then the Swedish Society and one organized earlier in Lund merged to form an official board.

After the revolutionary events of 1848 in France and Germany a wave of conservatism swept Europe. A new series of revivals excited

Swedish church people. Carl Johan Nyvall in Värmland and Per August Ahlberg and Hans Birger Hammar in Smaland fanned into flame fires that had been smoldering from former movements. As mission societies — aimed at home reform as well as foreign service — multiplied, the National Evangelical Foundation *(Fosterlandsstiftelsen)* attempted to keep the ferment within the church. The Conventicle Act of 1721 still stood, but it was widely circumvented. In the same year as the Foundation was born (1855) a Baptist congregation was begun in Stockholm. Liberal forces finally forced the repeal of the hated act in 1858. As in Denmark and Norway so also in Sweden some societies even held their own Communion services, first under a pastor, then with lay leaders. During his lifetime Rosenius counseled his followers in all the Scandinavian countries to remain in their national churches. But his successor, Lector P. P. Waldenström, pursued a more independent course, and after breaking with the church in 1872 on the doctrine of the atonement, he and his followers in the mission societies virtually separated in 1878 when they no longer required of their preachers subscription to the Augsburg Confession. The Mission Covenant thus became a church body, and the unity of the folk church was broken.

Within the church tension had grown between a high-church party with its center in Lund and a low-church party led from Uppsala. The Lund faculty aligned itself with Hengstenberg, Kliefoth, and Stahl. The ministry in its office of Word and Sacrament was transmitted through episcopal ordination. The Uppsala theologians looked with sympathy on lay participation in the organization and work of the church. Their viewpoint carried weight in Parliament, which in 1865 for the first time allowed the church its own convocation with lay representation. The initial steps of the convocation proved cautious, as evidenced by the new Catechism of 1878 and the Handbook of 1894.

The seventies and eighties were difficult decades. American Unitarianism was reflected in the religious philosophy of C. J. Boström, Pontus Vikner, and Viktor Rydberg. August Strindberg introduced a line of antichurch writers such as Ellen Key, Georg Brandes, and Karl Hjalmar Branting. The laboring class was indifferent when not hostile. The church suffered severe losses to the Free Churches. Thousands of serious-minded church people emigrated to America.

Mormons were active, as in Denmark and Norway. The Pentecostal movement grew out of Baptist groups. A turn for the better came before the end of the century. Verner von Heidenstam, Selma Lagerlöf, and Erik Karlfelt cleared the literary atmosphere of earlier naturalism. Christian thinkers acquired stature in poetry, history, and philosophy, for the church could point to Harold Hjärne, Bishop J. A. Eklund, Nathan Söderblom, and others. The shocks from the criticism of the Bible were tempered not only by an interest in Ritschl but also by new Luther study by Einar Billing and Söderblom. The World Christian Student Federation had its beginning at Vadstena in 1895, and after 1908 future leaders emerged from the youth movement led by Manfred Björkqvist.

Through strong episcopal leadership the Church of Sweden held its own and gained even more independence from the state at the same time as the state was unwilling to lose the stabilizing contribution of the church. But the unreadiness of the hierarchy to incorporate lay activity into the leadership of the church marked its leaders in the public mind as aristocratic and conservative. The clergy remained highly cultured leaders of worship in churches not attended by the populace. Yet there was a loyalty to the Lutheran Confessions and the liturgy, coupled with an awareness of the intellectual problems of the century, winning for the church a respect not given to individual groups living on meager revival fare. On a deeper level the orthodoxy of the official church was pietistic, as was apparent in its hymns, preaching, devotional literature, and religious poetry. The National Evangelical Foundation represented an active lay loyalty, and after 1909 a number of "Bible faithful" pastors and laymen emphasized the authority of Scripture within the missions of the church at home and abroad. For all its difficulties, Lutheranism in Sweden retained a unique unity of thought and purpose in the family of Lutheran national churches during the revolutionary 19th century.

The Church in Norway and Iceland

Freed from Denmark, Norway turned to the task of building a national culture and a state under a constitutional government. Shortly before its separation from Denmark it had received its own university. Here the theological professors S. B. Hersleb and S. J. Stenersen upheld confessional standards and trained pastors in a Biblical tradition. The bishops in Norway were supranaturalists in their theology, with a considerable Grundtvigian interest.

But the main theological figure was an unschooled peasant, Hans Nielsen Hauge — unschooled, that is, in university disciplines but at home in the Bible, the Catechism, Arndt, Pontoppidan, and Kingo. Moral seriousness made him critical of the looseness of the clergy. At the age of 25 he began to speak to people about the Word and the will of God. He had an unusual ability in manual arts and commercial ventures that made him doubly impressive as he taught peasants and small-business men the skill of both material and spiritual life. He organized followers and engaged in the business of shipping, milling — even distilling. His meetings were still unlawful because of the Conventicle Act, and authorities questioned his accounting procedures. Opposition from both church and state led to his imprisonment, and from 1804 to 1809 he was confined in Oslo. Long, drawn-out examinations did not free him until finally in 1814, when his health was broken. Martyrdom made him a national figure, and hardly a town in Norway but knew his friends and writings. He gave to the common people a serious, moralistic view of Lutheranism, but he also encouraged them to take an interest in their government. The church was still his home, and he asked his following to be loyal to it. His adherents gradually attained power and influence in church and society. The Conventicle Act was repealed in 1842 and religious freedom granted in 1845. Moravian groups had persisted in Norway. Under N. J. Holm the Norwegian Moravians joined the Haugeans to promote a strong folk participation in religious affairs. A Bible Society, a Tract Society, and a Missionary Society were evidences of connections with other lands.

Grundtvigianism was represented by men who imitated the Danish folk schools and were concerned about practical instruction. At the middle of the century W. A. Wexels was the central figure in this movement and in the capital. He shared Grundtvig's view of the church, the Creed, and the sacraments, and got his views into a new catechism. His high-church stand against lay activity won him the opposition of the Haugeans who also found fault with his teaching on the possibility of salvation after death. The leader of the Haugeans was the formidable Gisle Johnson, the dominant figure in the theological faculty. He was an effective preacher, a leader of revivals, and a critic in Kierkegaard's spirit of the official church. His theology was that of Erlangen, and with his colleague C. P. Caspari, an authority on the history and study of creeds, he held to a rigid theory of inspiration. For the rest of the century his students were leaders in the church. Their churchly Pietism found expression in the Landstad Hymnbook of 1869 and the revised liturgy of 1889.

In Norway as in Sweden the lay movement was responsible for much of the newer forms of activity. There were temperance societies and a seamen's mission. A Deaconess Home was founded on the model of Kaiserswerth. Foreign missions were supported by many groups. Lars Skrevsrud was a heroic figure whose success lay both in activity on the Santal field in India and in arousing missionary interest in Scandinavia. A pastor, Horatius Helling, instituted projects among the working class, even attempting a Christian Worker's Society. But, as elsewhere, both the intellectual and the working class were moved by antichurch forces. Bjoernstjern Bjoernson, Henrik Ibsen, Alexander Kielland and Jonas Lie made Norwegians aware of the non- and antichristian movements in European culture. Convinced Christian laymen, such as Jacob Sverdrup, tried to counteract the influence of Brandes and the Grundtvigian Christopher Bruun led the folk-school movement in the direction of economic reforms. But Gisle Johnson had given his following an anticultural, antiliberal image that weakened the church in its defense against the materialism of the age. Fredrick Petersen, the successor of Gisle Johnson, understood these forces but was unsuccessful with both liberal and conservative groups. Bishop Heuck, himself a theologian of the Erlangen school, aroused opposition to the university's theological faculty and in 1905 the appointment of a liberal professor caused a rupture that resulted in a separate faculty more conservative and churchly. Thus after 1908 there were two theological faculties within the church.

Haugeanism penetrated all religious forms in 19th-century Norway. Unlike Rosenianism, which separated from the Church of Sweden, the Norwegian revivals were almost entirely within the church. In this respect Norway resembled Denmark. The exception was a small Free Church which in 1877 separated from the Church of Norway, whose confessional position it retained but whose lack of discrimination in granting absolution and in admittance to the Lord's Table was the cause of separation. The isolated position of Norway saved it from the more violent cultural and social revolutions on the continent. Nationalism too united the people even if they disagreed on religious policies. Consequently Norway possessed a more homogeneous life than was possible in either Denmark or Sweden.

Iceland was retained by Denmark when it lost Norway. The middle line of Mynster and Martensen prevailed against both rationalism and Grundtvigianism. The education of the ministry was greatly strengthened by the establishment of a theological college in Reykjavik in 1847, which became the theological department when a university was founded in 1911. Under able leaders a new liturgy, hymnbook, and Bible translation were achieved in the closing decades of the 19th and the opening decades of the 20th century. In 1900 the bishop of Iceland was authorized to be consecrated in his own country and not as hitherto in Denmark. Schools were removed from the bishop's supervision in 1907, and all members of the church over 21 have been entitled to vote for the parish pastor since 1886. Observers of religious life in Iceland have remarked on an emphasis on the providence of God in preaching and an interest in spiritualism. The ordination promise since 1910 holds the pastor to preach the Word of God "as found in the prophetic and apostolic Scripture and in the spirit of our Evangelical Lutheran Church," the folk church of Iceland. Freedom for dissenters was granted in 1874. Controversy between the conservative and more liberal parties gradually gave way to more united efforts in meeting the challenge of a secular generation. Iceland and Denmark had a common king from 1918 until Iceland declared itself a republic in 1944. Its contacts with England and America led to the introduction of a Bible society, the YMCA, and an increase in church literature through a church press.

THE CHURCH IN FINLAND

It was the fate of Finland to fall under Russian rule in 1809. Yet its independent government and church structure were respected by the Moscow authorities represented by a governor general. Jacob Tengström, professor, bishop, and first archbishop, skillfully guided the church in its relationships to the new rulers. He directed the revision of the liturgy, the hymnbook, and the catechism, and took part in the founding of the Finnish Bible Society in 1812. The new church law of 1869 abolished the Conventicle Act, declared lay work legal, and afforded freedom for other denominations. The same law separated the school system from control by the church, but the Lutheran Church remained the church of the nation and was granted its own convocation to decide religious matters. Tension between Swedish and Finnish elements increased, and separate liturgical books were authorized. But in mission programs cooperation was possible — a Deaconess Institute, a Seamen's Mission, a YMCA, a YWCA, and a Student Christian Association were fruits at home. A Finnish mission society took up work in Amboland, South-West Africa, in 1868.

Distinctive of Finnish Lutheranism were its revivals. In eastern Finland Paavo Ruotsalainen (1777—1852) was acknowledged as leader. Self-educated in the devotional literature of Bunyan, Pontoppidan, Hollazius, Nohrborg, and the Moravian "Songs of Zion," he, like Hauge, emphasized a life in accordance with one's faith. With speaking in tongues, Finnish meetings often became ecstatic. Ruotsalainen saved the revival movement from these excesses. In western Finland a revival under pastors Jonas Lagus and N. G. Malmberg, the latter having come in contact in St. Petersburg with the Gossner revival, joined forces with Ruotsalainen. On the other hand Henry Renqvist preferred a "prayer revival," and F. G. Hedberg turned from Ruotsalainen to follow Rosenius. Hedberg wanted a firmer spiritual assurance than constant revivalism seemed to give. His followers called themselves the Evangelical party. Another revival group, called Laestadians from their leader, the Swedish revivalist Lars Laestadius, emphasized the duty of lay members to confess to one another and to receive absolution from one another.

Theologically the leadership of the church followed J. T. Beck of Tübingen. Professors A. V. Ingman and C. G. von Essen and Bishop Gustaf Johansson impressed on the clergy the Biblical theology of Beck. The university had moved to Helsingfors (Helsinki) in 1828. Its leading lights included the poets Runeberg and Z. Topelius, and E. Lönnrot, the collector of the Kalevala sagas. Their attitude was unfriendly to the pietistic revivals, but their circle was small. Meanwhile the church had to defend itself against increased Russification, which Finnish nationalism also tried to counter, and at the turn of the century Marxism infected the radical labor class. An apologetic for the Christian faith was put into contemporary terms by Bishops H. Rabergh and Georg O. Rosenquist. Revivalism, Swedish-Finnish tensions, Russian Orthodoxy, Free Church movements, and antireligious culturism combined to create complex problems for the Finnish Church in the century of Russian rule.

XVI

NEW PLANTINGS ON FIVE CONTINENTS

While the cold light of rationalism seemed to overlay the landscape of Christendom after the middle of the 18th century, new shoots of life appeared in many parts of the church. The universities were alive with speculation concerning the nature and source of the Christian faith. Governments were trying to bend the congregations and the ministry to political purposes. But deep in the ranks of believing Christians springs of new energy were breaking forth, and in the next century the missionary movement was to win for the church a historian's designation as "the great century" (Latourette).

THE MISSIONARY MOVEMENT

The movement coincided with the era of colonization by the new maritime powers of Europe. Holland and England took the places of Spain and Portugal in gaining new territories in Asia, Africa, and the islands of the South Seas. North and South America were shaped by influences of the Old World. The original Danish-Halle mission in Tranquebar, India, exercised a peculiar attraction. Some of the new efforts centered there, but gradually the whole world became the concern of Protestant missions, and missions of Lutheran churches extended to the ends of the earth.

GERMAN MISSIONARY SOCIETIES

In Württemberg there had been interest in India since Ziegenbalg's day. An Augsburg pastor, J. A. Urlsperger, organized friends of an active faith into a "Christendom Society" *(Christentumsgesellschaft)* in 1780. This soon merged with a similar group in Basel, and the Basel Society became an outstanding center with a number of daughter societies. The society came into contact with the new English enterprises — Bible and tract and missionary societies. In Berlin Pastor

Johann Jänicke of the Moravian congregation started a school for the preparation of missionaries, many of whom entered the employ of the Basel or the London Missionary Institute. Among the graduates of Jänicke's school were the famous pioneers in India and China, Karl Rhenius and Karl Gutzlaff. The Anglican Church Missionary Society employed Basel graduates until its insistence on episcopal ordination of pastors. Then Basel turned in other directions and began fields of its own until it gradually grew into one of the leading missionary organizations in Europe.

Its branch in Barmen combined with smaller societies in western Germany to become the Rhenish Missionary Society. This association directed its attention to southeast Africa, Borneo, Sumatra, New Guinea, Madang, and China. Especially successful was its mission among the Bataks on Sumatra under Ludwig Nommenson's leadership. Another branch of Basel was the North German Missionary Society, with a center first in Hamburg, then in Bremen. After a beginning in New Zealand, its main effort turned to western Africa. University and church leaders in Berlin organized a society in 1824, and another was started by a former Roman Catholic priest, J. E. Gossner, who before his conversion had acted as a secretary in the Basel Mission. Gossner's theory of self-supporting missionaries on native fields proved impractical, but his group was represented in India and Australia. Still another outgrowth of Basel was the Chrischona Institute in Württemberg.

These early societies grew up on ground prepared by Pietism, not least by the Moravian Brethren, whose genius was a missionary one. The impulse overleaped confessional boundaries, often taking on subjective tones of individuals rather than expressing the voice of churches. The high-church Anglicans therefore dissociated themselves from the Congregational London Society and made the Society for the Propagation of the Gospel their own organ, while friendly to the low-church Church Society. Likewise in Germany the self-conscious confessional Lutheran churches made the Leipzig Society their missionary agency. At its founding in 1836 it was made a branch of the Basel Society and was situated in Dresden, but moved to Leipzig in 1848. Its director, Karl Graul, was recognized as a leader in the theory and practice of missions and himself spent four years in India. He cherished the hope of uniting all Lutheran churches in his organization. Though only partially successful, his missionary journal, *Evangelisch-Lutherisches Missionsblatt,* reached far and wide. The society succeeded in obtaining much of the old Tamil field in India and thus continued the century-old Danish mission as the center of its field. Graul aimed for the upper classes and sought to win them as a whole rather than individually. The Leipzig attitude toward the caste system placed it in an unfavorable light with other missions who criticized its seeming acceptance of the ancient social divisions. After Germany entered the circle of colonial powers the Leipzig missionaries began work in eastern Africa. Here progress was rapid in Tanganyika (Tanzania), especially in the Kilimanjaro region, where by 1913 almost half of the children were in mission schools and the Christians numbered a considerable part of the population.

The insistence of the Leipzig leaders on a higher education of missionaries was not shared by another conservative German Lutheran mission, that of Hermannsburg. Its originator, Pastor Louis Harms, had joined in the activities of the North German Missionary Society but disapproved of its lax doctrinal position. With Leipzig he differed on the policy of recognizing caste. Believing that a group of Christians living among natives would testify most effectively to the Gospel, he sent a colony to Africa in 1865. The experiences of the mission necessitated a change to more conventional methods. Besides its field in the Telugu area of India, its workers were found in Persia and Australia.

A third center of positive Lutheranism in Germany grew up in the neighborhood of Nürnberg at Neuendettelsau. Here Wilhelm Loehe developed a colony that reflected his own firm, devotional, and missionary Lutheranism on a confessional basis. In opposition to the ambiguous unionism of his day he held to an evangelical clarity that was best guaranteed, he believed, by a strict and high view of the ministry. Yet he left a large place for the laity for cultivating liturgical worship and supporting a missionary activity at home and abroad. Loehe began a deaconess institute in Neuendettelsau, and he and his friends organized a society, published literature, and gathered funds for workers that were trained and sent first to North America, then to the Ukraine, Australia, and Brazil.

The confessional concern was strong also in the Breklum Society in Schleswig-Holstein, another group that had left the North German Society. And the Free Church of Hanover, which had separated from the State Church, held to an independent course abroad as well as at home. The Breklum Society operated in India, the Hanover Free Church in Natal and Transvaal in Africa.

SCANDINAVIAN MISSIONS

The same pattern of missionary societies of varying churchly character meets us in Scandinavia. Danish interest in the India mission had declined to the point that the old Tamil field was given over partly to English societies, partly to the Leipzig Society. Pastor B. Falk Rönne managed to revive efforts for the Greenland mission by the formation of a Danish Missionary Society in 1821. Later it began anew a field in India under missionary Carl Ochs, who left the Leipzig Society because of its policy in regard to the caste system. The Grundtvig party was not missionary in character, and the Danish Missionary Society came under the control of the Inner Mission. The Church of Denmark as such sponsored no field — all activity abroad was begun by independent societies. A Santal Mission in Bengal Territory, India, enjoyed support from both Danish and Norwegian societies. And both revered the memory of the founders, a Danish engineer, H. Borresen, and a Norwegian pastor, Lars Skrevsrud. Societies were organized for fields in the Sudan, Japan, and the Near East. A "Society for the Propagation of the Gospel among the Danes in America" was formed in 1869. To coordinate the programs of these various agencies a Danish Missionary Council was set up in Copenhagen in 1912.

In Norway the romantic figure of H. P. Schroeder, who in 1834 was directed to the Zulus by Robert Moffatt, dominated the early years of missions in that country, and until 1873 he had the support of the Norwegian Missionary Society which was begun in 1842 by most of the elements of the church, including the Moravian Brethren. In addition to the Zulu field in Natal the Norwegian Society carried on an extensive and successful program in Madagascar after 1866. Lars Dahle served first as missionary on that island, translating the Bible, organizing the field, instructing teachers, and then carried on as secretary of the society in Norway. Another, more low-church group which did not ordain its preachers either at home or on its foreign field, was the Norwegian Lutheran China Society begun in 1891. In 1901 the older Norwegian Missionary Society added China to its fields.

From 1835 the Swedish Missionary Society, besides aiding missionary endeavors among the Lapps, served as an agent for gathering mission funds from parochial societies and distributing these among older societies. The most popular missionary figure in arousing wide interest was Peter Fjellstedt, who had served in the Orient under the Basel Society. As the confessional movement gained ground, there was a desire for a distinctive Lutheran society. This eventuated in the formation of the Lund Missionary Society in 1845. Its first venture was directed toward China, but of its pioneers one missionary was murdered, the other had to return for reasons of health. The society then entered into negotiations with Leipzig, resulting in a long period of cooperation. The Swedish missionaries worked on the India field, with considerable support from their own country but under the direction of the German authorities. The association was not always harmonious. The Swedish men did not altogether approve of the caste policy of Leipzig, nor did they favor the exclusiveness of the Lutherans. But the arrangement was to continue even after the Lund Society merged with the Swedish Society in 1855. The resultant society was absorbed by the Church of Sweden in 1876. Greater independence from Leipzig was granted the Swedish workers after the turn of the century. In 1914 a separation was induced by the war.

The creation in 1874 of a Board of Missions of the Church of Sweden marked the beginning of a church mission which besides India assumed fields in Natal, South Rhodesia, and China. The Evangelical National Foundation, originally conceived of as an inner mission movement, expanded in 1855 into a society sending missionaries to Ethiopia and Eritrea and starting a seamen's mission with its first station in Constantinople. We have already noted how one part of the missionary fellowship under P. P. Waldenström separated from the Church of Sweden, forming the Mission Covenant. This body carried on its own extensive efforts in Russia, Persia, Alaska, in the Congo in Africa, and in Hupeh, China.

The Finnish Missionary Society, begun in 1859 as an independent agency enjoying church support, took up a field in Amboland, Africa. The Lutheran Gospel Association, similar to the Swedish Evangelical National Foundation, dates from 1873. Since 1900 it has had a field in Japan.

Thus from the opening of Jänicke's Mission School in Berlin in 1800 up to the outbreak of World War I Lutheran missionary societies in every Lutheran land had carried the Gospel to India, from Bengal to Tranquebar, to Madagascar, Borneo, Sumatra, New Guinea, to Japan and China, to Arabia and Persia, and in Africa from Ethiopia in the north to Transvaal in the south. In thousands of parishes groups of interested individuals met for study of Scriptures, for reading of mission periodicals, for prayer, and for collecting of funds. Strong schools for the training of missionaries grew up in Basel, Barmen, Hamburg, Leipzig, Stockholm, and Oslo. In a way never before realized a sense of the unity and duty of the church developed. The sacrifice of missionaries on new, untried, often unhealthy stations is a bright part of the story of the church and belies the lack of faith often attributed to the churches in this century. But we have yet to relate the record of the sending societies and churches in the continents of North and South America and of distant Australia.

THE AMERICAN FIELD — THE GENERAL SYNOD

From his arrival in 1742 Mühlenberg had steadily forged the German Lutherans in the American colonies into a new fellowship of faith. His son-in-law J. C. Kunze, like Mühlenberg a former Halle student, held the New York Ministerium to a confessional standard. But in all three of the earliest synods — Pennsylvania, New York, North Carolina — German rationalism and English deism made inroads. Kunze's successor as president of the New York body, Frederick H. Quitman, had been a student of Semler in Germany before his ordination by the Dutch Lutheran Church, which sent him to Curacao in the West Indies, whence he came to New York. His talents of leadership gave him eminence, and in sermons, catechism, liturgy, and hymnbook he tried to accommodate the Lutherans in America to the rational culture of his day. The Synod of North Carolina also had a rationalistic catechism by a Helmstedt graduate, John C. Velthusen, and had difficulty distinguishing itself from Episcopal and Moravian practices. The great influx of German immigrants after 1830 made for a compactness of settlements where Lutheran and Reformed often shared services of pastor and ownership of property.

As the frontier moved westward, missionaries of the Pennsylvania Synod followed into Ohio, where a separate synod was organized in

230

1818. A Synod of Maryland and Virginia was formed in 1820 by a conference of the Pennsylvania Ministerium, and in the same year four pastors of the Synod of North Carolina organized a separate Tennessee Synod. In 1824 the South Carolina Synod also grew out of the North Carolina body, while the Synod of Maryland and Virginia divided in 1829. In the rapidly growing congregations the problem was not only one of adjusting to a new language and new neighboring churches but of reconciling different traditions from the European home churches. The Swedish churches along the Delaware had lost their identity in amalgamating with the Episcopal Church, and some pastors and German churches in North Carolina, Georgia, and New York followed a similar course. Others saw no reason to deny a unionistic relationship between Lutheran and Reformed, which they knew from Germany after 1817. And Quitman, with an honorary doctorate from Harvard, was interested in "Americanizing" Lutheran theology even to the point of making it palatable to Unitarians.

The need for a unifying agency to guide the confused Lutherans in the older colonies, now states of the Union, inspired the organization of the General Synod in 1820. But suspicion of a centralizing power, fear of increasing use of English, and parochialism kept the larger synods out of the new body, and so its growth came mainly from the newer areas in western Pennsylvania, western New York, and South Carolina. The entrance of the New York Synod gave it more strength after 1837, and when the Pennsylvania Ministerium joined in 1853, the number of smaller synods in Ohio, Indiana, and Illinois had grown considerably. By 1860 the General Synod numbered two thirds of the American Lutherans (864 of 1,313 ministers, 164,000 of 235,000 communicants). But by that time new developments had already changed the course of the Lutheran Church in America. The older Lutheran synods were being challenged by fresh immigrations from Europe which had other answers for the problems of the church on both sides of the Atlantic.

LOEHE'S MISSIONARIES

Moved by missionary literature, Friedrich K. D. Wyneken of the Church of Hanover, educated at Göttingen and Halle, came to Baltimore in 1838 to work among fellow countrymen. He was employed by the Ministerium of Pennsylvania as a missionary, settling at Fort

231

Wayne, Indiana. His appeals back to Germany for help stressed the motive of loyalty and obligation to the faith and the church. One of his messages was read by Wilhelm Loehe in Neuendettelsau, who at once took up the cause for the brethren in America. Loehe decided that he could best help by preparing workers and gathering funds through an organization and a periodical. Wyneken had also interested Pastor Ludwig Petri of Hanover, who in turn combined efforts with Loehe and made his city a stopping point for the men from Neuendettelsau. His loyalty to the Confessions caused Loehe to demand the obedience of his emissaries to the Lutheran doctrines.

The first two workers were sent in 1842. In the United States they were directed to Columbus, where the Synod of Ohio was beginning a theological seminary. Loehe and his friends made the support of this school a project for which they sought books and candidates. One of the earliest and ablest men sent from Germany was Wilhelm Sihler, a doctoral graduate of Berlin and a former teacher in Dresden who had read Wyneken's appeal. He was highly esteemed by convinced Lutherans, and the Dresden Missionary Society sent him to join the Loehe men in Ohio, where he began his work in 1844. By 1846 the number of missionaries had risen to 22.

The Ohio Synod was a disappointment to Loehe and his workers. It was rent by discord, partly over the use of English, partly over theology. The conservative party opposed English as a language of instruction in the seminary, and Loehe felt, as this group did, that orthodox Lutheranism would suffer in translation. Theologically this party wanted to eliminate the phrase *Jesus spricht* (Jesus says) in the recitation of the words of institution in the Lord's Supper, believing that this formula weakened faith in His presence in the elements. Unable to win their case, the conservative party with the Loehe representatives withdrew from the Ohio Synod in 1845. Three years later the Ohio Synod unequivocally declared its adherence to the Symbolical Books, but it was too late for the Loehe men had now cast their lot with the Missouri Synod.

LOEHE AND THE MISSOURI SYNOD

The Saxon immigration, deceived by Stephan in Missouri, produced a remarkable leader in C. F. W. Walther. Coming from a long line of pastors, Walther had graduated from Leipzig University. His faith in the Word was firm. His experiences in the colony drove him to lay the foundations of his faith in the Bible and to determine his relationship to the church. He came to the conclusion that the Gospel, the sacraments, and the keys are God's gifts to a congregation faithful to the Scriptures and that such a congregation needed neither the ties with the homeland nor its ministry to be a true church. In 1844 he started a journal, the *Lutheraner,* which won readers in America and Europe and on new mission fields. Here was a call to a definite position in the evangelical faith and a proclamation of the Gospel as the true treasure of the church.

The Loehe groups joined with Walther's Missouri congregations and in 1846 at Fort Wayne, Indiana, formed a new Synod: the Evangelical Lutheran Synod of Missouri, Ohio, and Other States. Of the 16 pastors present slightly more than half were Loehe emissaries, but the leadership came from the Missouri contingent. In 1846 Sihler began a seminary at Fort Wayne which stressed the practical and missionary preparation of pastors, while the seminary at St. Louis gave the more basic, theoretical courses. The following year Loehe consented to transfer the Fort Wayne school to the Missouri Synod. Over 100 men were directed to the seminary or its synod by Loehe.

Already, however, tension was developing between Loehe and Walther. The Missouri Synod was composed of pastors and congregations, the pastors qualifying for voting participation in the affairs of Synod only if they served congregations and the congregations having the right to pass on the decisions of synod. Loehe, on the other hand, had adopted the doctrine that the office of the ministry was not dependent on the congregation but was an order derived from Christ Himself and transmitted through the rite of ordination. We have seen how this was an issue among Lutherans in Germany, and Walther entered into the discussion on the side of those who, like Johann W. F. Höfling, allowed a larger role to the laity. When Loehe discontinued aid to the Fort Wayne seminary, Wyneken and Walther went to Germany to confer with the Neuendettelsau pastor. The conversations were polite, but no change was effected on either side. While in Germany, Walther established contacts with many of the confessional leaders.

Especially meaningful was the relationship begun with the Free Church of Saxony, whose school at Steeden furnished the Missouri Synod about 250 students.

THE IOWA SYNOD

Despite differences with some of his own men in America, Loehe continued to minister wherever possible. In southern Michigan Württemberg Lutherans had been organized into congregations by Frederick Schmid, who with other Basel Society missionaries also attempted, beginning in 1833, to bring the Gospel to Indians around Ann Arbor. When F. A. Craemer, a well-educated and able Bavarian, responded to Wyneken's appeal, Loehe sent him, after ordination by Theodore Kliefoth, to Michigan. Working with Schmid's group, he was a leader in establishing a series of German colonies for which Loehe himself wrote the regulations, both material and spiritual — Frankenmuth, Frankentrost, Frankenlust, Frankenhilf. At Saginaw a "Pilgerhaus," or seminary, was begun for the training of teachers. This soon proved a point of contention, since the disagreement with Missouri made its graduates unacceptable. Only a handful of Loehe's own supporters stood by him, and Wyneken suggested that the group separate from Missouri areas and move to Iowa. So in 1853 a score of persons moved to Dubuque. They were joined the following years by others from Neuendettelsau. Foremost among the newcomers were the brothers Siegmund and Gottfried Fritschel, who for decades were leaders in the new synod, the Evangelical Lutheran Synod of Iowa and Other States, organized in 1854. Johann M. Reu, one of American Lutheranism's finest scholars, came in 1889.

Until 1925 the Iowa Synod benefited by recruits from the society in Neuendettelsau. Thoroughly conservative in its theology, the Iowa Synod was less rigid than Missouri, holding to the Confessions as the answer of the church to the issues of the 16th century but not a final answer to all questions. Following the desire of Loehe, the Iowa Synod remained German in its official language so that its minutes were still in German in the 1920s. A majority of the Texas Synod joined Iowa in 1895. This synod had its beginnings in 1850, when the Chrischona Institute near Basel sent missionaries to organize congregations among German settlers.

234

The doctrine of the ministry involved the Missouri Synod in controversy also with another German immigrant body. We have noted that because of resistance to the Prussian Union, John A. A. Grabau in 1839 led a Lutheran group from Prussia and settled in Buffalo and Milwaukee. In 1845 four pastors and ten congregations organized a synod called the Buffalo Synod. But the group had already lost adherents, for Grabau held to a theory of the ministry which made ordination the means by which Christ gave the congregation its ministry. Hence lay leadership in worship, even in the absence of a pastor, was denied to a Milwaukee congregation. Grabau's *Pastoral Letter* of 1840 sketched a definition of the pastor which made him a virtual dictator in the congregation. When some of his people joined Missouri congregations, Grabau protested their acceptance. Grabau as well as Walther visited Loehe and sought German support. Grabau found himself closer to Loehe's position, but Lutheran conferences in Leipzig and Bavaria counseled moderation and peace. In 1866 a majority of the pastors left Grabau for the Missouri Synod, and after Grabau's death in 1879 the remainder of the Buffalo Synod moved toward a more congregational polity. Eventually it was to find fellowship with the Iowa and Ohio synods.

Inasmuch as there was little communication between the various Lutheran bodies in Europe, it is not surprising that immigrant groups in the United States would at first keep to themselves. In addition, the walls of language created an isolation that endured into a second generation. For most of the 19th century the Scandinavian Lutherans built up individual synodical units.

Norwegian Synods

Immigrants from Norway carried with them divisions or tendencies of the homeland. Elling Eielsen brought the Haugean lay movement to this country with its emphasis on small gatherings for devotional purposes. He and like-minded countrymen organized in 1846 in Wisconsin The Evangelical Lutheran Church in America (known as Eielsen Synod), but its loose ties and individualism prevented its growth. When a decade later it sought to achieve more solidarity and discipline it encountered losses, and a repeated attempt in 1876 resulted in a new body — Hauge's Norwegian Evangelical Lutheran Synod in America. The conservative Church of Norway ministry was represented by able pastors from Norway — H. A. Stub, H. A. Preus, U. V. Koren, Laurentius Larsen — who formed the Norwegian Lutheran Synod in 1853. This synod was attracted to Walther, and from 1859 to 1883 educated its ministers at St. Louis. Another group thought the Eielsen Synod too weak and the Norwegian Synod too rigid. It entered into association with Swedish immigrants, helped form the Scandinavian Evangelical Lutheran Augustana Synod of North America in 1860, and remained with it for a decade. Then it left, only to split into two sections, one the Norwegian-Danish Augustana Synod, the other the Conference for the Norwegian-Danish Evangelical Lutheran Church in America.

When the predestination controversy broke out, the Norwegian Lutheran Synod was divided by an "Anti-Missouri Brotherhood," which in 1890 merged with the Augustana and Conference Norwegians into the United Norwegian Lutheran Church of America, representing about one half of the number of Norwegian Lutheran church members in America. A dispute over the fate of Augsburg College and Seminary, one of the schools in the merger, soon severed one faction from the union and brought about the Lutheran Free Church. The leader was Georg Sverdrup, of a prominent family in Norway. Conferences and negotiations looking toward a union of the Hauge Synod, the United Church, and the Norwegian Synod into one Norwegian body continued persistently.

THE AUGUSTANA SYNOD

The first Swedish pastors were influenced by the currents of revival connected with Schartau, Rosenius, Ahlberg, Wieselgren, and Fjellstedt. In Illinois they were dissatisfied with the theology of the General Synod and after a few years in the Synod of Northern Illinois organized their own body — the Augustana Synod. The separation in Sweden of the Mission Covenant was reflected in America by a similar independent body, and the synod had to resist a tendency to see in the Episcopal Church the counterpart of the Church of Sweden with its bishops. Only one third of the people from the Church of Sweden joined the Augustana churches that were rapidly spreading across the continent. Under the wise leadership of men like L. P. Esbjörn, T. N. Hasselquist, Olof Ols-

236

son, Erland Carlsson, and Eric Norelius the synod adopted a conservative Lutheran stand, with great interest in educational and charitable work. From Sweden it inherited a sense of liturgical worship and a spirit of ecumenical interest. After 1875 Augustana College and Theological Seminary was located in Rock Island, Illinois.

DANISH SYNODS

The missionary societies of Norway and Sweden included America in their scope and made grants to such pioneers as Claus L. Clausen of Denmark, J. W. C. Dietrichson of Norway, and Lars P. Esbjörn of Sweden. Denmark had a separate society for aid to Danes in America and in 1871 sent out men who a year later in Wisconsin laid the foundations for the Danish Evangelical Lutheran Church in America. This body was Grundtvigian in character, many of its pastors having attended the folk school at Askov. For a while a Grundtvigian folk school was attempted in Elk Horn, Iowa, but a more American style school was established at Des Moines, Iowa, in 1896. Danes who were sympathetic with the Danish Inner Mission separated in 1894 to form the Danish Evangelical Church of North America. It attracted a considerable number of those who had left the Norwegian-Danish Conference in 1884 to form a purely Danish group. In 1896 these two bodies merged in the United Evangelical Lutheran Church in America, with a school in Blair, Nebraska. The Danish divisions among the followers of Grundtvig and the Inner Mission in the Church of Denmark have thus been reflected among Danish Lutherans in the United States.

FINNISH AND ICELANDIC SYNODS

Likewise the Finnish Missionary Society looked on America as a field. In 1888 J. K. Nikander was called for work in the United States. His efforts resulted in the foundation of the Suomi Synod in 1890, uniting congregations of Finns especially in northern Michigan, Minnesota, the Dakotas, and Oregon. Several of its pastors came from the African field of the Finnish Missionary Society. An educational institution was founded at Hancock, Michigan. Another Finnish immigrant element, the National Evangelical Lutheran Church, organized in 1898, stood in relationship to the Finnish Lutheran Gospel Association, whose mission work was in Japan. Missionaries en route to Japan or back often visited the Finnish churches. The National Evangelical Lutheran Church in 1923 related itself to the Missouri Synod and joined it in 1964.

Small though its population, Iceland sent considerable numbers of its people to America, settling principally in the northwestern states and Canada. In 1885 the Icelandic Synod was formed, mainly of rural churches. A large congregation grew up in Winnipeg. The first president of the synod was Jon Bjarnason, who came as a missionary in 1877 and served as head of the synod for 23 years.

THE SLOVAK SYNOD

Lutherans emigrated also from Slovakia, but the church itself took no measures to care for the faraway brethren. A quarter of a century elapsed before a Slovak Evangelical Lutheran Synod was consummated in 1902 in Pennsylvania. Its contacts were mainly with the Missouri Synod, and in 1908 the synod joined the Synodical Conference.

AMERICANIZATION

Each of the immigrant groups was preoccupied with its own affairs, conserving and preserving much of its spiritual heritage while seeking to find a new home in a strange land. The Lutherans brought their religious books with them, followed orders of service from the home church, and used catechisms and hymnbooks in their mother tongue. Their attitude toward fellow Lutherans was one of questioning and caution. Only gradually did they find kindred spirits. In the first generation loyalty to church was expressed in a European tongue, and often a second generation grew up in an imported atmosphere as far as church life was concerned. The Pennsylvania and Ohio Germans as well as later immigrants fancied German would remain a living language in America. Also the Scandinavian churches were still using their fathers' languages into the 20th century.

Nor were the earliest attempts to translate Lutheranism into English encouraging examples. For all his urbanity and intellectual gifts, Dr. Quitman of New York was not representative of his generation, and his catechism had a slow sale. Even more "American" was the first president of Gettysburg Seminary, S. S. Schmucker. He had learned theology from the saintly J. H. C. Helmuth, but he became enamored of an American spirit that spent its energy in a vague ambition to unite the Protestant churches in order to counteract the Church of Rome.

Schmucker was esteemed by fellow leaders in America and Europe in the activity of the Evangelical Alliance. But when in 1855 he proposed a "Definite Platform" for a spineless Lutheranism, his own church repudiated him. He failed to see that the course of Lutheranism was not an imitation of revivalistic practices and confessional indifference. Paul Henkel in the Tennessee Synod and the confessional literature issuing from the press of his sons in New Market, Virginia, were the real legacy of Mühlenberg even in the older synods, and when the anti-unionism of the German confessional churches took root in the Midwest, along with the conservatism of Scandinavian churches that had not known any Prussian Union, the future was clear.

MOVEMENTS TOWARD UNITY

The decade of 1865 to 1875 marks a watershed in the history of the Lutheran Church in America. For in that decade the Ministerium of Pennsylvania broke with the General Synod and led in the formation of the General Council, which under C. P. Krauth's leadership for the first time translated the Lutheran faith into an American context. "The Unaltered Augsburg Confession," the Council declared in 1866, "is by pre-eminence the confession of that faith. The acceptance of its doctrines and the avowal of them without equivocation or mental reservation make, mark and identify that church which alone in the true, original, historical and honest sense is the Evangelical Lutheran Church." The council gathered under this banner, beside the Ministerium of Pennsylvania, the Ministerium of New York, the Pittsburgh Synod, the English Synod of Ohio, the Swedish Augustana Synod, and the German synods of Michigan, Minnesota, Canada, Illinois, and Iowa. Not all of these remained within the ranks, but the changes were in the direction of an even stricter body. For in 1872 the Synodical Conference drew together synods that followed the leadership of the Missouri Synod. These included Missouri, Wisconsin, Minnesota, Illinois, the Norwegian Synod, and the Ohio Synod. Later additions brought in the Michigan Synod, the Synod of Nebraska, and the Slovak Synod.

Doctrinal disputes, especially concerning the interpretation of the doctrine of predestination, led to the withdrawal from the Synodical Conference of the Norwegian and the Ohio synods, while in the General Council a long-standing issue was the policy of pulpit and altar fellowship (Galesburg-Akron Rule). In this development the General Synod itself was deeply affected. Its own progress drew it ever closer to a conservative position. Such also was the case in the General Synod of the South, which had separated from the General Synod during the Civil War. So few were the differences now between the General Council, the General Synod, and the General Synod of the South that union became increasingly possible.

Between 1820 and 1920 over 5 million Germans and more than 2 million Scandinavians came to the United States. Only a part of these of course were Lutherans, though most of the Scandinavians were nominally so, and the Lutheran Church lost thousands in the process of migration. But the inner unity in these various groupings of synods was a remarkable phenomenon, and the planting of the Lutheran churches on the new continent is a story both of sacrifice and of loyalty, often of heroism, and always of grace.

American Overseas Missions

Themselves the fruit of missionary endeavor, the American churches soon joined older societies in bringing the Gospel to other lands or pioneered on new fields. One of the early projects of the General Synod was to constitute a missionary society in 1837. It channeled aid to Rhenius in the Tinnivelly area in India and in 1841 sent "Father" J. C. K. Heyer, who had been a home missionary in the new Mississippi valley settlements, as its pioneer missionary to India. He located at Guntur and started labors in the Telugu country. In 1850 the North German Missionary Society transferred its field in Rajahmundry to the American church. Through Heyer the Rajahmundry mission in 1869 became the responsibility of the General Council, while the General Synod cared for the Telugu field and a new mission in Liberia, Africa. The General Synod of the South at first cooperated with the General Synod in India but after 1892 had its own field in Japan. The General Council added a Japanese mission in 1908. The Missouri Synod began a mission of its own in India in 1894 in proximity to the old Danish-Halle and Leipzig fields in Tranquebar. This has extended southward and westward in southern India. Before World War I the synod assumed a new field in China with a beginning in Hankow.

Thus all of the larger bodies had joined in world missions. But

240

also the smaller and independent synods displayed sacrificial interest. The Iowa Synod sent missionary funds to Neuendettelsau, the Ohio to Hermannsburg, the Buffalo to the Hanover Free Church field in South Africa. The Augustana Synod gathered money for the Hermannsburg, the Swedish, and the Norwegian societies, and after joining the General Council participated through its own missionaries in the Rajahmundry program. In 1908 the synod took over work in Honan, China, which a society had started in 1902. Despite their internal controversies the Norwegian bodies were able to work together in several foreign fields, often uniting their efforts with missionary societies in Norway. Madagascar, China, Africa attracted men and means. After the union of 1917 a unified policy was possible. And by 1913 a Union Lutheran Theological Seminary in China was an unusual example of united action by a number of churches, namely, the Norwegian and Finnish Missionary societies, three U. S. A. Norwegian bodies, and the Augustana Synod. Even the smallest of Lutheran bodies had a part in the missionary movement, for the Church of the Lutheran Brethren was represented in China and the Icelandic Synod in Japan.

SOUTH AMERICA

Immigration flowed also to South America, but here missionary aid was to come mainly from the northern continent. Early in the present century the Missouri Synod began gathering scattered German settlements into congregations — Brazil in 1901 and Argentina in 1913. Some pastoral activity was carried on in Buenos Aires, but not until the formation of The United Lutheran Church in America was an intensive ministry begun among the Slovak, German, and Hungarian Lutherans in this metropolis. Since 1666 Danish Lutheran pastors had been active on the Virgin Islands, which passed into the control of the United States in 1917. On the north coast of South America Dutch Lutheran pastors had established the church in 1743. In 1918 The United Lutheran Church assumed responsibility for the British Guiana ministry among Indians and Negroes. On Puerto Rico the Augustana Synod began a mission after the Spanish-American War of 1898.

AUSTRALIA

Quite different is the record in Australia. The Prussian Union, which drove Stephan and Grabau to North America, led A. L. Kavel to emigrate in 1838 with his followers to Adelaide. Other groups joined, one of them under Pastor G. D. Fritsche. Doctrinal and practical issues arose to divide the immigrants, with the result that Kavel became the head of the Immanuel Synod and Fritsche of the Evangelical Lutheran Synod of Australia. The latter gained recruits from the Dresden and Hermannsburg societies and after 1881 entered into relationships with the Missouri Synod, which trained its pastors for several decades until a Concordia College in Adelaide could supply pastors. The Immanuel Synod was associated for a while with the Victoria Synod, which was a Basel Missionary body, and the union was called the Evangelical Lutheran General Synod. But when the Victoria Synod persisted in following a unionistic Basel policy, one part of the Immanuel Synod joined with a synod in Queensland, which had been shepherded by Hermannsburg men and was known as the United German-Scandinavian Evangelical Lutheran Church of Queensland. Thus, in 1910, the Evangelical Lutheran Church Union was formed. It had the support of Hermannsburg and Neuendettelsau. The other part of the Immanuel Synod remained with the Victoria body and in 1889 was joined by the second Queensland synod, whose origin went back to workers from the Gossner Missionary Society, namely, the Evangelical Lutheran Synod of Queensland. This combined group continued to use the name of the Evangelical Lutheran General Synod.

MISSION AND UNITY

From a period when the life of the church seemed stifled by a rationalistic view of the world and the governments looked on the churches as necessary police and pedagogical forces of society had come the mighty missionary movement in the evangelical churches of northern Europe. In the Lutheran Church the force of the impulse not only created new agencies of inner mission work, as in the Fliedner, Loehe, and Bodelschwingh establishments in Germany and the Passavant institutions in the United States, but expressed itself also in a new independence and self-government of the church, making the Confessions of the church the standard of preaching, teaching, and discipline. It refused to conform to contemporary culture that went from rationalism through romanticism to secularism, materialism, and atheism. The preaching of the Gospel at home and to the ends of the earth took on

242

an aggressiveness and a boldness hitherto unknown in the Church of the Reformation. And on foreign fields even more than at home the various sections of that church were coming into contact with one another and into a form of cooperation that was to prove of immeasurable significance when the world of the 19th century was shaken to its foundations by the world wars of the next century.

XVII

THE SHAKING OF THE FOUNDATIONS

The year 1914 brought to an end an era in Western civilization. The unified Germany that had grown up around Prussia found itself in increasing difficulty with its neighbors — Russia, France, England. When war finally broke out, the flames spread throughout the world engulfing Turkey, Japan, Italy, and the United States. The old order was shaken to its foundations by four years of destruction. When peace was restored, the ancient structures of empires and boundaries of nations were gone. Germany was left to rebuild its government and institutions, but its possessions on the eastern edge of Europe were lost to Russia and its colonies over the earth divided among the victors. The Church of the Lutheran Reformation suffered severely in Europe, but in America a new force had developed that radically altered the situation of Lutheranism in the postwar world.

YEARS OF CRISES

What centuries of effort had failed to effect, the disaster of the war in Germany did produce — the separation of church and state. The new German constitution of 1919 proclaimed freedom of religion and of religious association. Yet the separation was not complete. The power of tradition was evident in the regulation that the state would still collect the tax for churches from citizens willing to support them. Religious instruction too continued in the lower schools, and the state supported the theological faculties. But inasmuch as the organs of state no longer exercised any administrative control in the churches, these were forced to develop self-government. Synods became the usual form, and a number of the provincial churches adopted the title of "bishop" for the chief officer. Thus Hanover, Saxony, and others used the term, but the Old Prussian Union Church retained the designation "general superintendent." In 1922 the 28 provincial churches, the

245

Landeskirchen, organized a Federation of Evangelical Churches. Each church retained its autonomy, but in the federation, or *Bund,* representatives were to meet every three years for counsel and fellowship in a conference, or *Kirchentag.* Through an executive committee efforts at cooperation were to be undertaken. But for a decade no great changes were made in the fragmented condition of the German evangelical churches. The pattern of 400 years persisted.

The decade of the 1920s was one of confusion in government and for people. To churches ministering to a nation depressed by defeat in war and by economic ills after the war the ringing voice of Karl Barth was a stimulant. For in his sermons and *Commentary on Romans* he pointed to the true strength of the Christian. The return to a study of Scripture was a healthful antidote to the barren speculation of much of prewar theology. The 1917 quadricentennial of the Reformation had been eclipsed by the war, but a new interest in Luther was advanced by the writings of Karl Holl. The collection of Luther's works in the Weimar Edition was also delayed by war, but new and more popular reprintings of Luther's works were issued as soon as publication was possible. Not only the church, however, was interested in Luther. In search of means for raising the morale of a dejected nation, political demagogs proclaimed Luther a national hero who could again give Germany an exalted position in Western culture. To stem a growing rationalism based on the central place of science in the new age, theology sought, in Karl Heim, to show the connection between faith and knowledge. But the times were too revolutionary for any synthesis — old or new. A mood of resignation and despair made interpretations of men such as those of Dostoevsky and Kierkegaard popular, while Christian scholars like Emil Brunner tried to find a basis for hope in a human nature created good, and Rudolf Bultmann talked of reinterpreting Scripture in terms of today rather than in the imagery of Scripture.

THE CHURCH AND HITLER

While the theologians wrote about a "theology of crisis," an even greater crisis was being fashioned for the churches. The spirit of despair, born of resentment against the Treaty of Versailles, of frustration amid quarreling victors, and of economic depression and social readjustment, found a voice in Adolf Hitler. How this peculiar

246

figure could charm a whole people from the working class to university professors is a tragic story whose end is chaos. But his goal encompassed also the churches, where he found supporters to help him. Even in a situation where church and nation are indistinguishable it is difficult to label as "Christian" nationalists whose program emphasized anti-Semitism. But the German Church League, the Thuringian German Christians, and the Christian German Movement, while varying in their hatred of the Jews and in their desire to rid the church of Judaism and its Old Testament, agreed that for them the Christian church was a German church. They could echo Hitler's challenge that the German nation and the German church should be characterized by German soil and German blood. Their call was for one German church instead of a score and more of provincial churches. This church would honor Luther while it opposed the Jews, the Marxists, the pacifists, and the internationalists. Their cause seemed on the way to victory when Hitler became chancellor in January 1933.

Already, however, the churches were beginning to react. A group of pastors under Hans Asmussen issued the "Altoona Statement," declaring that the church lives by the Word and its message cannot be dictated by the state. General Superintendent Otto Dibelius of Berlin fearlessly denounced the aims of the German Christians. The Federation of Evangelical Churches now tried to agree on a new constitution, even naming a bishop, Friedrich von Bodelschwingh, before any constitution defined his duties. In Düsseldorf a group of Reformed theologians, including Barth, asserted that the church had one leader — Jesus Christ. When a new church constitution was ready, elections were held. Hitler himself came to the aid of the German Christians, with the result that they gained control. In September 1933 a former chaplain in the army, a friend of Hitler, Ludwig Müller, was elected *Reichsbischof.* Müller had been leader of the German Christians in East Prussia and knew the tactics of the party. One of his moves was to incorporate the Evangelical Youth into the Hitler Youth organization. Wherever feasible he had non-Aryans retired from the ministry. Pastors were forbidden to speak on controversial subjects. Thus the German churches were supposed to be unified — by a political party.

During the same month that Müller became *Reichsbischof* a

Pastors' Emergency League came into being under the leadership of Martin Niemöller. Within a few months its membership grew to more than 4,000. These pastors claimed that they were bound only by Scripture and the Confessions in their preaching. They pledged aid to one another. From their pulpits they read protests against the encroachments of the state even though it often meant imprisonment, sometimes death. In 1934 a series of meetings, or synods, was held in which the pastors and churches protested the measures of Müller and his associates. These culminated in May in a synod at Barmen, where 18 provincial churches were represented by 139 delegates, of whom 53 were laymen. Here a "Theological Declaration Concerning the Present Situation" was adopted, along with an address by the leader, Hans Asmussen. The churches refused compliance with Müller's regime, pledged aid to non-Aryan ministers and students, and asserted that their organization rather than the *Reichsbischof* was the moral leader of the German churches.

The synod hoped that the Reformed and Lutheran churches would cooperate as one — a hope not realized. While Lutherans were active in the movement, there was a difference between their attitude and that of the Reformed. The latter, influenced by Barth, wanted a more complete break with the state, while the former were not ready to give the Barmen Declaration a place alongside the Confessions of the Lutheran Church. As long as confessional differences separated the churches, they could not act as if they were one. In August the Lutherans formed their own council to oppose the government's policies. They tried to work with Hanns Kerrl, who had been appointed minister for church affairs but found cooperation impossible since he assumed a dictatorial position. When war came, Hitler's regime brought all matters under a tyrannical government. Barmen as well as the council could only go underground, and imprisonment and death became the lot of the leaders of resistance. Hanns Lilje escaped death, but Dietrich Bonhoeffer was executed. Niemöller was held a prisoner by Hitler from 1937 to 1945.

LUTHERANS ON EASTERN BORDERS

The peace after World War I changed the eastern borders of Germany and affected sharply the Lutheran churches which had been a part of that region. Posen and Silesia were transferred to the newly

248

established nation of Poland. Some of the bitterest campaigns between Russia and Germany had been fought in this region, leaving devastation everywhere. In what had formerly been the German province of Posen the church had been a part of the Prussian Union. After the war there was a large emigration from what was now a Roman Catholic land, but in 1936 there were still 185 pastors among the 300,000 members of the Union Evangelical Church in Posen and Pomerelia. In Old Poland, with Warsaw as its center, was the Evangelical Church of the Augsburg Confession, with over 600,000 members. This church was divided into 10 districts, each with a senior functioning under a bishop, Julius Bursche being the first incumbent of the office.

Both the church in Posen and that of the Augsburg Confession included Polish congregations and pastors, and tension marred the relationships of the Poles with the Germans, who were in the majority. As the spirit of Polish nationalism rose, there were repercussions in the churches, and these increased as Ukrainians joined Lutheran churches around Stanislav. It was here in what had formerly been a province of Austria-Hungary that the Evangelical Church of the Augsburg and Helvetic Confession was organized in 1919. Many of the Ukrainians were converts from Roman Catholicism. A decade later the membership of this Lutheran-Reformed group was around 35,000 members. Oldest in point of history and most devoted in their Lutheran faith were the Polish churches in Silesia. They recalled with gratitude the fact that in the Counter-Reformation it was the Swedish king Charles XII who saved for them their church in Teschen.

The war which started in Austria proved to be the final chapter in the story of the Austro-Hungarian Empire, for it literally fell apart among the nationalities that had been clamoring for independence. Austria was cut down to a small area of German population. A new row of states emerged — Czechoslovakia, Hungary, Yugoslavia. Hundreds of thousands of Germans streamed back into Germany and Austria, but many remained; and the Lutherans among them associated themselves with the native-language churches. Burgenland, a portion of western Hungary, was added to Austria. Here Magyar was the language of some congregations. Otherwise the quarter million Lutherans in the Austrian Evangelical Church of the Augsburg Confession were

Germans. The new nation of Czechoslovakia (including the former Bohemia and Moravia) contained both German and Slovak Lutherans organized in two bodies — the German Evangelical Church in Bohemia, Moravia, and Silesia, a relatively small church, and the Evangelical Lutheran Church of the Augsburg Confession in Slovakia, counting some 400,000 members. After the Paris treaties Hungary was considerably reduced in size. The Hungarian Lutheran Church of the Augsburg Confession was scattered over the whole country, its half million members distributed in 15 districts, speaking Slovak, Hungarian, and German.

The new state of Yugoslavia (southern Slavs) was made up of various parts of the former Austro-Hungarian Empire. Here as in Czechoslovakia the Lutherans were divided into a German and a Slovak body. The German Evangelical Lutheran Church of the Augsburg Confession was constituted of groups formerly belonging to the Lutheran Church of Hungary. The Slovak body was made up of people of the former countries of Serbia, Croatia, and Slovenia.

The large Lutheran constituency in Transylvania — the Siebenbürgen colonies — as a result of the war found itself in the new nation of Rumania. It was accorded the title of the Evangelical State Church of the Augsburg Confession in Rumania, and its support came partially from church taxes. With over 500 congregations and almost 400,000 members it represented a large segment of the Lutheran Church in the east. In 1920 it received some congregations from Hungary, but 25 other congregations from Hungary formed their own body — the Evangelical Synodical Presbyterial Lutheran Church. They used the Hungarian, German, Slovak, and Rumanian languages and had a bishop as common head. Thus Rumania too counted two Lutheran churches — one German, the other mainly Hungarian.

The states on this eastern border of Europe were torn by internal conflicts — Slavs against Magyars, Magyars against Austrians, and both Slavs and Magyars against Germans. Freedom came to national communities with the breakup of the Austro-Hungarian Empire, but between World Wars I and II tensions between various groups and the Germans had injurious effects on church organizations. Yet loyalty to Luther's Catechism, the Augsburg Confession, Lutheran hymnody, liturgy, and devotional literature survived the secular divisions. The scarcity of pastors called forth lay leadership in the many small group-ings created by particular loyalties. World War II was to shake again the fragile ecclesiastical combinations that independence had brought into being.

LUTHERANS IN BALTIC LANDS

The collapse of one empire afforded independence in eastern and southeastern Europe, and the end of another brought a moment of freedom to northeastern states. For in its death the Russian Empire relaxed its grip on the Baltic provinces and on the Lutherans within Russia, though a more fearful tyranny was in the making. When the Bolsheviks ended the war with Germany, independence was tem-porarily allowed Estonia, Latvia, and Finland. The Estonian Church at once reorganized itself into district synods in which the parishes were represented and elected a bishop who was consecrated in 1921 by Nathan Söderblom, the archbishop of Sweden. The state church became a folk church in 1929 and was recognized by the state as a corporation with its own privileges. In 1934 these rights were recon-firmed, but the state asserted its right to approve elections of bishops and to annul the privileges. The people of the parishes had an oppor-tunity to call pastors and elect synod representatives but showed no great interest in exercising their rights, though they did vote to restore religious education into the schools in 1923.

The state deposed the bishop in 1939, and with the renewal of war between Russia and Germany the heavy hand of Russification fell on church and nation. Religious instruction in the schools was forbidden, as were religious publications and broadcasts. Religious books were confiscated and the theological faculty at Tartu was closed. Church property was nationalized, and congregations had to pay rent for its use and themselves raise the money for the salaries of the clergy. A breathing period returned when German troops occupied the country from 1941 to 1944, but Russia's eventual victory drove 80,000 people into emigration. Half of the clergy scattered to Sweden, Germany, Canada, and Australia. In 1945 only 77 clergymen remained of the 250 who five years earlier had ministered to a church of 900,000 members.

The development in Latvia was not greatly different, except that here relationships between Letts and Germans disturbed the peace of

251

the church. The Germans wanted autonomy, though they constituted only six percent of the population. They were given three places on the church council of nine, and the synod elected one Latvian and one German bishop in 1922 — both ordained by Archbishop Söderblom. It was a period of growth in congregational life. In 1922 a new hymnbook was issued for Latvia, a country which now included parts of Livland and Courland. In 1932 a new Lettish translation of the Gospels was published.

A strong romantic movement inspired a Lettish renaissance. The Lettish university at Riga boasted 11 faculties and 8,000 students. The church was drawn into this movement, but more for its sanction of national festivals than for its spiritual contribution. The pastors enjoyed high community standing because of their education, but there were few of them and their training was inadequate. Bishop Irbe (1922—1931) strove to steer a middle course, avoiding the national extremism. He established a church *gymnasium* and theological seminary and gave the church its constitution. But in the political struggle that involved expelling the Germans from the Dome Church in Riga he retired rather than yield to the nationalists. The state interfered with church affairs, and his successor had to accept a governing council that excluded German members. But the same fate awaited Latvia as Estonia. After 20 years of freedom, war would again bring Russian domination, this time in the form of a communist dictatorship.

When the czardom ended, there were over one and a half million Lutherans in Russia. The greatest concentration was in the valley of the Volga, where descendants of colonists from the days of Catherine II maintained their schools and churches. There were Lutheran parishes in Leningrad, the Ukraine, in the Caucasus, and even in Siberia. An Evangelical Lutheran General Synod of Russia had been organized in 1923, with Superintendent Theophilus Meyer as head, and a seminary established at Leningrad in 1925. After 1929 the communists instituted a policy of persecution. The seminary was closed in 1931 and most of the pastors were imprisoned or exiled. One large contingent on the Volga escaped to Manchuria, whence it was aided by the Lutheran World Convention to sail for Brazil. By 1935 a once-flourishing Russian Lutheran community had been dispersed and largely destroyed.

Lithuania too became a free republic in 1918. German, Lettish, and Lithuanian Lutherans each organized their own synod and looked forward to state recognition of their church. But World War II almost completed the elimination of Lutheranism, which World War I started by separating it from older churches.

Finland joined the group of free states in 1917. It had been able to retain a church structure under Russian overlordship and new forms were unnecessary. It had solved, too, its Swedish relationships without the animosity characterizing Latvian and German associations. A Swedish bishopric had been established for the Swedish (and German) congregations alongside the Finnish dioceses, and a Swedish theological school at Abo prepared the pastors for the Swedish parishes. The times brought a friendlier climate for the church, the cultured classes showing it more respect. But Marxism made approaches to the working class difficult. Yet the strong revival spirit of Finnish Christendom prevailed, continuing the pietistic character of the preceding century. Youth movements won many, and there was no dearth of theological students. The Church Convocation, meeting every five years, adopted in 1938 a new Bible translation and a new hymnbook. The war with Russia in 1940 cost Finland a great part of the Viborg diocese, resulting in mass evacuation and transfer of populations. Still the brave nation retained its independence — and the church its freedom.

THE SCANDINAVIAN CHURCHES

The other northern nations — Sweden, Denmark, Norway — succeeded in staying out of World War I, but their churches took a leading part in extending aid to the stricken regions after the war. It was therefore possible for them to continue normal courses, developing plans already under way. Sweden celebrated the quadricentennial of the Reformation by having ready a new translation of the Bible and a few years later added a section of new hymns to its hymnbook. In 1937 it completed a revision of the whole hymnbook, and in 1942 adopted a new handbook, or manual of Communion and other services and an order of pastoral acts. These new church books gave proof of disciplined church scholarship. Church vestments and art received renewed attention, and new church buildings in Stockholm and elsewhere betokened changes in architecture. In Denmark a new transla-

253

tion of the Old Testament was authorized in 1931, and a new interest developed in the field of liturgical music under the leadership of Thomas Laub. Norway completed work on a new service book in 1920 and had the luxury of two new hymnbooks, one in 1920, a revision of the official hymnal and more ecumenical in content, the other in 1925 in the older Norwegian language. A songbook of 1928 was more popular in spirit with revival hymns of Lina Sandell, Moody, and Sankey. In 1930 the bishops began to wear full episcopal regalia. The altar book of 1920 was the work of Gustav Jensen, a disciple of Loehe. To the list of revised service books should be added that of the church in Iceland, adopted in 1934.

Vital intellectual work was produced in all these countries. Danish writers renewed interest in both Grundtvig and Kierkegaard and called attention to the books of Holl and Barth. There was an earnest attempt to relate the Gospel to social needs of the day. This found expression in the Inner Mission program. Olfert Ricard, a leader in the YMCA, C. Skovgaard-Petersen, a writer and Bible teacher, Vilhelm Grönbeck, a professor, were Christian voices with wide audiences. Norway's Old Testament scholar S. Mowinckel gained international reputation. The hymn writers Bengt Stoeylen and Anders Hovden and the popular Inner Mission leader John Lunde contributed to the high standing of the church in Norway. Intellectuals in both Denmark and Norway were represented in the membership of the "Oxford," or Moral Rearmament, movement.

The year of the beginning of the war — 1914 — brought Nathan Söderblom to the archbishopric of Uppsala. He had already gained fame as a scholar of the history of religion. Now he turned his talents to the service of the Church of Sweden, enriching it in many ways. His genial personality won him friends in all classes, and he created a new climate of respect for the church among State- and Free-Church people. Coming from a pietistic parsonage he opposed formalism and stereotype. He fought for spiritual songs as well as stately hymns, and preaching should be in terms of the congregation. He made the bishops' conferences influential and inaugurated regular meetings of the bishops of all the Northern countries. He felt most deeply the unchristian character of war. In the dark days of World War I he appealed to Christian leaders in all lands to exert their influence.

254

Not until after 1918 could Söderblom bring interested people together to consider the place of the church in society. But in 1925 he assembled in Stockholm the first ecumenical gathering of modern times. The Christian Life and Work movement that he headed merged later with the Anglican-sponsored Faith and Order movement to create in 1948 the World Council of Churches. His capacity for friendship did much to reconcile Christians of warring lands after World War I, though death in 1931 prevented him from seeing the results of his endeavors. One of the unique achievements of his administration was the mutual recognition in 1922 by the Anglican and Swedish churches of the episcopal succession and the ministries of their communions.

Of all Lutheran leaders in the postwar period Söderblom's name ranks first. But other Swedish theologians contributed to the growing clarification of the meaning of the Gospel and to the ecumenical spirit among the churches. Gustav Aulén and Anders Nygren were widely read — the one interpreting the nature of the Christian faith, the other, of Christian love. Not that all were ready to follow the Söderblom leadership. The Danish bishop Harold Ostenfeld was an admirer and supporter, and Valdemar Ammundsen succeeded him as an ecumenical leader, but Archbishop Johansson of Finland opposed both the theology of Söderblom as "liberal" and the ecumenical endeavor. German churches were too busy fighting for their existence to participate, and their government after 1933 would allow no international contacts. But a light had been lit, and it brightened the way into a dark future.

Despite brilliant leadership, solid scholarship, improvement of places and ways of worship, and modern means of communication, attendance at church services and at Holy Communion remained small. The ties between church and school slowly dissolved. The churches in Scandinavia retained inherited privileges, but their influence steadily declined among a religiously indifferent population. Secularization and materialism seemed to grow with each new invention. New weapons of war threatened massive destruction. A kind of pessimism settled over men's minds and spirits as communism spread in Europe and Asia. Terms like "post-Christian" world were heard. The atom bombs that closed the tragedy of World War II cast vast shadows over the world. Lutherans of Europe looked hopefully across the Atlantic to their brethren in the New World.

The Lutherans of the United States had begun a new chapter. The 19th century was one of increasing immigration, especially into the midwestern and western states, while the older Lutheran settlements in the east and south sought to keep their identity in the multidenominational environment of a country where all religions had equal freedom. From the first a conviction grew that Lutherans should achieve some kind of unity despite their varied European backgrounds. We have seen how combinations were gradually effected in the General Synod, the General Council, and the Synodical Conference. But the new century was to be one of movements toward further unification.

Two major mergers occurred during World War I. One of these had long been in preparation. It was the union of three groups of Norwegians — the Hauge Synod with its emphasis on lay participation in the worship and work of the church, the Norwegian Synod, representing the orderliness and educated clergy of the Norwegian state church, and the United Church of 1890, which had gained flexibility from contacts with other Lutheran bodies. In 1917, the quadricentennial year of the Reformation, these bodies formed The Norwegian Lutheran Church in America, its half a million members representing 92 percent of Norwegian Lutherans in America. The Lutheran Free Church was not yet ready to join because of congregational polity, and a trio of small bodies remained aloof because of traditional divergences. The merged church consolidated its theological education in the seminary at St. Paul, Minn.

The following year a still larger merger brought together the oldest Lutheran organizations in the United States. While apart in the General Council, the General Synod, and the General Synod of the South, the Lutherans in the eastern and southern states had drawn together in missionary cooperation at home and abroad, in the preparation of a common hymnal and liturgy, in conferences among educators, church organizations, and students, and in a joint celebration of the quadricentennial of the Reformation. The time was ripe for union, and in 1917 a constitution was agreed upon by all members except the Augustana Synod, which hesitated because of language and structure peculiarities. The new church, The United Lutheran Church in America, was constituted in 1918. The Slovak Zion Synod was created in 1919, and the Icelandic Synod joined in 1942. Its 4,000 churches, 2,800 ministers, and 800,000 members made the United Lutheran Church the strongest single Lutheran body in the country, and its long history gave it influence in many relationships with other Protestant groups. Theological leadership was exercised by the seminaries at Philadelphia and Gettysburg.

Another significant merger followed in 1919. The synods of Wisconsin, Michigan, and Minnesota had been formed mainly out of German congregations. Strong influences from Loehe at Neuendettelsau, Harms at Hermannsburg, and Walther at St. Louis had led these synods into strict confessionalism and discipline. All had at one time been members of the General Council but had left it to join the Synodical Conference. In 1904 the Nebraska congregations of the Wisconsin Synod were granted the status of a synod, the District Synod of Nebraska, and it became the fourth member of the group known as the Joint Synod of Wisconsin, Minnesota, Michigan, and Other States. In 1917 the four bodies merged into one church, which concentrated the education of its pastors at Wauwatosa and later at Thiensville, Wis. Now known as the Wisconsin Evangelical Lutheran Synod, the body reports some 350,000 baptized members. Next to the Missouri Synod it was the largest component of the Synodical Conference.

Thus a large part of American Lutheranism had come together in doctrinal and organizational union in the course of three years. But the process was to go on. The postwar period saw a rapid decline in the use of other languages than English in the Lutheran churches. As the walls of separation crumbled, the various language groups recognized their similarity in doctrine, and in the expansion of their activities they met one another on many fronts. The year of the quadricentennial of the Augsburg Confession witnessed another advance in intersynodical commitments.

In 1930 the Joint Synod of Ohio, the Iowa Synod, and the Buffalo Synod merged. Loehe men had left their mark on the Ohio and Iowa bodies, while Grabau had fought for the freedom of his body from state control in Germany. The years in America mellowed the dictatorial powers of the clergy in the Buffalo Synod, and Ohio and Iowa found themselves in agreement on their attitude to the Confessions. All were faithful to the standards of the church, but they did not deem

257

it necessary to believe that the Book of Concord gives a final, complete answer to all questions that might arise in later centuries. So these synods united in the American Lutheran Church, keeping their seminaries at Dubuque, Iowa, and Columbus, Ohio.

AMERICAN LUTHERAN APPROACHES

Meanwhile The Norwegian Lutheran Church in America, the Augustana Church, the United Danish Church, and the Lutheran Free Church began to recognize how alike their mission and message were. In the same year as the American Lutheran Church was born, it joined with these other bodies in an association for edification, fellowship, and discussion of common programs, known as the American Lutheran Conference. It thought of itself as a mediating influence between the Synodical Conference, with its "conservative" theology, and The United Lutheran Church, more "liberal" in its theology and more American in its ways of work and expression. Because of its earlier relationship with the General Council, the Augustana Church felt least content with the role of the American Lutheran Conference.

In 1917 The Lutheran Church — Missouri Synod passed the million mark in its baptized membership, and in 1944 the million-and-a-half figure. In the latter year it counted over 4,500 congregations. The polity of the synod made the congregation the center of the life of the church, and no Lutheran body excelled it in the loyalty of its laity to the doctrine and practices adopted by the synod. In 1944 about 75,000 children were in the parochial schools of the church, which were maintained entirely by the contributions of members. The education of the ministry was carefully planned from parochial school through colleges and into the seminaries at St. Louis, Missouri, and Springfield, Illinois. The growth of the church had been steady, and the means used were the most modern. The "Lutheran Hour" was heard literally throughout the world.

The Missouri Synod had consistently affirmed doctrinal agreement as the essential basis for relationships with other Lutherans. It had carried on doctrinal discussions within its ministry, and it advocated theological conferences with other synods. Long negotiations had been held with the American Lutheran Church. The synod included districts in Canada and South America and was affiliated with Free Lutheran bodies

258

in Europe and the Evangelical Lutheran Church of Australia. Prior to World War II missionary work abroad was centered in India and China. In North America the Missouri Synod had pulpit and altar fellowship with the other members of the Synodical Conference, namely, the Joint Synod of Wisconsin and Other States, the small Norwegian Synod, and the Slovak Synod.

THE NATIONAL LUTHERAN COUNCIL

Most far reaching of the unifying forces in American Lutheranism was the National Lutheran Council. Its inception dates from the 1917 quadricentennial of the Reformation and the rudely interrupting events of America's entrance into World War I. The drafting of hundreds of thousands of Lutheran young men into war camps called for a ministry to them by their churches. In October 1917 the National Lutheran Commission for Soldiers' and Sailors' Welfare was established by most of the Lutheran bodies. A total of 150 camp pastors were appointed, and the commission enlisted 100 chaplains for the Army and Navy. A layman's organization, the Lutheran Brotherhood, served as an auxiliary. But the unusual circumstances of a nation at war called for a stronger agency.

In September 1918 the National Lutheran Council came into being, its constitution having been ratified by the United Lutheran Church, Augustana, the Norwegian Lutheran Church, the Lutheran Free Church, the Joint Synod of Ohio, the Iowa Synod, the Buffalo Synod, the United Danish Church, the Icelandic Synod, and later the Suomi Synod. The council was an agency of these bodies, speaking for them in matters involving the government and representing them to the nation. Its Division of Public Relations assembled statistics and disseminated information to the press. A *Lutheran World Almanac and Annual Encyclopedia* eventually grew to eight volumes and for the first time in Lutheran history sought to compile material from all the churches. The names of O. M. Pannkoke, G. L. Kieffer, and O. M. Norlie appear as pioneers in this field. The council also sought to coordinate the home mission programs of the many churches and to serve the interests of the multibranched inner missions. It stimulated the observance of the quadricentennial of Luther's Catechism in 1929 and of the Augsburg Confession in 1930. In the 1930s, under the leadership of

259

Dr. Ralph Long, the council increased its usefulness to member churches by steps taken to advance the cause of stewardship, by studies in the social responsibilities of the church, by establishing a department of welfare, and by expanding its publicity program.

THE COUNCIL AND THE LUTHERAN WORLD CONVENTION

The council's most dramatic program was the part it played in relief work and service to the cause of foreign missions in the years following World War I. The name of Lauritz Larsen is gratefully recalled as the early leader in the program of the council both at home and abroad. Early in 1919 commissioners were sent to Europe, who reported on the disasters that had befallen Lutherans in war-torn countries. Appeals for aid to Poland and the Baltic states brought immediate response from the American Lutherans, who quickly raised hundreds of thousands of dollars and gathered hundreds of tons of clothing. In 1920 Dr. John Morehead went as representative to Europe, and for the next 15 years his name was identified with an ever-growing association with European Lutheranism. Germany, Poland, France, and Russia were visited, and in every possible way assistance was given to suffering brethren. In the first decade of its existence the council raised around $8 million for relief of congregations, pastors, and institutions.

In 1923 the first world gathering of Lutherans took place in Eisenach. Morehead was named chairman of the continuing committee, and at the second gathering in Copenhagen in 1929 he was elected chairman of a small executive committee. At the Copenhagen meeting the Europeans were not yet ready for formal organization, and the name "Lutheran World Convention" implied no fixed structure. Much of the burden of the support of weak churches fell on the National Lutheran Council of the United States, whose funds were deeply cut by years of economic depression. When the third meeting of the World Convention was held in Paris in 1935, the German churches were feeling the effects of their government's control over finances, shutting off communication with their mission fields. Again the council came to the rescue, and only its solid backing in America and its international experience made it ready for the heavy calls World War II would make. A great part was played by Scandinavian churches in the relief measures adopted by the convention.

Soon after the war the council was instrumental in setting up the

Lutheran Foreign Missions Conference to consider the needs of Lutheran fields throughout the world, many of which had been deprived of German leaders and funds. Within the decade 1920—1930 the council raised $700,000 to aid in this program. Working with the Lutheran World Convention, the council was able to give emergency aid to the Berlin Mission fields, to the Breklum Mission in China, the Finnish China Mission, the Gossner Mission in India, and the Hermannsburg South Africa Mission. A brief survey will indicate the importance of happenings on the Lutheran mission fields of the world between the two world wars.

LUTHERANS IN ASIA

India, the oldest of missionary areas, exemplified the trend toward less dependence on European and American societies, though the world disorder caused by the wars of the nations retarded the movement. The Andhra Evangelical Lutheran Church, on whose field the General Synod, the General Council, the Augustana Synod, and The United Lutheran Church in America had labored, became an Indian church in 1927. In 1944 the presidency was placed in Indian hands. The Gossner Evangelical Lutheran Church, begun in 1844, dates as an autonomous church from 1919, when all the German missionaries had to leave. The Tamil Evangelical Lutheran Church was formally established in 1919, though its history goes back to Ziegenbalg and Pluetschau's day. The Church of Sweden, after assisting the Leipzig Mission, had taken over in 1914. The Tamil Church gave its head the title of bishop, who served as ordaining officer for the Evangelical Lutheran Church in Madhya Pradesh (Central Provinces), a fruit of the labors of the National Evangelical Foundation of Sweden; this church elected an Indian president in 1945. During and after World War II The United Lutheran Church in America helped the Breklum Society's mission in Jeypore, where in 1928 the Jeypore Evangelical Lutheran Church was founded. The Missouri Synod was able to extend its field in South India (begun in 1895) during this period, establishing a seminary in Nagercoil in 1928. The India Evangelical Lutheran Church came into being in 1958. The South Andhra work of the Hermannsburg Mission (begun 1865) was subsidized by the American Lutheran Church after 1930, and the South Andhra Lutheran Church was organized in 1945. The Danish Missionary Society was the supporting body of the Arcot Lutheran Church organized and given Indian participation in leadership in 1930.

The Japan Evangelical Lutheran Church, organized in 1922, was the fruit of work by the United Synod of the South, the United Evangelical Lutheran Church (Danish) of the United States, and the Lutheran Gospel Association of Finland. Since 1925 a seminary has been located in Tokyo.

The Batak Mission, which recalls the achievements of Nommensen, had grown to 100,000 members by the time of World War I. It was constituted a church in 1930. Lay leadership played a prominent part, and schools and medical stations went hand in hand with evangelistic work. But war, occupation by the Japanese, and political struggles were obstacles in the way of the desired development of the young church.

A tragic ending came to an extensive and intensive Chinese mission. Dedicated services of missionaries from Scandinavia, Germany, and the United States in the Honan and Hupeh provinces had resulted in a Lutheran Church of China in which 16 synods had produced a common liturgy, hymnbooks, and a theological seminary. The Missouri Synod had begun a prosperous work in Shanghai and Hankow, founding a seminary in the latter city in 1922. The United Lutheran Church had assumed responsibility for the Berlin Mission in Shantung in 1925. All of these fields were lost after 1938 when the communist regime followed the Japanese invasion.

LUTHERANS IN AFRICA

Every section of the Lutheran world became interested in Africa, though here too World War I played havoc with courageous beginnings. The Leipzig Mission in Tanganyika was cared for by the Augustana Church until 1926, when the latter took up its own work to the west in Iramba, central Tanganyika. When World War II broke out, 172 German missionaries had to leave. Again Augustana, with the help of Swedish societies, assumed the duties of missionaries of the Leipzig, Bethel, and Berlin societies. A Swedish society, Bible-True Friends, had started work in Ethiopia and Eritrea in 1911 — in 1948 they entered Kenya. The Danish Missionary Society and American Lutherans were in Sudan after 1913, while the American Lutheran Church continued earlier Norwegian projects in Madagascar. In South Africa the Berlin Society had begun as early as 1834. Cooperation in Natal and

Zululand began in 1912 between Berlin, Norwegian, and Swedish societies and was extended by the association of an American Mission in 1928, of the Hermannsburg Mission in 1938, and of the old Schroeder Mission in 1938. In the Cape region German immigrants formed congregations and organized a German Evangelical Lutheran Church of South Africa affiliated with the Church of Hanover. The Church of Sweden had an old mission in Rhodesia; and the Finnish Missionary Society had a mission in Ovamboland, ordaining the first native pastors in 1935. German immigrants made up the congregations which in 1926 formed the German Evangelical Lutheran Church in South-West Africa, while Rhenish missionaries worked among natives and formed a synod and established a seminary in 1938. On the west coast the United Lutheran Church inherited the mission in Liberia. The Synodical Conference began work in Nigeria in 1936.

LUTHERANS IN SOUTH AMERICA

South America combined characteristics of both a mission field and diaspora work. The Missouri Synod succeeded in building up a church of over 100,000 members in Brazil (the Evangelical Lutheran Church of Brazil) and Argentina (the Argentina Evangelical Lutheran Church) and incorporated them as districts into the North American organization. In Argentina schools were begun in Buenos Aires and Obera. In Brazil a college and a seminary were established in Porto Alegre for the training of pastors, including those using Portuguese. The General Synod of the United States laid the foundations of what became in 1948 the United Evangelical Lutheran Church of Argentina. It served both immigrants from many countries (Estonian, English, German, Hungarian, Latvian, Slovak) and Spanish-speaking natives. The German synods of Brazil, which had depended on help from the German Evangelical Church after World War I, soon found that the home church could do little. In 1949 they formed the Synodal Federation of the Evangleical Church of the Lutheran Confession in Brazil, establishing their own theological seminary. The La Plata Synod in Brazil, the German-speaking Evangelical Lutheran Church in Bolivia, the Evangelical Lutheran Church in Chile, and the German-speaking Evangelical congregations in Mexico all relate themselves to the Foreign Office of the Evangelical Church in Germany and are thus, in a sense, daughter churches of a foreign body.

263

Various missions have been started in South American countries by volunteer groups and then been taken over by church bodies in North America. Some also, as in the case of the Missouri Synod, have been initiated by a church or have been incorporated into a church body. The British Guiana Mission, for example, became a part of the Lutheran Church in America. And so there are Lutheran congregations and missions, usually small in number, in Bolivia, Colombia, Cuba, Ecuador, El Salvador, Guatemala, Honduras, Nicaragua, Panama, Paraguay, Peru, Uruguay, and Venezuela. In addition there are seamen's missions and foreign legation churches. By the time of World War II there were about half a million members in the Lutheran communities in Latin America.

LUTHERANS IN AUSTRALIA

Australia more than South America moved in the direction of confessional unity among both the older and the newer immigrants. Gradually the synods which represented the unionistic tendencies of the Basel missions were guided by Neuendettelsau and Hermannsburg men toward a more confessional position.

The Evangelical Lutheran Church Union and the Evangelical Lutheran General Synod merged in 1921 to form the United Evangelical Lutheran Church and established a seminary at North Adelaide, which since 1925 has educated the pastors of the united church. A movement then began to bring together the new body and the older, Missouri-related Evangelical Lutheran Synod, since 1941 known as The Evangelical Lutheran Church of Australia. After years of negotiation a union was consummated in 1965.

The convulsion of world war with its consequent destruction, exile, and emigration after 1914 affected every part of the Lutheran Church. For Germany it meant a revolution in the relations of church and state. For the churches the old boundaries between East and West were erased and new associations formed. The Scandinavian and American churches suffered least materially, but the spiritual life of all peoples underwent great changes. Most hopeful was the response of these churches to the needs of the afflicted. Out of the throes of the time was born the Lutheran World Convention, whose role in world Lutheranism remains to be recorded as we trace the events of the years since 1945.

XVIII

THE HOUSEHOLD OF FAITH

In the middle of the 19th century a combination of forces gave increasing vigor to a renewal of the identity of the Church of the Lutheran Reformation in Germany. The skepticism of a Hegelian philosophy made religious minds critical of its relationship to theology. The amalgamation of the territories of Germany into Bismarck's empire tended to bring the various interest groups closer together. The social problems faced by the church called forth the Inner Mission and challenged the love as well as the faith of the churches. In 1848 Johann Wichern appeared at a Kirchentag and demanded that the cause of the Inner Mission become a concern of all. Foreign missions had produced a host of societies at home, and leaders were faced with an interest that cut across confessional lines. Loehe and his friends sought to create new liturgical life in the congregations and found people who were ready to cooperate with them. In 1832 the memorial of the death of Gustavus Adolphus was widely observed — from it grew the Gustav Adolf Society to aid diaspora congregations in other lands. A revived Roman Catholic Church added urgency to the restoration of a self-conscious Lutheran communion.

THE GENERAL LUTHERAN CONFERENCE

Interestingly the plight of the pastorless Lutherans in America played a part in the revival. In coming together to help these brethren in the faith, leaders such as Petri in Hanover, Harless in Saxony, Kliefoth in Mecklenburg, and Loehe in Bavaria found fellowship and support for the deeper motive of a genuine faith. The event above others that made some kind of confessional stand imperative was the Prussian Union. Begun by Prussia in 1817 as an attempt of the state to enforce a religious unity, the program had expanded as more and more provinces were incorporated into the Prussian centralization of Germany. We

265

have seen that in some cases the protests took the form of emigration to North America and Australia. In others Free churches were the reply of Lutherans to the attempt to erase or ignore confessional differences. Not all the provincial churches were willing to adopt the union plan, but a large number were ready to consider a federation of German churches as suggested at the Wittenberg Kirchentag in 1848. The year was one of political unrest and for a while revolutionary parties seemed to be in the ascendancy. With their threat to the church, some bond of unity was desired. But the Lutherans were by this time convinced that such unity could rest only on confessional agreement.

When the Evangelical Conference, sometimes called the Eisenach Conference, was organized in 1852 to embrace all Protestant groups, many Lutherans declined participation and met separately the following year. There were important differences among them as to policies to be followed if the church was to have greater freedom from the state. Petri, Theodore Kliefoth, August Vilmar, and Loehe were among those who feared a majority rule in the church and were reluctant to place much power in the laity. But the growth of synods with synodical authority was inevitable, and Walther in America became a leader in what some European Lutherans considered a "democratization" of the church. Walther, however, coupled his program of lay participation with effective measures in lay education. The development in Bavaria, which followed Adolf von Harless rather than Loehe, strengthened the synodal polity. It gave the Lutheran Church freedom of expression by setting up separate organizations for Lutherans and Reformed.

Harless and others wanted nothing less than a union of all convinced Lutherans across territorial lines. In 1868 it was possible to convene the first all-Lutheran gathering, and so a General Lutheran Conference was organized at Hanover. Gottlieb Harless, Kliefoth, and Christoph Luthardt were the leaders. An early problem was how to include the Lutherans in both Union and Free churches. The conference had no legislative power. It aimed at developing the positive nature of Lutheranism and defending the church against unionism, Roman Catholicism, and secularism. The periodic conferences, held on the average every three years, also considered themes related to practical programs, such as Sunday observance, civil marriage, the care of the poor, and the aid of distressed Lutherans in other lands. In regard to the diaspora aid the conference sponsored its own "Chest of God" project apart from the Gustav Adolf fund that enjoyed general Protestant support. Until the end of the century the conference was a German assembly. In 1901 it moved across German boundaries to Lund, Sweden, and again in 1911 it met in Sweden, this time at Uppsala, and in 1925 at Oslo, Norway. Because the conference structure permitted the membership of Union churches, the stricter Lutheran members withdrew in 1907 and organized a separate body, the Lutheran *Bund,* or Alliance.

THE EVANGELICAL FEDERATION

The Evangelical Conference meanwhile sought to include in its membership all German Protestants. Before the government its executive committee represented the interests of all. After World War I its members were elected by the churches and thus spoke for them. In 1919 the committee met with representatives of the theological faculties and the Inner Mission and arranged for a *Kirchentag* at Dresden. Out of it grew in 1922 the *Kirchenbund,* or German Evangelical Church Federation, for the troubled conditions following the war made Protestant consensus necessary in matters related to secular authorities. The federation left its constituent members autonomous but hoped to present a united front to a confused government. The composition of the federation suggests the mixed nature of Protestantism in postwar Germany. There were the large Lutheran state or folk churches, such as those of Bavaria, Hanover, Mecklenburg, Saxony, Thuringia, and Württemberg. Free churches included those in Prussia, Baden, Hanover, Saxony, Hesse, and Hamburg. Then there were the Union and United churches, which comprised Reformed, Lutheran, and United congregations — in Hesse, Nassau, Baden, Bremen, Frankfort, and the Palatinate. The Lutheran and Reformed congregations were in the Evangelical Church of the Old Prussian Union.

THE LUTHERAN WORLD CONVENTION

In the preceding chapter we saw how the federation was taken over by the Hitler regime and how its jurisdiction was challenged by the Barmen group. At this point the General Lutheran Conference was approached by the National Lutheran Council of America. In earlier time there had been fraternal correspondence and exchange of visitors between the conference and the General Council of the Evangelical Lutheran Church in North America. But now the situation demanded common action by Lutherans in many parts of the world. The conference and the National Lutheran Council called together in 1923 the Lutheran World Convention in Eisenach. Leaders came from greatly differing churches — John A. Morehead, Charles Jacobs, G. N. Brandelle, F. H. Knubel from America; Superintendent Theophil Meyer from Moscow; Bishop Ludwig Ihmels from Saxony; Pastor Alfred Jorgensen from Denmark; Archbishop Söderblom from Sweden; Bishops Karlis Irbe and Peter Harold Poelchau from Latvia. Twenty-two countries sent 147 delegates to the first Lutheran world meeting in history. It was held in the wake of a world war, and its aim was to give spiritual and national aid to churches and missions suffering the effects of war on every continent. Only the American and Scandinavian churches were able to contribute funds in great amounts, and this they did until an economic depression paralyzed parishes in every country.

When the Lutheran World Convention held its second meeting in Copenhagen in 1929, the depression was beginning to show reduced budgets for relief and missions, and its full impact was reported at the third convention in Paris in 1935. Dr. Morehead had hoped for a more workable organization at Copenhagen, but European Lutheranism was neither then nor at Paris ready for a worldwide organization. He died in 1936 after a fruitful ministry in the name of world Lutheranism, directed partially from Geneva, where he shared his office with international Christian church relief personnel. Hanns Lilje was elected executive secretary, but World War II involved the German churches in resistance to Hitler, and once more the Lutherans of the world were divided by military powers. As soon as communication again was possible the American section of the Lutheran World Convention sent representatives to Europe. What Morehead had meant to the ravaged Lutheran churches after World War I was now duplicated by the tireless efforts of S. C. Michelfelder. The German churches had set up their relief organization known as *Hilfswerk*. The Lutheran World Convention geared its program to that of the German agency, and before the end of 1945 almost $150,000 had been given to aid churches in Germany, Finland, France, Holland, Norway, and Italy. Michelfelder

268

simultaneously headed the department of reconstruction of the World Council of Churches, relating the Lutheran efforts to those of the other churches. The magnitude of the task assumed by the National Lutheran Council of the United States led in 1945 to an organization of a separate agency, that of Lutheran World Relief. The Swedish section of the Lutheran World Convention had directed its assistance mainly to Poland, Germany, and the Baltic States.

THE LUTHERAN WORLD FEDERATION

The experience of three decades of war, depression, and international disorder finally persuaded Lutherans that to meet the changes of the day a world body should represent the whole church both to its members throughout the world and to political powers that were unaware of the effects of their decisions on spiritual communities. The Lutheran World Federation was born at Lund, Sweden, in the summer of 1947. Forty-six churches from 26 countries bound themselves to work through the federation. As a doctrinal basis the constitution repeated the formula agreed on at Eisenach in 1923: "The Lutheran World Federation acknowledges the Holy Scriptures of the Old and New Testaments as the only source and the infallible norm of all church doctrine and practice, and sees in the Confessions of the Lutheran Church, especially in the Unaltered Augsburg Confession and Luther's Catechism, a pure exposition of the Word of God." Commissions were set up to carry out the purposes of the new body. By the time of the Second Assembly at Hanover, Germany, in 1952 it was clear that the federation's activities could be grouped under three main departments — theology, world service, and world missions.

The first years of the federation had been filled with programs of relief to churches and mission fields. After Hanover the emphasis was on aid to refugees, of which the earth was full. At Lund it was decided that each country should set up a national committee through which the World Federation, with offices in Geneva, would act. From Lutheran World Service Norway and Finland each received over a million dollars for reconstruction. The largest grants went to Germany, at first through *Hilfswerk,* then through the German National Committee. Churches were rebuilt out of the rubble of destroyed cities. Inner Mission institutions were helped. Paper was provided for the printing of Bibles, hymnbooks, and catechisms. Aid amounting to $600,000 was given to churches in the East Zone. After the currency reform in 1948, West Germans were able to aid their brethren in the Russian occupation area.

The close of the war brought new states and changed boundaries. The nationalistic regimes on the eastern border of Germany drove multitudes into exile. It was estimated that one out of every ten Lutherans in the world became a refugee. Thirteen million Germans were expelled from the East; 125,000 Latvian Lutherans fled from Russian bondage into West Germany and Austria; 30,000 Estonians did likewise, their archbishop finding refuge in Sweden; 2,000 Hungarians sought new homes in Austria. Poles and Ukrainians joined the hundreds of thousands of refugees that West Germany had to house and feed.

After 1948 the Lutheran World Federation, in conjunction with the German churches, turned its attention to finding homes in other lands for the hordes of displaced persons. Some 20,000 Lutherans migrated to Australia, the Latvians and Estonians taking with them their own pastors. As a result the United Evangelical Lutheran Church in Australia doubled its membership. A total of 25,000 Estonians settled in Sweden where they formed their church in exile. In 1955 they were enabled to produce a new hymnal. The millions of refugee Germans had come from the Baltic provinces and what was now Czechoslovakia, Poland, Hungary, and Yugoslavia. During 1956 they streamed into West Germany at the rate of 25,000 a month. And 70,000 Lutheran refugees crowded into the now-small state of Austria. Through government and church agencies these East Germans were directed to new homes in both the Old and the New World. Many remained in Scandinavia or West Germany. The Lutheran World Federation, with which the Missouri Synod cooperated in manifold ways, gave travel grants to 18,000 displaced persons heading for Canada. Reception centers were established for the newcomers in Venezuela, Argentina, Brazil, Chile, Australia, and Scandinavia. A total of 40,000 Baltic and German Lutherans were admitted into Great Britain. Although Lutheranism was almost unknown there, the Lutheran Council of Great Britain was organized in 1948, made up of Estonians, Latvians, Germans, and Poles. The World Service of the Lutheran Federation engaged 57 churches in 29 countries in joint efforts.

270

By the date of the Third Assembly in Minneapolis, Minnesota, in 1957 the great work of reconstruction and resettlement had been accomplished. The interest of the churches could now be turned to theological discussion, liturgical reform, stewardship, evangelism, education, and closer ties between Lutheran churches in old and new lands. The nature of the federation itself received new attention, and the thought of the churches centered on the meaning of Lutheranism in the developing ecumenical consciousness. Thus at Helsinki, Finland, in 1963 the theme of justification by faith received major treatment by the Fourth Assembly. The federation also restudied its constitution and set up a foundation on research with reference to relationships with other Christian communions.

MINORITY CHURCHES IN FRANCE AND HOLLAND

The uniting power of the Lutheran World Federation is seen in its drawing into a family fellowship isolated communities of Lutherans whom historical circumstances had separated from their brethren. Such is the case of the Lutherans in France. Strasbourg on the Rhine had been a Lutheran stronghold in the days of Bucer. But Alsace and Lorraine were not only subjected to the forces of the Counter-Reformation. They were caught up in the age-old conflict between French and German armies. In 1802 Napoleon reorganized the Church of the Augsburg Confession, giving it state support. Created out of various traditions, bilingual, and synodical in government, the church never clearly specified its doctrinal position. On their ordination, however, pastors pledged loyalty to the Lutheran Confessions.

In 1871 France lost Alsace-Lorraine to Germany. The remaining Lutherans in France, around Montbeliard and in Paris, then organized a free Evangelical Lutheran Church of France. The Augsburg Confession was recognized as the basis of the new constitution that established a synodical government and provided for an "inspector," or superintendent, for each of the two districts. When Alsace-Lorraine was returned to France after the end of World War I, the Evangelical Lutheran Church of France chose to retain its independent status, but in 1950 it joined with the Church of the Augsburg Confession in the National Alliance of French Lutheran Churches.

In 1927 a group separated from the Church of the Augsburg Confession, protesting professed liberal practices. The resultant Free

271

Church of France and Belgium carries on some work also in the latter country and has contact with the Missouri Synod in the U. S. A. With a total communicant membership of about 150,000, these three French churches are a decided minority group.

Even smaller was the Lutheran communion in Holland, which welcomed the guidance and fellowship of the World Federation. The history of Lutheranism in this country goes back to the Reformation days when monks of Luther's Augustinian Order proved their faith by providing in 1523 the first martyrs in Brussels. Merchants and immigrants maintained a Lutheran congregation in Antwerp, under German leadership, despite the unfriendliness of the Reformed. In 1633 a church building was dedicated in Amsterdam, whence the Lutherans in New Amsterdam, or New York, received their first pastor. Holland was a center of rationalism, and in 1793 the Lutheran congregation was split by a conservative group that organized itself as the "Restored Evangelical Lutheran Church." A common interest in missions and renewed Luther research brought the parties together again — after the formation of the Lutheran World Federation. In 1955 the united church adopted a new liturgy and hymnal. The 65 congregations are organized in a synod composed of one third pastors and two thirds laymen. A seminary is affiliated with the university, and the church counts five women pastors. Pulpit and altar fellowship with the Dutch Reformed Church gradually became customary and was regularized in 1956. In 1960 some 35,000 communicant members made up the The Lutheran Church in the Kingdom of the Netherlands.

The Velkd and the Ekd

The postwar years from 1945 were years of consolidation and concentration for almost all Lutheran churches in various lands. In 1948 the greater number of the Lutheran churches in Germany realized a long-cherished desire for unity by the formation of the United Evangelical Lutheran Church of Germany (Vereinigte Ev.-Luth. Kirche Deutschlands=VELKD). Although some of the member bodies were bisected by the Iron Curtain that divides West and East Germany, around 20 million baptized members made up this first union of German Lutherans since the Reformation. The uniting churches were (in order of size) those of Saxony, Hanover, Schleswig-Holstein, Bavaria,

272

Thuringia, Mecklenburg, Hamburg, Brunswick, Lübeck, and Schaumburg-Lippe. The VELKD purposed to unify as much as possible the activities of these churches. Among its firstfruits were new liturgical forms for worship and ministerial acts. The Free churches did not join, continuing their objection to the former General Conference, namely, that the state churches included Reformed or United parishes, but they have been on friendly terms.

At the same time as the United Church came into existence, most of the Protestant bodies in Germany joined in establishing anew the German Evangelical Church Union (Evangelische Kirche in Deutschland=EKD). The various attitudes toward the Barmen Confessional group made the EKD a loose confederation of churches rather than a united church. Germany's three Protestant groupings were the result of centuries of history, the problem of union being complicated by different heritages of church-state relationships. Lutheran, Reformed, and United churches were not clearly delineated. As there were Lutheran parishes in Reformed churches (Baden, Palatinate), so there were Reformed parishes in the territorial churches of the VELKD, and in such EKD churches as those of Berlin, Brandenburg, Saxony, Westphalia, the Rhineland, and Hesse-Nassau Lutherans were in the majority. The predominantly Lutheran church of Württemberg was not a member of the VELKD but of the EKD. The Old Prussian Union, whose former churches were now largely under Russian control, also belonged to the EKD, though its membership included large Lutheran contingents. To the internal problems of German Lutheranism thus were added the profound questions of the future of the churches in communist-held lands.

MINORITY CHURCHES IN THE EAST

When the end of the war left all eastern borderlands in Russian hands, a radical change resulted in Lutheran constituencies. The 13 million Germans who left their former homes as a consequence of the Potsdam agreement of 1945 authorizing population transfers meant a mass evacuation of churches, parishes, and institutions. What had been German territory or Baltic free states now became Russian-ruled territory along with lands with new boundaries: Poland, Czechoslovakia, Hungary, Yugoslavia. Of the Germans still in Poland a decade after the Potsdam agreement no less than 300,000 returned to Germany when the Red Cross in 1955 arranged for permission to leave in order that families might be reunited, and another 70,000 had asked for a similar privilege. This meant the end of the German Lutheran Church — only the Polish part remained. Its 100,000 members experienced harassment both from the communist Russian authorities and the Roman Catholic authorities who had again made Poland a Roman stronghold.

Czechoslovakia proved more friendly to its Protestant population, assuming responsibility for the economic needs of parishes and theological seminaries. Thus the Slovak Evangelical Church of the Augsburg Confession received its own seminary in Modra near Bratislava. This body of over 400,000 members celebrated its 40th anniversary in 1959. Its two districts each had its bishop, a bishop-general supervising the church as a whole. The second Lutheran body, the Silesian Church of the Augsburg Confession, was a church of some 50,000 members using the Czech and Polish languages. Both Lutheran groups cooperated with the Ecumenical Council in Prague, which coordinated the work of the evangelical churches and helped them adjust to new political conditions.

The course of the Lutheran Church in Hungary was determined by vacillations in the policy of a communist government. Sweden and the National Lutheran Council of the United States gave substantial help to reconstruct the church in the new Hungary, a church numbering over 400,000 souls. Shortly after the Lutheran World Federation meeting in Lund, Bishop Ordass, one of two Lutheran bishops, was placed under arrest. Church government was placed in the care of bishops acceptable to the regime. The church in Hungary had experienced a spiritual revival under Zoltan Turoczy, who was elected bishop in 1939. He had made a deep impression on the clergy, who tried to resist the materialism of the age and who supported Bishop Ordass. The revolution of 1956 sent thousands of Hungarians into exile. Bishop Ordass was restored for a period until his retirement. The repression of the dissident political elements meant a pressure also on the Lutheran clergy to conform to the rule of the all-powerful state.

Yugoslavia combined numerous districts and faiths — Serbia, Croatia, Bosnia, Herzegovina; and Orthodox, Reformed, Lutheran, Roman Catholic. The upheavals of two world wars, including the departure of 100,000 Germans after 1945, left only small Lutheran churches in what was once territory of Austria or Hungary. A small German remnant remained in the form of the Evangelical Church in the People's Republics of Croatia, Bosnia, and Herzegovina, and the autonomous province of Voivodina. A Hungarian community in Serbia near the border of Hungary was called the Evangelical Church in the People's Republic of Serbia. A Slovak colony named itself the Slovak Evangelical Church of the Augsburg Confession in Yugoslavia. Near the Austrian border the old Slovenian Lutheran Church became autonomous in 1945 and was renamed the Evangelical Christian Church of the Augsburg Confession in the People's Republic of Slovenia in Yugoslavia. In Rumania the old Transylvania colonies recouped some of their emigration losses through an influx of Germans from other regions. They formed the Evangelical Church of the Augsburg Confession in the People's Republic of Rumania. The few Hungarians in Rumania continued in their Evangelical Synodal Presbyterial Church.

All these churches suffered persecution under the communist regime that tolerated them even as it sought to extirpate them. In East Germany the old Lutheran churches fought heroically against terrific odds. Especially difficult were the prohibitions against instruction of youth and the obstacles to theological training. Contacts across the borders became extremely rare. Similar conditions prevailed in Latvia and Estonia, where the attempt of those who remained to conserve the church were critically judged by fellow Lutherans in churches in exile. The extent of possible cooperation with an atheistic government was a problem variously solved in these countries under the cross. Lutheran churches in other lands were thwarted in measures they would gladly have taken for the relief of their brethren. In 1956 the Lutheran World Federation reviewed its program of aid to minority churches in a conference in Austria, and continuing help flowed through World Service. A second minority churches' conference in 1962 in Yugoslavia enabled the federation to learn where it could be of greatest help.

SCANDINAVIAN CHURCHES

The Scandinavian countries assumed a large share of the program of the Lutheran World Federation. This agency was instrumental in reconciling the people of Norway and Denmark with their former occupying powers, and together with the churches of Germany they bound up the wounds of war. Common problems have beset the churches of Sweden, Norway, Denmark, Finland, and Iceland. The shortage of pastors was met only in Finland. Ordination of women has caused considerable discussion. The secularization of schools did not crowd out religious instruction, though the time allowed for it was reduced. The relationship of church and state was not satisfactorily solved. In Sweden both parliament and the bishops studied what might happen if the Church of Sweden were to be disestablished. The Icelandic parliament in 1957 gave the church its own council. Lively contacts with other churches kept these countries in the forefront of the ecumenical movement, though the Norwegian Missionary Council voted against the World Council of Churches' incorporation of the International Missionary Council and retained its independence. The attendance at worship services in all these countries remained on a low level, giving rise to concern over the paganization of popular life. Yet religious literature and art and worship services by radio showed strong support of the church. Work among youth increased, and more lay leadership was encouraged in the parishes.

FURTHER MERGERS IN THE U.S.A. — A LUTHERAN COUNCIL

The post-World War II period witnessed another burst of unification among the Lutheran churches in America. The member bodies of the American Lutheran Conference discovered that there were no great differences in faith or practice among themselves and therefore desired a more organic union. One of their number, the Augustana Church, proposed a more comprehensive merger that would include The United Lutheran Church in America. Unable to win agreement on this point, Augustana withdrew from the negotiations. The remaining bodies went on to complete an organization and in 1960 formed The American Lutheran Church composed of the former Evangelical Lutheran Church (Norwegian), the American Lutheran Church (German background), and the United Evangelical Lutheran Church (Danish). In 1963 the Lutheran Free Church (Norwegian) joined this merger. Augustana and the United Lutheran Church were unsuccessful in effecting a larger union, and together with the American Evangelical Lutheran Church (Danish) and the Finnish Evangelical Lutheran Church (Suomi

276

Synod) they came together in 1962 into the Lutheran Church in America. Five of the seminaries of the merging bodies united in a new theological institution at Chicago, Illinois.

Thus in less than 50 years the majority of the many different nationalistic synods had coalesced into three large bodies, namely, the Lutheran Church in America with some 3 million baptized members, the Synodical Conference with almost as many, and The American Lutheran Church, which is somewhat smaller. Each of these groups included Canadian districts or divisions that had grown up in affiliation with bodies in the United States. These Canadian churches received a considerable influx of Lutherans after 1945 — in fact the 250,000 Lutheran immigrants equalled the number in already existing parishes.

Differences within the Synodical Conference caused the Wisconsin Synod and the Norwegian body to withdraw in 1963, leaving the Missouri Synod and the Synod of Evangelical Lutheran Churches as sole members. In its steady growth the Missouri Synod found itself more and more involved with other Lutheran churches, both during and after World War II. It had joined in common enterprises that involved negotiations with the government, in relief work in Europe and on mission fields, in educational and charitable agencies, in conferences, and in the capacity of an observer had followed the assemblies of the Lutheran World Federation. When the merger of synods among its members left the National Lutheran Council a company of two rather than of eight members, Dr. Paul Empie, the executive secretary of the council, proposed a successor body that should include the Missouri Synod. Preliminary theological conversations made clear the large areas of agreement among the four churches: The ALC, LCA, Missouri Synod, and the Synod of Evangelical Lutheran Churches. Formation by these churches of the Lutheran Council in the United States of America (LCUSA) at Cleveland, Ohio, Nov. 16, 1966, brought practically all Lutherans in the United States and Canada into a cooperative organization. By common agreement all participating bodies shall take part in the theological studies of the council.

COMMON PROBLEMS

The substantial consensus among American Lutherans in matters of faith and polity was matched by the similarity of problems affecting

277

all of them. The movement of population from country to city and the rapid deterioration of older city centers have threatened long-standing city parishes. The resources of the churches are strained to build new edifices in mushrooming suburban housing projects. The integration of residential sections both in the North and in the South is causing deep disturbances. But beyond physical changes are the profound spiritual problems accompanying a secularization of life. Only the Missouri and Wisconsin Synods have succeeded in maintaining a parochial school system. All the churches are faced with a divorcing of religious exercises from the public schools. On the level of higher education greater attention is being given to a ministry in the great state institutions. Both on the lower and the higher educational level the church has had to compete with new advances in educational practices and with the facilities of the public schools. The use of radio, television, and the press have kept the churches abreast of the means of communication. In the field of service the growth of the welfare state has influenced the means of aid by the churches to their members. Loneliness rather than poverty is the lot of many whom the ministry of parishes has not reached.

The rising cost as well as the standard of living has demanded a measure of sacrifice from the membership of the churches that has not been fully met. As a result the projected programs at home and abroad have not been realized. The ministry has been held to high standards despite calls for more pastors and for more varied forms of ministration. The adoption of the *Service Book and Hymnal* in 1948 after 15 years of common preparation by all except the Synodical Conference marked a milestone in the liturgical life of the American churches. Steps are now being taken to make a revision with the cooperation of the Missouri Synod in the hope of uniting all the Lutherans in America in their use of liturgical forms and hymnody. Common to all the churches is the question of relationships on the local level to other churches — the Protestant, Orthodox, and Catholic.

AUTONOMY AND FELLOWSHIP

In the contracting world of modern communications the Lutherans of Europe and America have come closer to the younger churches of other continents. Both the destructive forces of world wars and the

278

constructive programs of missionary societies and of the Lutheran World Federation have contributed to a spirit of fellowship in the household of a common faith. In this household the younger members have attained a maturity that made autonomy a natural condition. And that autonomy has been tested by the exigencies of war and the growing nationalism of independent nations. Everywhere missions have grown into churches, and churches have joined themselves in synods and federations — even sometimes into regional church bodies — which call for new types of relationships to missionary societies and the "home" churches. Consolidation and concentration has been the direction of development in all parts of the Lutheran world, young and old. A few examples will illustrate what has happened and is happening in the missionary areas.

The Ethiopian Evangelical Church Mekane Yesus in 1958 merged the former missions of the Swedish Evangelical Mission Society, the Hermannsburg Society, the Norwegian Lutheran Society, the Icelandic, the Danish, and the American Lutheran agencies into one native church. In Tanganyika (now Tanzania) the seven churches that had grown out of the labors of missionaries from almost all the European and American churches united in 1964 to form the Evangelical Lutheran Church in Tanganyika. The various mission churches of southeast Africa, with one exception, united in 1960 in the Evangelical Lutheran Church in Southern Africa, Southeastern Region. The Northern and Southern Transvaal synods merged into the Evangelical Lutheran Church (Transvaal Region) in 1962. A Council of Churches on Lutheran Foundation carries on common educational projects for its members — mission, German, and indigenous church bodies — in southeastern and southwestern Africa, the Transvaal and Cape regions, and the Orange Free State. These churches have close ties also with Scandinavian, German, and American Lutherans. The Free churches of Germany support both a German Free Synod in South Africa and a mission to Zulu people. The Wisconsin Synod has laid the foundation of churches in Nigeria and Rhodesia.

The communist victory in China drove missionaries of all churches out of the country. They scattered far and wide. Many went to Japan where new churches were founded by missionaries of the Missouri Synod, the Wisconsin Synod, and Norwegian bodies. Older missions of the Japanese Evangelical Lutheran Church were reinforced by new forces from the Augustana and Suomi churches and from the Danish Society. Chinese refugees on Taiwan began to build a church in 1951. They were joined by missionaries of Scandinavian and American bodies. A seminary was established in 1957, and church work was extended to Taiwanese as well as Chinese. Other Christian refugees began a Lutheran congregation in Hong Kong in 1954 and soon included workers of German, Scandinavian, and American churches who had fled from China. The Lutheran World Federation sought to aid and coordinate efforts by many groups in many languages.

After World War II the Missouri Synod also began work in the Philippines, Korea, Hong Kong, and New Guinea. In New Guinea the Evangelical Lutheran Church of Australia extended its field, and the old mission of the Neuendettelsau Society that had been taken over by the American Lutheran Church because of war conditions organized itself in 1956 into the Evangelical Lutheran Church of New Guinea. This church and the Batak Church in Indonesia are the largest of all Lutheran mission churches. The Batak Church drew up a confession of faith in 1951 that satisfied the conditions of membership in the Lutheran World Federation. In 1954 it established Nommensen University. Its activity, however, is hampered by internal dissension and by the fact that it is a part of a nation whose population is 95 percent non-Christian.

The dimensions of the missionary program of the Lutheran churches are suggested by the fact that World War II cut off the relationships of 2,000 missionaries from their home bases. The significance of the aid rendered by the Lutheran World Federation in the years of emergency is to be measured not only in terms of the $8 million channeled through it mainly by the Church of Sweden and by American, Australian, and Canadian Lutherans, but in terms of the fellowship established with the million members of the younger churches in Tanzania, Sudan, Nigeria, Sumatra, New Guinea, Madagascar, India, Palestine, and the remote corners of the earth.

As the missions grew into congregations and congregations made up churches that related themselves to the older communions of the Lutheran Reformation, the younger churches found themselves faced with questions of relationships to other Christians in their own vicinity.

In India, the oldest Protestant missionary field, this problem had become acute when Congregationalists, Presbyterians, Methodists, and Anglicans formed the Church of South India in 1947. Slowly the Lutheran churches had become autonomous and chose their own leadership. Inspired not only by Swedish example but by Anglican orders and by native needs, some of the Lutheran mission churches adopted the title of bishop for their highest office; in other churches the term president prevailed. In all of them the synod became the legislative organ, with an executive council or diocesan chapter as an intermediary between the synod and its head. This became the form also on other fields — in Africa and Asia. Native leaders in all Protestant missions came to have a decisive voice in the administration of their churches at home and in international conferences. At Edinburgh in 1910 they had no part, but they were participants at the Jerusalem Conference of the International Missionary Council in 1928, and even more so at Tambarene (near Madras) in 1938. After the war — in conferences at Whitby in 1947, Willingen in 1952, and Ghana in 1958 — the younger churches have been on equal footing with the representatives of the older, and all have been concerned with the question of their mutual dependence and of unity in the common Lord.

So far the Lutheran churches have not been party to the union churches in India, China, Japan, the Philippines, and North India. But the decision to join in the Church of South India is now a problem before the Tamil Evangelical Lutheran Church and its bishop, Rajah Manikam. Unsolved too is the question of the relationship of churches that join united churches to their former brethren. Thus by a curious development the same problem faces the newest of churches in the Lutheran family that has concerned the oldest of the territorial churches in Germany. As Free churches have found some kind of answer to the question of their relationship to the secular government, they now must find an answer to the problem of their relationship to other churches — Lutheran and non-Lutheran, local and ecumenical.

What has held together these many different kinds of churches in Germany, Austria, the Eastern borderlands, the Baltic provinces, Scandinavia from Finland to Greenland, the churches of North and South America and Australia, and the missionary churches of Asia and

281

Africa and the islands of the seas through all the shifting situations of over four centuries of modern history? Certainly not language or culture or form of organization or administrative genius. The one common denominator is a Christian faith. Its simplest and most universal expression has been found in Luther's Small Catechism. It has opened the doors to the Scriptures, which have everywhere been accepted as the foundation of the faith as well as its complete revelation.

For the Lutheran of every color and climate the hymnbook has expressed the meaning of the faith for his own life. For the pastor and teacher the Augsburg Confession and the entire Book of Concord have provided the interpretation of Scripture in the preaching and teaching ministry. Out of faith in the Word and Sacrament, which have constituted the contents and spirit of worship and the guidance of thought and action, has come the prayer to live and to work in obedience to the Christ revealed in the Word. In the fellowship of the congregation of believers near and far the Lutheran Christian has seen his purpose in life and fulfilled his calling as a member of the body of Christ. He has experienced and confessed the grace of God in Jesus Christ through the Spirit living in His church.

XIX

WORD AND SACRAMENT IN THE CONGREGATION

The Church of the Lutheran Reformation was no new church. It sought to develop the life of the congregation in a manner in accord with the institution of Christ and the apostles rather than in the pattern of many of the theories and customs that had grown up in the course of the earlier centuries. In the various countries where it was established the Reformation recognized historical differences. It has been called a conservative movement because it rejected only those teachings and practices which were contrary to the Scriptures, its recognized constitution of the church.

ARCHITECTURE

Its conservative nature allowed the Lutheran Reformation to continue the use of the church buildings in which the reformers had worshiped. Only one altar was necessary — all side altars for private masses were removed. Karlstadt had wanted to remove sculpture and painting, but Luther quelled this impulse. Only objects that were considered conducive to the adoration of the Virgin and the saints were not tolerated. The proclamation of the Word and the administration of the sacraments gave pulpit and altar and font a new emphasis. No new form of architecture was required, only a renovation of the old temples. The regions of southern Germany near Switzerland made the renovation more complete. In Scandinavia few changes were made, medieval paintings on walls and ceilings remaining as before. Indeed until the ravages of the Thirty Years' War made it necessary, few new church buildings were erected. Within the existing structures the tendency was to bring pulpit and altar closer together; and as congregational singing increased, the organ was brought into view. Thus the position of the pulpit above the altar, and the organ above both, became a common one in the Lutheran churches in the 17th and 18th centuries.

283

In new churches the long rectangular form was preferred, with the altar often in the center of a long wall, but circular and cruciform types were also erected. Galleries were popular and were often installed in old as well as new edifices. The Frauenkirche, or Dom, in Dresden was widely acclaimed, but its stone material and five galleries made it very costly in proportion to its capacity. Some hailed it as *the* Lutheran form of church architecture, but actually its builder, George Baehr, was influenced by Roman models. In Sweden Nicodemus Tessin, leading court and church architect, gave the country richly decorated baroque buildings where Renaissance influences provided more light for the congregation and design and color in altar and pulpit. The massive altarpiece by Precht in the Uppsala Cathedral followed the altar of St. Ignatius in the Jesuit Church of Rome. The romantic movement in Germany brought new interest in Gothic, especially its English form, and in 1861 the Eisenach Conference of Lutheran Churches placed Gothic first on its list of ecclesiastical art standards. The World Wars destroyed buildings and theories, and postwar buildings have been smaller and less pretentious. The church realizes that it no longer sets cultural standards, and so its buildings are more functional than before. The "Notkirchen" of O. Bartning have often become permanent.

Despite attempts during the past three centuries to define "Lutheran architecture," it seems evident that there is no such unique type. Lutheran congregations have worshiped in every kind of structure, only asking that there be access to font and altar and that the pulpit be visible and the preacher audible to all. A new appreciation of the Lord's Supper has favored a separation of pulpit and altar, and so the pulpit is usually placed between altar and people. Choir and organ are to the side of the chancel or on a rear gallery. The church encourages every art, and some temples have become national shrines, such as the Trondheim Cathedral in Norway, the Gnadenkirche in Tesch, and the Copenhagen Dom with Thorwaldsen's statues. But the size, type, and furnishings of the church building have been determined in accordance with fashions of the age, the needs and artistic talents of the people, and the environment, traditions, and resources of the land. As the church has become independent of the government and dependent on its professed membership, its architecture has passed from a monumental style to one meeting the needs of the particular congregation. While at first missionaries built churches on the new mission fields in the style of their homeland, today native Christians are being encouraged to build edifices for worship consonant with their climate, culture, and religious endowment. Good church architecture is an offering of the finest of artistic talent to the worship of God.

LITURGY

While the Reformation evolved no distinctive architecture, it did produce a liturgy that has achieved a remarkable uniformity in the churches of various lands. Luther regained for the church a sacrament in place of the sacrifice of the Mass, making the Communion, in the vernacular, conform to its Biblical origin. Most of the other contents of the service — the ancient service of the catechumens — were retained. The church year was kept, and parts appropriate for each Sunday and festival — musical rubrics, lessons, prayers — were continued. New importance was attached to preaching, for the proclamation of the Gospel was the heart of the service, and preaching and sacraments should make clear to the people the truths of Scripture. Luther wanted to keep the Latin responses that boys could learn in school, but gradually the singing became altogether vernacular, and hymns replaced the Kyrie, the Introit, the Gloria, the Gradual, the Credo, the Preface, and the Agnus Dei. The period of orthodoxy stressed the teaching element in worship, and the Catechism was given a place in the service. In general the didactic overshadowed the prayer elements so that prayers were moved from the altar to the pulpit and there made into opening and closing parts of the sermon. The service became a preaching service, with Communion celebrated only monthly or even less often — quarterly and in some places only once a year. Pietism paid less attention to congregational worship than to personal edification in small groups for Bible study and prayer. Rationalism made the church a school for community concerns. Not until the 19th-century renewal did the service regain its sacramental character and give the altar equality with the pulpit.

How complete a liturgical consensus has been reached is apparent today in the recent *Agenda,* or forms of worship, adopted by the Church of Sweden in 1942, by the Lutheran churches of the United States in 1958, and by the United Evangelical Lutheran Church of Germany in 1954. All of these consider a service with Communion as normal though recognizing that a service without Communion is both proper

285

and common. Four divisions are distinguished: Introduction, Word, Sacrament, Conclusion.

The Introduction includes (a) singing by congregation or choir or both; (b) Kyrie (in a litany form in the American liturgy); (c) the Gloria in Excelsis (abbreviated in the Swedish); (d) the Collect for the day.

The Word section is made up of readings from Scripture: the Epistle and the Gospel — the pericopes of ancient use (the American service includes a series of Old Testament selections). The congregation responds with a Hallelujah, or the choir with a Gradual, following the Epistle, and with the Creed or a creedal hymn after the Gospel. Then follows a hymn in keeping with the Gospel of the day, the sermon, music during the offering, and a general prayer. When Communion is not celebrated, the service may go on to the Conclusion, consisting of response, benediction, and hymn.

The Communion section begins with a response by the congregation to the pastor's Sursum Corda (lift up your hearts), followed by the Preface, to which the congregation replies with the Sanctus, then the Verba, or Words of Institution, which may be incorporated in a Prayer of Thanksgiving and for the gift of God's Spirit; the Our Father; the Agnus Dei; the distribution of bread and wine at the altar.

The conclusion includes prayer (in the American liturgy the Nunc Dimitis before the prayer), thanksgiving, and benediction.

In all these forms the service proper may be preceded by a confessional section that consists of a confession of sin by the congregation and a declaration of absolution by the pastor. This element goes back to the Reformation and to the desire to retain confession and absolution, not as a sacrament in the Roman sense but as a pastoral ministry to the people. Luther opposed an obligatory confession and a rite that had degenerated into an annual confession at Eastertime before Communion. Various efforts were later made to recover the practice of voluntary confession to the pastor, who could comfort the penitent with a direct absolution. In Finland the Laestadian group held to confession to lay members, who absolved one another. But individual confession disappeared except in special instances.

At the same time the church tried to guard against thoughtless

286

participation in Communion. In the 16th and 17th centuries catechization became a means of pastoral counseling. But the general substitute for the confessional became a congregational confession that Luther had fashioned out of the medieval priest's personal confession before Mass. This was used in Lutheran congregations before Communion and retained its place even where the service was not followed by a celebration of the Sacrament. The fact that it was a group confession caused Pietists to question whether the pastor could declare direct absolution, and in some cases the declaration was made conditional — "if this be your sincere confession." Often the confession was made the subject for a separate service sometime during the week before Communion. In today's *Agenda* there is a separate service leading up to absolution. It is questioned whether such a service need be a prerequisite to Communion, just as others question the role of the confessional service in the service without Communion. The persistence of the custom indicates the desirability of preserving the confessional as a ministry to the individual, but it also points in the direction of a more private and direct meeting between pastor and people.

PREACHING

Even before the Reformation preaching had been cultivated by the friars, but the sermon was not a necessary part of the Mass. In some of the early Lutheran liturgies a preaching service preceded the service. With Luther's emphasis on the proclamation of the Word, the sermon soon assumed a major place in the service. Since preaching was essentially an exposition of Scripture, the sermon followed naturally on the reading of the Gospel for the day. Luther's genius as a teacher and speaker made him a model — but one which none could match. Yet his method of exposition was imitated. Sermons were based on the pericopes, on Bible books, and on series of hymns. Exposition, however, soon developed into the practice of finding a doctrine in the text and of teaching it to the people.

Preaching in the period of orthodoxy was didactic and catechetic. The structure of the sermon as taught in the theological schools was very formal, with numerous divisions and subdivisions. Every sermon, according to one theory, should include five parts — a doctrine, its defense, an exhortation, condemnation of errors, comfort for the believer.

287

Despite the great changes that took place in secular thought after the Thirty Years' War, preaching turned in on the concerns of church doctrine alone, usually in a polemical tone against other churches. Pietism reacted against this sterile dogmatism without focusing attention on the changing world. Rather it appealed to the emotions and experiences of concerned individuals. Conversion of the member — and of the pastor — was its objective. Necessary as this was, it neglected other phases of the Word. It produced conventicles rather than a congregation. Yet the Biblical quality was present in preaching, and both orthodoxy and Pietism knew great preachers, such as Johann Arndt, Spener, Francke, and Bengel. The writings as well as the sermons of these men, often collected in postils, or sermon books, had wide influence. Johann Rambach, Magnus Friedrich Roos, Heinrich Mueller, Gerhard Tersteegen, and Johann Freylinghausen were names known throughout the Lutheran world, and the influence of the Moravian Zinzendorf was felt in both the Old and the New World.

The teaching function of the preacher reached its ripeness in the Enlightenment. But rationalism brought this function down to one of a community wise man — if not a community policeman. The rationalistic preacher meant much to the economy and order of his age, but his preaching did not rise above the secular, or natural, order. Even the valiant effort of Schleiermacher to reach the cultured of his age by a psychological interpretation of religion represented only a natural theology, though of a high order.

The French Revolution acted as a moral earthquake to shake men's confidence in natural goodness. On the one hand it produced agnosticism and atheism. On the other it drove men back to deeper wells of inspiration. The celebration of the Reformation anniversary in 1817, the renewed historical study of Scripture, the falling back on the Confessions necessarily changed the climate of preaching. Some tried in vain to stem the secular development or to reconcile it to theology. Others carried forward the Württemberg interest in Biblical studies, especially J. T. Beck, the Blumhardts, and S. K. Kapff. The confessional position was reinforced by Petri of Hanover, Luthardt of Leipzig, and Loehe of Neuendettelsau; and the liturgical life of the congregation through worship and sacrament received new impetus. A definite separation took place between the Biblical and confessional preachers and

288

the representatives of a liberal culture-Protestantism. The catastrophic results of the wars of the present century have carried forward the former rather than the latter tendency. The study of Luther, the influence of Karl Barth and the dialectical theology, the experience of the Confessional Church after Barmen, and the liturgical renaissance have strengthened the conviction that the preaching of the church has its power from Scripture and not from rapidly changing secular fashions. Yet the church realizes that it cannot withdraw from the world and therefore resists the temptation to become a liturgical monastery far from the currents of contemporary life. Preaching has become less formal, briefer, more direct, and tied to congregational life and worship. The church's perennial task is to hear the Word of God and to communicate that Word to its generation.

HYMNODY AND CHURCH MUSIC

Extraordinary in the story of the Christian churches is the development of hymnody and church music in the congregations of the Lutheran Reformation. Choir music was known in the liturgy of the medieval church, and the efforts of Luther to preserve some of the rich Gregorian chants are well known. But congregational singing had no important place even though hymns were constructed on some of the notes the people heard in the liturgy. The Reformation transformed the service from a Mass celebrated by a priest in the presence of a congregation to a corporate worship of pastor and people, and through its hymns the response of the communicants made them participants in the worship. The 38 hymns that Luther wrote were built on previous material — psalms, canticles, medieval sequences, popular songs. They stressed God's deeds for man without excluding man's response to the grace of God. They were hymns of proclamation and prayer, and because of their objective character they have kept their place through the centuries. The period after Luther brought hymns of a more personal nature. Often they were written for private use and later found their way into the official hymnbooks. Paul Gerhardt, Philipp Nicolai, and J. Heermann gave the church some of its greatest hymns.

Pietistic hymn writers described their experiences, which often were exemplary but just as often sentimental and exaggerated in their emotion-filled compositions. The hymns of the period of rationalism

289

stressed man's duties and moral perfections. Besides those of Christian Gellert few survived, but the zeal of the era in preserving older hymns deserves gratitude. The romantic movement too renewed interest in earlier hymns, while the confessional and liturgical revival brought back the structure of the church year with its appropriate hymns. The official collections were not ready to admit the revival songs that flourished in the 19th century, though sometimes these gained entrance in appendices or were used in special collections.

Every Lutheran country has produced its own hymn collections, and these have reflected the period of their publication. German hymns by Luther, Gerhardt, and Nicolai are in almost all hymnbooks, but each country has incorporated its own contributions. Enduring hymn writers include Kingo, Brorson, and Grundtvig in Denmark; Landstad in Norway; Wallin and Franzén in Sweden; Tranoski in Slovakia. Gradually a consensus has developed that a hymnbook should be ecumenical and that one part of the church has a right to use the creations of any other part. Thus the newer books embody hymns of all ages and denominations. While early German Lutheran congregations tended to sing only hymns of Luther, the most recent collections in both Europe and America cross all creedal lines. The American Lutheran *Service Book and Hymnal* includes ancient Latin and Greek hymns, medieval compositions, and hymns of many denominations — even a Negro spiritual. Modern collections are carefully edited and show sensitivity to high poetic and musical standards. The Lutheran congregations are indeed singing congregations and have a unique heritage of hymnbooks.

Originally the words of Reformation hymns were set to a fixed melody. Melodies, however, were soon regarded independently, and so various hymns might use the same melody. The singing of the Bohemian Brethren had effect on Lutheran hymnody, though the latter tended to unison singing while the former enjoyed polyphonic forms. Before the days of printed hymnbooks the congregation sang hymns from memory. This restricted the number used and also slowed down the tempo, which was usually in a grave, slow manner. Lukas Osiander of Nürnberg introduced in 1586 a boys' choir singing in parts while the congregation sang in unison. Even four-part congregational song was not unknown. The use of the organ, which originally did not accompany congregational singing but was played between verses, also aided

290

in slowing the tempo. The organist, furthermore, was tempted to make his preludes, interludes, and postludes the primary music.

From 1700 to 1850 congregational singing suffered and did not improve until the liturgical renewal gave it greater value. Rationalism had little interest in singing and was satisfied to use many hymns to the same melody, and so the average congregation seldom knew more than a score of tunes. In the middle of the 19th century the Lutheran churches heeded the appeal of E. M. Arndt for some uniformity both in hymnbooks and in melodies. Saxony alone had 75 different hymn-books. In 1852 the Eisenach Conference called for a nucleus of hymns and for rhythmic singing instead of the monotonous isometric style. A German Evangelical hymnbook resulted, which the Bavarian Church was first to adopt in 1854, followed by other provincial churches. The new hymnbook of the Evangelical Lutheran Church of Germany followed the pattern of a nucleus used in common, with additional hymns in special editions of the member churches.

Out of the heritage of the church's music, especially its chorales, Johann Sebastian Bach created cantatas, Masses, and instrumental masterpieces. He shares with Michael Praetorius, Dietrich Buxtehude, and Schütz a foremost place of honor in the history of church music, but no one has excelled in quantity and quality his proclamation of the Gospel in music. Nathan Söderblom designated him as a "fifth evangelist." Bach retold the Passion story of St. Matthew and St. John. He wrote organ music to illustrate parts of the liturgy, several series of cantatas based on texts of the church year, motets to express the contents of various Scripture verses, and his Mass in B Minor was a musical exposition of the Communion service in his church in Leipzig.

In accordance with the usage of the time, Bach used not only the organ but also the violin, the whole orchestra, and several choirs, making a symphony of sound as he in his way proclaimed the message of the church and expressed its prayer and praise. Combining a German heritage with French and Italian influence, Bach stood at the end of an age, an age that saw the alienation of a secular culture from the church. Just as the monumental style departed from church architecture, so music went on to its own historical development outside the temple — to concert, sonata, opera, recital. For its part the church, retaining its treasures from Bach, sought greater self-consciousness in

291

its liturgical and hymnodical experience. L. M. Lindeman of Norway explored folk tunes, and T. M. Laub of Denmark followed the lead of Germany back to earlier chorale music of the congregation. In Sweden renewed study broke the hold of J. C. Haeffner's rigid style and led the way to rhythmic singing. Today church musicians are seeking to enrich public worship not only by encouraging intelligent congregational participation but also by improving the contributions church choirs can make in appropriating treasures from former periods, as well as by encouraging compositions that add to those treasures.

The Reformation succeeded in transforming and conserving the main service of worship, with traditions reaching back to the earliest centuries of the Christian faith. It was less successful in the observance of the daily services, which had found their use in monasticism and were hardly congregational in character. Of the *horae,* or hour services, the church retained in some measure Matins and Vespers, and these mostly in urban parishes, which could count on boys' choirs in the schools. Even these city churches felt the pedagogical purpose of orthodoxy and concentrated on preaching or catechization. Pietism contributed little, though Biblical study and prayer and hymn singing in the conventicles quite well matched the goal of the hours services, except for the critical tone these groups assumed toward the church. Rationalism had little understanding of discipline in worship. Only in rather recent times have interested groups in various parts of the church sought to give order to daily hours of devotion by recovering elements of the hour services. This has included experiments in putting to congregational use liturgical music for the Canticles, the Te Deum, and the Psalms.

SACRAMENTS AND RITES

The medieval church had organized the ministry of the parish around seven sacraments. The Reformation restricted the term sacrament to the two which Christ had instituted, Baptism and the Lord's Supper. We have noted how the Sacrament of the Altar was reinterpreted according to its Scriptural origin and how the practice of confession retained what was the early purpose of the Roman sacrament of penance. In the Sacrament of Baptism the Reformation emphasized the unmerited grace of God that encompasses the child from birth. It gradually divested the baptismal act of a whole series of customs that

292

had accumulated through the centuries — making the sign of the cross, giving a child salt, opening of the ear, exorcism and renunciation of the devil, anointing with oil and chrisma, putting on of a white dress, giving of a candle. In deference to popular ideas the omission of these symbolic gestures took place slowly. Only one of them produced discussion among the theologians — exorcism, or the driving out of evil spirits. Some reformers defended the practice, some even wanted it kept because Calvinists opposed it. The custom has perpetuated itself into modern times, but the direct command is usually changed into a prayer for deliverance from the power of the evil one. The mode of baptism has come to be the pouring of water thrice on the child's head, though immersion and sprinkling are permitted since the form is considered of secondary importance.

The periods of Pietism and rationalism saw the sacrament often shift from the church to the home and become a family affair, but its restoration in the 19th century into the church gave prominence to the place of the font in the church — at the entrance or near the chancel — and laid increasing emphasis on the duty of parents and sponsors to have the child reared in the knowledge of the faith into which he had been brought in Baptism.

CONFIRMATION

Confirmation had become a sacrament in the Roman Church, though less a confirmation of baptism than of a relationship established between the child and the church through the bishop's making of the sign of the cross on the child's brow. This episcopal ceremony disappeared in the Reformation Church. But the need of instructing the child was present, especially in an evangelical church that looked on Scripture as its authority. Luther had given the congregation a handbook in his Small Catechism, to be used by the head of the household. This became the textbook of the Lutheran Church in the following centuries and in every land. Catechetical instruction entered into the worship service in orthodoxy, and catechetical examination was an essential part of the parish ministry and discipline. The terrible effects of the Thirty Years' War included deterioration of religious instruction in schools and homes and churches. In his program for reform Spener made the practice of instruction a regular preparation for Communion and the rite of confirmation a desirable one. This custom spread and

293

gradually the liturgy of the church came to include an order of confirmation. It was tied to baptism, and so it was often interpreted as the child's own assumption of obligation, which in baptism had been undertaken by parent or sponsor. In principle, however, Baptism was a gift of God and needed no confirmation. But the youth now declared his faith publicly and was admitted to full privileges in the congregation, especially Holy Communion.

Confirmation has thus become a requisite for responsible participation in the Lord's Supper and for membership in the congregation. The trend has been to require fewer promises on the part of the youth in the confirmation rite and to make it more of an intercession by the congregation for its youth and a sharing of the blessings of the fellowship of the church. As a symbol the laying on of hands by the pastor is a prominent part of the rite. This act is reminiscent of the laying on of hands in the ordination of the pastor. In confirmation there is an "ordination" into the universal priesthood of believers into which the child was called in baptism.

MARRIAGE

Marriage too had become a sacrament in the pre-Reformation church. The evangelical no less than the Roman Church held marriage to be a holy estate. By degrees the medieval hierarchy had taken the natural order of matrimony — the consent of the individuals concerned — out of the secular sphere and made marriage by the priest obligatory for the Christian. The Lutheran Church recognized the authority of the secular government in this area and reserved to it the right of determining prohibited relationships. The medieval church had gained much both in prestige and in money by referring forbidden cases to bishops or even to Rome. As the secular governments asserted their jurisdiction by demanding — in some countries — civil marriage for all, the evangelical churches conceded this right and, unlike the Roman authorities, considered such marriages valid. The church, however, could still expect its members to seek its blessing and to regard Christian marriage as implying a higher than secular appreciation of the meaning of marriage.

When civil marriage precedes the church ceremony, the latter becomes a blessing and an admonition. Where the civil government allows it, the pastor may, and sometimes is expected to, act as a servant

294

of the state in declaring groom and bride as man and wife. In such matters as divorce and birth control the policies of modern Lutheran countries are determined as much by secular governments as by the churches, for although the churches can proclaim higher standards, they may not exercise control of civil affairs. They are to keep before their people the obligations of Christian matrimony and the duties of parents and children who profess to follow Christ.

BURIAL

Extreme unction as a sacrament disappeared from the churches of the Reformation. Yet this represented no loss of care for the dying. The parish ministry continued its service of prayer and intercession, but the elimination of the doctrine of purgatory from the evangelical faith removed the popular fear of dying without a priestly rite. Burial of the dead still commanded reverence, and the grave was hallowed by prayer and thanksgiving. Slowly the age-old prohibition against the burial of suicides within the parish cemetery walls was broken down, and the attitude of the church has turned to one of greater understanding both of the afflictions of man and of the mercy of God. In our day cremation has become permissible. Even prayer for the dead has in some places slowly and subtly insinuated itself into the church despite the evangelical fear of believing in the merits of men — even of saintly men and women. But turning directly to the fount of mercy, the church can pray: "For the sake of Jesus Christ judge him not according to his sins, and according to Thy mercy awaken him to eternal glory."

Symptomatic of the great social changes that have engulfed the church is the disappearance of the church cemetery. In the urban conditions of our time the parish church with its surrounding, well-kept cemetery grounds is but a memory.

ORDINATION

Ordination, another sacrament of the medieval church, was radically transformed in the Reformation, for it had to do with a concept of the church which the reformers rejected. In the Roman theory the pope had received from the apostle Peter all authority and with the bishops ruled the church on earth. The bishop ordained the priest, who thenceforward had the right to offer the sacrifice of the Mass in which bread and wine changed into the body and blood of Christ. For none of this did Luther find a basis in Scripture. Rather by Baptism every believer became in God's sight a priest who could receive forgiveness of sins, offer prayer and intercession, and encourage fellow believers.

Yet order was necessary in the congregation, and out of the universal priesthood the congregation called men into the ministry. The minister, however, did not have a higher status in the sight of God than the layman. Ordination in the Lutheran congregation was a public confirmation of the call of the pastor to serve a body of fellow believers in a ministry of preaching, sacrament, and spiritual counsel. In an emergency the congregation itself could ordain, but normally the candidate would be formally set apart by the laying on of hands by other pastors as representatives of a larger communion of believers.

Two emphases have characterized ordination in the Lutheran congregations, one indicating the divine institution of the ministry as obedience to the command of God above subservience to the congregation, the other deriving the office from the universal priesthood. The advocates of the former have tended to favor the episcopal ordination, while exponents of the latter have been willing to admit laymen to participate in the examination of candidates and in the laying on of hands. Other divisions have arisen over the question of the ordination of women, which has occurred in Denmark, Sweden, and Slovakia. Nowhere is an essential distinction made between bishop and other clergy, except in function; and no part of the church believes ordination by bishops in apostolic succession is essential. Beyond these differences of viewpoint a unity has existed in the affirmation that the essence of the office is the proclamation of the Word and the administration of the sacraments. The truth of apostolic succession lies in a faithful transmission of the Gospel, and while no indelible character is given in ordination, a perpetual obligation is laid on the pastor to enrich his people with the means of grace, whose efficacy is guaranteed through no human arrangement but by the gift of the Spirit. Therefore His coming and presence is implored at every ordination.

Something of the reaction of the Church of the Reformation to the pressures of secular change has been mirrored in the dress of its clergy. In southern Germany, under Swiss influence, the ancient vestments disappeared, and through most of Germany the academic robe

296

not only imitated Luther but accentuated the role of the preacher as a teacher. Along with other professions the clergy in many places retained the bands, which in Denmark and Norway floriated into ruff collars. In an almost unique way the Swedish Church kept its vestments — alb, chasuble, stole — and bishops and archbishops wore regalia of medieval pattern, though sometimes in northern regions the walrus tooth took the place of ebony in the mitred bishop's staff. Along with the liturgical and confessional renewal of the 19th century came an appreciation of this heritage, so that Lutheran bishops today can be distinguished from other clergy. In Europe the ministers often wear the chasuble at the altar. In America they appear in surplice and stole — the latter in seasonal colors. True to the Augsburg Confession, the church considers these matters adiaphora, that is, things neither commanded nor forbidden by Scripture; but the attention paid to vestments of clergy and choir, to altar and chancel paraments, and to vessels for Baptism and Communion do reflect a concern that the work of the church be carried on reverently and in conscientious orderliness.

POLITY

In the Reformation the power to ordain theoretically came from a communion of congregations rather than, as in the Roman view, from a hierarchy. But with age-old conditions confronting them, the reformers could not go about reorganizing parishes. For centuries the parish priests had been set there by their bishops, and bishops had been responsible to Rome. And the whole system was inextricably interwoven with secular governments with whom the church divided its rule over vast treasures of land and buildings — also over matters of marriage, taxation, and education. At first Luther had hoped that enough bishops would join the reform movement to facilitate the continuance of church order. When this failed, the new parishes depended on the secular authorities in cities or on landed estates to help secure evangelical pastors. If the authorities were friendly, they assumed the obligation of membership and leadership in the congregation, becoming a sort of episcopacy over parishes in their domain. They depended on theological teachers who helped prepare and ordain pastors, and with the theologians they instituted periodic visitation of churches and schools. The system of secular authority over the congregations developed in Germany, usually administered by a commission of lay and clerical members called a consistory. When the bonds between church and state loosened in the 19th century, the church gained greater independence through the establishment of synods. After the wars of the first half of the 20th century the church achieved full authority to manage its own affairs and elect its own spiritual leader, often called bishop.

The Scandinavian churches never lost their independence altogether. The Swedish Church succeeded in keeping the episcopate unbroken, and the congregations or episcopal chapters through the centuries exercised relative freedom in the calling of pastors and in the administration of parish affairs. Denmark temporarily lost the episcopal system but gradually regained it. In the days of Grundtvig and the Inner Mission the parishes received extraordinary freedom to organize themselves. In Norway, despite the Haugean movement, church and state remained closely tied together. In its relationship to the school system the parish church retained more privileges than the other northern churches. Strangely, Finland's difficult course under Russian rule led to an arrangement in 1869 which gave the church greater freedom than any other Lutheran state church enjoyed, while still receiving financial support from the public treasury.

The ideals of the Reformation found their closest approximation when the political developments left the congregations free to organize and administer themselves. In the American system the state exercises no authority in the churches. Lutheran doctrine strongly emphasizes the distinct roles of the two realms, the spiritual and the secular. It grants the state jurisdiction in the realm of the secular and asks for the church freedom to preach the Word and administer its sacraments, to regulate its own life, and to choose its own leaders. In countries where the national church is constitutionally Lutheran and the state supports the economy of the church, the state still exercises certain supervisory and approving functions, but everywhere the church aims for independence in its spiritual ministry. Where independent of secular authority and state support, the Lutheran congregations have learned to support themselves. Yet they do not interpret their freedom to mean silence in judging the life of the state. The proclamation of the Word includes the social and economic conditions under which members of church and state live. The preaching of Law and Gospel covers the whole of life whether the church is a part of or apart from the machinery of secular government.

CHURCH AND SOCIETY

The distinction between Law and Gospel is the more important as the secular state has during the recent centuries taken over areas of human concern long under the care of the church, such as charity and education. Care of the sick, the poor, the orphan, the aged have come to be a part of the program of the modern welfare state. Education, which from kindergarten to university was nourished by the church, has slowly passed from the hands of parish councils and church chancellors into the hands of community and state officials or of corporations. In the field of charity the church seeks more than the care of the body, and on mission fields its institutions set standards for secular hospitals and homes. Where the state has taken over school systems the churches have established their own programs of religious education and tried to influence higher education through church colleges. In the preparation of its ministry the European churches have in most cases depended on state-supported universities, whereas churches in America and elsewhere have established their own theological seminaries.

Thus, with roots deep in the earlier centuries, the congregations of the Lutheran Reformation developed the Biblical principles of the church, embracing all the experiences of the parish people from baptism through confirmation to marriage and burial, hallowing each by the Word and Holy Communion. Generation after generation a body of believers grew in grace and was able to meet the trials and crises of community and nation. Where exile or emigration forced members of parishes into new environments, they were able to plant a new community — with or without a resident pastor. On the frontiers of the East or the West, facing foes of both body and soul, a group could meet to sing cherished hymns, read parts of a familiar liturgy or sermons from well-worn postils, and teach children the Small Catechism until in time a pastor could come to administer the sacraments and lead in the building of a church where a bell would be installed to call the members to regular worship. So, as a vine extends its tendrils, the congregations of the lands of the Reformation struck new roots in Transylvania, in Siberia, in the major lands of North and South America, and in Australia. From the life of these parishes went the founders of new congregations in Asia, Africa, and the islands of the seas. The Word penetrated into all the experiences of the individual, all levels of society, and all parts of the world. Through a ministry bound by Confessions interpreting the Word, a communion of saints was realized in countless communities whose character was influenced by men and women praying for the hallowing of God's name, the doing of His will and the coming of His kingdom on earth as in heaven.

In recent years the churches have tried to bridge the gap that separates their ministry from leaders of thought and action in an increasingly secular world by instituting evangelical academies. One of the earliest was the Sigtuna Stiftelse in Sweden, growing out of a Christian student movement before World War I. Since the end of World War II academies have multiplied in Germany. Representatives of various professions are invited to meet with leaders of the church in periods of discussion and fellowship where both sides may discuss the needs of the day. It is the hope of the churchmen that they may thereby establish communication with representatives of medicine, law, journalism, government, labor, and other community spokesmen, interpreting the message of the church to such as do not understand or misunderstand the relevance of the Gospel in modern society. This, too, is the purpose of the American church colleges.

THEOLOGICAL SCHOLARSHIP

The revolutionary changes that have taken place in the relationship of the churches to one another, to education and philanthropy and the welfare state, and to a materialistic and secular culture today pose great problems to the ministry of Word and sacraments. Not only has there been a divorce of church and government, but since the middle of the 18th century secularism has steadily pushed the church aside. A philosophy of life has developed apart from Christian teaching. Sometimes science has been considered as the source of all meaningful knowledge. More often materialism has reigned, subjecting the marvelous discoveries of the physical and biological sciences to human control and offering them for the enrichment of man's life. The satisfaction of the senses has become a sufficient ideal. The ideology of communism presents such a philosophy in its ultimate form, used by its advocates as a means to political power.

Despite the achievements of the modern mind, the fundamental problems of humanity remain. Poverty grips much of the world's population — in the face of the riches of some countries. The relations between races of different color have never been more acute. While bodily health has often improved, mental health has become a paramount issue. And despite two world wars in this century, the world still trembles in apprehension of another, more devastating nuclear war. What is the message of the church in such a world? Some have doubted that the church has any other message than the comfort of an eschatological hope. Others have given themselves entirely to contending with social, economic, and political questions. Between these extreme positions the teachers of the Church of the Reformation have sought both to strengthen the faith of its people and to relate that faith to the problems present in this generation. The curriculum of theological education therefore stresses the Biblical sources of Christian faith by close attention to the meaning and interpretation of Scripture. It also puts increasing emphasis on the application of the Gospel to the real problems of the individual and of society. These are problems of all people, and the Lutheran Church joins all disciplines in quest of knowledge. It seeks the *Christian* answer to the questions of mankind.

Theological investigation thus moves across ecclesiastical boundaries. But the confessional consciousness of Lutheran teachers has received new significance as the Lutheran World Federation has opened means of communication between different countries. German theological works have circulated inside and outside the church ever since the Reformation. Whereas the majority of Lutheran publications a century ago were confined to Scandinavia or Germany or the United States, journals and conferences and conventions today make common property of the achievements of any part of the church. In the American churches the names of Henry Eyster Jacobs, Franz Pieper, Conrad Lindberg, and M. Reu were little known outside their synod, though they mediated much of European theology to this country. Today the works of Werner Elert, Paul Althaus, Peter Brunner, Hermann Sasse, Edmund Schlink, and Adolf Köberle are translated and read in other languages; and Gustaf Aulén, Anders Nygren, Yngve Brilioth, Sigmund Mowinc-

301

kel, and Kristen Skydsgaard are known in all Lutheran seminaries. American students go to Europe to study with Rudolf Bultmann, Gerhard von Rad, Joachim Jeremias; and Europeans come to America to view methods of organization, evangelization, stewardship, and pastoral counseling. A steady flow of exchange goes on between the older and the younger churches.

Thus the treasures of scholarship and ministry are available to all who want to learn. Publications such as the Weimar Edition and the new American Edition of Luther's Works, the volumes of the *Wörterbuch*, the new encyclopedias, such as *Die Religion in Geschichte und Gegenwart, Nordisk Teologisk Uppslagsbok, The Encyclopedia of the Lutheran Church,* and excellent journals of the various bodies and of the Lutheran World Federation have lifted the level of the church's scholarship and made it known in other communions. While realizing its difference from a world of secular culture, the church must nevertheless be able to understand the world if it wishes to speak to such a culture.

XX

THE CHURCH CATHOLIC AND
THE CHURCH OF THE LUTHERAN REFORMATION

Luther's purpose was to restore to the church its original character. Over the centuries Rome had introduced innovations that obscured the real nature of the one, holy, catholic, and apostolic church. These novelties in the Mass, the hierarchy, and the papacy, insofar as they were contrary to Scripture, had to be eradicated. The real mission of the church was to proclaim the Gospel and to administer the sacraments. By recalling Christians to this charter the Reformation was bringing the church back to its true foundation. Traits emphasized by the Reformation as marks of the original, Scriptural church were the proclamation of the Word, the Sacrament of Baptism, the Sacrament of the Altar, the practice of confession and absolution, the function of an ordained ministry, the use of the Apostles' Creed and the Lord's Prayer, a worship of prayer, praise, and thanksgiving, daily suffering under the cross, the sanctified life of members, obedience to temporal government, and the honoring of marriage. All these marks of the church are but different aspects of the Gospel, which is the good news of the forgiveness of sins by a gracious Lord through Jesus Christ, received in faith and creating a new life in Christ. Not the initiation of a new church, therefore, but a reaffirmation of the church of the Word was the genius of the Lutheran Reformation.

A COMMUNION OF FAITH

The reformers had at first hoped for a general council that would reform the churches by setting them on a Scriptural foundation. But the medieval hierarchical institution centered in Rome was so entrenched and so involved in the aims and rivalries of the nations of Europe that no free church council could ever be realized. Instead the Council of Trent, under the domination of the papacy, refused to heed the call for reform. It did effect some improvements, but set for itself the task of suppressing everywhere the efforts at real reform, a task in many places effected by the Jesuits acting in conjunction with favorable secular rulers.

Faced by such resistance the reformers could bring about changes only where clergy and secular authorities were willing to cooperate and to defy the papal claims to absolute rule. So began the slow, often discouraging process of organizing communities under new spiritual leadership. This could not be done without a clear statement of the faith professed by the reformed pastors and congregations. The Augsburg Confession was such a statement, making very clear that "we have introduced nothing, either in doctrine or in ceremonies, that is contrary to Holy Scripture or the universal Christian church." Clarification of the Augustana articles led to discussions and controversies for half a century, until the Book of Concord became an accepted constitution of churches accepting the Lutheran Reformation. While the Formula of Concord was not received by all Lutheran churches, it did represent a major victory in welding together a great number of Christians in a common statement of faith. The alternative might have been a general disintegration of these communities.

The Reformation could not be realized by isolated congregations. The church of the Word was a communion of the faithful, and the Christ, who was the Head of the church, included in His body all who lived by and in Him. In his Large Catechism Luther had described the church on earth as "a little flock or community of pure saints under one head, Christ. It is called together by the Holy Spirit in one faith, mind, and understanding. It possesses a variety of gifts, yet is united in love without sect or schism. . . . Through it he gathers us, using it to teach and preach the Word. By it he creates and increases sanctification, causing it daily to grow and become strong in the faith and in the fruits of the Spirit." Thus the earthly church is an instrument by which Christ, the Word, creates a holy people, and a true church is known by its faithfulness to its Lord. There were many people of God in the Roman Church because it too had the Word, but the encrustations on that church prevented it from exhibiting clearly and fully the free grace in Christ. The churches of the Reformation were to be judged by their allowing the Spirit to call, gather, enlighten, sanctify, and keep and unite believers in the true faith. In these churches too were un-

304

worthy members, but the churches were in the church catholic insofar as they proclaimed the fullness of the grace of God. For the church is catholic in the degree that it witnesses to the wholeness of the temple of which Christ is the Cornerstone.

The Course of the Roman Church

Instead of a church reformed and united, the following centuries beheld increasing division and bitterness among Christians of Europe. The Church of Rome turned to force, to the Inquisition, to education in its attempt to win obedience. It became increasingly dependent on national governments despite its declared sovereignty over them. The Peace of Westphalia confirmed the Roman Church's loss of much of northern Europe. Elsewhere growing nationalism threatened its power. France asserted an independent policy, placing bishops and orders in constantly increasing numbers under royal authority. Austria replaced Spain as the leading Roman power, but the Enlightenment made Joseph II more tolerant than Rome could endure. The Edict of 1781 gave Evangelicals in the Hapsburg territories new hope. For the papal power the French Revolution was a catastrophe, to be followed by the liberation of Italy from the temporal rule of the Vatican. Frightened by secularism and materialism, Roman Catholics saw in the papacy a last resort, and the ultramontane party ascribed to it broader spiritual authority as its secular power diminished. The pope retired into an isolation from which he condemned all modernism as error. At the Vatican Council in 1870 his faithful followers declared him infallible when he speaks *ex cathedra,* that is, when as supreme head of the church he proclaims a doctrine for the whole church. Meanwhile more creative forces among the lower clergy and the laity sought to meet the challenge of social and economic problems by benevolent programs, such as the charitable labors of the followers of Vincent de Paul and the educational work among the poor by the associates of Jean Baptiste de la Salle and the Saint Sacrament Compagnie of Paris.

The Jesuits fell on evil times. They had earned the jealousy of competing orders and were involved in difficulties with colonial powers, trade associations, and national governments. Within the church their accommodating methods brought on them condemnation by Jansenists in France and also by the Curia in Rome. They were excluded from

Portugal, France, and Spain, and finally in 1773 the pope was induced to suppress their order, which in 1750 had numbered 22,000 members. Other orders turned into directions favored by the times. St. Germain des Pres, Parisian center of the Benedictine congregation of Saint-Maur, became famous for the historical research of Jean Mabillon and fellow monks. The lives of saints and of the fathers, especially St. Augustine, and the authenticity of ancient documents were subjects of study. Some of the results were disturbing to the cult of the saints, but other orders furthered popular devotion in the form of contemplation of the Sacrament and of the heart of Jesus. The adoration of Mary and the development of Mariology reached their culmination in 1950 when the dogma of the Assumption of the Virgin Mary to the throne of heaven was promulgated. This decree and that of papal infallibility separated the Roman Church even farther from the churches of the Reformation, justifying their protest against doctrines not based on Scripture.

Despite the course of the papal church after Trent, there were some who hoped for reconciliation. Spinola, a Roman bishop of Dalmatia, traveled far and wide in the latter part of the 17th century visiting Lutheran princes and theologians in the hope of finding a formula for union — but in vain. The famous French preacher and bishop Jacques Bossuet carried on a correspondence with the philosopher Leibniz, but the demand of the latter for a new council to supersede Trent was coolly received. The conversion of some rulers proved sensational — Christina of Sweden, Christian August of Saxony, the dukes of Holstein, Brunswick-Lüneburg, and Württemberg — but with little other effect on their subjects than to increase popular resistance to papal emissaries. What mellowing there may have been between Lutherans and Romanists was due to a general spirit of tolerance engendered by the philosophy of rationalism. As governments became neutral, the masses tended toward indifference to the claims of theologians. Tradition, inheritance, and status more than religious conviction determined church membership until a 19th-century spiritual renewal in both communions revealed unreconciled divergences.

LUTHERANS AND ORTHODOX

With even less mutual understanding the Lutherans and the Orthodox faced each other on the borderlands of Europe and Asia. Melanchthon had hoped to establish a relationship with the Greek patriarch, for in 1559 he wrote Jeremiah II a personal letter and sent him a Greek translation of the Augsburg Confession. Later, Tübingen theologians carried on a lengthy correspondence with Constantinople, emphasizing points of agreement between the two churches, but the only result was an invitation for the Lutherans to join the true original church — the Orthodox. The Greeks were not interested even in theological discussion. Closer contacts were found in Poland and the Baltic countries. In Poland and the Ukraine the Orthodox and the Roman Catholics were locked in bitter conflict, for by offering certain privileges Rome tempted the Orthodox to become Uniate churches. Here the Lutherans could only be onlookers, but they discovered that any Protestant-minded Orthodox theologian, such as Cyril Lucas, would find little sympathy among fellow Orthodox teachers. In the middle of the 19th century many peasants of Latvia and Estonia thought they might be better off as members of the Orthodox Church than as members of Lutheran parishes run by their overlords — mainly German nobles. Conversions ran into the thousands, embarrassing even the Russian authorities. When after 1905 the disappointed converts could legally return to Lutheran congregations, the tide turned. Finland staunchly held its own against St. Petersburg and Moscow, even occasionally trying to teach the illiterate Orthodox in their territory to read. Here the contact was less irritable since the Finnish Orthodox Church was subordinate to Constantinople rather than the Third Rome. We may date the beginning of a real catholic interest by Lutherans in Orthodoxy to 1925, when Greek religious leaders accepted the invitation to the Stockholm Conference.

LUTHERANS AND REFORMED

The early controversy between the followers of Luther and those of Zwingli divided the reformers into groups that have persisted to the present day. When the Swiss and the Germans met at Marburg in 1529, they were able to agree on 14 points, but on the 15th — the doctrine of the Lord's Supper — they could not unite. The indefatigable Bucer continued his search for a common formula, and some progress was achieved in the Wittenberg Concordat of 1536. Differences in attitudes toward Scripture and on the interpretation of the mode of the presence of Christ in the Sacrament, however, were not reconciled. Melanchthon made matters worse by his revision of the Augsburg Confession in 1540, for he obscured the connection between the elements and the body and blood of Christ in order to satisfy the Swiss. The Lutherans recognized the difference between Zwingli and Calvin but were not satisfied with Calvin's determination of the presence of Christ in the Sacrament.

The separation between the Lutherans and the Swiss was widened by differences in forms of worship and the exercise of discipline. Political conditions deepened the bitterness. From the Peace of Augsburg (1555) to the Peace of Westphalia (1648) the Calvinists were not legally entitled to the privileges enjoyed by the Lutherans. Real as the differences were, they were magnified by polemical theology until Lutherans sometimes felt that they were closer to Rome than to Geneva. Where church and government were closely identified, as in German territories or Scandinavian countries, every attempt was made to keep out Calvinist doctrines. Where both Lutherans and Reformed were minority groups fighting for survival against the Counter-Reformation, they could, as in the 1570 Polish Consensus of Sandomir, combine for common defense. Close relationships were avoided mainly because Calvinism spread into countries with few Lutheran congregations — France, the Netherlands, and Scotland.

But isolation of nations was no longer possible. Currents of trade, students, and books flowed between them as they had done earlier, then aiding the Reformation. The teachings of Georg Calixtus at Helmstedt had permanent consequences. He advocated a return to the theology of the first centuries and, like Jacob Acontius, a distinction between fundamental and secondary articles in the Confessions. Despite the opposition of the dominant orthodoxy his irenic spirit was carried far and wide by influential students. John Dury, a Scotch Presbyterian, had come to know the divisions among Protestants in Holland, France, and Germany as well as in his homeland, and in the midst of the Thirty Years' War he tried to interest Gustavus Adolphus and English diplomats for peace among the Evangelicals. David Pareus of Heidelberg meanwhile was teaching a friendlier spirit between the confessions — one of his pupils was Amos Comenius, the renowned leader of the ecumenical Brethren. These were indeed solitary voices in centuries when no real approach was made by the Reformed and Lutheran authorities to each other. Yet they were continuing evidences of the troubled consciences of Christians who realized that the situation was a denial of the creed each professed, namely, the unity of the church of Christ. At present the renewed conversations between Lutherans and Reformed both in Europe and America awaken hopes of better relationships.

INTERCONFESSIONAL LITERATURE AND MISSIONS

Although secular governments and theological faculties could not effect close relationships between Christians, another movement achieved far more success. This was the wave of devotional literature that crossed all boundaries in a manner church historians have inadequately portrayed. Most influential of all were the works of Johann Arndt, whose *True Christianity* is probably the most ecumenical book since the Reformation. Arndt, a Lutheran pastor, transmitted into Lutheranism a strain of medieval mysticism originating in Augustine and St. Bernhard. More than this, he knew by heart portions of the devotional writings of the Greek monk Makarios, whose works were published in Germany after 1594. Arndt's *Four Books on True Christianity* came out between 1606 and 1609 and were soon translated and read throughout Protestantism, leaving deep traces in Pietism and Puritanism. Likewise the mystical writings of Arnold, Boehme, and Tersteegen found their way through confessional barriers. The international contacts of Pietism facilitated the interchange of literature. English books gained immense popularity in Lutheran lands, especially Richard Baxter's *Saints' Everlasting Rest,* Bunyan's *Pilgrim's Progress,* and Arthur Dent's *True Conversion.* As hymns were translated into many languages hymnbooks grew increasingly ecumenical. Beneath the storms of theological controversy a form of piety grew unobtrusively, nurtured by light and streams from many directions.

The fruits of such popular devotion were gathered in the great harvest of interconfessional activities after the last decades of the 18th century. The Inner Mission movement in Switzerland and Germany owed something to the charitable activities of French Catholics. Its workers were enlisted from Reformed and Lutheran parishes alike. The swelling number of foreign mission societies inaugurated a new period of interconfessional cooperation. Bible and tract societies enjoyed nondenominational support. Emigration, exile, and travel contributed toward a mellowing of traditional attitudes and to a growth of fellowship between Christians of different origins and training.

309

Not always was the experiment of a new relationship happy or successful. When Frederick of Prussia tried to impose both a common consistory and a common liturgy on his churches, he met stout resistance. But the union movement persisted, resulting in strange combinations. In some provinces a kind of consensus was established between the confessions. Some combinations permitted each confession to have its own catechism and worship. When Germans from these provinces came to Pennsylvania, they would erect a union church where one edifice and pastor served both Lutheran and Reformed, the one holding to Luther's, the other to the Heidelberg, Catechism.

In this confused state of church relationships the revival of Lutheranism took place. The Lutheran leaders who came together after 1868 in the General Conference in Germany were intent on identifying the foundations of the Church of the Lutheran Reformation. Only against this background can the word "unionism" in Germany be understood. No comparable situation developed in Scandinavia. Here the emigration of dissenters led slowly to the granting of privileges by the state and finally to full freedom for non-Lutherans, but their numbers were never large enough to challenge the state churches. In the United States the immigrants found themselves in a political system where the government left the churches to their own decisions. Many were lost to the church of their fathers, but slowly the Lutheran churches found their identity and their fellows in the faith. Their relations with other Protestants were entirely voluntary and had none of the character of forced "unionism," as in Germany. All in all, while the Prussian Union was an expression of catholicism in the evangelical churches, the experiment did more harm than good, setting back rather than advancing the cause of improved confessional relationships. Not only did it fail to unite Lutherans and Reformed in any meaningful way, but it caused a serious cleavage between Lutherans themselves.

FEDERATION AND UNION IN GERMANY

Over a century passed after the ill-starred Prussian Union before another event of an entirely different nature brought together the followers of Luther and Calvin in Germany. In 1922 as a result of World War I the churches in Germany set up the Evangelical Church Federation to enable them to deal with the new government. A decade later, when Hitler came to power, the German Christians, a party subservient to him, attempted to take over the control of all churches. So palpably false was the claim of the German Christians to be following the Confessions in their plan to build a national, anti-Semitic church that opposition immediately arose among pastors of both Reformed and Lutheran churches.

Inspired by Karl Barth, a movement arose to make a common stand against the Berlin administration. Some felt the times called for a new confession. Accordingly at Barmen in 1934 a free synod of both communions declared that the church was based on the Word, and Christ alone was its leader. The synod claimed to represent the true organization of the churches and through a committee directed them during the perilous years that ended with the collapse of Germany in 1945. Then the question whether Barmen constituted a new church fellowship, including fellowship at the Lord's Table, pressed for an answer. Many answered the question affirmatively, holding that the Barmen Declaration did not mean an abandonment of the older Confessions but was an advance beyond them. Leaders of the Lutheran churches, however, asserted that a new confession could come about only by properly constituted negotiations between both churches.

As a result no union was effected. The churches did join in a federation, the EKD, or Evangelical Church in Germany, but the majority of Lutheran churches formed the VELKD, or United Evangelical Lutheran Church of Germany. The federation contained Reformed and United churches, the Church of the Prussian Union, and Lutheran churches. It has had to confine itself to cooperation in matters of administration, representation, and extension, while the VELKD has adopted a common liturgy, a common core of hymns, common forms for pastoral rites, and common rules for parish life. Discussion seeking closer bonds has proceeded within the EKD. A comprehensive study of the Lord's Supper produced a considerable measure of agreement in the so-called Arnoldshain Theses. But after 400 years the separation at Marburg has not been bridged in Germany. Rather other issues have been raised. The Reformed have been critical of the Lutheran reluctance to attack modern ethical problems though showing tolerance of liberal Scriptural exegesis. The Lutherans have claimed a more correct inter-

311

pretation of the relationship of Law and Gospel in preaching and teaching, and have considered the Reformed view of the kingdom of God superficial, lacking eschatological dimension. Yet a sense of obligation to lift the controversies to a higher ecumenical level has been growing.

LIMITED INTERCOMMUNION IN SCANDINAVIA AND GREAT BRITAIN

The Scandinavian countries have agreed to certain mutual relationships with the Church of England. Especially Sweden and Finland, with an unbroken succession of bishops, have been approached by the Anglican Church, and both communions now allow each other's members at their altars, their pastors in each other's pulpits, and each other's bishops at their consecrations. Visitors from Denmark, Norway, and Iceland are invited to Anglican altars, and Anglicans away from their churches are admitted to altars in these countries. Both Swedish and Finnish churches have made clear that they do not hold apostolic succession essential. Therefore they do not accept the Anglican distinction between their churches and those of the other Scandinavian countries. To the invitation of the Church of Scotland that there be mutual admission of members away from home to each other's Communion table all the Scandinavian churches have responded favorably.

NATIONAL CHRISTIAN COUNCILS

In general the practice of the Lutheran churches everywhere has been to require agreement in doctrine as a condition for participation in the Lord's Supper. But there has been a growing willingness to enter into cooperation with other Protestant churches in meeting common problems of the times. Regional or national associations have been organized on every continent, and Lutherans have had a part in many of them. In the United States the Federal Council of Churches early in the century failed to win Lutheran bodies, but many of them joined the National Council of Churches formed in 1950. Lutheran churches hold membership in federations in Argentina, Uruguay, Brazil, and Mexico. Most of the constituent members of the Federation of Evangelical Lutheran Churches of India participate also in the National Christian Council of India. Similarly Lutheran churches in Africa are members both of Lutheran associations and of the Christian Councils of Tanzania or of South Africa. In Europe, where the EKD embraces most of the German churches, Lutherans are found in ecumenical councils in Austria, Hungary, Czechoslovakia, and Poland, and French Lutherans are members of the Protestant Federation of France.

THE WORLD COUNCIL OF CHURCHES

The drawing together of Christian churches has been an impressive phenomenon of this century. The greater mobility of populations, the many emigrations, and the improvement of communications hastened a consolidation of Christendom as it faced the complex social problems of the 19th century. The Evangelical Alliance, the YMCA and the YWCA, the international student movement, the peace movement, and above all the worldwide missions of the churches created new forms of interrelationships between individual Christians. The Edinburgh Missionary Conference of 1910 became a watershed in Christian history. From that date streams of church life began to flow in the direction of ecumenicity. Rudely shattering as the consequences of World War I proved to be, they yet made more urgent the call for common action by Christians. An American Episcopalian, Bishop Brent, headed the Faith and Order movement; a Swedish Lutheran, Archbishop Söderblom, that of Life and Work.

Lutherans responded to the challenge of both movements. In the Stockholm Conference they showed readiness to take part in a program of attacking social and economic wrongs as well as personal sins. At Lausanne they declared their intention of entering the ecumenical ranks as a confessional unit rather than as parts of geographical groups; and they contributed significantly to the emphasis on the teaching of the grace of God, which characterized the Edinburgh Conference of 1937. A considerable portion of world Lutheranism joined in the formation of the World Council of Churches at Amsterdam in 1948. In the short history of the council no one has given more in the position of leadership than the chairman of its Central Committee, Franklin Clark Fry, president of the Lutheran Church in America. In 1965 almost one fourth of the member churches in the World Council were Lutherans representing every part of the world, and next to the Orthodox the Lutherans constituted the largest confessional group. They have played leading roles in the council's commissions on Faith and Order, international relationships, interchurch aid, and in the department of world missions.

313

In joining in the ecumenical endeavor the Lutheran churches have insisted on their confessional character. The World Council, they have helped make clear, is not a church but a meeting of churches that do possess a unity no less real because it is limited. These churches own a common Baptism and an obligation to regard every baptized Christian as a member of the universal household of God. They profess a common faith in Christ as the Son of God, the Redeemer and Lord of the world. They do not all agree on the interpretation of Scripture and the nature of its authority, but the measure of agreement they do hold as followers of Christ justifies the form of common confession they make before the world in the council. Here they find opportunity to study the Scriptures together, meet in common prayer, and work together in evangelism and missions.

The Lutherans are not ready to hold common Communion services or allow indiscriminate attendance at their own altars, for this sacrament to them is the most intimate of all the experiences of the church with its Lord, and they believe a common confession as to the meaning of His presence is required for a worthy celebration. But the temple of God, which one enters at Baptism, is spacious enough to permit many forms of fellowship until all can kneel together at the Communion table. No less than other Christians, Lutherans consider unity at the Table as a goal, but they do not look on it as a means toward the goal. Even among themselves pulpit and altar fellowship has not been achieved everywhere, a condition deplored at the 1962 Lutheran World Federation meeting in Helsinki. Nor are all Lutheran bodies in either the Lutheran World Federation or the World Council of Churches. Yet all feel the obligation to bring the various parts of the Church of the Reformation together to chart the way to any larger unity.

Lutheran churches in the World Council have borne witness to the nature of the unity they seek. Their own history has proved true the assertion of their confession that the preaching of the Word and the administration of the sacraments can take place in many forms of organization. They have witnessed to the church catholic in regional and national councils, in folk churches and free churches, in congregational, presbyterian, or episcopal polities. Their own ideal of unity is in a consensus of what is preached, taught, and practiced, and

314

though they recognize tradition — they themselves exhibit a variety of traditions — they hold that the essential tradition is a faithful transmittal of the Word of God in Scripture as their supreme authority. For their own understanding of what is central in Scripture they accept the Confessions, which declare man's justification by the grace of God alone through faith alone as the heart and core of Christian truth. The significance of apostolic succession is not in a series of laying on of hands but in a confession of faith in accord with the apostolic message. The church is not a judge but a servant of the Gospel, and its service is the proclamation of the Word to the world. The Gospel creates the church by the Spirit, and its unity is in the witness it bears to Christ, its Head and Lord.

LUTHERANS AND VATICAN COUNCIL II

Thus the Church of the Lutheran Reformation has little interest in a worldwide unity of organization. Its ideal of unity determines its attitude not only toward Orthodox and Protestant churches in the World Council but also toward the reforms of the Roman Church through Vatican Council II. The remarkable change which Pope John XXIII inaugurated when he called together the bishops of the Roman Church to chart a changed course in the modern world included an approach to Protestants as "separated brethren," which reversed a 400-year condemnation of the churches of the Reformation. The losses which the Roman Church suffered through war and communism may have had something to do with the papal call for new measures. The advance, too, of the ecumenical movement by the participation of the Orthodox Church created a challenge to the Church of Rome. In 1925 the pope snubbed the Stockholm Conference, but in 1961 official Roman observers attended the New Delhi meeting of the World Council. Recent advances in Biblical studies had transcended church boundaries, and historical research had changed the Roman evaluation of Luther and the church of his day. The pope even asked for forgiveness of the sins that his church may have committed against the churches of the "separated brethren." The changes sanctioned by the Vatican Council, such as the celebration of the Mass in the vernacular, greater participation by the laity, and the admission of a collegiality of the bishops in the administration of the church are strangely reminiscent of demands made 400 years ago.

315

Lutherans welcomed these unexpected approaches from Rome. Already during and after the war years friendly discussions had taken place between Roman and Lutheran theologians, such as those arranged by Prof. Edmund Schlink of Heidelberg. The Lutheran World Federation encouraged the conversations carried on with Roman representatives under the leadership of Prof. K. E. Skydsgaard of Copenhagen and set up an institute at Strasbourg for interconfessional research, directed by Vilmos Vajta. In the United States a new irenic note was heard in Jaroslav Pelikan's book *The Riddle of Roman Catholicism.* At the same time the Evangelical Lutheran Church of Germany cautioned against premature optimism. Official observers of the Lutheran World Federation at Vatican Council II have given objective accounts of happenings, emphasizing the difference between discussion and decision and decision and implementation.

Lutherans have appreciated the respect newly accorded them and have readily admitted sins of unbrotherliness on their side. Yet they have entertained no intentions of a "return to Rome," to which they have been invited. They have neither recognized nor expressed any desire for a worldwide church centered in Rome, an attitude they have shared with the Orthodox churches. They have noted that the Council of Trent's condemnation of *sola fide* (by faith alone) still stands. Nor have they seen any trend in Rome away from traditions lacking Scriptural authority. On the contrary, the new dogma of the Assumption of Mary was followed in 1964 by the papal decision that Mary is the mother of the church. The policy of Rome on mixed marriages has not been materially changed. Nor has any change been recommended in the form of papal consecration, and so the successor of John XXIII was addressed at his coronation: "Receive the triple-crowned tiara and know that you are the father of princes and kings, the ruler of the world, the vicar of our Savior Jesus Christ on earth, to whom be honor and glory forever."

A FREE GENERAL COUNCIL

The reaction of the Church of the Lutheran Reformation to both the superficial oneness of all Christians called for by some Protestants and the pretentious unity of a papal hierarchy was clearly stated by Söderblom, a Lutheran ecumenical pioneer: "The proud idea of a sole world-conquering organization of the church is for the purity of religion a perilous one and has for all time perished. Now the idea of the universalism of Christendom must be realized in the respect the separate communions have for each other as co-workers or competitors. The sense of the whole is strengthened in the degree that the particular communion boldly carries out its purported duties. If a new *corpus evangelicorum* is to be established, not as a political creation but as a truly catholic attitude without sectarian self-sufficiency, it cannot be through a mixing or disregarding of those differences which in reality are character forming. In a dynamic catholicity we need a sharper perception of the authentic gifts of grace in our church. Faithfulness to our own heritage is accompanied by respect for the ideals of others." These words were written before the reformation of John XXIII, but Söderblom would gladly have welcomed the Roman Church into a *corpus Christianum* on the terms now governing the World Council of Churches. Indeed, were the Church of Rome to join in that council, or in a similar organization, on equal terms with other Christian churches, we might behold the fulfillment of the prayers of the 16th century for a free general council. A common Christian faith already present might be exhibited there, and also a hope for more complete harmony as the various communions grow into full unity in Christ.

The Church of the Lutheran Reformation came into a world where ancient empires were disintegrating, new continents were being explored, and a new learning was revealing secrets of the earth and the heavens. Today, again, new nations are replacing old kingdoms, a mysterious universe of space is being discovered, and revolutions are taking place in the minds of men of all races and colors. Are the unexpected changes in the relationships of churches a movement of the Spirit of God who seeks to proclaim anew the unmerited grace of God in Jesus Christ, the Alpha and the Omega of the world?

SELECTED BIBLIOGRAPHY

ENGLISH

Andersen, Oskar. *Survey of the History of the Church in Denmark.* Copenhagen, 1930.

Arden, G. Everett. *The Augustana Heritage.* Rock Island, 1963.

————. *Four Northern Lights: Men Who Shaped Scandinavian Churches* (Ruotsalainen, Hauge, Grundtvig, Rosenius). Minneapolis, 1964.

Arntzen, Arnliot M. *The Apostle of Norway, Hans Nielsen Hauge.* Minneapolis, 1933.

Baepler, Walter A. *A Century of Grace.* St. Louis, 1947, rev. 1963.

Bainton, Roland H. *Here I Stand: A Life of Martin Luther.* New York, 1950.

————. *The Reformation of the Sixteenth Century.* Boston, 1952.

Bergendoff, Conrad. *Olavus Petri and the Ecclesiastical Transformation in Sweden.* Philadelphia, 1965.

Boehmer, H. *Road to Reformation.* Philadelphia, 1946.

Brilioth, Yngve. *A Brief History of Preaching,* trans. Karl Mattson. Philadelphia, 1965.

Burgess, Andrew S. *Lutheran World Missions, Foreign Missions of the Lutheran Church in America.* Minneapolis, 1954.

Carlson, Edgar M. *The Reinterpretation of Luther.* Philadelphia, 1948.

Cochrane, Arthur C. *The Church's Confession Under Hitler.* Philadelphia, 1962.

Craig, J., trans. (anon. author). *History of the Protestant Church in Hungary From the Beginning of the Reformation to 1850.* Boston, 1854.

Daniel-Rops, Henri. *The Church in the Seventeenth Century,* trans. J. J. Buckingham. London, 1963.

Dau, W. H. T. *Ebenezer. Reviews of the Work of the Missouri Synod during Three Quarters of a Century.* St. Louis, 1922.

Dillenberger, John. *God Hidden and Revealed.* Philadelphia, 1953.

Dunkley, E. H. *The Reformation in Denmark.* London, 1949.

319

Duruy, Victor. *History of the Middle Ages,* trans. E. H. and M. D. Whitney. New York, 1891.

Ecumenical Review, I (Autumn 1948) ff. World Council of Churches, Geneva.

Elert, Werner. *The Structure of Lutheranism,* trans. Walter A. Hansen. St. Louis, 1962.

Encyclopedia of the Lutheran Church, The, ed. Julius Bodensieck. 3 vols. Minneapolis, 1965.

Erikson, Erik H. *Young Man Luther.* New York, 1958.

Figgis, John N. *Studies of Political Thought from Gerson to Grotius 1411 to 1625.* Cambridge, 1900.

Forell, George W. *Faith Active in Love.* New York, 1954.

Fortescue, Adrian. *The Orthodox Eastern Church.* London, 1929.

Gavin, Frank. *Seven Centuries of the Problem of Church and State.* Princeton, 1938.

Gierke, Otto. *Natural Law and the Theory of Society, 1500 to 1800.* Cambridge, 1934; Boston, 1957.

Haapanen, Alfred. *Our Church: Suomi Synod, the Finnish Evangelical Lutheran Church in America.* Hancock, 1945.

Hunter, Leslie Stannard, ed. *Scandinavian Churches.* London, Minneapolis, 1965.

Jacobs, Henry Eyster. *A History of the Evangelical Lutheran Church in the United States,* 6th ed. New York, 1912.

————. *Works of Martin Luther.* 6 vols. Philadelphia, 1915—32.

Katz, Peter. *Nathan Söderblom: A Prophet of Christian Unity.* London, 1949.

Kidd, Beresford J. *The Counter-Reformation 1550—1600.* London, 1933.

Kjaer, Jens C. *History of the Church of Denmark.* Blair, Nebr., 1945.

Koch, Hal. *Grundtvig,* trans. Llewellyn Jones. Yellow Springs, Ohio: Antioch Press, 1952.

Koestlin, Julius T. *Life of Luther,* trans., ed. J. G. Morris. Philadelphia, 1883.

Krauth, Charles P. *The Conservative Reformation and Its Theology.* Philadelphia, 1871.

Latourette, Kenneth Scott. *A History of the Expansion of Christianity.* 7 vols. New York, 1937—45.

Lehmann, E. Arno. *It Began at Tranquebar,* trans. M. J. Lutz. Federation of Evangelical Lutheran Churches in India, 1956.

Lindsay, Thomas M. *A History of the Reformation.* 2 vols. New York, 1906—7.

Lowrie, Walter. *A Short Life of Kierkegaard.* New York, 1946.

Luther, Martin. *Luther's Works,* American Edition, 55 vols. St. Louis, Philadelphia, 1955—.

Lutheran Cyclopedia, ed. Erwin L. Lueker. St. Louis, 1954.

Lutheran Directory. I. *Lutheran Churches of the World;* II. *The Lutheran World Federation.* Berlin, 1963—64.

Lutheran World, The, I (1954) ff. Geneva.

Lutheran World Almanac and Annual Encyclopedia. 8 vols. National Lutheran Council, 1921—37.

Lutheran World Review, I (1948) ff. Geneva.

Mackinnon, James. *Luther and the Reformation.* London, New York. 4 vols. 1925—50.

McNeill, John T. *The History and Character of Calvinism.* Oxford, 1954.

Molland, Einar. *Church Life in Norway, 1800—1950,* trans. Harris Kassa. Minneapolis, 1957.

Murray, Robert, ed. *The Church of Sweden Past and Present,* trans. N. G. Sahlin. Malmö, 1960.

Nelson, E. C., and E. L. Fewold, eds. *The Lutheran Church Among Norwegian-Americans.* 2 vols. Minneapolis, 1960.

Neve, J. L. *A Brief History of the Lutheran Church in America,* 3d rev. ed. Burlington, Iowa, 1934.

Nygren, Anders. *Agape and Eros,* trans. A. G. Hebert and Philip S. Watson. Philadelphia, 1953.

Nyholm, Paul. *The Americanization of the Danish Lutheran Churches in America.* Minneapolis, 1963.

Pauck, Wilhelm. *The Heritage of the Reformation.* Glencoe, Ill., 1961.

Prenter, Regin. *Spiritus Creator.* Philadelphia, 1953.

Reed, Luther D. *The Lutheran Liturgy.* Philadelphia, 1947.

Reu, M. *Luther's German Bible.* Columbus, 1934.

Rouse, Ruth, and Stephen Charles Neill, eds. *A History of the Ecumenical Movement, 1517—1948.* Philadelphia, 1954.

Rupp, Gordon. *Martin Luther.* London, 1945.

———. *The Righteousness of God.* London, 1953.

Sabine, George H. *A History of Political Theory,* 3d ed. New York, 1959.

Scharf, J. L. *Wilhelm Loehe's Relation to the American Church.* Heidelberg, 1961.

Schwiebert, E. G. *Luther and His Times.* St. Louis, 1950.

321

Sentzke, Geert. *Finland: Its Church and Its People.* Helsinki, 1963.

Shaw, Joseph M. *Pulpit Under the Sky: A Life of H. N. Hauge.* Augsburg, 1955.

Sheatsley, C. V. *History of the Evangelical Lutheran Joint Synod of Ohio and Other States.* Columbus, 1919.

Solberg, R. W. *As Between Brothers: The Story of Lutheran Response to World Need.* Minneapolis, 1957.

Streeter, B. H. *The Rise of Christianity* (Cambridge Ancient History XI). Cambridge, 1956.

Sundkler, Bengt. *The Church of South India: The Movement Towards Union 1900—1947.* London, 1954.

Tappert, Theodore G., Jaroslav Pelikan, Robert H. Fischer, and Arthur C. Piepkorn, trans. *The Book of Concord.* Philadelphia, 1959.

Thompson, James Westfall. *History of the Middle Ages.* New York, 1931.

Troeltsch, Ernst. *The Social Teaching of the Christian Churches,* trans. Olive Wyon. 2 vols. New York, 1931.

Vajta, Vilmos. *Church in Fellowship: Pulpit and Altar Fellowship Among Lutherans.* Minneapolis, 1963.

———— and Hans Weissgerber, eds. *The Church and the Confessions: The Role of the Confessions in the Life and Doctrine of the Lutheran Churches.* Philadelphia, 1963.

Wahlstrom, Eric. *My Father Worketh.* Rock Island, 1945.

Walker, Williston. *History of the Christian Church.* New York, rev. ed. 1959.

Watson, Philip S. *Let God Be God: An Interpretation of the Theology of Martin Luther.* Philadelphia, 1948.

Wentz, Abdel Ross, ed. *The Lutheran Churches of the World.* Geneva, 1952.

————. *Lutheran Churches of the World.* Minneapolis, 1957.

————. *A Basic History of Lutheranism in America.* Philadelphia, rev. ed. 1964.

Williams, George H. *The Radical Reformation.* Philadelphia, 1962.

Wordsworth, John. *The National Church of Sweden.* London, 1911.

GERMAN

Benz, Ernst. *Wittenberg und Byzanz.* Marburg, 1949.

Beyreuther, Erich. "Die Erweckungsbewegung," in *Die Kirche in ihrer Geschichte,* Vol. IV. Göttingen, 1963.

Deindoerfer, Johannes. *Geschichte der Evangelisch-Lutherischen Synode von Iowa und anderen Staaten.* Chicago, 1897.

Die Bekenntnisschriften der evangelisch-lutherischen Kirche. Deutscher Evangelischer Kirchenausschusz, Göttingen, 1930.

Fagerberg, H. *Bekenntniskirche und Amt in der deutschen konfessionellen Theologie des 19. Jahrhunderts.* Uppsala, 1952.

Fleisch, Paul. *Hundert Jahre lutherischer Mission.* Leipzig, 1936.

Geissler, Bruno, und Günther Stökl. *In Oriente Crux: Versuch einer Geschichte der reformatorischen Kirchen im Raum zwischen der Ostsee und dem Schwarzen Meer.* Stuttgart, 1963.

Gensichen, Hans-Werner. "Missionsgeschichte der neueren Zeit," in *Die Kirche in ihrer Geschichte,* Vol. IV. Göttingen, 1961.

Grundmann, Herbert. "Ketzergeschichte des Mittelalters," in *Die Kirche in ihrer Geschichte,* Vol. II. Göttingen, 1963.

Grundmann, Siegfried. *Der Lutherische Weltbund.* Grundlagen Herkunft-Aufbau. Köln, 1957.

Hauck, Albert. *Realencyklopädie für protestantische Theologie und Kirche,* 3d ed. Leipzig, 1896—1908.

Hermelink, Heinrich. *Geschichte der Evangelischen Kirche in Württemberg von der Reformation zur Gegenwart.* Stuttgart, Tübingen, 1949.

Heyer, Friedrich. "Die katholische Kirche vom Westfälischen Frieden bis zum Ersten Vatikanischen Konzil," in *Die Kirche in ihrer Geschichte,* Vol. IV. Göttingen, 1963.

Hirsch, Emanuel. *Geschichte der Neueren evangelischen Theologie.* 5 vols. Gütersloh, 1960.

Holl, Karl. *Gesammelte Aufsätze zur Kirchengeschichte,* 3 vols. Tübingen, 1928—1932.

Koehler, J. P. *Geschichte der Allgemeinen Evangelisch-Lutherischen Synode von Wisconsin und anderen Staaten,* I. Milwaukee, 1925.

Lau, Franz, und Ernst Bizer. "Reformationgeschichte Deutschlands bis 1555" in *Die Kirche in ihrer Geschichte,* Vol. III. Göttingen, 1964.

Luther, Martin. *D. Martin Luthers Werke.* Weimar, 1883—.

Lutherische Monatshefte, I (Jan. 1962) ff. Hamburg.

Moeller, Bernd. "Spätmittelalter," in *Die Kirche in ihrer Geschichte,* Vol. II. Göttingen, 1966.

Müller, Karl. *Kirche, Gemeinde und Obrigkeit nach Luther.* Tübingen, 1910.

Müller, Karl F., und Walter Blankenburg. *Leiturgia: Handbuch des evangelischen Gottesdienstes.* 5 vols. I. *Geschichte und Lehre des evangelischen Gottesdienstes;* II. *Der Hauptgottesdienst;* III. *Der Predigtgottesdienst*

323

und der tägliche Gottesdienst; IV. *Die Musik des evangelischen Gottes-dienstes;* V. *Der Taufgottesdienst.* Kassel, 1954—.

Planck, G. J. *Geschichte der protestantischen Theologie von der Konkordien-formel an bis in die Mitte des achtzehnten Jahrhunderts.* Göttingen, 1831.

Religion in Geschichte und Gegenwart, 3d ed. Tübingen, 1957—62.

Rietschl, George. *Lehrbuch der Liturgik,* ed. Paul Graff. Göttingen, 1951—52.

Ritschl, A. *Geschichte des Pietismus.* Vols. 1—3. Bonn, 1880—86.

Schlink, Edmund. *Theologie der lutherischen Bekenntnisschriften.* München, 1948.

Seeberg, Reinhold. *Lehrbuch der Dogmengeschichte.* Leipzig, 1917—30.

Siegmund-Schultze, Friedr. *Ekklesia: Eine Sammlung von Selbstdarstellungen der Christlichen Kirchen.* II. *Die Skandinavischen Länder;* IV. *Die Evan-gelische Kirche in Österreich;* V. *Die Osteuropäischen Länder.* Gotha, Leipzig, 1935—38.

Solberg, Richard W. *Kirche in der Anfechtung. Der Konflikt zwischen Staat und Kirche in Mitteldeutschland seit 1945.* Berlin, 1962.

Stephan, Horst. *Geschichte der deutschen evangelischen Theologie seit dem deutschen Idealismus,* 2d rev. ed. M. Schmidt. Berlin, 1960.

Stupperich, Robert, ed. *Kirche im Osten: Studien zur osteuropäischen Kirchen-geschichte und Kirchenkunde,* Band I, 1958—. Stuttgart and Göttingen.

Tholuck, Friedrich August. *Das kirchliche Leben des siebzehnten Jahrhun-derts.* Berlin, 1861.

Wittram, Reinhard. *Baltische Kirchengeschichte.* Göttingen, 1956.

SCANDINAVIAN

Arsbok för den norske kirke (Annual since 1952). Oslo.

Aulén, Gustaf. *Den Kristna Gudsbilden.* Stockholm, 1927.

———. *Den Kristna Försoningstanken.* Stockholm, 1950.

Bang, A. C. *Den norske kirkes historie.* Kristiania, 1912.

Gustafsson, Berndt. *Svensk Kyrkohistoria.* Stockholm, 1957.

Helgason, J. *Islands kirke.* Vols. 1 and 2. Copenhagen, 1922—26.

Holm, Rurik. *Studier tillägnande Magnus Pfannenstil.* Lund, 1923.

Holmquist, Hj. *Den Senare Medeltidens Kyrkohistoria.* Stockholm, 1914.

———. *Handbok i svensk kyrkohistoris,* 1—3. Stockholm, 1948—52.

———. *Medeltidens Kyrkohistoria.* Uppsala, 1910.

——— and H. Pleijel, eds. *Svenska Kyrkans Historia:* II. *Den senare medel-tiden 1274—1521,* Y. Brilioth. Stockholm, 1941; III. *Reformations*

324

tidevarvet 1521—1611, Hj. Holmquist. Stockholm, 1933; IV. 1) *Svenska kyrkan under Gustav II Adolf 1611—1632*, Hj. Holmquist. Stockholm, 1938; V. *Karolinsk kyrkofromhet, pietism och herrnhutism 1680—1772*, H. Pleijel. Stockholm, 1935; VI. 2) *Neologien, romantiken, uppvaknandet 1809—1823*, E. Liedgren. Stockholm, 1946.

Koch, Hal. *Danmarks Kirke gennem tiderne*. Copenhagen, 1960.

———— and Bjoern Kornerup, eds. *Den danske Kirkes Historie*. I. *Den Aeldre Middelalder Indtil 1241*, Hal Koch. Copenhagen, 1950; II. *Sen Middelalderen 1241—1448*, Niels Knud Andersen. Copenhagen, 1962; IV. *Det Laerde Tidsrum 1536—1670*, Bjoern Kornerup. Copenhagen, 1959; *Pietismens Tid 1699—1746*, Johannes Pedersen; *Oplysningstiden 1746—1799*, Bjoern Kornerup. Copenhagen, 1951; VI. *Tiden 1800 to 1848*, Hal Koch. Copenhagen, 1954; VII. *Tiden 1849—1901*, P. G. Lindhardt. Copenhagen, 1958.

Linderholm, Emanuel. *Sven Rosén och Hans Insats i Frihetstidens Radikala Pietism*. Uppsala, 1911.

Lindhardt, Paul G. *Den nordiske Kirkes Historie*. Copenhagen, 1945.

Lindroth, Hjalmar. *Lutherrenässansen i nyare svensk teologi*. Stockholm, 1941.

Nordisk Teologisk Uppslagsbok. 3 vols. Lund, Copenhagen, 1952—57.

Norvegia Sacra 1—20 (Annual), 1921—1940. Oslo.

Olsson, Herbert. *Grund problemet i Luthers Socialetik*. Lund, 1934.

Rundblom, Oscar. *Svenska Förbindelser med Leipzig-Missionen 1853—1873*. Lund, 1948.

Schmidt, Wolgang. *Finlands Kyrka Genom Tiderna*. Uppsala, 1940.

Svenska Kyrkans Arsbok (Annual, since 1920). Stockholm.

Welle, Ivar. *Norges kirkehistorie*. Oslo, 1948.

Westin, Gunnar. *I den svenska frikyrklighetens genombrottstid*. Stockholm, 1963.

Index

327

Confession, Confutation of, 62
Diet of 1, 60, 66, 71, 73, 92, 112
Peace of 72-73, 74, 85, 139
August, Elector, of Saxony 115, 173
Augustana College and Theological
Seminary 237
Augustana Variata 112
Augustine, St. 6, 33
Augustinian Order 19, 32, 34
Aulén, Gustav 255, 301
Australia, Ev. Luth. Church of 264
Ev. Luth. General Synod 242
Ev. Luth. Synod 242
Immanuel Synod 242
Queensland, Ev. Luth. Synod 242
Union, Ev. Luth. Church 242
Victoria Synod 242
Austria 88, 102, 143, 148, 150, 195,
198, 249-50
Avignon 10

Babylonian Captivity of the Church,
Luther's 43
Bach, Johann S. 127, 291
Baehr, George 284
Baelter, Sven 184
Baier, Johann W. 134
Baird, Robert 215
Balle, Nicolai E. 179, 180
Baltic 3, 12, 150-51
Ban of excommunication 45
Bang, Peter 132
Bang-Karin 186
Bapst, Valentin 135, 136
Baptism, Luther's ritual for 51
Barany, Georg 164
Barmen Missionary Society, *see* Mis-
sionary Societies
Barmen, synod at 248, 288, 311
Barth, Karl 246, 288, 311
Bartholomew's, St., Day Massacre 108,
140
Bartning, O. 284
Basel 48, 76, 80, 83; *see also* Mission-
ary Societies
Council of 10, 26
Bastholm, Christian 179-80, 181
Batak Prot. Christian Church 226,
262, 280
Batory, Stephen 105, 142
Baur, Ferdinand C. 205
Bavaria 2, 9, 11, 65, 144, 209
Baxter, Richard 154, 171, 309
Bayle, Pierre 179
Bayly, Lewis 154

Beck, Johann T. 208, 222, 288
Beck, Vilhelm 213
Bel, Matthias 164
Belgic Confession 141
Bellarmine, Robert 109, 171
Bengel, Johann Albrecht 158, 165
Benzelius family 184
Bergen (Norway) 159
Bergen Book 117
Berkenmeyer, William 190
Berlin 156, 165, 174, 198; *see also*
Missionary Societies
Bern 76, 83
Bernhard of Clairvaux 7, 18, 135, 137
Bethel, *see* Missionary Societies
Bible, German, Luther's 48-50
Bible societies 210, 212, 215, 219,
221, 222
Bible translations 19, 23, 28, 47-50,
89, 93, 95, 96, 97, 164, 189,
193, 221, 253
Biel, Gabriel 35
Billing, Einar 218
Birgitta, Saint 14
Bishop (Lutheran) 80, 94, 97, 131,
245, 261, 280, 298
Bjarnason, Jon 238
Bjoernson, Bjoernstjern 220
Björk, Eric T. 189
Björkqvist, Manfred 218
Bodelschwingh, Friedrich von (born
1831) 242
Bodelschwingh, Friedrich von (born
1877) 247
Bodin, Jean 172
Boehme, Jacob 166, 182, 215, 309
Bohemia 3, 11, 20, 24, 66, 87, 88,
101, 139, 142, 145, 149, 196
to 197
German Ev. Church of A. C. in
250, 274
Bohemian Brethren 20, 25, 87, 89,
165
Bohemian Confession 87
Bolivia, Ev. Luth. Church in 263
Bologna 6, 8, 71
Boltzius, John M. 191
Bonaventura 8, 20, 135
Bondage of the Will, Luther's 56
Bonhoeffer, Dietrich 248
Boniface, Winfrid 3
Boniface VIII 10, 18
Borga 188
Borneo, Rhenish Miss. Soc. in 226

328

329

330

Ethiopian Ev. Luth. Church Mekane
Yesu 279
Evangelische Kirche in Deutschland
273, 311
Faith and Order 255, 313
Falckner, Justus 190
Fant, Michael 184
Farel, William 83
Ferdinand, duke of Austria, emperor
65, 66, 67, 70, 72, 74
Ferdinand II, king of Hungary and
Bohemia, emperor 142-44
Ferrara, Council of 26
Feudalism 9, 15, 53, 57, 75
Feuerbach, Ludwig 214
Fichte, Johann G. 204, 215
Finland 13-14, 97-98, 148, 162, 163,
185-86, 188, 199, 221-23, 253;
see also Missionary Societies
Finnish Lutherans in N. America 237,
259, 276, 280
Finno, Jacob 136
Fischer, Jacob B. 164
Fischer, Johann 164
Fjellstedt, Peter 229, 236
Fjellstrom, Pehr 188
Flacius, Matthias 71, 89, 116, 118
Fliedner, Theodore 210, 242
Florence, Council of 26
Font, baptismal 283, 293
Formula Missae, Luther's 51
France 3, 9, 10, 20-21, 26, 65, 81, 84,
102, 108, 139-40, 146-47, 172,
203, 271; see also French
France, Ev. Luth. Church of 271-72
Francis of Assisi 20
Franciscan Order 6, 14, 20
Francis I (France) 41, 63, 67, 69
Francke, August Hermann 156, 158,
161-62, 164, 191-92, 195, 198
Frandsen, Peder 181
Frank, F. H. R. von 209
Franzén, Frans M. 184, 290
Frauenkirche, Dresden 284
Frederick
(Denmark) I 92; IV 159, 193
(Prussia) I 198; II 174, 198
(Roman Emperor) II 105
(Palatinate) III 85, 145; IV 145;
V 145, 146, 150
(Saxon Elector) the Wise 40,
41, 45
Frederick William (Prussia) III 206;
IV 206

Free Churches, France 271, Germany
206-207, Norway 220-21
Freedom of a Christian, The, Luther's
44
Freedom, religious 72-73, 243
French Church of the Augsburg Con-
fession 271
French Lutheran Churches, National
Alliance of 271
French Revolution 180, 203, 288
Freylinghausen, Johann 162, 288
Fritsche, Gotthold D. 242
Fritschel, Siegmund and Gottfrid 234
Fry, Franklin Clark 313
Fünfkirchen 196

Galesburg-Akron Rule 240
Gallican Rite 4
Geijer, Erik G. 215
Gellent, Christian 290
General Council 239, 256, 262, 268
General Synod 231, 239, 240, 256,
261, 263
General Synod, South 240, 256, 262
George, duke of Saxony 65
Gerhard, Johann 133, 134, 135
Gerhardt, Paul 136, 137, 173
German Christians 247
German Mass, Luther's 53, 85
Germany 3, 9, 13, 20, 43, 54, 58, 64,
75-76, 96, 139, 149, 150
Gerson, John 22, 26
Gezelius, John 132, 136, 163
Giessen University 132, 158
Gjoe, Mogens 92
Glück, Ernest 164
Gnesio-Lutherans 113
Göttingen University 76
Goeze, Johann 176
Goiske, Rosenstand 179
Good Works, Treatise on, Luther's 42
Gorka family 90
Gossner; see Missionary Societies
Gossner, Johannes 210, 222, 226
Grebel, Conrad 55
Gothus, Laurentius P. 131, 132
Grabau, John 207
Graul, Karl 226
Gravamina 64
Greenland 13, 159, 228
Gregory I, Pope 4
Gregory VII, Pope 10, 13, 14, 17, 18
Gregory XIII, Pope 108
Greifswald University 76, 114

Infallibility, papal 305-306
Ingman, Anders V. 222
Inner Mission, German 210, Danish 213, 237
Innocent III, Pope 18, 21
Inquisition, Roman 106, Spanish 12, 19, 20-22, 82, 105
Institutes of the Christian Religion 83-84
Interim, Augsburg 71, 80, 97, 113; Leipzig 71; Prague 87
Iramba 262
Irbe, Karlis 252, 268
Italy 8-9, 10, 12, 15, 27, 63, 82, 106

Jacobs, Charles M. 268
Jacobs, Henry Eyster 301
Jänicke, Johann 196, 210, 226
Japan 229, 237, 240, 262, 279, 280
Jensen, Gustav M. 254
Jeremiah II, Patriarch 307
Jeremias, Jeremiah 302
Jerome of Prague 24
Jesuit Order (Society of Jesus) 82, 103, 108, 139, 140, 142-43, 144, 154, 174, 187-88, 195, 305-6
Jeypore Luth. Church 261
John II, Bishop of Abo 14
John Frederick, elector of Saxony 68
John George, elector of Saxony 145, 146
John III, king of Sweden 142
John XXIII, Pope 315
Johansson, Gustaf 254
Johnson, Gisle 220
Jonsson, Finnur 181-82
Jonsson, Gisli 136
Jonsson, Hannes 181-82
Jorgenson, Alfred 268
Joseph II, Austria 197
Julius, bishop of Würzburg 144
Julius, duke of Brunswick 115, 116
Julius III, Pope 71
Juslenius, Daniel 163
Justification 35, 36, 39, 100, 113, 115, 116, 117, 133, 315
Juusten, Paul 98

Kaiserswerth 210, 220
Kant, Immanuel 177, 204, 215
Kapff, Sixt K. 288
Karlfelt, Erik 218
Karlskrona 161
Karlstadt, Andreas 41, 50, 53, 91

Kavel, August L. 241
Kempis, Thomas a 28, 135
Kenicius, Peter 131
Kenya 262
Kepler, Johannes 177
Kerrl, Hans 248
Kiellin, Carl and Samuel 162
Kierkegaard, Sören 213-214, 246
Kingo, Thomas 135, 181, 219, 290
Kirchenrat 81
Kirchentag 246, 265, 267
Kliefoth, Theodore 207, 209, 234, 265, 266
Klopstock, Frederick 179, 204
Knapp, Albert 208
Knoll, Michael 190
Knöpken, Andreas 90
Knös, Anders 185, 215
Knox, John 142
Knubel, Fredrick 268
Köberle, Adolf 301
Kocherthal, Joshua von 190
Königsberg 80
Koren, Ulrik V. 236
Krauth, Charles P. 239
Krman, Daniel 164
Kunze, John C. 230

La Plata Synod in Brazil 263
Laestadius, Lars 216, 222, 286
Lagerlöf, Selma 218
Lagus, Jonas 222
Laity 156-58, 186, 209, 214, 227, 262, 296
Landahl, Martin 215
Landstad, Magnus B. 220, 290
Lange, Joachim 157
Lange, John 91
Lappland 158, 188
Larsen, Laurentius 236
Larsen, Lauritz 260
Laski, John 90
Lateran Council, Third 18, 105; Fourth 10, 105
Latin in worship 52, 126, 285
Latvia 3, 91, 142, 151, 164, 165, 200-201, 251-52, 270, 307
Laub, Thomas M. 254, 292
Laverson, Peter 181
Law and Gospel 42, 58, 119, 153, 159, 298-99, 312
Leibnitz, Gottfried W. 175, 306
Leipzig 24, 41, 70, 81, 95, 114, 158, 194

337

338

p. 129 In period of orthodoxy, by Alean prevailed.

p. 305 Arndt's 4 Books of True Xᵗⁱⁿ"

p. 320 Forell, "Faith Active in Love"